Radicalism in the Wilderness

Radicalism in the Wilderness

International Contemporaneity and 1960s Art in Japan

REIKO TOMII

The MIT Press Cambridge, Massachusetts London, England

First MIT Press paperback edition, 2018

Cover image: GUN, *Event to Change the Image of Snow*, 1970. Documentary photograph of performance art. Photo © Hanaga Mitsutoshi.

This book was set in Minion and Avenir by the MIT Press. Printed and bound in the United States of America.

Library of Congress Cataloging-in-Publication Data

Names: Tomii, Reiko, author.
Title: Radicalism in the wilderness : international contemporaneity and 1960s art in Japan / Tomii, Reiko.
Description: Cambridge, MA : The MIT Press, 2016. | Includes bibliographical references and index.
Identifiers: LCCN 2015039695 | ISBN 9780262034128 (hardcover : alk. paper) | ISBN 9780262535311(paperback)
Subjects: LCSH: Art, Japanese—20th century. | Contemporary, The, in art.
Classification: LCC N7355.4 .T66 2016 | DDC 709.52/0904—dc23 LC record available at http://lccn.loc.gov/2015039695

10 9 8 7 6 5 4 3 2

To Jeff
For our life together, love together

CONTENTS

ACKNOWLEDGMENTS

This book, which examines aspects of 1960s art in Japan and explores a methodology of world art history, has taken shape in two stages. It involved a long journey of discovering postwar Japanese art, studying it when few guideposts were in sight, and seeing the field of my study grow. The development of the book itself was slow and gradual, as I began to deliberate on methodological strategies to place Japanese "contemporary art" (*gendai bijutsu*) in the global 1960s. Accordingly my expression of gratitude is twofold: for people who were key to the evolution of my scholarship; and for individuals and institutions that supported this book project from inception to fruition.

* * *

1984. The journey began. After four years of studying Western art history with Professors Kimura Shigenobu and Tsuji Shigebumi of Osaka University, who had taught me how to see art and how to think about art, I left for Austin, Texas. There I spent another four years to learn how to historicize art and how to articulate ideas about art under the guidance of Professors Linda D. Henderson and John R. Clarke. Having earned a Ph.D. in postwar American art history from the University of Texas at

Austin, I still progressed slowly. There were yet another four years of apprenticeship in New York with the late Bhupendra Karia, who taught me how to curate art, how to archive art, and how to speak about art globally at the Center for International Contemporary Arts (CICA).

1994. I found what would turn out to be my life's project: to study 1960s Japanese art. Working closely with Alexandra Munroe on the book *Japanese Art after 1945: Scream against the Sky* (1994), I saw in postwar Japanese art an exciting, challenging, and ultimately rewarding subject of serious study. A pioneer of the field and partner in crime, with whom I had first worked on CICA's Kusama Yayoi retrospective (1989), Alexandra has since inspired and encouraged me with her expansive visions. *Scream* was followed by a series of projects and assignments that fed into my scholarship. Among them, I was particularly blessed to be involved with two exhibitions, *Global Conceptualism* at the Queens Museum of Art (1999) and *Century City* at the Tate Modern (2001), which helped me comprehend the global stakes of my study.

2004. An expansion was taking place. I saw more graduate students, scholars, and curators taking interest in postwar Japanese art. That was why, a year before, with Miwako Tezuka I had co-founded PoNJA-GenKon, a listserv group for those interested in the field. The group has since become our intellectual home and site of collaboration. (This acronym stands for *Po*st-*N*ineteen forty-five *J*apanese *A*rt Discussion Group / *Gen*dai Bijutsu *Kon*dankai.) Through global networking, I found like-minded conspirators in Hiroko Ikegami and Ming Tiampo, and the whole field became my partners in spirit. My study, too, expanded thanks to collaboration with other scholars. In especial, Joan Kee encouraged me to reflect on the deeper meaning of "contemporary art" for her guest-edited issue of *Positions* (Winter 2004); J. Thomas Rimer offered me an opportunity to go beyond *Scream* in narrating 1960s art in his anthology *Since Meiji* (2011); and Midori Yoshimoto worked with me to examine Japanese collectivism in the whole 20th century in our guest-edited issue of *Positions* (Spring 2013). These works became the core of my exploration of 1960s art in Japan in a broader context.

2014. This volume finally began to take a concrete shape and vision. And the journey will continue.

* * *

In my study, those who lived through the time I examine have always been inspirations for me. It has been a privilege and pleasure to know the practitioners highlighted in this book: the late Matsuzawa Yutaka, The Play's Ikemizu Keiichi, and GUN's Horikawa Michio and Maeyama Tadashi. They have been untiringly responsive to my queries and requests, and I am humbled by their generosity.

After Matsuzawa's unexpected death in 2006 (nobody around him thought he should pass away on a numerologically insignificant date), I worked closely with his family, especially his daughter Matsuzawa Kumiko and her husband Haruo, whose commitment to their father's art has been exemplary. They spearheaded ongoing research at the artist's residence in Shimo Suwa. Researchers include Aoki Masahiro and Sakagami Shinobu; Yūgakkai (Kubodera Yūji, Maiya Eiichi, and Watanabe Akira); and Matsuzawa Yutaka Moving Images Preservation Project (Hosoya Shūhei, Itami Hiroshi, Kosaka Mayu, Shimada Yoshiko, and myself), all of whom have generously shared their findings with me.

As a frequent editor myself, I am keenly aware that no book either writes itself or publishes itself. At the MIT Press, I am immensely indebted to Roger Conover, who placed complete faith in my book idea, sight unseen. We share a passion for book making and a desire for new ways to narrate art history. His quiet encouragement has been a source of energy in pressing forward. The painstaking support and assistance provided by Justin Kehoe, Matthew Abbate, and Yasuyo Iguchi have made this a very handsome book.

A number of colleagues kindly read parts of my draft in various stages and offered me valuable input. My appreciation for their time and thought goes to Jane Farver, Jaimey Hamilton Faris, Hashimoto Azusa, Justin Jesty, and Judith Rodenbeck. In particular, I am grateful to Alexandra Munroe for her astute reading and to Hiroko Ikegami and Ming Tiampo for their patience, encouragement, and advice.

A dear friend since Austin and trusted editing partner, Kathleen M. Friello, copyedited the submission manuscript with her usual diligence, care, and sensitivity, which I have treasured so much. She also compiled an index.

My research has been assisted and supported by a community of specialists and colleagues. A special note goes to Nakajima Masatoshi and Nakajima Yasuko, who worked with me and taught me the depth of art documentation for almost two decades since the time of CICA. An effective and attentive research partner for this project is Kikkawa Hideki, with whom I have exchanged enjoyable banter on seemingly dry documents and publications. Likewise, I had fun sharing moments of discovery with Uesaki Sen at Keiō University Art Center, Tokyo, and Katherine Alcauskas, then at the Department of Drawings & Prints at the Museum of Modern Art, New York. Miyata Yūka generously provided me with Matsuzawa-related documents from the archives of Naiqua Gallery. I am proud to be a member of Oral History Archives of Japanese Art, a group of scholars who have conducted interviews with scores of cultural practitioners and from whom I have learned much.

I am blessed with numerous colleagues, academic and professional, who generously shared with me their knowledge, research, and expertise. The late Jane Farver was an early supporter and a collaborator with whom I worked on *Cultural Melting Bath* (1997), the first New York solo presentation of the Chinese contemporary artist

Cai Guo-Qiang, and the landmark *Global Conceptualism* (1999), among other projects; I will always remember her forward-looking vision for non-Western contemporary art. With admiration I have learned much from the work of KuroDalaiJee (Kuroda Raiji). I value scholarly collegiality and professional friendship extended to me by Kawasaki Kōichi, Masuda Tomohiro, Fergus McCaffrey, Miko McGinty and Rita Jules, Yasufumi Nakamori, Seki Naoko, Shin Misa, Eric C. Shiner, Tsuji Yoshitaka, Midori Yamamura, and Mika Yoshitake. I have enjoyed the exchange of ideas that varyingly fed into this book with Christophe Cherix, Chiba Shigeo, Doryun Chong, John Clark, Kevin Concannon, Jane DeBevoise, Donna De Salvo, Fujii Aki, Hirai Shōichi, Honnami Kiyoshi, Ikegami Tsukasa, Inaga Shigemi, David Joselit, Kajiya Kenji, Kataoka Mami, Katō Mizuho, Kawatani Shōko, Kimura Eriko, Kumagai Yūko, Kurokawa Noriyuki, Matsushita Yuri, Mitsuda Yuri, Morita Hajime, Hammad Nasar, Nishikawa Mihoko, Nose Yōko, Amy Plumb Oppenheim, Ashley Rawlings, Satō Tsuyoshi, Tabata Yukihito and Yamamoto Hozu, Takiguchi Akiko, Elizabeth Tinsley, Jeffrey Weiss, Anne Wheeler, Bert Winther-Tamaki, Michelle Wong, and Ayelet Zohar.

Photo research was capably aided by Callie Jones, a fellow Texan. Assistance was also provided by Chiba Yumiko, Takayuki Fujii, Fujii Yūko, Kunii Aya, Senoo Aya, Sarah Watson, and Yokota Shigeru. Those who graciously granted the permission to reproduce and furnished the images are separately credited. Special thanks are due to Nakajima Kō, who discussed his photographs of Matsuzawa Yutaka; and Hanaga Tarō, who showed me the photo archives of his late father Hanaga Mitsutoshi and, together with his associate Inagaki Akihiko, kept me abreast of the progress of their digitizing project. Takako Oishi-Marks designed the maps and diagram. Part of my photo research was funded by a Short-term Research Travel Grant to Japan from the Northeast Asia Council of the Association for Asian Studies, with the support of the Japan-U.S. Friendship Commission.

I cherish friendship extended to me over years by those who lived through the 1960s and 1970s, including Jon Hendricks, Hikosaka Naoyoshi, Hirata Minoru, Minemura Toshiaki, Ushio Shinohara, and Noriko Shinohara, who together remind me that art is created by living souls who breathe the air of their times.

On a personal note, above all I thank my parents, Tomii Miwako and the late Toshio, for letting me pursue my dream even before I knew what that dream would be. My mother-in-law, Lorraine Rothstein, always takes interest in my work and reads all my English publications. Our family friends René Balcer and Carolyn Hsu Balcer keep a window open for us to a wider world beyond the borders. Last but not least, I could not have built my scholarship and written this book without the love, patience, and support of my husband Jeffrey Rothstein. His warm presence and company have sustained me in my life as a transplanted New Yorker and my work as an independent scholar. This book is dedicated to him with my utmost love and appreciation.

NOTES TO THE READER

This volume, with its focus on post-1945 Japanese art, generally follows the style guidelines established in the fields of Japanese studies and art history. However, it has also become necessary to adopt a set of rules used in the field of post-1945 Japanese art history which reflect the emerging reality of globalization that surrounds both contemporary Japanese art and its scholarly and museological studies.

ROMANIZATION

In transliterating the Japanese language, the modified Hepburn Romanization system has been employed. A notable deviation from the original Hepburn is the use of "n" before b, m, and p (e.g., *shinbun*, *Anpo*).

MACRONS

Macrons are used to indicate long vowels in Japanese names and words (e.g., Takiguchi Shūzō). Commonly known place names and words adopted into English are given without macrons (e.g., Tokyo).

PERSONAL NAMES

Japanese and other East Asian names are given in the traditional order, surname first. Exceptions are made for individuals who primarily reside outside their native countries *and* adopt the Western system. In this volume, they include Shūsaku Arakawa, On Kawara, Yoko Ono, Ushio Shinohara, and Yasunao Tone.

GROUP NAMES

Postwar artists' collectives employed diverse naming strategies, frequently combining Japanese and English or other foreign words (e.g., Group Ongaku) or creating easy-to-remember abbreviations (e.g., Bikyōtō). In this volume, their names are rendered in the forms established or preferred in the field.

KATAKANA

Katakana is a syllabary used in modern Japanese to transcribe loan words from foreign languages. In Japanese diction, even when a given foreign word has been translated into Japanese (e.g., "avant-garde" into *zen'ei*, 前衛), the original word may continue to be used in its *katakana* form (e.g., *avangyarudo*, アヴァンギャルド) to signal a subtle difference of signification or a sense of novelty or sophistication, depending on the context.

MEASUREMENTS

Measurements are given in metric. Below are quick conversions.

1 inch = 2.54 centimeters (10 centimeters is approximately 4 inches)

1 yard = 0.9144 meters (1 meter is approximately 1 yard)

1 mile = 1.6093 kilometers (3 kilometers is approximately 2 miles)

1 ounce = 28.3495 grams (100 grams is approximately 3.5 ounces)

1 pound = 0.4535 kilograms (1 kilogram is approximately 2 pounds)

GLOSSARY

FREQUENTLY USED JAPANESE TERMS

āto	art
avangyarudo	avant-garde
bijutsu	art
dantai	artists' organizations and exhibition societies, customarily holding annual salons
gainen	concept
geijutsu	Art with a capital "A," or the arts
gendai	contemporary
kannen	meditative visualization (Buddhism), idea (modern)
kindai	modern
kontenporarī	contemporary

obuje	derived from *objet(s)*, meaning "readymade or junk objects," or "works made of *objets*"
zen'ei	avant-garde

FREQUENTLY USED ABBREVIATIONS

Kyoto Modern	The National Museum of Modern Art, Kyoto
Mainichi Contemporary	*Contemporary Art Exhibition of Japan*
Mainichi International	*International Art Exhibition, Japan* (aka Tokyo Biennale)
Nagaoka Contemporary	Museum of Contemporary Art, Nagaoka
Tokyo Modern	The National Museum of Modern Art, Tokyo
Trends	*Trends in Contemporary Japanese Art* exhibition
Yomiuri Independent	Yomiuri Independent Exhibition

FREQUENTLY CITED PERIODICALS

Asahi shinbun (Asahi [Morning sun] newspaper)

Bijutsu hihyō (Art criticism)

Bijutsu jānaru (Art journal)

Bijutsu techō (Art notebook)

Geijutsu Shinchō (Arts of Shinchō [new tides]), published by Shinchō-sha

Mainichi shinbun (Mainichi [Everyday] newspaper)

Mizue (Watercolor)

Yomiuri shinbun (Yomiuri newspaper)

Radicalism in the Wilderness

PROLOGUE

THREE IN THE WILDERNESS

1964, Shimo Suwa: Matsuzawa Yutaka

In the wee hours of December 3, 1964, Matsuzawa Yutaka, arguably the most important conceptualist in Japan, opened the exhibition *Independent '64 in the Wilderness* at Nanashima Yashima Highland in Nagano Prefecture in central Japan. Following the sudden announcement of the suspension of the annual Yomiuri Independent Exhibition earlier that year, his endeavor was part of a movement among artists to self-organize independent exhibitions in order to extend Yomiuri's postwar legacy. Unlike other such exhibitions, however—for that matter, unlike any other exhibitions—Matsuzawa's eschewed all the material trappings of an art exhibition through the radical principle of "vanishing of matter" (*busshitsu shōmetsu*) which the artist had discovered six months earlier. Most significantly, he completely eliminated the heart of any exhibition, the physical presence of artworks. Not that no artist participated. Indeed, more than a handful of works were submitted, or more accurately transmitted, according to the method specified in the call-for-entries ad: "Please keep your entry in your hand and deliver the formless emission from it (imaginary work) to the exhibition site. Any delivery method will do. [...] Those who wish to enter may start contacting in material and/or immaterial ways" (figure 0.1).[1] Notable entries included the painter Ikeda Tatsuo's *Alpha Orionis of Constellation Orion at Midnight, December 9* and the poet-critic Takiguchi Shūzō's *Delivery of Subway Trains for the Opening of the Takadanobaba-Kudanshita Stretch of Tōzai Line on December 23.*[2] Only at an exhibition of *kannen* (meditative visualization) could one entertain such outrageously "bizarre" and "merry" displays without any concern for labor and cost, as the ad suggests. All Matsuzawa needed to do was post the ad in an art journal to instigate the mental movement of like-minded practitioners residing far from his headquarters, the Void/Imaginary Space Situation Research Center, in his hometown of Shimo Suwa.

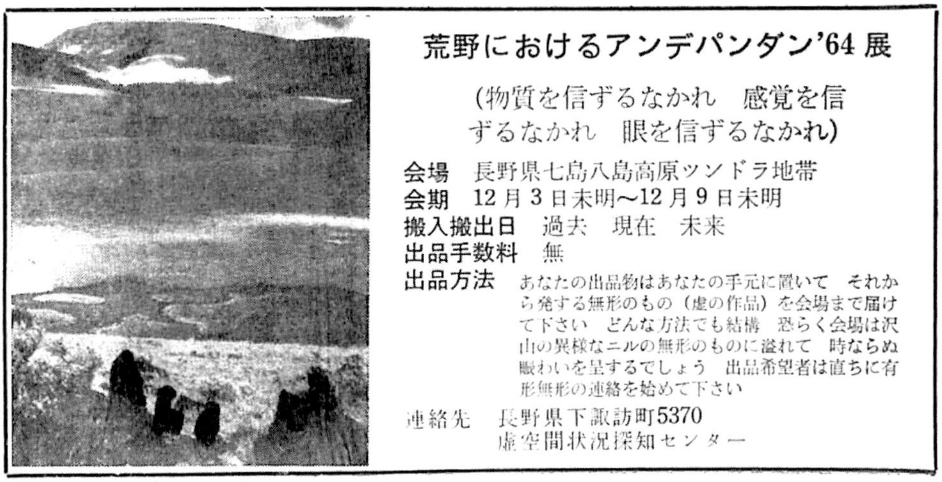

FIGURE 0.1
Matsuzawa Yutaka, *Independent '64 in the Wilderness*, 1964. Magazine ad, reproduced from *Bijutsu jānaru* (October 1964): 51. See facing page for a translation.

Independent '64 in the Wilderness

Don't believe matter
Don't believe senses
Don't believe the eye

Site:
Tundra Field, Nanashima Yashima Highland, Nagano Prefecture
Period:
Before daybreak, December 3, to before daybreak, December 9
Installation/Deinstallation Dates:
Past, present, future
Entry Fee:
None
Entry Method:
Please keep your entry in your hand and deliver the formless emission from it (imaginary* work) to the exhibition site. Any delivery method will do. It is very likely the site will be filled with many bizarre, formless things of Nil, making the exhibition a rare, merry occasion. Those who wish to enter may start contacting in material and/or immaterial ways.
Please contact:
Void/Imaginary Space** Situation Research Center
5370 Shimo Suwa-chō, Nagano Prefecture

Translator's notes:
* "Imaginary" as in "imaginary numbers" which, combined with "real numbers," constitute complex numbers in mathematics.
** "Void/Imaginary Space" is translated from 虚空間, which combines "imaginary space" (kyo kūkan), as opposed to "real space, in mathematics and 虚空 (kokū), or "void," in Buddhism.

1968, Shionomisaki: The Play

On August 1, 1968, the artist Ikemizu Keiichi and his fellow members of The Play, an Osaka-based collective of "Happeners" (*hapunā*), embarked on two fishing boats from the port of Kushimoto. The town was located near the Shionomisaki cape at the southernmost tip of Japan's main island. After some three hours of travel, they arrived at the open sea, more turbulent than expected. At 33°05′ N, 135°41′ E, having come as close as possible to the Japan Current, they ceremoniously released a humongous fiberglass egg the group had built into the ocean with a slight hope that the egg might reach the continental U.S., riding first on the Japan Current and then on the Alaska or California Current (figures 0.2, 3.5). Their voyage began in midmorning and was over before sunset. But their *Voyage: Happening in an Egg* had only begun, as the oval construction 3.3 meters long and 2.2 meters wide continued on, bearing their group name and other information. One month later, it was seen improbably floating in the waves by a ship, which telegraphed its sighting at around 155°10′ E. Thereafter nothing was heard of their egg. Yet it unmistakably carried "an image of liberation from all the material and mental restrictions imposed upon us who live in contemporary times."[3]

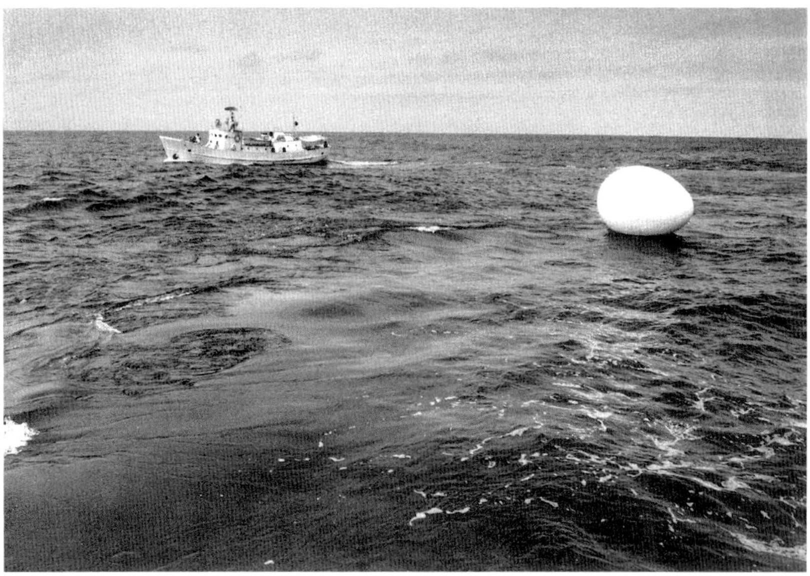

FIGURE 0.2
The Play, *Voyage: Happening in an Egg*, 1968. Documentary photograph of performance art. © The Play.

1970, Niigata: GUN

On February 11, 1970, four members of the local collective GUN spread out onto a dry riverbed of the Shinano River.[4] As with many other rivers in Japan, large and small dry riverbeds (called *kasenjiki* administratively or *kawara* colloquially) flank the Shinano, the longest river in the country, which begins in the Japan Alps, runs through Niigata prefecture, and flows into the Sea of Japan. At about the midpoint of its run, in the city of Tōkamachi, the vast area of the riverbeds forms an enticing blank canvas when thickly covered by snow. This was an idea that GUN, an acronym for Group Ultra Niigata, had entertained for some time. The group's titanic ambition was now being realized with the assistance of their photographer friend Hanaga Mitsutoshi from Tokyo. He helped them secure permission to use the dry riverbed from the Ministry of Construction and receive a donation of a massive amount of pigment, valued at some 450,000 yen (the equivalent of $1,250 at the time), from a large chemical company that specialized in colorant. Equipped with a pesticide sprayer borrowed from a local farmer, they painted a colorful abstraction on the snow. The location was a veritable no-man's land, deserted and avoided. In the region known for the heaviest snow in the country, the thickly snow-covered fields with yet more falling snow represented less a joyous playground than a reminder of the burdens such severe weather brought to everyday life. Hence the title of the project, *Event to Change the Image of Snow*, referred to a transformation of hardship into a pleasant surprise (figure 0.3, plate 1). Four days later, the seven GUN members reprised the act. Each time, the gorgeous color field abstraction they created was eclipsed by the constantly falling snow within 30 minutes.

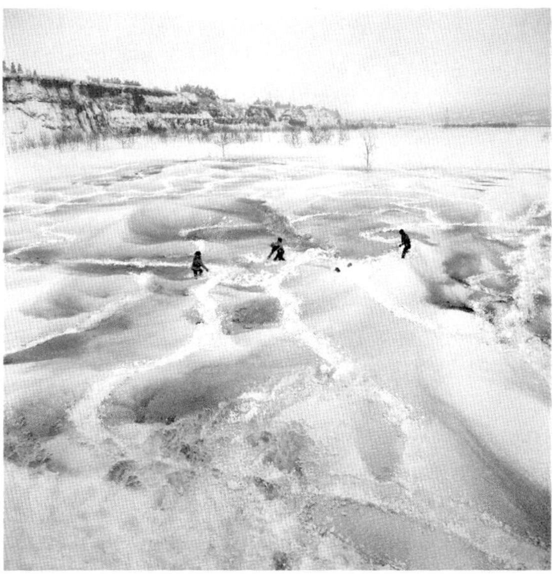

FIGURE 0.3
GUN, *Event to Change the Image of Snow*, 1970. Documentary photograph of performance art. Photo © Hanaga Mitsutoshi. (Also plate 1.)

WHERE WAS THE WILDERNESS?

These three protagonists of this book—Matsuzawa Yutaka, The Play, and GUN—were among many individuals and collectives who made Japan one of the world's major frontiers of vanguard art in the decades following World War II. Since the mid-1950s, when Gutai (shortened from "Gutai Art Association") declared its desire for an "international common ground,"[5] Japanese artists had indeed come a long way to claim international contemporaneity as they developed distinct practices parallel to, and often antecedent to, their counterparts in Euro-America and other parts of the world. They eventually demonstrated the state of international contemporaneity in a clearly visible and tangible manner at *Tokyo Biennale 1970: Between Man and Matter*, an exhibition held at the Tokyo Metropolitan Art Museum and sponsored by the Mainichi newspaper company, where 40 international artists, 28 of them participating from abroad, demonstrated their shared conceptualist and post-minimalist concerns.

By 1970, the diversity of vanguard practices in Japan, locally called *gendai bijutsu* (literally "contemporary art"), was phenomenal. It ranged in aesthetic and expressive possibilities from the technology-based intermedia of Expo Art[6] to the phenomenological Mono-ha and post-minimalism, to diverse kinds of conceptualism, to performance art indoors and outside.[7] The generational depth was just as impressive. Such prewar veterans as Yoshihara Jirō and his fellow abstractionist Saitō Yoshishige watched over the postwar generations as elder statesmen, with Yoshihara leading the Gutai group in Osaka and Saitō teaching at Tama Art University in Tokyo. Having emerged from the ill-fated annual Yomiuri Independent Exhibition (which was suspended in January 1964), many practitioners of Anti-Art (*Han-geijutsu*) went on to develop mature voices, as new art school graduates and younger artists rapidly struck out on their own to form the Non-Art (*Hi-geijutsu*) contingents in the post-Yomiuri years. Their habitats were also vast. Regional subcenters mushroomed during what I call the "expanded 1960s" from Hokkaidō to Kyūshū, making the whole archipelago a space of contemporary practices (figure 0.4). The institutional vista expanded in step as well. Two national museums of modern art were instituted in Tokyo and Kyoto, while a small number of commercial galleries specializing in *gendai bijutsu* emerged, with rental galleries (*kashi garō*) filling in the gap and sometimes serving as alternative spaces. Some contemporary artists desired yet more adventurous options, going out into the streets and beyond the city limits. Accordingly, to understand the full scope of *gendai bijutsu* and its radicalism in 1960s Japan, looking at the center—that is the capital, Tokyo—is barely enough.

In this book, *Radicalism in the Wilderness*, we follow, among the most inventive practitioners, one artist and two collectives who more or less consistently made the wilderness their habitats. The notion of "wilderness," a key word for understanding postwar Japanese art history, requires some explanation. The three opening episodes

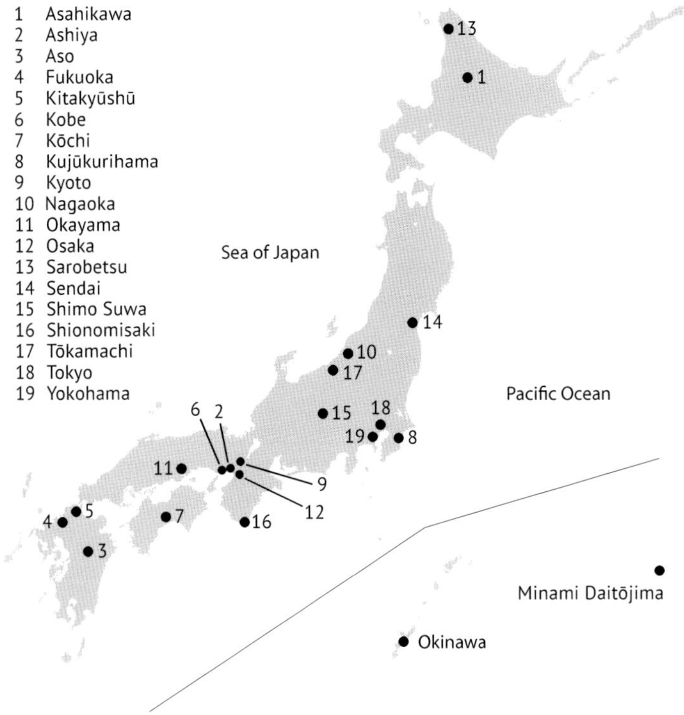

FIGURE 0.4
Map of Japan. Designed by Takako Oishi-Marks.

saliently demonstrate these artists' affinity with "no-man's land," each episode representing one of their earliest radical acts—in their institutional critique and intervention into the everyday. In this regard, the title of Matsuzawa's exhibition is emblematic: *Independent '64 in the Wilderness*, where "wilderness" is a desolate landscape or *kōya* (荒野). However, in this book, "wilderness" has several layers of meaning. Signifying more than remote landscapes, it metaphorically invokes "out there." One example of "out there" is outside the norms in thinking (both in the context of everyday life and art making), as in the case of Matsuzawa. He took a serious interest in parascience and parapsychology, as much as in non-Zen Buddhism and contemporary physics, in formulating his theory and practice of Psi, which he structured as an art of *kannen*, or "meditative visualization." Another "out there" is "out of Tokyo," the outside status that applies to all three protagonists as well as many others working in a number of subcenters. (Given Tokyo's peripheral location compared to Euro-American centers, "out of Tokyo" was doubly "out there.") In 1960s Japan, activities in the wilderness in this sense, or regionalism, were labeled the "regional avant-garde."[8]

Wilderness has a further historical association: *ya* (野) in *kōya* stands for being "outside of the seat of power," either by circumstance or by choice, in the traditional East Asian vocabulary. In China, politicians "descend to the wilderness" (*xiaye*, 下野) when they lose their positions in the court and the government; literati painting was part of this tradition, with scholar-painters withdrawing from the seat of power to critique the officially sanctioned academic painting. In modern Japan, "being in the wilderness" (*zaiya*, 在野) gained a positive connotation of not participating in the institutional systems—whether the government, corporations, or academia. In art, in 1914, when disgruntled artists departed from the government salon *Bunten* (short for the Ministry of Education Exhibition) and formed their own organization Nika-kai (Second Section Society), they proudly declared themselves to be *zaiya*, starting a modern tradition of *zaiya* (non-governmental) artists' organizations. In the complicated history of modern collectivism in Japan,[9] however, *zaiya* organizations which by definition are supposed to be anti-establishment nonetheless by the 1930s became part of the salon-based art establishment that dominated Japan's art world. In this process, the *zaiya* organizations were instrumental in propelling the evolution *and* acclimation of modernism in prewar Japan. The avant-garde, or *zen'ei*, and *zaiya* salons overlapped to a small degree, but the form of collectivism taken by the former was frequently short-lived small groups, situated on the margins of the art world. In the postwar years, to dismantle the status quo consisting of both the government salon and *zaiya* salons, a series of countermeasures were instituted, one of them being the inauguration of the Yomiuri Independent Exhibition in 1948.

Organized by the Yomiuri newspaper company, the Yomiuri Independent thus prepared the stage for the coming of the 1960s avant-garde of Anti-Art, as is well known. At the same time, it was the beginning of the mainstreaming of *zen'ei* (the avant-garde) as *gendai bijutsu*. Although contemporary art would not become part of mainstream culture until much later (that is, with the generation of Murakami Takashi and Nara Yoshitomo and later), by 1970 it became a force to reckon with in the official art world, even though conservative critics loathed its incomprehensible nature and the general public found it puzzling and inaccessible. Wilderness was in this regard a flip side of the mainstreaming of contemporary art. These two vectors complemented each other: wilderness served as a space for experimentalism literally outside the box, while a different kind of experimentalism progressed inside the box of the museum and gallery space.

By focusing on the wilderness in this sense, this book will uncover an aspect of postwar Japanese art less visible—yet by no means less important—than that of mainstreaming contemporary art, which has in the past received a considerable amount of attention with beneficiaries including Takamatsu Jirō and Mono-ha, to just name a few. Of the three protagonists of this book, Matsuzawa and The Play imaginatively and resourcefully conducted their experiments in the post-Yomiuri years. Joined by the slightly younger GUN, they would extend the spirit of wilderness beyond 1968 and into the 1970s; when called upon, they brought the wilderness into the mainstream sites of the museum. Their choice to be in the wilderness, as much as their innovative practices, positions them among the most radical examples of 1960s art in Japan. Even though Japan is a small country, its condensed yet dispersed urban populations and geographical complexities give it many distinct locales. In this regard, it is imperative to counterbalance the frequent metropolitan and cosmopolitan focus in the study of postwar and contemporary practices of Japan. This book thus offers a new in-depth look into local history by using as entry points three key figures in the wilderness who represent three different generations, three non-Tokyo locales, and three interconnected tendencies of conceptualism, performance art, and land art.

LINKING LOCAL AND GLOBAL

If the first task of this book concerns local history, the second task involves world art history—how to incorporate this local study into a global narrative of postwar art. Making a simple acknowledgment that, say, Matsuzawa's practice constitutes a pioneering example of global conceptualism and inserting it into (adding it to) an ever growing encyclopedic reservoir of knowledge has, unfortunately, proven to be inadequate. We only need look at two thematic survey exhibitions, *Voids* at the Centre Pompidou in Paris (2009)[10] and *Invisible* at Hayward Gallery in London (2012),[11] in which examples of Matsuzawa's empty gallery and invisible work were absent, despite the prominent place afforded to him in the landmark exhibition *Global Conceptualism* at Queens Museum of Art in New York (1999) a decade earlier.[12] How can we *actively* incorporate into a global narrative of postwar art 1960s Japan in general and Matsuzawa's conceptualism, The Play's Happenings, or GUN's land art in particular? In other words, how can we bridge national histories (area studies) and transnational histories? How can we connect the local and global? This is a challenge that this study tackles.

In considering these questions, 1960s Japan serves as a paradigmatic site of world art history, because of its discourse of "international contemporaneity," or *kokusaiteki dōjisei* (alternately *kokusaiteki dōjidaisei*), which underscored the rise of *gendai bijutsu*, as well as the accompanying discourse of *gendai*, which prefigures today's discourse on contemporaneity in contemporary art.[13] In a sense, with its state of internationalization far less complicated than today's globalization, 1960s Japan is a microcosm in which we can conduct a theoretical and methodological exploration in our attempt to formulate a world history of modern and contemporary art. It has to be remembered that in the second decade of the 21st century, Eurocentrism is not yet a thing of the past. We have begun to deconstruct and decenter art history but barely know how to regroup and narrate in a decentered manner. This is what is at stake in this book. As indicated by its subtitle, *International Contemporaneity and 1960s Art in Japan*, this book proposes to look at 1960s art in Japan as a case study and examine it through the theoretical and methodological lens of this concept, international contemporaneity.

In the discourse of 1960s Japan, "international contemporaneity" is a geohistorical concept, one that liberates us from the inevitable obsession with the present inherent in "contemporaneity" as used in the English construction of "contemporary art" (whose basic meaning is "art of present times") and helps us devise an expansive historical framework to construct a multicentered world art history. Beyond its analytical value for examining the facts of synchronicity, the spatiotemporal formulation of international contemporaneity also foregrounds the agency of artists, critics, and others who lived through the 1960s with differing degrees of its awareness. With international contemporaneity as lived experiences, perception was as important as fact, if not more. Yet perceptions of the parties involved were limited by their existence in their particular time-space coordinates. It is therefore necessary to introduce the retrospective view of international contemporaneity by employing two comparative concepts, *connections* and *resonances*, and examining their *similar yet dissimilar* characteristics. These concepts serve as a basis for exploding the ingrained Eurocentric narrative of postwar art, creating clusters of *narrative tangents* which at once shatter and capitalize on the linearity of our narrative mind.

Radicalism in the Wilderness: International Contemporaneity and 1960s Art in Japan offers a two-pronged strategy for a world art history: foregrounding the local and the presumed periphery and building the global from the bottom up. Its focus on the wilderness, then, has an additional perspective of local within local, elucidating the center-periphery relationship within a locale. Yet these categories were never stable in the dynamic decade of the 1960s, when the artists in the wilderness could enter a conversation with the international, whether directly—as demonstrated by Matsuzawa's mail-art campaign—or indirectly through the perception and experience of international contemporaneity within their locale.

1 INTRODUCTION TO "INTERNATIONAL CONTEMPORANEITY" AND "CONTEMPORARY ART"

In the early 21st century, the idea of the "global" is unavoidable in thinking about contemporary art. As "world art history" or "global art history" necessarily comes to the fore in the discipline of art history,[1] we have begun to develop methodologies to create a shared sense of history that at once encompasses diverse localized stories and illuminates the complex state of contemporaneity, wherein diverse parallel phenomena exist at a given time and multiple stories tangle together. An incremental "adding more" or "inserting more" to the existing paradigm is never enough.[2] If we focused on merely "adding more," even could we build a Babelian encyclopedia of information we would quickly exhaust our resources—that is, the space and time of discourse. What we need are ways to expand and amplify—ultimately ways to devise different narratives.

This book has a twofold goal: to narrate an aspect of local history in 1960s Japan that I call the "wilderness," and to link it to world art history. As an introduction, chapter 1 likewise has a twofold goal: to present a set of methodological concepts for world art history and to outline a larger framework for the wilderness in the local history. The former is predicated on the notion of "international contemporaneity" (*kokusaiteki dōjisei*), a local term that conceptualized the country's relationship to the external world in the dynamic decade of the 1960s; and the latter is embodied in an overarching story of "contemporary art" (*gendai bijutsu*), which, transmuted from the avant-garde (*zen'ei*), was informed by an expanding sense of "international contemporaneity." Indeed, the rise of "contemporary art" accompanied by the discourse of *gendai* (the contemporary) and the articulation of "international contemporaneity" are twin pillars of 1960s art in Japan that distinguish it from many other locales.

Derived from the local discourse at the time, these two ideas were prescient concerning the rise of "contemporary art" in the globalized art scenes of the 21st century and the intensifying discourse on the "contemporary."[3] In this respect, 1960s Japan can be retroactively reclaimed as a seminal episode in the 21st-century discourse on the contemporary.[4] Of particular import is its historicized view of *gendai*—conceptualized as a shift from *kindai* (the modern)—which is often obscured in the current discussion of contemporary art.[5]

At the same time, with its prescient articulation of history, 1960s Japan can also serve as a laboratory of world art history in which methodologies may be formulated and their efficacies tested. Some may wonder whether such locally specific ideas are conducive to, or even meaningful in, globalizing art history. On the contrary: as will be outlined below in the section "A Proposal for Methodology," when recast as a geohistorical concept, "contemporaneity" serves as an expansive tool for decentering the ingrained Eurocentrism and opening up our discipline to examine a multiplicity of contemporary and vanguard practices worldwide. In theory, the methodology of contemporaneity constitutes not a familiar top-down (or "center-out") approach but a bottom-up (or "periphery-in") strategy, through comparative readings of various locales. In practice, a comparative perspective derived from "international contemporaneity" prompts us to consider "connections" and "resonances"—two modes of connectedness that can be deciphered as "similar yet dissimilar" phenomena. "A Proposal for Methodology" is complemented by "An Overview of History," since the theoretical and historical foundation of the methodology of contemporaneity lies in the particular yet prescient state of 1960s art in Japan.

A PROPOSAL FOR METHODOLOGY: "INTERNATIONAL CONTEMPORANEITY" AND BEYOND

A Brief Note on "International Contemporaneity"

Language at once reflects and defines what the speakers think. What is at stake is more than linguistic, with a multitude of unknowables hidden behind the facade of words. So it is with the key term of this book, "international contemporaneity" (*kokusaiteki dōjisei*), along with its companion term "contemporary art" (*gendai bijutsu*). Loaded with local implications, these terms were embedded inextricably in Japan's historical and cultural conditions and, in turn, defined the shape of local art discourse. As such, it is useful to decipher these two terms in light of the goals of this book.

The best place to begin is the word *gendai*—a Japanese equivalent of "contemporary"—which links "contemporary art" and "international contemporaneity," but differently from the current discourse on contemporary art. A convenient noun-adjective, *gendai* signifies a concrete sense of time ("[of] our era" and "[of] today"), with a distinct connotation of "times after *kindai* (modern times)," although the demarcation point from *kindai* to *gendai* is fluid. When it was combined with art (*bijutsu*) to form *gendai bijutsui* in the early 20th century, it initially meant "today's art" but soon acquired a layer of meaning as "new art" and "vanguard art."[6] By the mid-1960s, the association of *gendai bijutsu* with vanguard practices was firm. Critically, the moment of rupture was pinpointed at gestural abstraction, thanks to the discourse of *gendai* established by the critic Miyakawa Atsushi (discussed further in "An Overview of History"). The mainstreaming of the avant-garde cemented this sense of rupture and *gendai* came to assume an aura of historicity, not only as an area of practice distinct from the modern practices of painting and sculpture that date back to Meiji Japan in the late 19th century, but also as a periodization term signifying that which comes after *kindai bijutsu* (modern art 近代美術). In English, "contemporary art" took a different path to shed its generic meaning of "today's art" to become a critically loaded concept: it followed "postmodern art" of the 1980s and 1990s before it came into frequent use in the 21st century and began to invoke the discourse of "the contemporary" and "contemporaneity." *Gendai bijutsu* (現代美術) thus parallels "contemporary art," but their historical places differ. In Japan, the *katakana* rendition of *kontenporarī āto* (コンテンポラリー・アート) has been increasingly used to update *gendai bijutsu* as an equivalent of the 21st-century English discourse of "contemporary art."

The English counterpart, "contemporary," is more complicated, for it has two dictionary definitions: "happening or beginning now or in recent times" and "existing or happening in the same time period; from the same time period,"[7] with a synonym of the latter being more matter-of-factly "contemporaneous." The former corresponds to *gendai* and the latter to *dōji* and *dōjidai*. Accordingly, the noun form "contemporaneity" has to perform double duty as the noun form of both "contemporary" as *gendai* and "contemporary = contemporaneous" as *dōji*. When discussion concerns the critical and theoretical dimension of "contemporary," the compound form of "the contemporary" is often used customarily paired with "the modern," which is a bigger mouthful than the Japanese pair, *gendai* and *kindai*, equipped to connote both abstract/theoretical and concrete dimensions. Given the theoretical weight "contemporary" carries today, it is almost tempting to propose an English neologism of "contemporarity" in parallel with "modernity" to bestow on it the dignity it deserves.

As this exposition makes clear, in the construction of "international contemporaneity," translated from *kokusaiteki dōjisei* and its alternate form *kokusaiteki dōjidaisei*, "contemporaneity" has a distinct meaning of "contemporaneous." (In *dōjisei*, the versatile suffix *sei* makes an abstract concept out of a common noun.) As a linguistic matter, *gendai* and *dō(ji)dai* are *not* interchangeable, but in art discourse of 1960s Japan, *dōjisei* (*dōjidaisei*) became a key word in the field of *gendai bijutsu*, precisely because while *kindai bijutsu* was long saddled with belatedness, *gendai bijutsu* managed to overcome belatedness, with Japanese vanguard practices not only catching up with but also paralleling Euro-American counterparts in significant ways. This sense of reckoning evidently demarcated *kindai* from *gendai* in art, as the avant-garde was increasingly legitimized and came to the fore (i.e., mainstreamed) in the art world as *gendai bijutsu*. The addition of the spatial word "international"—that is, "between nations"—to the temporal term "contemporaneity" emphasized Japanese art's interface with the external world. In brief, the construction of "international contemporaneity" and "contemporary art" are fundamentally geohistorical, reflecting Japan's self-conscious assessment of its place vis-à-vis the external world (primarily Euro-America) and in the history of art.

"Contemporaneity" as a Geohistorical Concept

Taking a cue from "international contemporaneity" in the discourse of 1960s Japan, this book proposes to define "contemporaneity" as a key critical and methodological concept. The goal is to develop a methodology for narrating world art history of modernism, especially for the postwar period when art practice was increasingly internationalized and became contemporaneous—the development that prefigured today's globalization. Rather than treating "contemporaneity" as a measurement or signification of the present (now), I propose to define it as a measurement of the past (history) with geographical implications. In other words, contemporaneity is conceptualized as a geohistorical concept that enables us to understand both "facts" and "perceptions/lived experiences" of history. Indeed, in 1960s Japan, after having long measured their progress in modernism against Western counterparts, artists and critics reached a reckoning that "We are contemporaneous with them at this point." This awareness or observation marked a crucial moment in Japanese art history because of the country's status as a latecomer to modernism. A sense of contemporaneity thus engendered was tinged with urgency—urgency of interfacing and negotiating with the external world in a new light. This made the contemporaneity they felt more than a fact; it was a moment they had to live through.

In parallel with this lived experience, geohistorical contemporaneity can be understood as seeing something occurring contemporaneously *with* something else and living through it with that awareness. At a minimum, two entities are required for contemporaneity in this sense to be perceived and experienced. If so, we can extend 1960s Japan's experience into a more general formula: contemporaneity can be defined as a given locale's perception regarding itself and the outside world, one empirically shaped by its interface with another locale and/or the outside world. In other words, contemporaneity is as much objective "fact" as subjective "perception," which encompasses concrete awareness, observation, or experience. These two do not always coincide, partly because the former might only be obtained with the benefit of hindsight. Therefore, it is vital to sort out fact and perception in writing history. Even this gap in and of itself becomes a subject of study, since the gap is a measurement of distance between locales, most typically the putative center and the presumed periphery.

A few theoretical potentials are immediately recognized. Applied to world art history, contemporaneity as a geohistorical concept can be an analytical tool for measuring relationships between two locales at a given historical time and can help us plot transnational relationships. Moreover, the geohistoricity of contemporaneity enables us to put in perspective the moment(s) of reckoning of contemporaneity in each locale within its local history, for such a perception is at once objective and subjective. As such, geohistorical contemporaneity can serve as a strategy for decentering, for it is inherently comparative and it enables a view from the periphery, not just the center. As such it brings at least two (and potentially more) locales into discussion and generates a space that is open for multiple viewpoints to operate in, prompting a reexamination of the established narrative.

It is notable that the prescience of Japanese art discourse was in no small part informed by its perceived position at the periphery of modernity vis-à-vis the putative center that is Euro-America. The condition of a given locale necessarily affects its view of itself and of the outside world. What may be called Japan's "peripheral vision" was more attuned to the changing environment than the "central sight." It would not be surprising if, say, in Tokyo and New York the respective viewpoints toward the outside world were different, because by the 1960s New York had begun to assert its dominance in the international art world following the rise of Abstract Expressionism and solidified it with Pop Art. On one side, Tokyo saw the international tendency of gestural abstraction as a "shared experience" of many regions of the world; for that matter, many locales—Eastern Europe, Latin America, and other parts of Asia—embraced gestural abstraction as an international language. On the other side, New York saw it as a sign of "American triumph." Not so parenthetically, it may follow that Abstract Expressionism should be considered yet another "local" phenomenon of gestural abstraction within a global context. With this understanding, it is imperative to separate the *perception* of "(international) contemporaneity" and the *fact* (state) of "(international) contemporaneity."

When the agency of artists and others in a given locale is incorporated into the equation, the study of contemporaneity foregrounds a given locale and its specific contexts, exploding the center-periphery paradigm and relativizing the putative center(s)—as just demonstrated with gestural abstraction and Abstract Expressionism. Although contemporaneity is formulated on the appearance of similarity (visual or conceptual), the methodological goal is to uncover specific differences (being dissimilar) hidden underneath. In seeking contemporaneous parallel practices, we must look at their "similar yet dissimilar" characteristics. The investigation of the "local" is then the focal point of world art history's interest in contemporaneity, because whereas "similar" allows us to see a global picture, "dissimilar" anchors us to a local manifestation. In this respect, local and national histories serve as basic and indispensable building blocks in considering transnationality, although they are by no means the only component in world art history. It cannot be overstated that the more global we want to be in our investigation, the more local we need to be in our attention.[8]

Comparing "Similar yet Dissimilar": "Connections" and "Resonances"

Deployed as a methodological tool, contemporaneity functions to link "local" and "global," offering nodes of geohistorical narrations for examination. It frames them in the global-local coordinates rather than through the politically and historically inflected terms of center-periphery. Put differently, it becomes an important task for world art historians to seek out and examine linkable "contact points" of geohistory. "Contact points" is a methodological term, encompassing, but not limited to, actual events of "interfaces."[9] There are two basic ways to find contact points, corresponding to two modes of connectedness. They can be historically offered as actual interactions and other kinds of links, or retrospectively acknowledged in the form of visual or conceptual similarity even where few or faint links existed. I call the former "connections" and the latter "resonances."

Connection is more obvious and more direct, encompassing events that actually happened; in this interface, two parties may know each other personally, or at least one party knows of the other. Granted, the connectedness of 1960s art was a corollary of the growing connectedness of the whole postwar world engendered by, among other things, the ease of international travel and the dramatic expansion of communication and mediatization. However, when we factor in the lived experiences of Japanese artists, connections were not as direct as we might expect, often made through exhibitions and publications.

Resonance is far more indirect and post hoc in nature but as vital as connection in our study.[10] In resonances, there may have existed little actual linkage between two parties at the time, but a visual or conceptual parallel can be found often retroactively. Connections alone are not sufficient to link global and local in narrating world art history. By studying resonances, a good number of which can be found in 1960s art, we will have more contact points to link local and global and hence more possibilities for decentering and exploding the hitherto Eurocentric and closed narrative.

Connections have been uncovered in recent scholarship. The cross-pollinations among the Fluxus hubs, including Tokyo, readily come to mind. (It should be noted, however, that many Tokyo Fluxus artists began their conceptualist works prior to the occurrence of connections with Fluxus and thus also represent a case of resonances.) Yoshihara Jirō's discovery of Jackson Pollock's painting in 1951 was an important moment in the prehistory of Gutai. The news of American Pop Art in 1963 directly inspired the Anti-Art practitioner Ushio Shinohara to invent his *Imitation Art* series in 1963–1964. As demonstrated in this book, both The Play and GUN were aware of Allan Kaprow's Happenings and adopted the transliterated *katakana* term *hapuningu*; and The Play developed their own discourse of Happenings to support their practice. Except for his brief stay in New York in 1955–1956, the conceptualist Matsuzawa Yutaka's connections began in 1970, the year when he was invited to *Tokyo Biennale 1970* (figure 5.1), a major occasion of incoming interface. In that year, his affiliation with the Amsterdam-based Art & Project gallery began; and he launched the mail-art networking project *World Uprising* in 1971, thereby generating a series of outgoing interfaces.

As for resonances, an obvious example is Matsuzawa, who began to probe the possibilities of the invisible in art in the 1950s in an isolated environment with no real interlocutors either inside or outside Japan. By 1964 he established the organizing principle of *kannen* (meditative visualization), in parallel to the rise of conceptualism worldwide but with no contact with other conceptualists until later. The Play's *Voyage: Happening in an Egg* (figure 0.2) of 1968 had an unknown counterpart in the Swiss artist Herbert Distel's 3-meter egg sculpture of 1968, which was released into the ocean in 1970 under the title of *Project Canaris*.[11] A few years after inaugurating their 10-year project *Thunder* in 1977 (figure 6.13), a mountaintop observatory of lightning, the group learned that it had coincided with Walter De Maria's *Lightning Field*, also from 1977 (figure 6.12); they introduced themselves to De Maria by sending a letter in English, but no response came back.

There are many notable examples of synchronicities in 1960s Japan, making it a land of resonances. To mention a few more, the transgressive naked rituals staged by Zero Dimension (Zero Jigen), based in Nagoya and Tokyo, echo the raucous *Meat Joy* by Carolee Schneemann in New York and the abject performances by the Vienna Aktionists, all from the mid-1960s. In 1963 and 1964, just one year apart, practitioners proposed the idea of "Capitalist Realism" in West Germany (Manfred Kuttner, Konrad Lueg, Sigmar Polke, and Gerhard Richter) and in Japan (Akasegawa Genpei); Akasegawa's "Capitalist Realism" was an early theoretical entry in his epic project *Model 1,000-Yen Note Incident* (1963–1974). By the time Non-Art arose in the late 1960s, connectionless resonances occurred less frequently, due to the increasingly efficient mediatization of the art world; in Japan, certainly art journalism was following the developments overseas more closely than in the early 1960s. This makes the resonance between The Play and De Maria an extremely rare case.

In both connections and resonances, visual and conceptual similarities serve as the methodological and critical link to be investigated through comparison, a foundational tool of contemporaneity. Needless to say, comparison is nothing new in art history. In particular, the study of connections has long been part of the discipline, and they are very much present especially in transnational art history. Resonances, too, have been part of our intuitive experience in associating something unfamiliar with something familiar. For example, when the art historian Irving Sandler visited Gutai's first New York exhibition in 1958 at Martha Jackson Gallery, he annotated the checklist by associating American lookalikes to Gutai artists, such as Jackson Pollock to Kanayama Akira (his toy car painted abstraction) and Paul Jenkins to Motonaga Sadamasa (his poured painting).[12] We may go so far as to say that such a mnemonic or associative device is a natural part of art appreciation and art historical pedagogy. What is crucial to how we structure world art history is what we do with such associations. In New York, what Ming Tiampo calls "flattening"[13] happened, triggering the then default reaction through which unfamiliar forms from the periphery were made familiar by comparison under the assumption of periphery as derivative: the critic Dore Ashton devastatingly remarked that Gutai paintings resembled Pollock twice removed from the original (Japan from New York mediated by Paris, London, and other locales).[14]

In this discussion, however, we also have to remember that the Eurocentric equation of the center-periphery with the original-versus-imitation paradigm[15] has not been limited to Euro-America. Japan and other peripheral locales were equally prone to it. Worse, since the center would hold the authority to accord historical legitimacy, the margin more often than not relentlessly deployed the center's discourse that it had assimilated and internalized. A stunning example existed in 1960s Japan in what I call the "imitation discourse" waged by the art monthly *Geijutsu Shinchō* in its special feature, "Japan's Glory Upheld by Imitators," in 1969. Most egregiously, the magazine's 20-page album that compiled the sins of Japanese imitators included Sekine Nobuo's landmark Mono-ha work, *Phase—Mother Earth* of 1968, an alleged imitation of Claes Oldenburg's *Hole* from 1967 (figures 1.1, 1.2). In this case, historical amnesia compounded reverse chauvinism: the editorial declared Oldenburg as "the originator of hole digging" despite several existing local precedents (table 1.1).[16]

Contemporaneity frequently manifests itself through similarity in form, idea, and strategy. Therefore it is not enough merely to point out similarity between two (or more) instances. Similarity constitutes a starting point, not the goal in and of itself. Comparison to tease out the "similar yet dissimilar" natures of two or more works should rather be taken as an opportunity to delve beneath surface resemblance or correspondence and explore local knowledge in a contextualized reading. This strategy is an antidote to the troublesome problem of "original versus imitation," putting in perspective the presumption of the flow of influence from the center to the periphery and

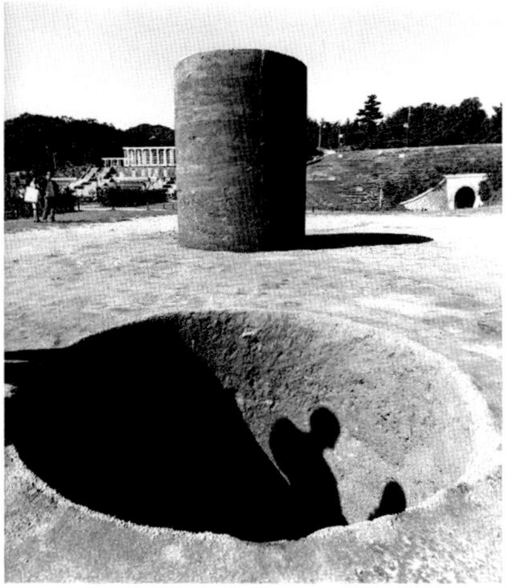

FIGURE 1.1
Sekine Nobuo, *Phase—Mother Earth*, 1968. Documentary photograph of site-specific sculpture at Suma Detached Palace Garden, Kobe. Photo © Murai Osamu.

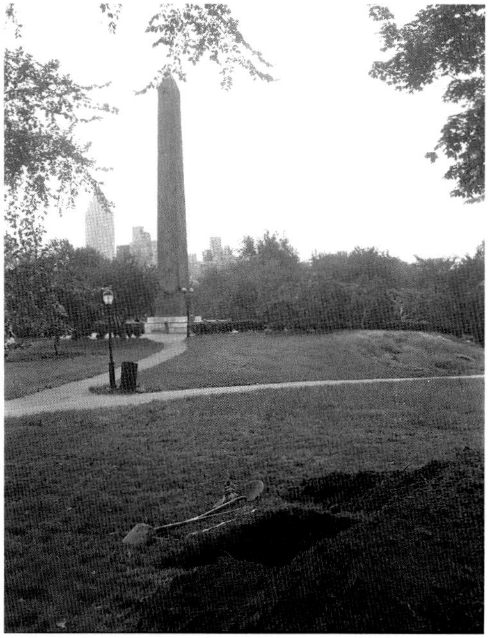

FIGURE 1.2
Claes Oldenburg, *Hole*, 1967. Documentary photograph showing a hole dug in Central Park. New York City Parks Photo Archive.

TABLE 1.1
Hole Digging in Japan and New York

1956	Yoshihara Michio, *Discovery*, created for *Outdoor Gutai Art Exhibition*, Ashiya.
1960	Walter De Maria, an untitled concept of digging a hole and covering it, published as "Meaningless Work" in *An Anthology* (March 1960).
1962	Miyazaki Junnosuke, an untitled performance of digging six or seven square six-foot-deep holes, on the beach of Fukuoka, for Kyūshū-ha's overnight program, *Grand Gathering of Heroes*.
1963	Yoko Ono, *Cloud Piece*, published in *Grapefruit* (1964).
1965	Group "I," *Hole*, *Independent Art Festival*, Gifu.
1967	Claes Oldenburg, *Hole (Placid Civic Monument)*, created for *Sculpture in Environment*, Central Park, New York.
1968	Sekine Nobuo, *Phase—Mother Earth*, created for *1st Kobe Suma Rikyū Park Contemporary Sculpture Exhibition*.
1968	Sol LeWitt, *Buried Cube Containing an Object of Importance but Little Value*, made by Dick van der Net.

grounding the study in a more nuanced multi-locale perspective. For example, understood through a contextualized comparison, the hole diggings by Oldenburg and Sekine cannot be more different than, say, Pollock's drip painting and Shiraga Kazuo's foot painting.[17] Not only did their holes vary morphologically; the visual difference was also informed by their contrasting concerns: Oldenburg's antiwar action and Sekine's topological thought experiment. Such an intrinsic difference is reinforced by a more extrinsic reading: whereas Oldenburg's hole digging heralded his future monuments in urban settings and would retrospectively earn him the status of a pioneering Earthworks artist,[18] Sekine's hole digging constituted the big bang moment of the Mono-ha movement.

Since the 1960s constitutes a watershed of contemporary art when many innovations and experiments emerged, it remains a basic task for art historians to establish a precise chronology of events. Nonetheless, the competition for priority—and a narration of history based on the embedded ideology of linear modernist progress—is not merely limiting but often futile, because there almost always exists a prior instance somewhere in this vast world characterized by contemporaneity and multiplicity, as the example of hole digging demonstrates. Our task is further complicated because history writing is never a precise science. A link between two similar works, or the lack thereof, may sometimes have to remain speculative. Sekine's knowledge may be reliably presumed from circumstantial evidence, in line with that of his fellow artists.[19] And he should have known at least one Japanese precedent, that by Group "I" from 1965, which was the talk of the town back then (figure 6.9). Still, it is what he did with such knowledge that is crucial. The same applies here: even though we might not question Oldenberg's unawareness of Group "I" (with a presumed unilateral flow of information from the center to the margin), we need to examine the possibility of his knowledge of Walter De Maria's unrealized concept of 1960. And again, applying the same logic to the New York artist: even if he did know it, what counts is what he did with such knowledge. What is at work in these cases of knowing precedents and responding to them inventively is "interpoetics," as proposed by Ming Tiampo, who adopted and updated Harold Bloom's reflections on influence and originality in *The Anxiety of Influence* (1973).[20] It goes without saying that "conspicuous imitation"—lazy imitations that do not even try to understand, let alone transcend, the originals—remains a serious concern and must be distinguished from the creative learning of interpoetics. This is precisely why "similar yet dissimilar" must be examined through contextualized comparison.

A fascinating coincidence is "Capitalist Realism," the same name coined for two different practices in Düsseldorf and Tokyo less than one year apart. As the chronology demonstrates (table 1.2), it is most likely that Akasegawa was unaware of the German project, but we can never be sure.[21] Our starting point of comparison, then, is the works themselves, and examining how dissimilar they are. Indeed, they are as

TABLE 1.2
Early Days of "Capitalist Realism"

Late 1962–early 1963	Akasegawa, residing in Tokyo, identifies paper currency as an object of close observation for his Anti-Art project and begins painting *Morphology of Revenge*, a 100-times-magnified realistic replica of the 1,000-yen note (figure 6.6). He continues his painstaking reproductive work until 1968, without finishing the painting.
February 1963	Akasegawa uses the mechanical reproduction of the 1,000-yen note for an announcement of his solo exhibition at Shinjuku Dai-ichi Gallery in Tokyo. After this first *Model 1,000-Yen Note*, he has more notes printed to use for his works and performances.
May 1963	Richter et al. coin the term "Capitalist Realism" to promote their self-proclaimed "first German Pop Art exhibition," held at a butcher shop in Düsseldorf.
October 1963	Richter and Lueg stage *Living with Pop: A Demonstration for Capitalist Realism* at the Berges furniture store in Düsseldorf.
January 1964	Akasegawa is investigated by the Tokyo Metropolitan Police for currency imitation.
February 1964	Akasegawa publishes "On 'Capitalist Realism'" in *Nihon dokusho shinbun* (Japan book-readers' newspaper) and defines his mechanically reproduced money as *Model 1,000-Yen Note*, to counter the legally defined criminal concepts of "imitation money" and "counterfeit money."

different beyond the shared term as Sekine's and Oldenberg's hole digging is beyond their shared urge—a "primal" urge, perhaps—of digging the earth. Under the rubric of Capitalist Realism, Richter and Lueg illuminated the middle-class values and the repressive mechanisms of Germany's postwar era by displaying themselves as commodities at a furniture store; in their case, the immediate inspiration came from a news story on Pop Art they found in *Art International*.[22] Akasegawa formulated his theory of Capitalist Realism in response to his becoming the target of a criminal investigation for "currency imitation" in his mechanical reproduction of the 1,000-yen note.[23] He coined the concept of *model*, as opposed to the legal concepts of *imitation* and *counterfeit*, which enabled him to examine state power by scrutinizing its financial instrument, usually too mundane for a second look. His super-realism was in practice facilitated by the use of mechanical reproduction (printed money) and illustrator's techniques (painted money).[24]

Coincidences happen, of course, but in this case we can look toward a larger postwar condition that the German and Japanese practitioners shared, prompting in both cases a critical investigation of capitalism. In both of these former Axis powers that achieved "economic miracles" under the Cold War order, vanguard artists increasingly turned to the everyday as the object of their investigation. If the postwar politics and economy are too broad a correlation (since this also applies to other industrial countries), their individual political and cultural backgrounds reveal a narrower scope of commonality. Among the four Germans, Richter, born and raised in East Germany, once worked as a Socialist Realist painter, while Akasegawa was keenly aware of art and politics of the Eastern Bloc, having come of age in the 1950s when one of the progressive painting practices in Tokyo was Social Realism in the vein of Communist-inflected Reportage Painting. These hidden but shared inspirations and references, if not direct connections, are indicative of the widespread state of international contemporaneity during the 1960s.[25]

Connectedness does not write itself into history. That is why we need to actively identify contact points by uncovering connections and especially resonances and articulating their similar yet dissimilar nature. But how can we make our study more than the sum of multiple connections and resonances? If they are essential building blocks of world art history, how can connectedness be coherently narrated without being broken into disparate fragments? Once art history is decentered through locating contact points, a next step is to *regroup* them.

Exploding the Narrative: Contemporaneity and "Narrative Tangents"

In constructing world art history, contemporaneity offers an organizing principle, wherein connections and resonances, two markers of contemporaneity, serve to generate contact points with varying degrees of connectedness that can be examined in terms of their similar yet dissimilar nature. These contact points constitute components of multiple narratives. A strategy of world art history, contemporaneity helps us construct and amplify a narrative from bottom up (or "periphery in"), rather than imposing a top-down (or "center-out") abstract framework. Whereas contemporaneity is an overarching macro concept, it becomes a micro concept when deployed in any particular instance. As a foundational tool, comparison of connections and resonances creates contact points that puncture the established Eurocentric narrative. Contact points will open up the existing narrative and paradigm, creating intersecting tangents of perspectives. With each contact point, the rigid linearity of the familiar narrative is loosened, and new narrative tangents will be drawn in reflection of a local logic and context, with contemporaneity binding them together.

As mentioned in the previous section, area studies and local art histories are building blocks of a world art history that is truly transnational. If the knowledge base of local histories in question is weak, there is more than a considerable risk that comparison becomes superficial. When we construct narrative tangents, we do not just pinpoint "dots," that is, individual works or artists, but rather we look at "flows," that is, stories with local contexts, which by definition involve local topography and

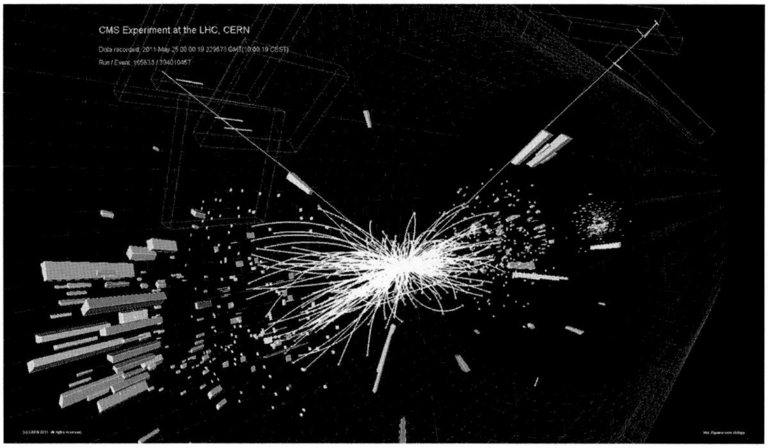

FIGURE 1.3
A typical candidate event in the CMS Standard Model Higgs Search, with two high-energy protons (in red towers) and tracks of other particles produced in the collision (yellow). © 2011 CERN. (Also plate 2.)

channels of continuity. "Dots" may be subject to superficial comparison or, worse, easily overlooked altogether. Of course, by adding their metadata (certain monographic background information), we can make dots bigger, but still dots are dots. In contrast, "narrative flows" form a more expansive unit and hopefully a more effective unit of knowledge that makes learning of local (national) histories not optional and cursory but compelling and integral—because in world art history, comparisons become far more meaningful if contact points become "entry points" to further look at local histories.

This methodology may be likened to the scientific visualization of hypothesized yet invisible subatomic particles by means of the modern cloud chamber or the contemporary particle collider, also known as atom smasher (figure 1.3, plate 2).[26] In a sense, we all know in abstraction that there are many histories both inside and outside the established and entrenched Eurocentric paradigm. The problem is that they often remain invisible and require orchestrated "atomic collisions" to make them tangible and available to study. Comparison is one such method, opening up the linear master narrative and revealing the possibility of additional and alternate narrative tangents passing through or originating from each contact point. If comparative art history may not necessarily create a new master narrative, it can generate multiple clusters of stories. Which is to say, while comparisons help us "decenter" Eurocentrism, narrative tangents enable us to proceed with the next step: "regrouping" the decentered parts.

Let us take a concrete example in order to illustrate how narrative tangents may work in linking global and local art histories. Thanks to the recent development of scholarship in the English- and Japanese-speaking spheres, Gutai offers itself as a good case to explore. For a long time, what was perceived as Gutai's "return" to painting after its burst of innovative experiments was viewed negatively, for it does not fit the linear evolution of the avant-garde history that moves from painting to performance art by way of assemblage and environment, more or less modeled on Allan Kaprow's formulation. Although both Kaprow and Gutai learned from Pollock's drip painting as their point of departure, Gutai took a different path. We can draw two narrative tangents from the fateful connection Yoshihara made with Pollock in 1951, when he personally saw two drip canvases by the American artist, along with other American abstractions, shown first as part of that year's Yomiuri Independent Exhibition and then brought to Osaka, his hometown.[27] Since Yoshihara had thought long and hard of ways to create a new painting culture since the end of World War II, he immediately recognized Pollock's bold newness and candid take on materiality, when few other Japanese artists or critics even took note of the American's work.[28] Three texts Yoshihara published in 1951–1953 on Pollock reveal the profound impact Pollock had on the future Gutai leader, who conducted in-depth research on the nature of drip painting, concluded Pollock's discovery was very "original," and saw the possibilities of painting beyond modernism.[29] This narrative tangent, short as it may be, comes out of a significant case of "resonance" with other Pollock discourses at the time, including those not only by Clement Greenberg, Harold Rosenberg, Michel Tapié, and Allan Kaprow but also by many others who dialogued with Pollock's art elsewhere. When these are regrouped comparatively rather than seen individually, they become a cluster of narrative tangents.

This mini tangent of Yoshihara's Pollock discourse morphs into a larger tangent after the founding of Gutai in 1954, when younger artists joined Yoshihara's endeavor to create a new painting culture. In their efforts under Yoshihara's rigorous leadership, Gutai members imaginatively thought of *e* (pronounced *eh* and signifying "picture" in Japanese). As Murakami Saburō, one of the lead members, would recall later, the idea of *e* enabled the members to interpret painting in "expanded manners," allowing them to create installation and performance works as pictures.[30] Thus, Tanaka envisioned *Work (Bell)* of 1955 as a picture that demarcates the exhibition site as a mental pictorial space through its ringing sounds; and her *Stage Clothes*, performed for the first *Gutai on the Stage* presentation in 1957, was an exercise in changing abstract color compositions. Likewise, for Shiraga Kazuo, his brutally performative *Challenging Mud* was intended to extend his foot painting by deploying the whole body and create what can be called a "mud picture" (figure 1.4). The adaptation of "*e* = picture" as their creative concept allowed the Gutai members to construct a new painting culture in both painterly and performative manners, outside of the Western

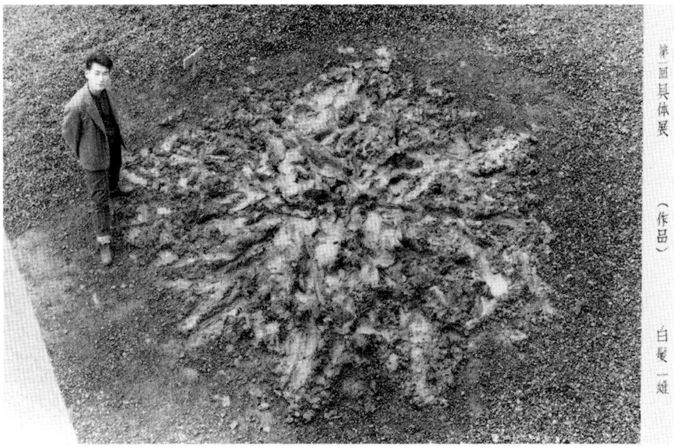

FIGURE 1.4
Shiraga Kazuo standing next to *Challenging Mud*, at *1st Gutai Art Exhibition* at Ohara Kaikan, Tokyo, 1955. Postcard. Courtesy of Amagasaki Cultural Center.

logic of modernist painting. At the same time, in embodying their search for the ethics of freedom informed by Japan's postwar democratic ideal, it adds a further localized theoretical dimension to their radical adventures.[31] Starting from American abstraction and mediated by Yoshihara's study of Pollock, this narrative tangent markedly differs from the familiar Euro-American narrative of performance art and Happenings emerging *in defiance of* gestural abstraction. It thus accords Gutai a place of distinction in a cluster of storylines emanating from gestural abstraction in general and Pollock in particular.

The examples I have examined in this section are from 1960s Japan, but if contact points are explored in various locales and possibly different periods, the pool of our accumulated knowledge can be reorganized and made more pertinent than if such examples are understood individually. The degree of a given locale's connectedness may affect the result: 1920s Japan may not be as explosive as 1960s Japan, and 1960s China is less connected than 1980s China. No doubt the 1960s is a treasure trove of contemporaneity, ripe for further investigation through this methodology.[32] Also important to keep in mind is that just as an event in world art history can create a cluster of narrative tangents, the same applies to an event in national art history that reanimates it. In fact, one merit of thinking in terms of clusters of narrative tangents is to circumvent the intuitive linearity of our history-writing mind. It is not unlike mapping a river with numerous tributaries and branches—but more three-dimensionally, factoring undercurrents below its surface at different locations. Or even creating a weather map of sorts, with a mass of cold or hot air varyingly affecting areas it passes through depending on their topographies, or tropical storms arising simultaneously from oceans separated by continents.

AN OVERVIEW OF HISTORY: THE RISE OF "CONTEMPORARY ART"

The Expanded 1960s of Japanese Art

The diversity of vanguard practices and their international contemporaneity make 1960s Japan an important site to study in the global postwar. The evolution of these practices was complex, and neither an imposition of Western logic nor facile comparisons do justice to its significance. To unpack it in the context of world art history, it is beneficial to introduce an order that reflects local ideas, whose diversity and complexity equal local practices.[33] Toward this end, I have developed a simplified diagram spanning two decades, or the "expanded 1960s of Japanese art" from 1954 to 1974 (figure 1.5, plate 3). Consisting of three major tendencies or movements—Gutai, Anti-Art (*Han-geijutsu*), and Non-Art (*Hi-geijutsu*)—this outline not only parallels the general development of global tendencies—from gestural abstraction to Pop Art, from minimalism to conceptualism and post-minimalism—but also takes into account the local discourses that accompanied local manifestations of these tendencies.

The 1960s as presented in this diagram differs from the calendar definition or the geopolitical definition of the decade. In postwar Japan, the decade is geopolitically defined by *Anpo*, or the U.S.-Japan Security Treaty, which was first signed in 1951, along with the San Francisco Peace Treaty that brought Japan back into the international community and ended the U.S. Occupation. The *Anpo* treaty allowed American troops to be stationed in Japan, turning Japan into America's forward base for its Asian military operations in the Cold War order. The decennial renewal of the treaty, in 1960 and 1970, thus became a flashpoint of domestic politics, with the anti-*Anpo* struggles creating major political turmoil at both ends of the decade. The 1960 demonstration against the *Anpo* revision was fierce, resulting in the resignation of the

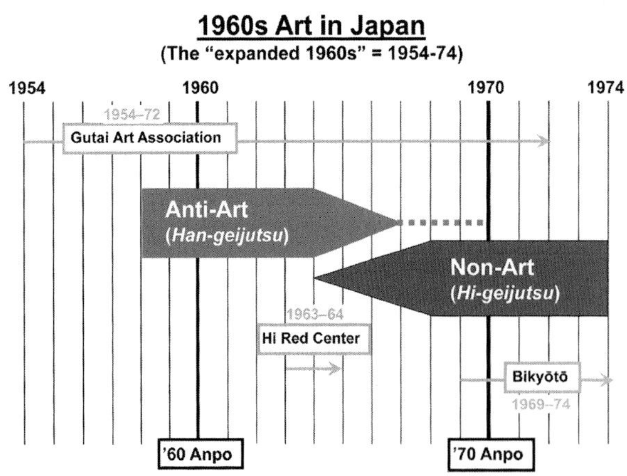

FIGURE 1.5
Chronology of Japanese art in the expanded 1960s. © Reiko Tomii. (Also plate 3.)

whole cabinet under Prime Minister Kishi Nobusuke. After this devastating lesson, the state vowed not to repeat a similar fiasco at the time of the treaty's 1970 extension. Toward the end of the decade, as the student movement and the anti-Vietnam War protest converged with the anti-*Anpo* movement, the state accordingly made every effort to crush opposition, bringing about the near collapse of the New Left with smoldering effects for another few years. If the year 1960 introduced an era buoyed by the country's high economic growth and increasingly affluent consumerist life but with an undertone of political anxiety, the year 1970 ushered in an era of apathy, or *shirake* (resulting from the political defeat of the left), and an expanding lifestyle of leisure (awakened by and promoted after Expo '70), with economic threats felt from the global oil and currency crises.[34]

Apart from this geopolitical calendar, the 1960s in reference to art in Japan can be understood in an expanded sense, spanning from 1954 to 1974. (Instead of "the long 1960s," I use the adjective "expanded," because the decade as defined is not only long but immensely expandable, with other tendencies often seamlessly added on, as will be explained.) The expanded decade begins with Gutai, founded in the city of Ashiya, west of Osaka, in 1954.[35] On the one hand, Gutai's radical experiments in "performance paintings" of many varieties prefigured the global 1960s tendencies including installation art and performance art (figure 1.6). On the other hand, their painting experiments set the precedent for gestural abstraction in Japan, before the so-called "Informel Whirlwind" (*Anforumeru senpū*) struck Japan. With the publication of its namesake journal, Gutai was a highly discursive collective, articulating their desire for a new art that encouraged the ethics of freedom in the aftermath of the country's defeat in World War II under the totalitarian regime whose aggression had had ruinous consequences in the Asia Pacific regions.

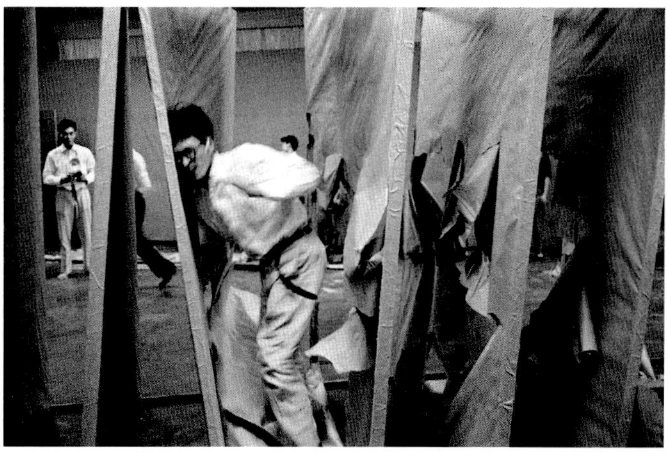

FIGURE 1.6
Murakami Saburō, *Passing Through*, 1956. Documentary photograph of performance at *2nd Gutai Art Exhibition*, Ohara Kaikan, Tokyo, 1956. Photo by Ōtsuji Kiyoji; Ōtsuji Seiko Collection, Musashino Art University Museum & Library, Tokyo. © Ōtsuji Seiko.

Anti-Art began in 1958, partly prompted by the Informel Whirlwind, which unleashed a new generation of vanguard artists. In 1960, another impetus came from the pent-up energy amplified by the historic *Anpo* protest.[36] The Anti-Art practitioners rebelled first within the frame of painting and then quickly went beyond it, as they avidly incorporated everyday objects in their works. The proliferation of assemblages with junk and readymade objects, called *objets* (derived from the French *objet* and pronounced *obuje*) in the Japanese art lexicon, characterized Anti-Art (figure 1.7), but the practitioners even transcended the institutional boundary of art, infiltrating the public sphere, as exemplified by Hi Red Center and Zero Dimension, among others (figure 1.8). The term *Han-geijutsu* was attributed to the critic Tōno Yoshiaki, who used the label of "junk anti-art" in 1960 in discussing the work of Kudō Tetsumi shown at that year's Yomiuri Independent Exhibition, which served as the main arena for vanguard artists. His usage derived from the historical Dada and the postwar context of Neo-Dada/Nouveau Réalisme, but it took on its own life in Japan's art world and stuck as *the* defining term of the early 1960s. Tōno was challenged by the critic Miyakawa Atsushi in the Anti-Art debate, in which the latter famously theorized Anti-Art as the "descent to the everyday," which became a formulation as influential in the 1960s as Clement Greenberg's "flatness" was to New York art.[37] Not coincidentally, Miyakawa's rise with his cerebral approach to art criticism that hinged on developing the discourse of *gendai* in the early 1960s bridged the 1950s and 1960s. Influential from the expanded 1960s onward, the so-called Big Three critics (Tōno, Haryū Ichirō, and Nakahara Yūsuke) emerged in the 1950s, while younger critics (Ishiko Junzō and Lee Ufan, as well as Fujieda Teruo and Minemura Toshiaki) came to the fore in the late 1960s and exercised their influence in the 1970s and beyond. Following Miyakawa, they were keenly aware of the significance of *gendai* and endeavored to divine the meaning and direction of *gendai bijutsu*.[38] Since Anti-Art constituted the fervent assault on the modern (*kindai*) construct of "Art" with a capital A, or *geijutsu*, it had a broader critical implication than the parallel Euro-American terms of Neo-Dada, Nouveau Réalisme, and Pop Art, and it became an umbrella term for Japanese critics to discuss all of those Euro-American tendencies together.

One possible culmination point of Anti-Art is January 1964, when Yomiuri announced the suspension of its independent exhibition, the movement's unofficial flagship, although the practice of Anti-Art continued beyond this date. The next possible culmination point is 1967, when Anti-Art's theoretical claim "against Art" was rescinded in Akasegawa Genpei's ill-fated and theoretically complex *Model 1,000-Yen Note Incident*. In this saga, which originated in the mechanically reproduced 1,000-yen note, the artist was criminally investigated, tried, and ultimately found guilty. In the process, the artist chose to disown his Anti-Art stance to defend his freedom of expression.[39] The ultimate culmination point is 1970, the year of Expo '70, Asia's first world's fair held in Osaka. On this occasion, many Anti-Art practitioners worked to

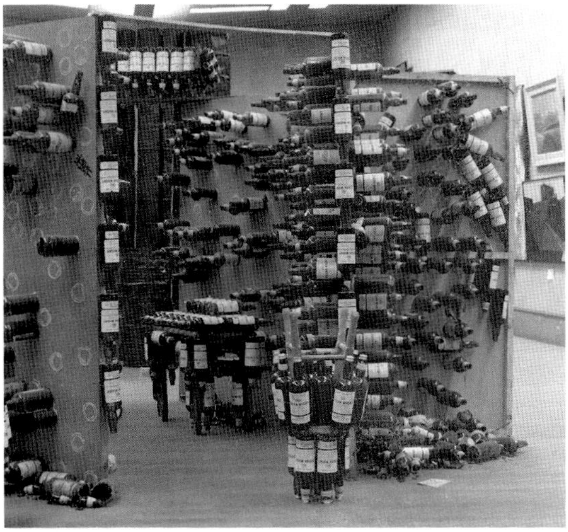

FIGURE 1.7
Yoshimura Masunobu, *Mr. Sadada's Reception Room*, 1961. Installation view at the Yomiuri Independent Exhibition at Tokyo Metropolitan Art Museum in 1961. Photographer unknown; Takiguchi Shūzō Papers (c. 1945–1979), Keiō University Art Center, Tokyo.

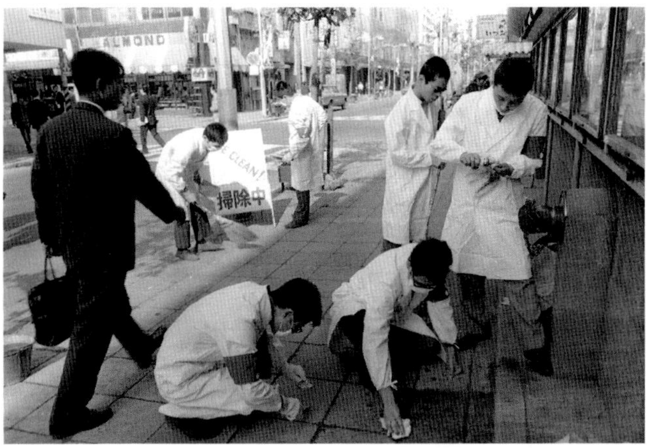

FIGURE 1.8
Hi Red Center, *Cleaning Event* (officially known as *Be Clean!* and *Campaign to Promote Cleanliness and Order in the Metropolitan Area*), October 16, 1964. Documentary photograph of performance. © Hirata Minoru.

produce big-budget corporate pavilions.[40] The cultural left considered Expo '70 the state's ploy to distract attention from the *Anpo* struggle, and condemned the artists' cooperation with this state project as a devolution of the avant-garde.

Non-Art (*Hi-geijutsu*) took over when Anti-Art lost its momentum mid-decade, making its presence known in 1968. Unlike the impassioned Anti-Art, Non-Art was more sober and somber, focusing on the critique of the institutions of *bijutsu*, or "art" with a lowercase "a." If Anti-Art ultimately embraced the idea of "making something" in its sometimes chaotic manner, Non-Art decidedly pursued the ideology of "not making" (*tsukuranai koto*) in three different directions: conceptualism, Mono-ha (School of Things) (figure 1.9), and performance art. The term Non-Art is taken from a special feature, "Voices of Emerging Artists," in the February 1970 issue of *Bijutsu techō*, which was subtitled "From the Horizon of Non-Art."[41] Among the texts in the feature, the roundtable among Mono-ha's core group centering on Lee Ufan and Sekine Nobuo served as the group's founding manifesto and presented the discussion of "not making."[42] Much like the idea of "dematerialization," coined in 1967 by Lucy Lippard and John Chandler to acknowledge the departure from the material reliance on conventional painting and sculpture, Mono-ha's rhetoric of "not making" concerned their defiance of the convention of art making in pursuit of a different mode of production.[43] If Mono-ha envisioned involving the viewer in phenomenological experiences through their works, the pioneering conceptualist Matsuzawa Yutaka decisively eschewed any materiality in his work from 1964 onward in order to facilitate the development of the viewer's latent mental faculties.

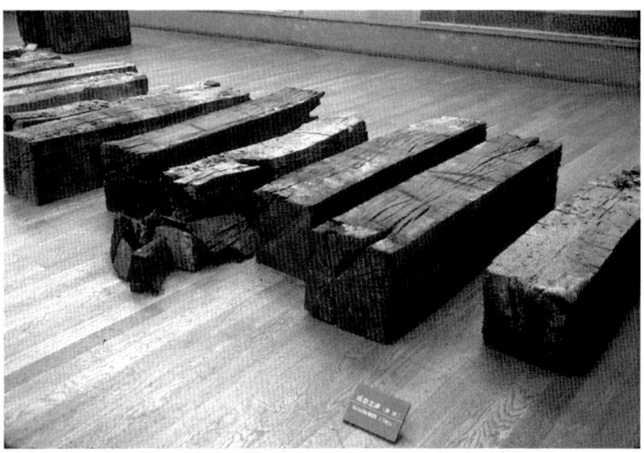

FIGURE 1.9
Narita Katsuhiko, *Sumi 7–22*, 1970. Installation view at *Tokyo Biennale 1970* at Tokyo Metropolitan Art Museum. Photo by Horikawa Michio.

The definite beginning point of Non-Art is assigned to 1968, the launch year of Mono-ha[44]—not 1964, the launch year of Matsuzawa's art of *kannen* (visualized meditation)—partly because Mono-ha was the more theoretically vocal proponent of Non-Art and more visibly signaled the rise of *gendai bijutsu* in the mainstream art world. However, as this book will reveal, Matsuzawa was not alone in the wilderness, joined there by The Play and GUN as well as his Nirvana School. Metaphorically speaking, beyond their wildernesses was a farther "out of bounds" terrain, so to speak. Those found in this realm were Zero Dimension and fellow Ritualists (Gishiki-ha), who categorically rejected the institutional space and irreverently mounted anti-Expo protests while embracing the "anarchy of the body," in the memorable words of the art historian KuroDalaiJee (figure 3.4).[45] Between the two non-mainstream domains, while the mainstream considered the wilderness a useful resource to tap when deemed beneficial or expedient, "out of bounds," a golf term, metaphorically signified "completely outside the playing field" of the institutional space.[46] In recognition of the relevance of their work, Matsuzawa, The Play, and GUN were all summoned to the mainstream exhibitions (discussed in the next section). In the late 1960s and into the 1970s, Non-Art was intellectually and morally entwined with leftist politics. In both art and politics, the status quo was the designated Enemy No. 1. Significant in this context was the presence of Bikyōtō (short for Artists Joint-Struggle Council), a Non-Art collective, founded in 1969 at Tama Art University in Tokyo in the midst of the student movement (figure 1.10). Whereas its pre-1970 activism focused on the institutions of art, such as the museums, as well as the salon exhibitions and other large-scale exhibitions, its post-1970 projects interrogated what they called "internal institutions" that should emerge in an artist's mind even if she or he was outside the institutional space.[47] Ultimately in 1974, one of its subgroups, the Second Bikyōtō Revolution Committee, made a pact of "not making or exhibiting at all" during the year 1974, pushing the Non-Art ideology of "not making" to a logical conclusion. And this extremity marks the terminal date of Non-Art and the expanded 1960s.

This is a highly abbreviated outline of Japanese art in the expanded 1960s, spanning over two decades from Gutai to Bikyōtō. However, it can be amplified with subnarratives that entwine with the core narrative. For example, Jikken Kōbō/Experimental Workshop, a collective contemporary to Gutai, pioneered in technology-based intermedia and prefigured Environment Art (*Kankyō geijutsu*), which would emerge in the mid-1960s and play a central role in Expo '70.[48] The development of modernist painting traversed all three movements, while a tendency called "graphism" (*gurafizumu*) that arose in mid-decade reveals proximities of vanguard art to graphic arts and print culture, adding a social and popular dimension.[49] In the lively underground scenes, visual cultures—such as experimental theater and film, vanguard manga and animation, and Butoh dance—flourished, concurrent to and often merging with Anti-Art and Non-Art.[50] Although not easy to integrate seamlessly, artists such as Yoko Ono

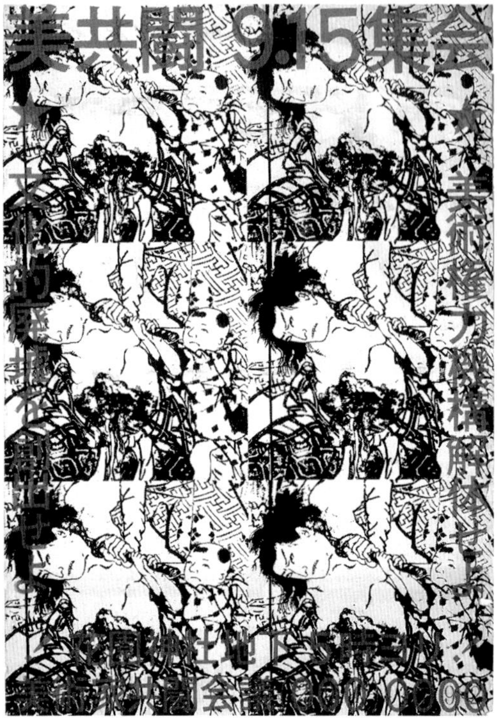

FIGURE 1.10
Bikyōtō, *Bikyōtō 9/15 Meeting*, 1969. Poster, designed and printed by Hikosaka Naoyoshi; framed, 73.2 × 51.8 cm. Collection of Hikosaka Naoyoshi.

and Kusama Yayoi (who was in New York in the 1960s) had frequent or extended contacts with their homeland to form independent narrative tangents.

It should be noted that an intensely eventful unfolding of Japanese politics can also be amplified in this simple diagram, using the two *Anpo* struggles as benchmark events. Local and national struggles for Okinawa, for example, which was ruled by the U.S. until 1972 and has since continued to serve as a major American military base in East Asia, intersected with the *Anpo* struggles, for anti-*Anpo* signified both anti-militarism and anti-Americanism. From a geopolitical perspective, the rise of contemporary art and its mainstreaming, as examined in the following section, were part of the rise of the nation-state Japan as an economic force in the Cold War order. The emergence of a new art echoed the country's assertion of a new identity on the international stage on par with the U.S. and other advanced industrial countries. Yet it is rather reductive to seek a one-to-one causal relationship between art and politics. Not that Japanese contemporary artists were apolitical. As has been carefully studied with Gutai and Lee Ufan, politics was latently present in their work as they profoundly reflected on the ethics of their expression. By looking at their intent in its ethical scope, we can at once honor their commitment to expression and their lives as thinking beings.[51] This proves true for Matsuzawa, The Play, and GUN, who were all deeply concerned with the historical and sociocultural state of the world, if not of the nation of Japan per se. Another important factor to consider in this respect is the fact that Japan's art world was a highly sophisticated modern entity that had steadily evolved from the late 19th century onward. The art establishment itself thus represented a status quo of the first order. This gives a political significance to the act of revolt against its entrenched territorialism as much as its conventionalized aesthetics. The mainstreaming of contemporary art, as will be discussed, has to be understood in this context, for this strain of radicalism arose from within the system rather than from outside.

Mainstreaming of the Avant-Garde: Another Post-Yomiuri Story

The post-Yomiuri years began in January 1964, when the Yomiuri newspaper announced the termination of its annual independent exhibition, inciting a number of developments in vanguard circles. The adventures in the wildernesses, the topic of this book, are but one of them. While the sudden loss of the reliable museum venue sent the unaffiliated artists scrambling to figure out their next moves, unbeknownst to them their habitat was expanding dramatically. Complementing the wilderness activities, this transformative development effected the "mainstreaming of the avant-garde," which went hand in hand with the steady expansion of infrastructures for *gendai bijutsu* (table 1.3).

The infrastructural development was already set in motion in 1963 on the museum front. In that year, a Kyoto branch of the National Museum of Modern Art, Tokyo, was opened (hereafter "Kyoto Modern" and "Tokyo Modern"). Whereas the Tokyo Modern had paid occasional attention to *gendai bijutsu* since its opening in 1952,[52] the Kyoto Modern instituted an annual survey of *gendai bijutsu*, titled *Trends in Contemporary Japanese Art*.[53] For this survey, the Kyoto Modern selected 20 to 30 mostly young artists who had produced notable works in the previous year, thereby offering an indicator of the state of contemporary art. After the branch was upgraded to a full-fledged museum as the National Museum of Modern Art, Kyoto, in 1967, the annual survey continued through the ninth in 1970.[54]

In 1964, in the northern regional city of Nagaoka, Niigata Prefecture, the Museum of Contemporary Art, Nagaoka (hereafter "Nagaoka Contemporary"), was founded as the country's first-ever museum of contemporary art by Komagata Jūkichi, a local banker and private collector.[55] Not only did the Nagaoka Contemporary boost the local atmosphere of vanguard art, encouraging the formation of GUN (chapter 4); it played a national role by instituting an annual competition to "proactively contribute to the advancement of *gendai bijutsu*."[56] Reflecting its agenda of collecting international contemporary art, the Nagaoka Contemporary invited foreign artists and jurors to its annual competition, known as *Nagaoka Contemporary's Award Exhibition*, from the second year onward. Modest though it may be, its effort for internationalism—inviting American, Italian, British, and West German artists and judges in 1965, '66, '67, and '68 respectively—was significant. The competition served as a foundation for the museum's collections (award-winning works entered the collection), while its judging process that was open to the public was instrumental in acclimating both the international and the contemporary in the mainstream art world.

A distinctly Japanese area of institutionalization was the cultural programs organized and financed by newspaper companies. In particular, three national dailies—Asahi, Mainichi, and Yomiuri—offered a broad range of arts programming, which included exhibitions of European modernism in the immediate postwar years. They effectively defined postwar Japan's mainstream cultural landscape, while the public sectors prioritized economy over culture in recovery efforts. Yomiuri's annual independent exhibition was an attempt to democratize the art world by circumventing the entrenched salon system dominated by the artists' organizations.

In the post-Yomiuri years, the void left by Yomiuri was filled by its rival company, Mainichi. Just as Anti-Art cannot be discussed without Yomiuri's independent exhibition, the transformation of the avant-garde as *gendai bijutsu* cannot be discussed without the role played by Mainichi.[57] In 1952 and 1954, Mainichi began its twin biannual exhibitions, respectively *International Art Exhibition, Japan* and *Contemporary Art Exhibition of Japan* (hereafter "Mainichi International" and "Mainichi Contemporary"). Unlike Yomiuri's independent exhibition, Mainichi's exhibitions were establishment affairs complete with awards, and their conservative nature was slow to change. In 1961, Mainichi emulated the prestigious Venice and São Paulo Biennales by changing the official English title of the international biannual to "Tokyo Biennale." In 1962, the company added a juried "open-call" section to the by then invitation-only Mainichi Contemporary, offering vanguard artists a valuable opportunity for entrance into the official art world. However, a real retooling geared toward "contemporary art" and "international contemporaneity" did not begin until 1967, when the newspaper company added three judges from abroad to the hitherto Japanese-only jury panel charged with selection of awardees for the Mainichi International. The year 1969 was originally slated for the Mainichi International according to the two exhibitions' alternating calendar. However, Mainichi decided to showcase its international biannual in the same year as Expo '70, and instead presented the Mainichi Contemporary in the 1969 slot with a complete overhaul. It put the establishment practices in perspective (through a retrospective with select award-winning works from earlier Mainichi exhibitions), took the temperature of what was truly new (through a "Frontiers of Contemporary Art" section organized by the critic Haryū

TABLE 1.3
Mainstreaming of *Gendai Bijutsu*

1952	The National Museum of Modern Art, Tokyo ("Tokyo Modern") opens.
	The Mainichi newspaper company inaugurates the biannual *International Art Exhibition, Japan* ("Mainichi International").
1954	The Mainichi newspaper company inaugurates the biannual *Contemporary Art Exhibition of Japan* ("Mainichi Contemporary").
1961	The official English name of "Mainichi International" is changed to *Tokyo Biennale*.
1962	A competitive "open-call" section is added to "Mainichi Contemporary."
1963	The Kyoto Branch of the Tokyo Modern ("Kyoto Modern") opens and inaugurates its annual survey *Trends in Contemporary Japanese Art* (continued through 1970).
1964	Museum of Contemporary Art, Nagaoka ("Nagaoka Contemporary"), opens and inaugurates *Nagaoka Contemporary's Award Exhibition*.
1967	Foreign judges are added to the jury panel of "Mainichi International."
1968	*Kobe Suma Rikyū Park Contemporary Art Exhibition* is inaugurated.
1969	The thoroughly revamped "Mainichi Contemporary" includes the invitational section "Frontiers of Contemporary Art" (curated by Haryū Ichirō). Its competitive sculpture section is divided into *Rittai* A and *Rittai* B sections, where *rittai* literally means "three dimensions."
	Hakone Open-Air Museum inaugurates *Contemporary International Sculpture Exhibition*.
1970	"Mainichi International" is organized as *Tokyo Biennale 1970: Between Man and Matter* (curated by Nakahara Yūsuke).
	The Tokyo Modern presents *August 1970: An Aspect of Contemporary Art* (curated by Tōno Yoshiaki).
1971	"Mainichi Contemporary" includes the invitational section "Man and Nature" (curated by Haryū Ichirō). Its competitive sections are streamlined into two sections, *Heimen* (two dimensions) and *Rittai* (three dimensions).

Ichirō), and tried to discover young talents (through a juried open-call section). It even took a drastic measure to make the sculpture section commensurate with the state of vanguard practice: a new rubric, *rittai* (literally "three dimensions"), was introduced and the section was split into categories A and B, with A encompassing conventional sculpture and B absorbing anything else. Then came the 1970 Mainichi International, under the title of *Tokyo Biennale 1970: Between Man and Matter*, curated by the critic Nakahara Yūsuke, which put Tokyo on the map of international art and gave an indisputable demonstration of international contemporaneity for the first time in postwar Japan.

All these reforms in Mainichi's twin biannuals were single-handedly engineered by Minemura Toshiaki, a young staffer at Mainichi's culture enterprises department, who would go on to become an influential art critic from the 1970s onward.[58] In tandem with a few other large-scale exhibitions, such as the open-air sculpture competitions at the Suma Detached Palace and Hakone's sculpture garden, newly instituted in 1968 and 1969 respectively, Minemura's reforms decisively enhanced the visibility and legitimacy of vanguard practices as *gendai bijutsu* in the mainstream art world.

The banner year for the mainstreaming of *gendai bijutsu* was 1969. Along with the "Frontiers" section of the Mainichi Contemporary, the Kyoto Modern's *Trends* exhibition highlighted Non-Art tendencies, thus reiterating the growing sense of international contemporaneity in vanguard practices that were quickly dematerializing. In 1970, capitalizing on this development, Nakahara Yūsuke created a very concrete sight of international contemporaneity in his Tokyo Biennale, assembling works from Japan *and* abroad that reflected the latest trends of conceptualism, minimalism, and post-minimalism as well as video and performance art. By no means were artists passive participants in this development. Without their indefatigable innovations and experimentation, that is, without any relevant art to display, these institutional efforts would certainly not have happened.[59] In this sense, a fortuitous symbiosis marked the evolution of 1960s art in Japan.

Yet the backlash was as strong. Conservative critics attacked the incomprehensibility of *gendai bijutsu*, and Minemura left Mainichi partly due to the poor attendance at the 1970 Tokyo Biennale. The 1971 Mainichi Contemporary continued Minemura's reforms without him: the open-call competition section was streamlined into two categories, *heimen* (two dimensions) and *rittai* (three dimensions); the invitational section, "Man and Nature," was organized by Haryū in a collegial competition with Nakahara's *Between Man and Matter* from the year before. After these three critically important iterations, however, the newspaper company reconfigured the biannuals to make them less polemical and more palatable to the establishment.

The gallery scenes changed in tandem with the aesthetic evolution. It is almost a cliché to say that there was little market for contemporary art in 1960s Japan. Few vanguard artists could make a living by making art; this was a major difference between, say, Tokyo and New York or Paris. Yet a handful of commercial galleries began to support younger artists in the 1960s. Especially Tokyo Gallery and Minami Gallery contributed greatly to internationalizing and mainstreaming *gendai bijutsu*. Both galleries added lead Gutai members to their rosters,[60] with Minami in particular actively bringing both the persons and the works of Euro-American artists (Jean Tinguely, Robert Rauschenberg, and Jasper Johns, among others) to Japan upon Tōno's recommendations.

Emblematic in the post-Yomiuri years were two solo exhibitions held at Tokyo Gallery in 1966, featuring Takamatsu Jirō and Ushio Shinohara. For the two main protagonists of the Anti-Art movement, these were their first ever solo ventures at a commercial gallery. The results could not have been more divergent. Takamatsu presented an installation based on his cerebral and subdued *Shadow* series, which he began in 1965 to pursue his theoretical interest in the gap between cognition and perception—the interest already manifesting itself in his Anti-Art string works. His critical achievement and subsequent commercial success resulted in a long relationship with the gallery which would also support his sometimes unsalable works, such as his conceptualist piece of number-bearing stones in 1969 (figure 4.5). Appointed as a lecturer at Tama Art University in 1968, Takamatsu cut a dandy figure as a star of *gendai bijutsu* and was considered a leading practitioner until his death.[61] Shinohara, on the other hand, gravitated toward Pop Art as his mid-decade endeavor. At Tokyo Gallery, he showed the gaudy fluorescent *Oiran* series, which followed the ironical *Imitation Art* series. Known for his bad-boy image that exemplified the junk and action side of Anti-Art, Shinohara received some critical attention with his Pop *Oiran*,[62] but the exhibition was a commercial bust. Despite his inventive efforts to keep pace with a general move toward intermedia and technology art, he remained underappreciated and frustrated, and in 1969 left for New York. He settled there permanently to continue his prolific art making, which has gained him admiration yet yielded only sporadic financial success.[63]

A definitive local factor, theoretical *and* economical, was Expo '70, in which many vanguard artists were involved along with other cultural practitioners. If money was at issue with the marketization (commodification) of the avant-garde in 1960s New York, money became a bone of contention around Expo '70 among the avant-garde in 1960s Japan, who were otherwise financially deprived. To realize a futuristic vision of the first world's fair in Asia, an unprecedented amount of money was budgeted, and contemporary artists were mobilized to collaborate with architects and designers to produce technology-based intermedia environments of *Kankyō geijutsu* (Environment Art). We cannot simplistically equate their Expo participation with a betrayal of the vanguard ideal.[64] However, financial reward had long eluded the avant-garde since prewar Japan, and the slow mainstreaming process that was taking place during the 1960s barely translated into monetary terms. In reality, therefore, it was not Takamatsu but Shinohara who was closer to the norm for vanguard artists. Since the infusion of money into contemporary art was strictly tied to Expo '70, the impression made by the windfalls was all the more inevitable: Expo corrupted the avant-garde. Most typically, Akasegawa Genpei blasted Environment Art as a "money-soaked anti-establishment."[65]

The end of *zen'ei* (the avant-garde) was not a novel notion. As early as 1962, the critic Haryū Ichirō suggested the end of the prewar-style avant-garde in the mold of Dada that, in his conception, would rally like-minded artists under a single program or principle.[66] By 1970, the mainstreaming of the avant-garde was near completion. Instead of the punitive term "*neo*-avant-garde," the term *gendai bijutsu* replaced *zen'ei*. In retrospect, what was lost with *zen'ei* was amply compensated for by *gendai bijutsu*. The latter connoted a set of determinedly new forms of practice that departed from the modern conventions of *yōga* (Western-style painting, but typically easel-sized oil painting) and *Nihonga* (Japanese-style painting). *Gendai bijutsu* shed the sense of belatedness that saddled Japan's art of *kindai* (modernism) and asserted a state of international contemporaneity with Euro-American counterparts. If Anti-Art degenerated into the "money-soaked" Environment Art that embellished Expo '70, a new generation in the guise of Non-Art now carried the banner of contemporary art. Mono-ha perfectly fit the bill. Such Mono-ha artists as Sekine Nobuo, Lee Ufan, and Suga Kishio shared an interest in cognition and perception with Takamatsu, the face of *gendai bijutsu* who bridged Anti-Art and Non-Art via Environment Art and what I call Tricky Art, a tendency for visual trickery centering on *Tricks and Vision: Stolen Eyes*, a 1968 exhibition jointly held at Tokyo Gallery and Muramatsu Gallery.[67] However, Mono-ha artists outgrew the engagement with Tricky Art to produce large-scale impermanent installations. In particular, Sekine's work won award after award in 1968–1969, with each prize financing the next project, beginning with the Mainichi Contemporary (1968 and '69) and continuing with the Nagaoka Contemporary's Award Exhibition (1968) and the outdoor sculpture competitions at Suma (1968) and Hakone (1969). The winning streak was enhanced by his solo exhibition at Tokyo Gallery in 1969 and triumphantly culminated in his selection as a Japanese representative, along with the New York-based Shūsaku Arakawa, at the 1970 Venice Biennale by the critic Tōno Yoshiaki.

Nothing more eloquently demonstrated the completion of the mainstreaming of the avant-garde as *gendai bijutsu* than *August 1970: An Aspect of Contemporary Art*. This exhibition was curated by an influential critic (Tōno) and sited at an institution (the Tokyo Modern) to present mostly Mono-ha artists as the fresh face of contemporary art, ready to ascend the ladder of a new mainstream in Japanese art. In the domestic rise of contemporary art, *August 1970* was perhaps the most important event in 1970, more so than that year's Tokyo Biennale, because the future for museum-sanctioned contemporary art was set in course. In the construction boom of prefectural and municipal museums that began in 1970, reflecting the country's thriving economy, modern and contemporary art museums, not newspaper companies, became the primary engine of contemporary art. In this new environment, *gendai bijutsu* became an object of desire and legitimacy, while *kindai bijutsu* was revered as part of the historicized past.

Discursive Origins of International Contemporaneity in 1960s Japan

Situated in the far eastern end of the Eurasian continent, the archipelago of Japan faces the vast span of the Pacific Ocean to the east. In ancient times, culture, along with political, economic, and social systems, came from the continent (China) and the peninsula (Korea) across the western sea; in modern times, they came from the West, which meant Europe and the U.S. As Japan avidly absorbed and assimilated external influences while nurturing its own culture, it was historically conscious of its isolated place away from the center. Belatedness was an unspoken characteristic of its relationship with the outside world, particularly after the mid-19th century when the construction of modernity became the nation's mandate and aspiration.[68] After the defeat in World War II, with the urgency of being part of the international community, the idea of "internationality" (*kokusaisei*) and "world relevance" (*sekaisei*) came to the fore, underscored by the persistent anxiety over belatedness as a non-Western latecomer to modernism.[69]

In 1951, the critic Takiguchi Shūzō deployed the term "world relevance" to ask in a comparative sense: How would the current works of Japanese art fare side by side with Western works?[70] This was a vital question at the time of Japan's reentry into the international community, with the signing of the San Francisco Treaty in 1951 allowing Japan to send its artists to the Venice Biennale in the following year.[71] The debate over internationality continued throughout the 1950s, on the pages of *Bijutsu hihyō* (Art criticism) and other art magazines.[72] This topic deserves further study that goes beyond the scope of this book. Suffice it to say, as the critic Tōno would later recall in the 1970s, the nature of internationality in 1950s Japan differed from that in the subsequent two decades, because the former was shaded by the country's inferiority complex toward European art since the late 19th century.[73] Or, rather, the internationality discourse of the 1950s can be characterized by "aspiration," that is, the question of how to achieve internationality and create art equipped with world relevance. This was more transparently the case with such traditional arts as *ikebana* (flower arrangement) and ceramics that endeavored to produce "avant-garde" forms to shed the taint of wartime nativism, but this international aspiration was widely felt in culture in general, including art and architecture. Interestingly, the peripheral locale of Mexico figured prominently in the internationality discourse of the 1950s as an alternative modernity, thanks to *An Exhibition of Mexican Art* at the Tokyo National Museum in 1955.[74] Mexico became an object of aspiration and emulation, as exemplified by On Kawara's move there in 1959.

The discursive shift that Tōno referred to was prompted by the introduction of Art Informel in 1956 and the infatuation with gestural abstraction that swept even the more conservative part of the art world. Most important among the critical responses was "After 'Informel'" by the critic Miyakawa Atsushi. This award-winning essay of 1963 was praised by the elder critic Takiguchi as having "struck an epistemic hoe"[75] into the at best inconclusive and at worst confused Informel discourse. For example, among the Big Three critics, Haryū Ichirō left the best, though very dense, criticism,[76] while Nakahara Yūsuke mostly circumvented the movement and Tōno Yoshiaki contributed a tardy "homage" with little criticality (in his own words).[77] Miyakawa's innovation was to propose the discourse of *gendai* as a new value system, as opposed to *kindai* (modernity).

> Although people have already started talking about *gendai* kaiga [*contemporary* painting, emphasis original], as opposed to *kindai geijutsu* [modern art], they just distinguish from *kindai* what has stylistically become a matter of fact. However, *kindai* is not merely a style concept [*yōshiki gainen*]; it constitutes a value concept [*kachi gainen*], underlined by an intense consciousness and sensitivity of *kindai* first recognized by Baudelaire.
>
> Paradoxically speaking, having so long deemed *kindai* a synonym of *contemporain* [*kontanporan*], we now reach a point at which we should not relegate *gendai* to the generic concept of *contemporain*, a point at which we should redeem in advance *gendai* from *contemporain*.[78]

Miyakawa benefited from his late entry into art criticism in authoring "After 'Informel,'" his veritable debut piece, well after the Informel movement transmuted into Anti-Art. A theorist conversant with French critical theory, the young critic saw the state of international contemporaneity as a given that allowed him to freely discuss any artists he chose to in making his argument.[79] In this regard, the *gendai* he proposed to articulate was expressly universal, not locally specific. Which is to say, he understood the state of international contemporaneity as a fact and assumed an omniscient perspective. His writing, indeed, reveals his explicit Eurocentrism, as his discussion centers primarily on the work by Euro-American artists.[80]

Miyakawa's claim for *gendai* was more empirically supported by two of the Big Three. In 1965, Tōno authored a volume entitled *Contemporary Art: After Pollock*, ostensibly Americanizing Miyakawa's periodization.[81] Haryū was engaged with the notion of international contemporaneity more locally than Miyakawa and more explicitly than Tōno. He first went for contextualization in his short survey of two decades of postwar Japanese painting in 1966, "Postwar: Toward the Formation of International Contemporaneity." He clearly declared,

> I see the crux of the problem that separates [today] from the prewar period in the fact that Japan's contemporary art has been, like it or not, submitted to worldwide perspectives and trends and the consciousness of international contemporaneity has been formed.[82]

On the one hand, he saw the "divide between *kindai* and *gendai*" in the rise of mass society (*taishū shakai*) which coincided with Art Informel. On the other hand, he decisively associated the claim for international contemporaneity with the post-Yomiuri works by mostly Anti-Art artists, which in his view embodied the imminent end of modern individualism. He delineated the shape of contemporary art at that time, by grouping Miki Tomio (known for his obsessive "ear" motif), Shūsaku Arakawa ("diagram painting"), and Ushio Shionohara (Pop-inspired *Imitation Art* series) among others under the rubric of "Fictional Realism."[83] Significantly, the moment of reckoning for Haryū came in 1967 when he visited the Paris Biennale, in which Japan had participated since its inauguration in 1959. He used his experience to open his contribution to "12 Japanese Artists Who Can Compete Internationally," a special feature in the January 1968 issue of *Geijutsu Shinchō*.

> Last fall, at the [5th] Paris Biennale, three Japanese artists, including one photographer, received awards. Standing in the chaotic junkyard-like gallery, which reminded me of the Yomiuri Independent Exhibition, I found Japanese works revealing distinctly original ideas. I don't think I was being partial to our native sons. Nakahara Yūsuke, the commissioner [of the Japanese representation], and I talked about several other Japanese artists who would equally have cleared the [international] judgment, had their works been shown here.[84]

Three award winners were Takamatsu Jirō, a star of contemporary art; Miki Tomio, a fellow Anti-Art practitioner working then in the vein of Environment Art; and Takanashi Yutaka, a photographer who would join the vanguard collective Provoke in 1968. The two artists were at the forefront of the increasingly mainstreamed *gendai bijutsu*, and their inclusion signaled the positive attention it received from an official segment of the art world charged with selecting Japanese representatives for large-scale international exhibitions.

Haryū's pride was amplified by the favorable treatment Japanese sculptors received at the Guggenheim International Exhibition from the curator Edward Fry in the same year. His recollection of Paris speaks loudly, given the long-held desire for a latecomer to modernity to achieve a perceived international standing on the world stage. What he did not explicitly say was equally important: Japanese vanguard artists had finally caught up with Euro-America. With this confidence, likely borrowing from Miyakawa's playbook, he cheered for a new art by a new generation of artists:

> Today, all over the world, we need artists who have crossed this fault line [Informel] and developed their own methodologies to decisively confront the issues of civilization and humankind, to challenge the problem of time-space in a whole manner. As far as Japan is concerned, [...] we have finally achieved consciousness of the "contemporary" [*kontenporarī*] in the sense of "international contemporaneity." It is natural that the younger generation has quickly eschewed the domestic standard and the establishment hierarchy. The works by artists in the forefront, albeit still in a small number, contain kernels of ideas that are capable of transforming art worldwide.[85]

If the emerging Miyakawa made a theorist's detached observation, the veteran Haryū articulated an insider's earnest appraisal based on his experiences. In other words, while Miyakawa took "international contemporaneity" as a fact, Haryū discussed it as a matter concerning "consciousness." When he organized the "Frontiers of Contemporary Art" section for the 1969 Mainichi Contemporary, he expressed his curatorial premise through the "self-awareness" of international contemporaneity and "disappearance of distance" in perception. Haryū later rightly took credit for popularizing the idea of international contemporaneity in the 1960s.[86] With his conceptualization of it as "consciousness" and "perception,"[87] he left an important critical legacy for world art history, teaching us the importance of the "perception" of international contemporaneity in the late 1960s in Japan.

Haryū's affirmative vision is but one factor in the discourse of international contemporaneity. His idea had both allies[88] and detractors. As touched upon above in the section "A Proposal for Methodology," the most sensational attack came from the art magazine *Geijutsu Shinchō* with its August 1969 special feature, "Japan's Glory Upheld by Imitators." While the 20-page album visually put forth the "imitation discourse," the critic Ōshima Tatsuo, who contributed the lead essay, bitterly lamented "contemporary mannerism" and the "catching up and overtaking" mentality that characterized the obsession of "overcoming modernity," which resulted in nothing more than "hybrid contemporaneity, stateless cosmopolitanism, or uniformity of the ultramodern avant-garde."[89] It is notable that Ōshima's objection to international contemporaneity boils down to "similarity" and lack of national, regional, or local distinction, as implied by such words as "uniformity," "hybrid," and "cosmopolitanism." He evidently saw the root cause of all these symptoms in an "imitation" rampant in Japan, even though he acknowledged that some resemblances might be accidental.[90] Thus understood, Ōshima's imitation discourse serves as a cautionary tale of world art history in which contemporaneity is a key critical and methodological concept. The comparative methodology of "similar yet dissimilar" is not only an antidote to the debate of originality versus imitation, but also a means to resist the smothering sameness that contemporaneity may bring about.

Another objection concerned the uncritical acceptance of international recognition as the criterion of international contemporaneity. In 1969, considering the state of contemporary art in Japan, the critic Fujieda Teruo rightly saw a "passive" form of internationalism in Japan's art world buoyed by the news of Japanese artists receiving positive attention at the 1967 Guggenheim International and winning awards at such major international venues as the 1967 Paris Biennale and the 1968 Venice Biennale.[91] This was—and indeed still is—a thorny issue for Japan in the periphery. Fujieda issued a stern admonishment against "enjoying having international contemporaneity" and instead proposed the exercise of a rigorous criticism correctly leveled equally against Japanese art and Western art in order to transcend modernism.[92] Related to this is Lee

Ufan's objection, made in 1968, to Japanese critics who "wield foreign-made yardsticks," in a "groundless false fashion of international contemporaneity."[93] In 1972, when Lee dialogued with Fujieda on the state of Japanese art, he expanded on this point.

> Be it action painting or Informel, the most serious problem is that Japanese critics never discussed [the phenomenon] with their own words. Not that there is no action painting or Informel, Primary Structures or Minimal Art, Pop Art or Op Art, in Japan. Yes there are, but [many aspects of these works] diverge from what these terms [usually] signify. Generally speaking, these terms would do. [...] But take for example Pop Art. Japanese Pop works contain issues that the word Pop cannot capture, that will fall outside it. [...] In these cases, critics should have identified terminology to address such aspects and [along with it] accept [the phenomenon of] Pop Art into Japan.[94]

It is as though Lee foresaw the challenge of world art history more than 40 years ago, pointing out the need to see "similar yet dissimilar" aspects of parallel practices. As a theorist-artist, Lee certainly practiced what he preached by inventing a set of terms to discuss Mono-ha. For us in the 21st century, the challenge is bigger. Yet in studying 1960s art, we have the advantage of the remove of time, which allows us to reexamine the history thus far narrated and narrate it anew.

* * *

Eventually, the project of world art history will require more than individual efforts in order to create a collective and collaborative scholarship.[95] This book provides a trial for the methodology, as proposed in this section, in a small dose using a paradigmatically significant site, 1960s Japan. The next three chapters (chapters 2–4) will be devoted to laying out local knowledge of the three practitioners in the wilderness, Matsuzawa Yutaka, The Play, and GUN. The last two chapters (chapters 5–6) will build on the previous monographic chapters and examine connections and resonances. A study of connections, chapter 5 will identify specific contact points by looking at how these practitioners "lived through"—that is, consciously participated in—international contemporaneity. Chapter 6 is a study of resonances that examines their works "in retrospect," giving them retrospective assessments, in order to create contact points beyond their lived experiences and place their works in a transnational comparative framework.

In theory, such a "transnational" framework should be global, incorporating pertinent works for comparison from, for example, Korea, India, Brazil, or any other areas that offer contemporaneous and similar works.[96] Nevertheless, in practice chapters 5 and 6 will hew closely to Euro-America, mainly in reflection of Japan's historical circumstances. Above all, in their lived experiences the Japanese artists most frequently interfaced with Euro-American art, which constituted their primary point of reference for both contemporaneity and internationalism, as illustrated above. Still, it should be remembered that Japanese practitioners had to negotiate a treacherous terrain of contemporaneity—treacherous because even though modernism certainly entered a new phase, which the Japanese embraced by calling the avant-garde *gendai bijutsu*, neither the perception nor even the reality of "center-periphery hegemony" ever disappeared. Their struggles will be a crucial topic for connection studies of 1960s Japan.

Another critical factor is the reality of postwar Japan shaped by its vexing history. While most non-Western regions suffered colonialism in modern times, Japan was a colonizer that emulated the Euro-American powers and made the twin claims of nationalism and pan-Asianism to justify its military aggression. After its defeat in World War II, nationalism became an untenable intellectual position, making internationalism an ideal philosophy in culture—although in politics, the conservatives persisted in keeping alive the longing for emperor-centered nationalism. What is more, the American Occupation and the subsequent security alliance with the former occupier pushed the nation more toward Euro-American internationalism than toward the nationalism of self-determination embraced by the former colonized countries as an effective foundation for decolonization. Thus, in postwar Japanese art, Euro-American practices are more readily comparable and more historically germane than those of, say, India,[97] as a starting point. (As will be suggested in epilogue, expanding this study to a broader scope is the next logical step.)

At the same time, we cannot afford to avoid the problematics of the center-periphery ideology in world art history. In order to decenter, amplify, and regroup, we need to address not just the periphery but also the center through comparison. Indeed, the goal of this book is to place analytical pressure on the center and on Eurocentrism from the direction of 1960s Japan through the methodology of contemporaneity.

2 MATSUZAWA YUTAKA'S WILDERNESS OF NIL

A quintessential master of the wilderness, Matsuzawa Yutaka cuts a singular figure in 1960s art, locally and globally. From the very outset of his career, which began in the immediate postwar years, he quietly explored ways to express the invisible in art, informed by his distrust of material civilization. His ultimate goal was to transcend the modern norm of Enlightenment rationalism and humanism, which he believed had produced military technologies that had taken humanity to the brink of extinction. His endeavor thus constituted first and foremost an intervention into the institution of mind that dictates how to think and what to think. But making art his medium of choice, he inevitably called into question the whole institution of art.

By the mid-1960s, his long and persistent search resulted in a distinct brand of conceptualism. Art is an inherently material practice that engages the visible. When it engages the invisible, as it has done from the time of ancient religious art to modern Symbolism, abstraction, and Surrealism, it still materially deploys the visible. This inevitably made Matsuzawa's aspiration to express the invisible invisibly an almost impossible proposition, and his search for an elegant solution demanded much trial and error. At the core of his visionary and immaterial conceptualism was his theory of Psi (*pusai* in Japanese pronunciation). Its development was tortuous and enigmatic, as the beginning of any new theory might be. Intellectually voracious, Matsuzawa conducted extensive research into the known and unknown, Eastern and Western, new and old realms of knowledge to formulate his ideas. Three disciplines proved to be useful: parapsychology, contemporary physics, and non-Zen Buddhism, all of which involve the visualization of the invisible, rationally or irrationally, through the mental faculties. Transdisciplinary in his search, the artist eventually merged these different meditative methodologies under the rubric of *kannen*, which has a double meaning of "idea," as in modern metaphysics, and "meditative visualization," as in Pure Land Buddhism. Thus was born his "art of *kannen*" (*kannen bijutsu*).

The complex evolution of Matsuzawa's art was punctuated by three decisive moments in 1945, 1956, and 1964. The first was when he witnessed the ruins of Tokyo after the March 1945 firebombing, which exposed the fragility and futility of material civilizaton, pushing him to a lifelong search for the invisible. The second took place in February 1957 when he discovered in New York a late-night radio program on station WOR specializing in things paranormal, which opened his eyes to a realm of the unknown beyond the five senses and prompted him to develop his theory and practice of Psi. The third was when he had what is known as a "Revelation" on June 1, 1964, which culminated in his adaptation of *kannen* as his principal methodology, setting his conceptualism in full motion. His engagement with conceptualism is thus divided into two phases, before and after the Revelation. Accordingly, chapter 2 is divided into two parts: the first part is pre-Revelation, during which time he established himself as Mr. Psi; and the second part examines his post-Revelation development and his radical reconstruction of art through *kannen*.

THE MAKING OF MR. PSI: TOWARD CONCEPTUALISM

A Transdisciplinary Mind: From Shimo Suwa to New York and Back

Born in 1922 in Shimo Suwa in central Japan, Matsuzawa Yutaka spent his impressionable teenage years in his native town during the so-called Fifteen Year War, which extended from 1931, when the Imperial Japanese Army caused the Manchurian Incident, to 1945, when Japan was defeated in World War II.[1] He advanced to Waseda University in Tokyo to study architecture in 1943. Thanks to his major, which the state deemed part of science and technology and hence vital for the war effort, Matsuzawa was exempted from conscription but mobilized to work at a factory in Niigata away from Tokyo in February 1945.[2] Accordingly, he did not experience the historic U.S. firebombing of Tokyo in March 1945. Still, when he came back to Tokyo, he was stunned to see many parts of the capital razed to the ground, literally presenting a landscape of nothingness (figure 2.1). Although he must have understood the overwhelming American military might in abstraction, he had to face the weight of reality in an extreme form.

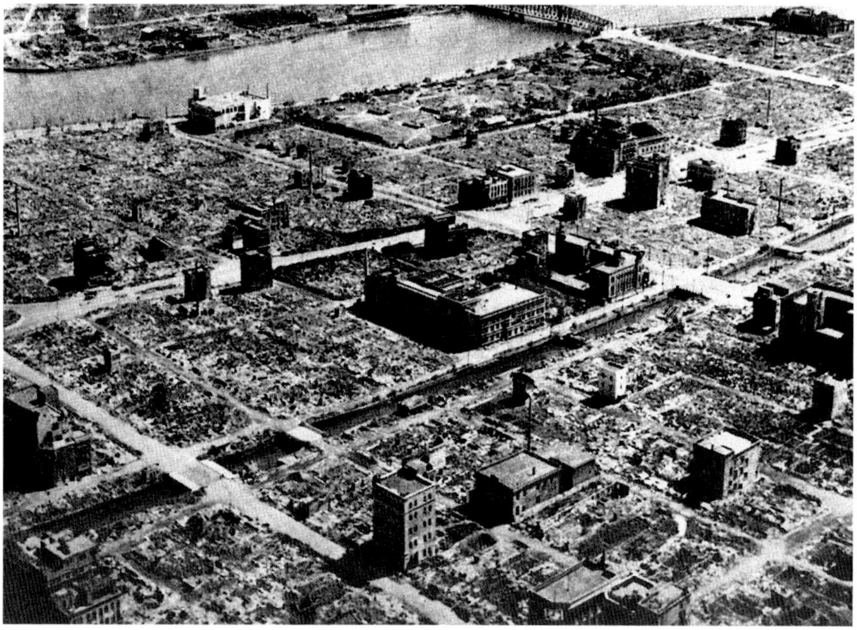

FIGURE 2.1
Tokyo after the U.S. firebombing (Hamachō and Shinbashi areas), 1945. Photo © The Mainichi Newspapers.

His graduation thesis in 1946, "Plan for Fujimi Highland Artists' Colony,"[3] speaks loudly of his disenchantment with material civilization. In his thesis essay, entitled "On the Ruins," he poetically wrote: "That which humans make will eventually perish, humans will eventually perish." This sentiment was enforced in a speech he made at the school's reception for new graduates in which he proclaimed: "I don't believe in the solidness of iron and concrete. I want to create an architecture of soul, a formless architecture, an invisible architecture." Implicit here is the fundamental worldview that would shape his art: his faith in art and his distance from the center. In the postwar state of tabula rasa, as a rebuilding project, he proposed to create a community for artists in his home region away from Tokyo's urban civilization. His rejection of material culture was underscored by his critique of human-made civilization that had brought about war. Such words as "soul," "formless," and "invisible" signaled the beginning of his search for the invisible.

Upon graduation, he helped to build housing for Occupation Army officers. But in 1948, after two years, he gave up on architecture altogether and returned to his hometown. He soon took up a position teaching mathematics at night high school. The nighttime teaching allowed him to devote the rest of his time to his research, as he took up poetry and painting, both of which he had begun to dabble in during his college years. In order to overcome the barrier of the Japanese language, he composed nine "Symbol Poems" in 1954, while launching a research project to construct an "operational hypothesis on a universal language,"[4] foraging through such sources as Leibniz's philosophy and French Lettrism. By then, however, he had also grown frustrated with the communicative limitation of language as such, and eventually shifted his focus to art.[5] During this time, the issue of communication firmly emerged as his goal in his search for the invisible.

On the art front, having been trained in architecture and having shifted to art from poetry, Matsuzawa had a strong sense of mission to expand the scope of art as serious reflections on human civilization. Unconstrained by a traditional art education, he thought outside the box and aimed to "add that which has not existed."[6] His transdisciplinary thinking helped him enormously, as did his voracious intellectual curiosity, combined with his deep commitment to the invisible.

From 1952 onward, he sent his work to the annual Yomiuri Independent Exhibition and the annual salon of the Bijutsu Bunka (Art Culture) Association, a vanguard exhibition society established in 1939 with a strong Surrealist contingent. Intensely interested in signs and symbols, by 1952 he added to his intellectual arsenal cybernetics and general semantics (via *ETC: A Review of General Semantics*)[7] as well as UFOs and parapsychology. The fruits of his research were poured into his art, as evidenced by *Time-Space for Telepathy* of 1954, now lost (figure 2.2). Billed as "solid painting," a cube delineated by metal pipes was filled with abstract shapes which would change their aggregate appearance as the viewer walked around it. According to his chronology, he further experimented with new material in two "chemical paintings," *010101* and *011011*, which he produced in January 1955 in collaboration with the photographer Kitahara Isao by pouring photographic sensitizer and other chemicals over rusty sheets of galvanized iron; they were presented at the inaugural exhibition of Alpha Art Circle (Arufa Geijutsu Jin), established around him in 1954 (figure 2.3).[8] In collaboration with younger poet Kaneko Shōji, Matsuzawa was instrumental in authoring the manifesto which called for a "true avant-garde art" in a post-atomic age that would transcend not only the categories within culture—i.e., art, poetry, and music—but also the boundaries between the humanities and sciences.[9] (Kaneko would later join Matsuzawa again as a member of the Nirvana School in 1970.)

An innovative interdisciplinary collective was short-lived, however, mainly because its driving force, Matsuzawa, left for the U.S. on a Fulbright fellowship in the summer of 1955 to expand his horizons. He spent one academic year at Wisconsin State College-Superior (now University of Wisconsin-Superior), as a visiting scholar whose proposed research theme was the "objective measurement of beauty."[10] At one point, he entertained the idea of going to MIT to study with Gyorgy Kepes, but he declined an invitation from the former New Bauhaus teacher.[11] He moved instead to New York on a Japan Society fellowship in the summer of 1956, affiliated with

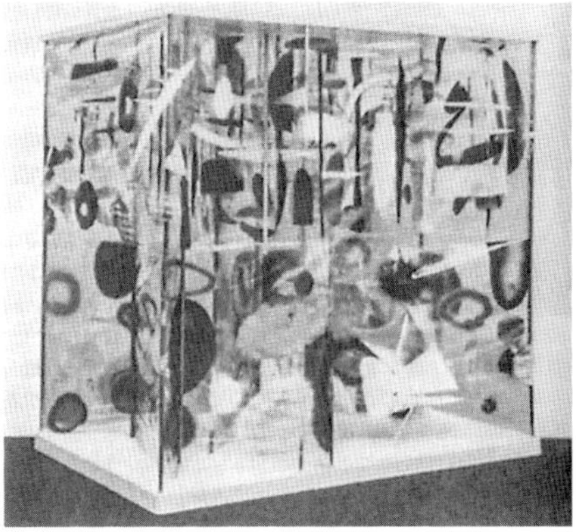

FIGURE 2.2
Matsuzawa Yutaka, *Time-Space for Telepathy*, 1954. Whereabouts unknown. Reproduced from *Kikan*, no. 13 (1982): 46.

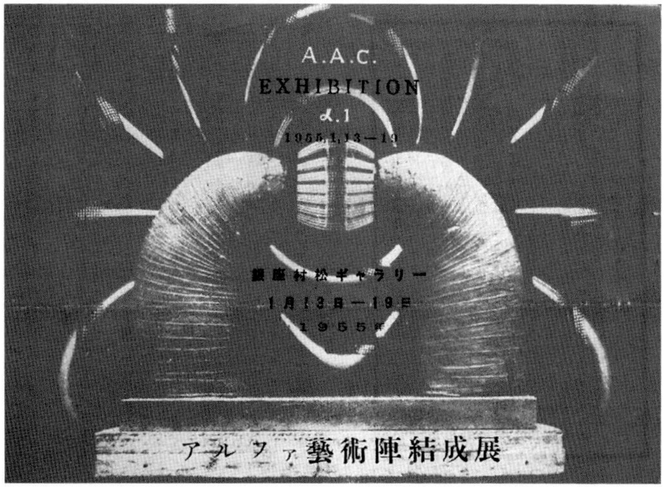

FIGURE 2.3
Alpha Art Circle Inaugural Exhibition, 1955. Exhibition brochure. Collection of Matsuzawa Kumiko.

Columbia University to study religious philosophy and art history. For his grand plan to "comprehend what has and has not been done in art, present and past, East and West,"[12] a real site of research was the city of New York, an emerging capital of international art. His residence on West 66th Street was convenient to visit the Midtown galleries, the Museum of Modern Art, and most importantly the Donnell Library, a major circulating branch of the New York Public Library just opened in 1955 across from the museum on 53rd Street. Among the new art he had witnessed in New York were Pollock's retrospective at the Museum of Modern Art and Rauschenberg's work shown probably at Leo Castelli. He also visited I. Rice Pereira, the abstract painter with a spiritual bent,[13] and tried to seek out the reclusive Joseph Cornell.[14]

How his mind worked can be gleaned from a letter he sent soon after his arrival in New York to the poet-critic Takiguchi Shūzō, with whom he had been in contact since 1953.[15] In this letter, published in the September 1956 issue of *Bijutsu hihyō* (Art criticism),[16] Matsuzawa sounded unimpressed by the Brooklyn Museum's national print annual.[17] However, he was delighted to see a pair of Japanese Buddhist mandalas juxtaposed with a Jain cosmic diagram in the museum's Asian gallery (figures 2.4, 2.5). A sense of the pan-Asian cosmic vision compelled him to speculate about how well today's artists responded to the needs of the whole of humanity. As he saw it, the problem lay in the inability to communicate among peoples as well as the paucity of connection among what he called "peaks" of knowledge in various specialized disciplines; in order to advance the thinking of artists, philosophers, and scientists alike, they must look into the "valleys," or the borders of disciplines. The idea of "valleys" of knowledge appears to have come from his prior exchange with Takiguchi on *trans/formation*,[18] the short-lived art annual published by Wittenborn, which Matsuzawa had seen in New York. Excited by this avowedly interdisciplinary magazine, he even made an arrangement with the publisher to send a copy to Takiguchi in Tokyo. Matsuzawa must have been thrilled, for example, to see the theoretical physicist Werner Heisenberg's "The Quantum Theory: A Formula That Changed the World" side by side with the vanguard composer John Cage's work (in "4 Musicians at Work"), in the third issue published in 1952.[19] The magazine's goal to provide a "world review" for "art, communication, environment," as its cover proclaimed, evidently struck a chord in the Japanese artist who had had his own interdisciplinary venture through Alpha Art Circle. The magazine confirmed that his conviction was not mistaken and was shared by some others an ocean away.

The "loneliest yet most productive"[20] period in his life concluded with a mind-altering experience. On February 2, 1957, his 35th birthday, he located one of the "valleys" of the unknown with a huge reservoir of potential. According to Matsuzawa, precisely at 2 am, the insomniac artist happened to tune his Motorola radio to WOR, then transmitting from New Jersey. The program was hosted from midnight to 5:30 am by Long John Nebel. A pioneer in late-night talk radio, Nebel had just begun his inventive talk show in August 1956, deploying a novel format of panel discussion and focusing on "strange and unexplained phenomena," interspersed with such normal topics as economics and medicine. In 1950s America, UFOs and ETs were hot topics, with the first season of *The Twilight Zone* soon to come to television in 1959. Nebel's show was an instant hit, attracting a tremendous loyal following.[21] Although Matsuzawa had become aware of UFOs and other paranormal phenomena in Japan, he was struck by the vivid intensity of hearing contactees personally recounting their experiences on the air and mediums channeling spirits on the spot. For a studious artist, the program, called "The Party Line," was ideally packed with panelists, invited specialists, and other guests seriously conversing on diverse topics ranging from astrology and spiritual mediums to mathematics, physiology, and clinical medicine, from hypnosis and yoga philosophy to engineering and religion.[22] In one awe-inspiring episode that he heard, a medium channeled Yada who had presumably lived in the Himalayas 500,000 years ago.[23] After one month of immersion in Nebel's radio show, Matsuzawa had enough and decided to go home, cutting short his one-year fellowship tenure in March 1957. After seeing Gyorgy Kepes in Boston and Mark Tobey in Seattle, he arrived in the port of Yokohama via Hawaii on April 1, with his transdisciplinary arsenal fully stocked.

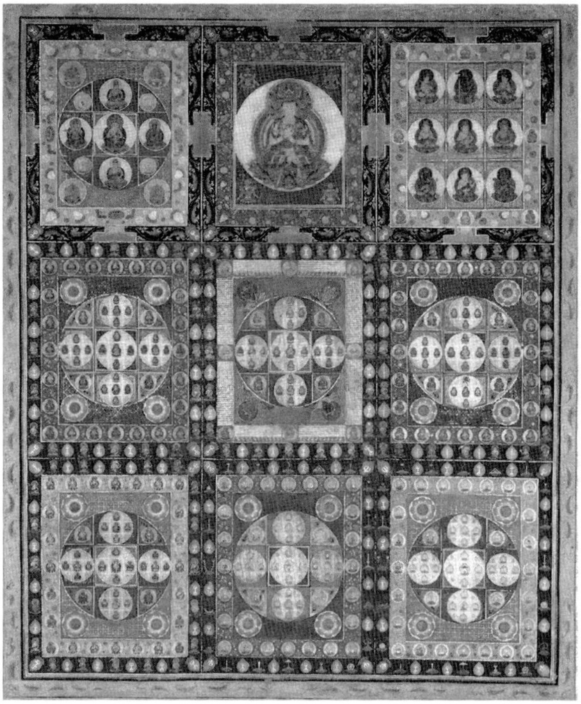

FIGURE 2.4
Diamond World Mandala (*Kongō-kai Mandara*), unknown artist, 13th century, Japan. Opaque watercolor, ink, and gold on silk; overall: 214.7 × 127.3 cm. Brooklyn Museum, Museum Collection Fund, 21.240.1.

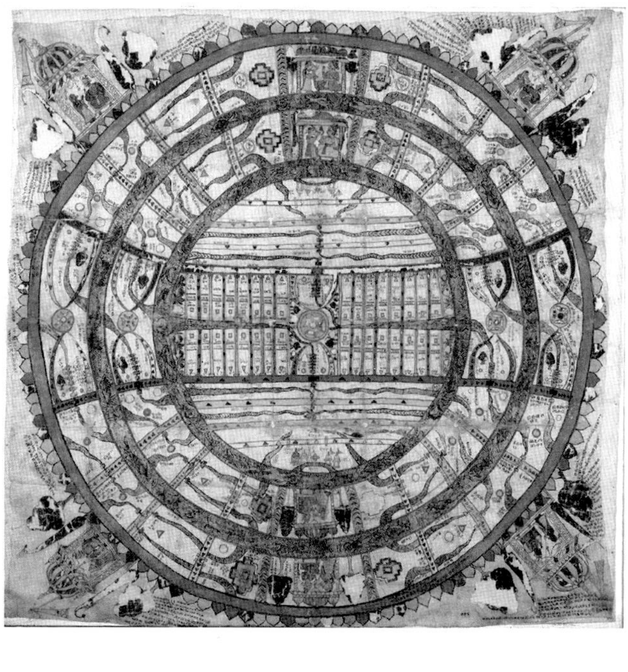

FIGURE 2.5
Diagram of the Universe (*Kshetrasamasa*), unknown artist, Western Indian Style, 18th century, India. Opaque watercolor on cotton; sheet: 64.5 × 64.5 cm. Brooklyn Museum, Brooklyn Museum Collection, X899.2.

Theory and Practice of Psi: Before "Revelation"

Matsuzawa needed some time to sort out his New York experiences, but by the spring of 1958 he was back on track, participating in the annual Yomiuri Independent Exhibition. From then through 1963, Yomiuri's annual exhibition became a main venue in which to present his research results to the art world. Among diverse ideas he had absorbed in New York, parapsychology was a primary influence, as signaled by his adoption of the word Psi. This initially appeared in the title of the 1959 series of Surrealist abstractions, *Psi Bird*, which was followed by *Meaning of Psi*, a series of panels, in 1960. It evolved into *Psi Altar*, consisting of *Meaning of Psi* and two *Psi Chambers*, in 1961; *Peep into the Psi Tortoise, the Winged Secret Rules*, a box with collage and assemblage elements, in 1962 (figure 2.6); and *Invitation to Psi Zashiki Room*, an *objet*-based installation, in 1963.

As Matsuzawa explained in "From Cybernetics to Mandala," his 1960 text published in the art monthly *Geijutsu Shinchō*, Psi derived from what parapsychology defines as "psi powers," or "cognitive abilities beyond the five senses such as precognition and clairvoyance."[24] Matsuzawa must have seen a way to activate an untapped potential of the human mental faculty and a powerful model for seeing the invisible and perceiving the intangible in this "science" (which had gained a considerable level of legitimacy through academic research undertaken in the U.S. in the 1950s, most notably by J. B. Rhine of Duke University). Above all, parapsychology studies telepathy and clairvoyance, which are the power to see what the ordinary eye cannot see, and spiritualism, or the power to channel and allow us to hear through a medium ordinarily inaudible voices of the dead. True to his transdisciplinary mind, Matsuzawa did not focus on just one idea. In his view, indeed, any single discipline, deployed in isolation, was inevitably limited, but by combining several branches of knowledge they would "complement each other and answer the question: What is humanity, what is psyche, what is the universe?"[25] Art was a frontier site in which advanced disciplines could work together.

General semantics offered another foundation with what he understood as its basic tenet, that "Human achievements are based on the use of signs," although he was critical of its mechanistic treatment of signs related to such essential concepts as time and God.[26] Through the early 1960s, indeed, he devised numerous signs of his own, which he considered to "amount to my signatures that repeat themselves unconsciously while I am drawing."[27] Of particular importance was the bird in *Psi Bird* of 1959, which might signify the liberated flight of mind. In the 1959 series, it was often reduced to its wings; it was eventually condensed into a symbol reminiscent of the Japanese *hiragana* ひ and employed in the flier for *Invitation for Psi Zashiki Room* (figure 2.7, plate 4).

The significance of the 3-by-3 mandala format for Matsuzawa's art, which first appeared in the 1960 series *Meaning of Psi*, cannot be overstated, as it would serve as

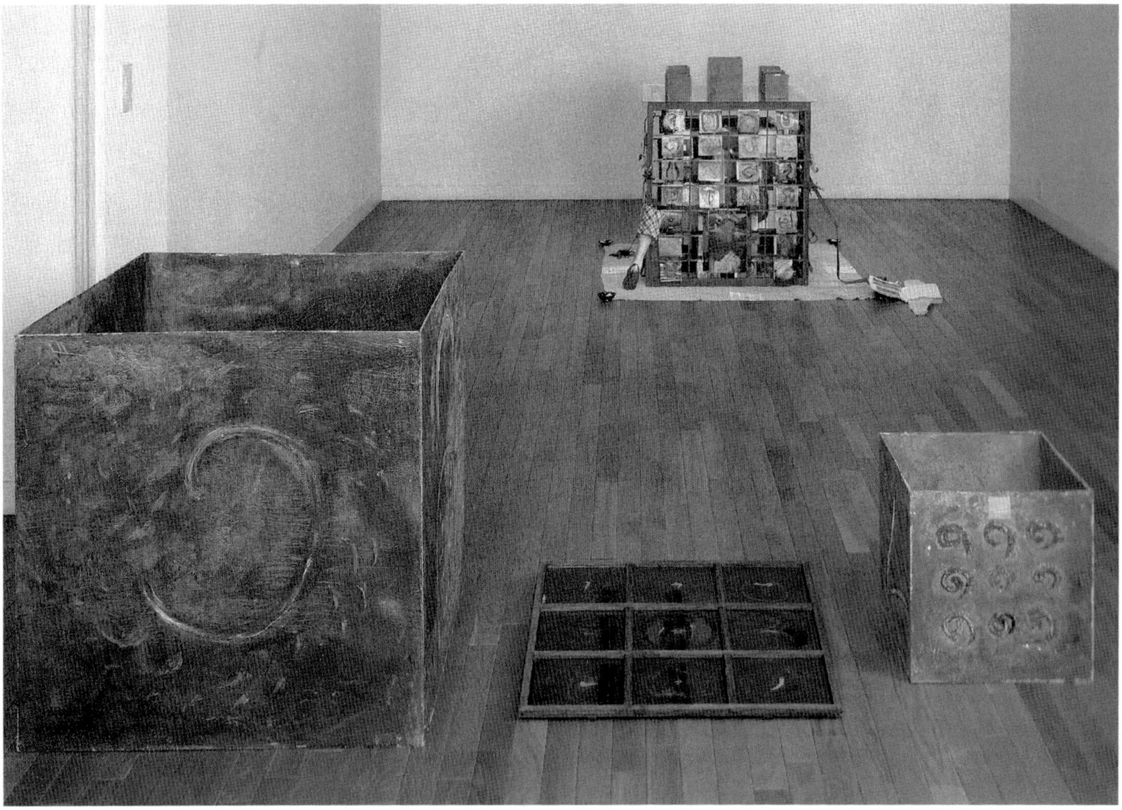

FIGURE 2.6
Matsuzawa Yutaka, *Psi Chamber YM*, *Meaning of Psi*, and *Psi Chamber SM* (aka *Psi Altar*), 1961; and *Peep into the Psi Tortoise, the Winged Secret Rules*, 1962 (back). Installation view, 1997. Mixed media; *Psi Chamber YM*: 90 × 90 × 90 cm, *Meaning of Psi*: 75 × 75 × 3 cm, *Psi Chamber SM*: 45 × 45 × 45 cm, *Peep into …*: 85 × 85 × 92 cm. Collection of Matsuzawa Kumiko. Reproduced from *To Spiritualism: Yutaka Matsuzawa 1954–1997* (Kawaguchi: Kawaguchi Museum of Contemporary Art, 1997), 22.

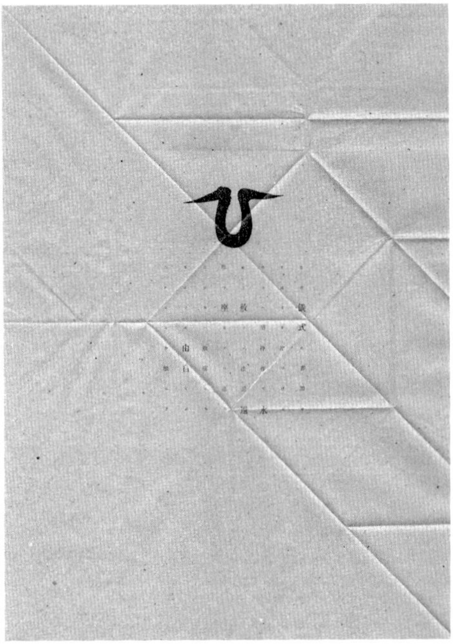

FIGURE 2.7
Matsuzawa Yutaka, *Invitation to Psi Zashiki Room*, 1963. Letterpress; 35 × 25.6 cm. Takiguchi Shūzō Papers, c. 1945–1979, Keiō University Art Center, Tokyo. (Also plate 4.)

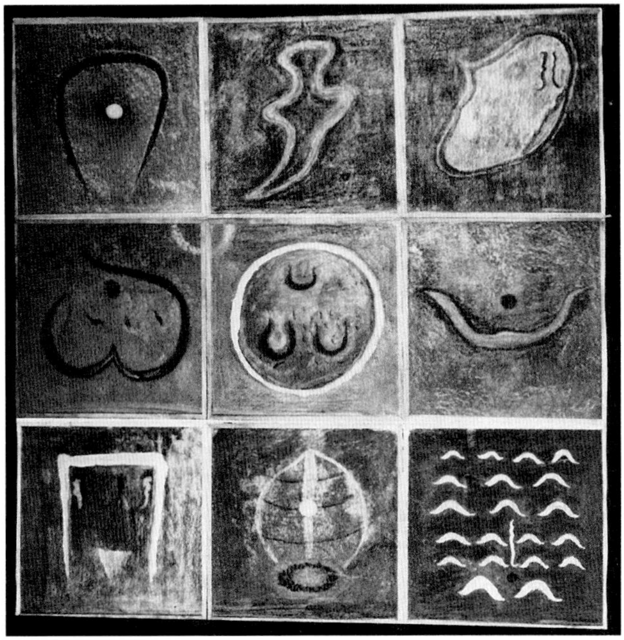

FIGURE 2.8
Matsuzawa Yutaka, *Meaning of Psi*, 1960. Whereabouts unknown. Reproduced from *Mizue* (June 1960): 8.

his compositional foundation throughout his life (figure 2.8). A staple of traditional iconography in Japanese art, the mandala meant for him a system that "combined a scientific measurement and a paranormal mystery to express the universe."[28] It not only became a versatile container of his signs but also provided a ritualistic dimension of sign reading. Unlike Exoteric Buddhism, which centers on the "open" teachings of Buddha Śākyamuni, Esoteric Buddhism centers on the "secret" teaching of Dainichi Nyorai (Sanskrit: Mahāvairocana), or "Great Omnipresent Illumination of Light," who presides over the Diamond World and the Womb World (figure 2.4).[29] In the Diamond World mandala, the 1-to-9 descending reading (clockwise from center) and the 9-to-1 ascending reading (counterclockwise toward center) embody two opposite paths for enlightenment, with 1 being the seat of Dainichi: in the former (1 to 9), Dainichi comes down to the masses to teach, whereas in the latter (9 to 1) the masses rise to enlightenment aided by Dainichi (figure 2.9).[30] Although Matsuzawa would later simplify the reading and always specify the 1-to-9 descending order in his work, for *Meaning of Psi* he prescribed three readings—1 to 9, 9 to1, and 1 through 9 all at once—so that the viewer would have three different transcendental time-space experiences.[31]

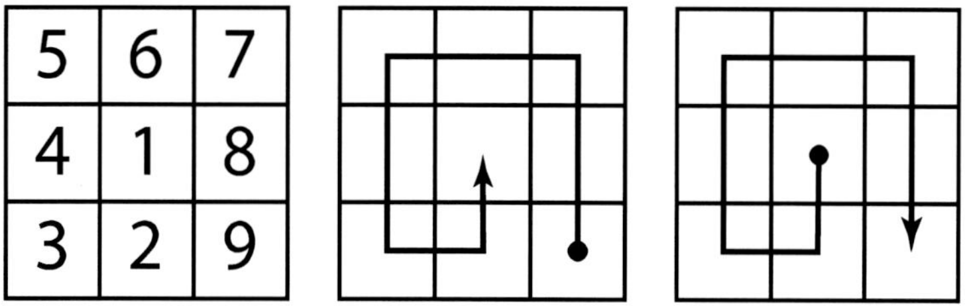

FIGURE 2.9
Readings of the Diamond World Mandala: Matsuzawa's 1-to-9 Numbering (left), Ascending Order (center), and Descending Order (right). Designed by Takako Oishi-Marks.

At this point, science only played a small role with the panel series. He invoked cybernetics and associated its binary system (0 and 1) with the front and back sides of each grid in order to double the reading options.[32] He also invoked contemporary physics in one of his panels, subtitling it *In Reference to Heisenberg's Cosmic Equation*. It is not clear which equation of Werner Heisenberg Matsuzawa meant by "cosmic equation," but he had in mind the physicist's attempt to describe the whole universe in one equation, much as the mandala does in one diagram.[33]

This was intricate enough. Yet Matsuzawa further complicated his relentless pursuit with a three-dimensional upgrade, which he nicknamed *Psi Altar*. It consisted of two *Psi Chambers*, large and small, flanking *Meaning of Psi* laid on the floor (figure 2.6) and accompanied by a flier, the first text-only work Matsuzawa produced outside of poetry (figure 2.10). The flier, titled *On "Meaning of Psi" and "Psi Chamber,"* among other things explains a ritual to be performed by the viewer with *Psi Altar*. The goal was clearer, if not simpler, than the 1960 panel. As the flier explains, the viewer must read the signs on the lidless boxes in two ways, "Vibration Type" and "Recurrence Type" (respectively indicated by the left and right cross-shaped diagrams in the flier). In either case, the viewer will have to "walk around the chambers, bend and stretch your back, and bend your neck," to see the signs the artist drew on the inside and outside of the boxes. Such physical contortions must be performed as the viewer "solemnly" gazes at the "ultra-topological" structure, so that the whole act will constitute a "ritual" that will "generate Psi," which in the flier is defined as "spiritual spatiotemporal matter." Progressing beyond his early attempts, the artist now managed to define his Psi in his own words. Indeed, the flier reveals a sense of accomplishment by boldly declaring, "*Nil novi sub sole*" (Nothing new under the sun) and "My idea is neither new nor strange." He invoked a litany of names, ranging from a Christian mystic to Buddhist monks to a parapsychologist (J. B. Rhine), from a geometer to a non-Euclidian mathematician to a cybernetic pioneer (Norbert Wiener), in order to contextualize and

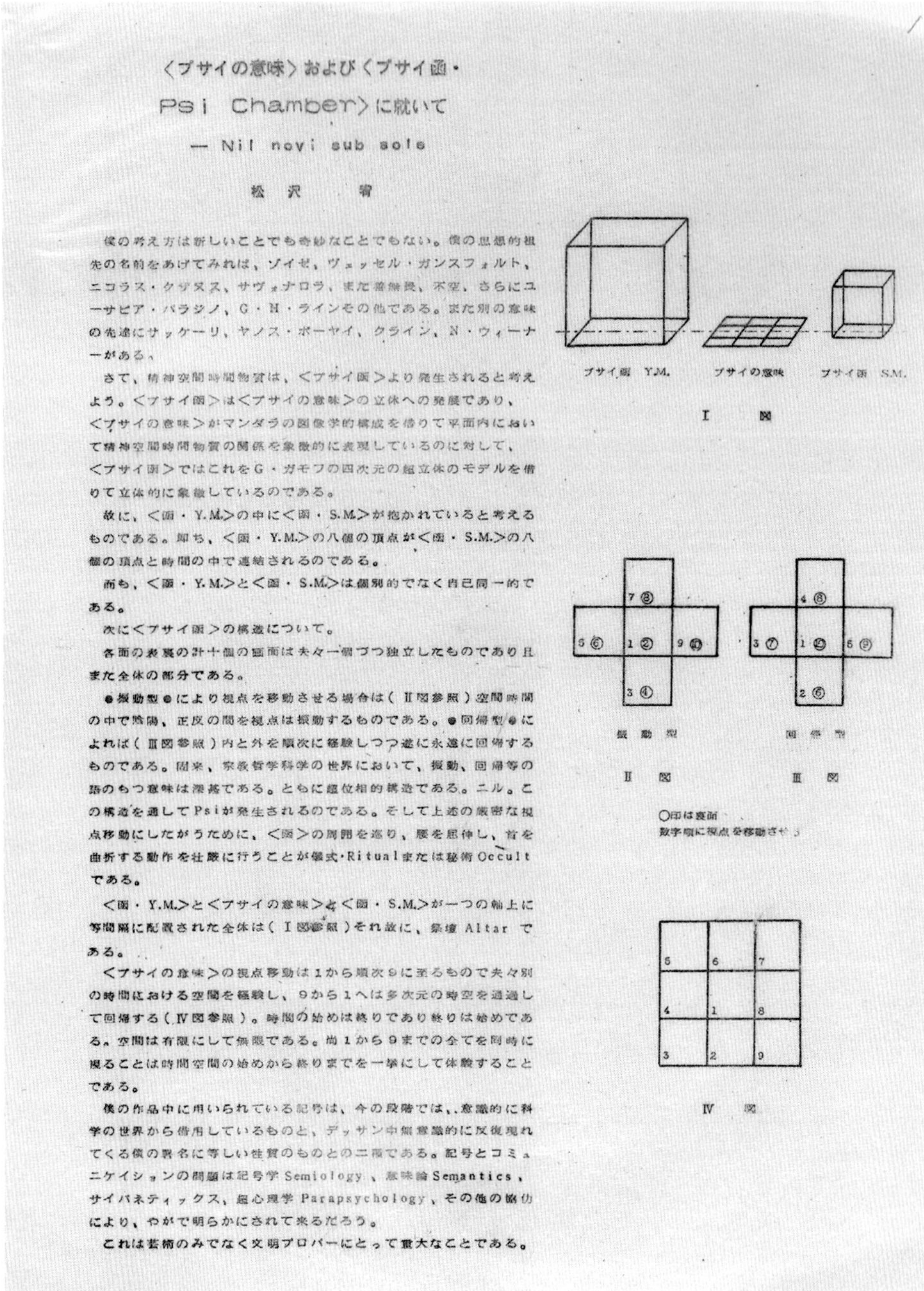

〈プサイの意味〉および〈プサイ函・Psi Chamber〉に就いて

— Nil novi sub sole

松沢　宥

僕の考え方は新しいことでも奇妙なことでもない。僕の思想的祖先の名前をあげてみれば、ゾイゼ、ヴェッセル・ガンスフォルト、ニコラス・クザヌス、サヴォナロラ、また普化、不空、さらにユーサピア・パラジノ、G・H・ラインその他である。また別の意味の先達にサッケーリ、ヤノス・ボーヤイ、クライン、N・ウィーナーがある。

さて、精神空間時間物質は、＜プサイ函＞より発生されると考えよう。＜プサイ函＞は＜プサイの意味＞の立体への発展であり、＜プサイの意味＞がマンダラの図像学的構成を借りて平面内において精神空間時間物質の関係を象徴的に表現しているのに対して、＜プサイ函＞ではこれをG・ガモフの四次元の超立体のモデルを借りて立体的に象徴しているのである。

故に、＜函・Y.M.＞の中に＜函・S.M.＞が抱かれていると考えるものである。即ち、＜函・Y.M.＞の八個の頂点が＜函・S.M.＞の八個の頂点と時間の中で連結されるのである。

而も、＜函・Y.M.＞と＜函・S.M.＞は個別的でなく自己同一的である。

次に＜プサイ函＞の構造について。

各面の表裏の計十個の画面は夫々一個づつ独立したものであり且また全体の部分である。

●振動型●により視点を移動させる場合は（II図参照）空間時間の中で陰陽、正反の間を視点は振動するものである。●回帰型●によれば（III図参照）内と外を順次に経験しつつ遂に永遠に回帰するものである。閑来、宗教哲学科学の世界において、振動、回帰等の語のもつ意味は深甚である。ともに超位相的構造である。ニル。この構造を通してPsiが発生されるのである。そして上述の厳密な視点移動にしたがうために、＜函＞の周囲を巡り、腰を屈伸し、首を曲折する動作を壮厳に行うことが儀式・Ritualまたは秘術Occultである。

＜函・Y.M.＞と＜プサイの意味＞と＜函・S.M.＞が一つの軸上に等間隔に配置された全体は（I図参照）それ故に、祭壇 Altar である。

＜プサイの意味＞の視点移動は1から順次9に至るもので夫々別の時間における空間を経験し、9から1へは多次元の時空を通過して回帰する（IV図参照）。時間の始めは終りであり終りは始めである。空間は有限にして無限である。尚1から9までの全てを同時に視ることは時間空間の始めから終りまでを一挙にして体験することである。

僕の作品中に用いられている記号は、今の段階では、意識的に科学の世界から借用しているものと、デッサン中無意識的に反復現れてくる僕の署名に等しい性質のものとの二種である。記号とコミュニケイションの問題は記号学 Semiology、意味論 Semantics、サイバネティックス、超心理学 Parapsychology、その他の協力により、やがて明らかにされて来るだろう。

これは芸術のみでなく文明プロパーにとって重大なことである。

FIGURE 2.10
Matsuzawa Yutaka, *On "Meaning of Psi" and "Psi Chamber,"* 1961. Stencil copy; 33.2 × 24.2 cm. 1 of 71 items in *The Whole Works, 1961–1971*. The Museum of Modern Art, New York, Art & Project/Depot VBVR Gift, 2007. Digital Image © The Museum of Modern Art/Licensed by SCALA / Art Resource, NY.

legitimize his endeavor to reach the invisible through Psi.[34] Still, protestation of legitimacy alone would not engender legitimacy if the theory was not comprehensible. Morphologically, he also faced a physical barrier: no more expansion was possible beyond the four dimensions of time-space. In other words, Matsuzawa had hit a dead end.

To break the impasse he went for an enigmatic maximalism, as embodied by his 1962 presentation at the Yomiuri Independent Exhibition, *Peep into the Psi Tortoise, the Winged Secret Rules*, which expanded on the theme of the box (figure 2.6). Most notably, however, his enigmatic maximalism quietly advanced at his home out of public view. His compulsion concerning sign drawing developed into a preoccupation with object making. He literally emptied the family's large storehouse which held precious artifacts and obsolete household articles accumulated over generations, many of which were preserved in traditional wooden boxes. He was especially fond of these boxes,[35] which he brought into one of the large *zashiki* reception rooms in his house. He varyingly placed his own works or readymade objects in them or embellished them with collages. Other items—sketchbooks, natural objects, and such—were also brought in. The result was the so-called *Psi Zashiki Room*, which quickly achieved a celebrity status and into which only a privileged few were invited (figure 2.11).

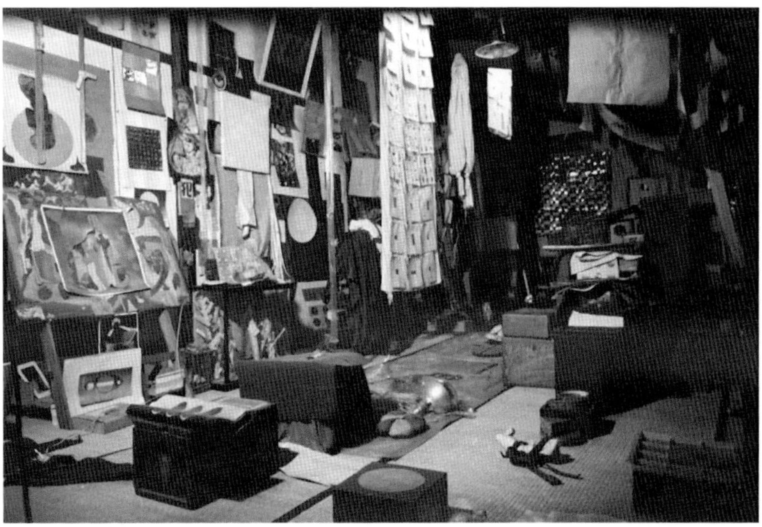

FIGURE 2.11
Matsuzawa Yutaka, *Psi Zashiki Room* in Shimo Suwa, 1969. Photo © Hanaga Mitsutoshi.

Nascent Conceptualism: Apparatus, Operation Manual, Container

Matsuzawa later recalled his pre-Revelation period as his "fetish" phase.[36] This is an apt self-assessment, given the many drawings, boxes, and other objects he had obsessively made and compulsively accumulated in his *Psi Zashiki Room*. However, his conceptualism arose from this "fetish" phase, as he developed a set of strategies that would serve him well after 1964. In addition to the use of language which began with the 1961 flier, he also started to devise a few strategies to fundamentally reconceptualize the nature of art making during this period. His strategies involved three aspects: artwork as apparatus, use of language as operation manual, and gallery as container.

From around 1960, Matsuzawa made a gradual departure from the idea of "artwork as an autonomous object." He later recalled that he stopped thinking about "individual phenomena" in favor of considering the universe as a whole.[37] In practice, this led him to stop working within the constraint of the pictorial frame, let alone the convention of representation as such, a vestige of which his *Psi Birds* series of 1959 still retained. Rather, he endeavored to construct "apparatuses" (*sōchi*)[38] that would encourage an active effort on the viewer's part. Among the first apparatuses he made was *Meaning of Psi*, in which he borrowed the traditional mandala format of Esoteric Buddhism. It should be noted that the mandala contains the whole Buddhist cosmology in a single diagram and, in this sense, itself constitutes a superb "apparatus" that engages Buddhist devotees. In the artist's adaptation, *Meaning of Psi* would activate the viewer's mind and induce in it a complex set of transcendental time-space experiences. In the 1961 *Psi Altar*, the ensemble as a whole constituted an apparatus to activate the viewer's body and mind to perform a ritual.

If a work is presented as an apparatus that functions differently from a conventional painting or sculpture—i.e., a thing to be looked at—some sort of instruction is necessary for it to be properly employed. For the 1960 *Meaning of Psi*, "From Cybernetics to Mandala,"[39] a text the artist published in *Geijutsu Shinchō*, at once offered a theoretical exegesis and a guide for use; taken together it constituted an operation manual for his apparatus, so to speak. For the 1961 *Psi Altar*, he did not rely on a third-party publication but had his text printed as a flier and presented it as an integral part of the altar (figure 2.10). Typeset and initially printed on pale green paper,[40] the flier is not only a well-thought-out text but a well-crafted object. Indeed, the artist was conscious of the fact that this was the very first among his text-based artworks outside of poetry writing.[41] Following it, his Yomiuri entries for 1962 and 1963 both entailed fliers. A flier for *Invitation to Psi Zashiki Room* is another exquisite production (figure 2.7, plate 4). It bears a symbol similar to an inverted Greek Ω (or Japanese *hiragana* ひ reminiscent of a flying bird) and an invitation copy below, all printed in black on dusty rose. Laid in an 8-by-8 grid (to be read in a clockwise spiral from the center), the text is arranged like a concrete poem with large and small fonts mixed. It constitutes another operation manual for the viewer to use the object presented in the exhibition:

> Invitation to *Psi Zashiki Room*: The manner is as follows: when you come to the room, put away wings and be seated properly on the floor [*seiza*, knees folded and flat on the floor, with the bottom resting on the soles of the feet]. Feel free to touch thoroughly to participate in this rite. Never ever touch breasts.[42]

Interestingly, Matsuzawa used the flier literally as an "invitation" by sending it to Takiguchi Shūzō, with a note informing the Tokyo-based critic that he would be at the exhibition site on the opening day.[43] To put the 35-by-25-cm sheet of *Invitation* in a regular letter envelope, he devised a kind of conceptual *origami*, neatly folding it into a compact size. (Following the creases, we can reconstruct how he folded it.) Residing in the remote Shimo Suwa, Matsuzawa went on to use mail art as an important tool to reach those in Tokyo and elsewhere, but the beginning of his mail art was rather prosaic and cumbersome.[44] Distance was also a latent element in the three-mat sampling of *Psi Zashiki Room* that Matsuzawa displayed at the Yomiuri Independent Exhibition, but this installation pushed his "artwork as apparatus" one step farther. Not unlike Robert Smithson's "Site/Non-Site," it linked the exhibition hall in Tokyo, where the sampling was presented, and the remote site, his home in Shimo Suwa, where the whole 24-mat version resided. *Invitation to Psi Zashiki Room*, then, performed a dual duty of inviting the viewer to a partial presentation at the Yomiuri exhibition and pointing to the whole of it.

In a significant pre-Revelation development, he had his first solo exhibition in September 1963 at Aoki Gallery, a newly established commercial venue specializing in Surrealism and closely associated with the critic Takiguchi Shūzō.[45] An occasion to use the whole space of a gallery with the sympathetic support of the gallery owner Aoki Toshi resulted in two new ideas: the gallery as container-apparatus and the substantial incorporation of contemporary physics.

If the partial *Zashiki* at the Yomiuri Independent in the prior spring was a ritual apparatus, the whole *Psi Zashiki Room* could be considered as a mega ritual apparatus filled with diverse mini apparatuses. A next logical expansion could then be a "gallery space as an apparatus." This was precisely what he did at his very first solo exhibition, with his text-based work *On Another Work in Another Container, or On Cutting*, accompanied by a mandala diagram (figure 2.13). Defining the gallery space as a "hard container" holding a "hard work" and the viewer's "hard body," he asked the viewer to envision a "soft version" and an "imaginary version" of them through her "sense mind" in the past, present, and future (see translation in appendix). The focus is the viewer's mental act of envisioning the soft and the imaginary (as opposed to the real) while in the gallery, which contained the viewer and a work. In principle, indeed, any gallery and any work would do, with the gallery-container serving as an apparatus for this exercise of "sense mind." At the same time, just like in his *Psi Zashiki Room* at home, many smaller apparatuses were assembled in the gallery-apparatus. Distance

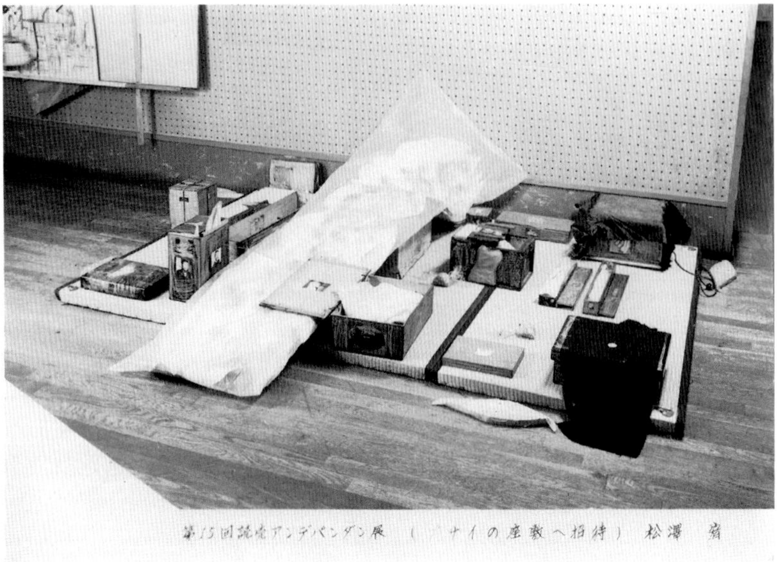

FIGURE 2.12
Matsuzawa Yutaka, *Invitation to Psi Zashiki Room*, 1963. Exhibition postcard. Takiguchi Shūzō Papers, c. 1945–1979, Keiō University Art Center, Tokyo.

was again incorporated in the work: it is notable that he minimized the need for the viewer to be in this hard container (Aoki Gallery) to experience mini apparatuses on display, because the artist intended his work to "communicate" toward the ψ (psi)—i.e., psyche—of a remote viewer willing to "persistently meditate."[46] The scheme of "gallery space as an apparatus" thus had two future implications. One was the possibility of an "empty gallery as an apparatus" engaging the viewer's mind; the other was that of an "exhibition at a remote site." For both, he would produce a few important post-Revelation examples, as will be discussed.

As important as the conceptualization of "gallery as container" was the substantial introduction of contemporary physics into his theory of Psi. In fact, this was the first time he used the Greek character ψ (psi), as seen in the exhibition title, *Matsuzawa Yutaka According to ψ*.[47] The text of *On Another Work* likewise uses the Greek character. Prior to this exhibition, he had usually written it out as *pusai* (プサイ) in *katakana* syllabary to render it phonetically. Moreover, at this exhibition he evidently spoke of the ψ function—a key element of quantum physics that represents the wave function and figures prominently in the works of Werner Heisenberg and Erwin Schrödinger—when he explained his work to one curious critic who reviewed the exhibition. The critic Miki Tamon wrote that Matsuzawa's "work by Psi was unusual. His strange theorization based on the ψ function is so mystical that it almost sounds like religion."[48] On another note, particle physics clearly informed the "hard-soft-imaginary" triad of *On Another Work*. Particle physics had previously been quietly referenced with *Psi Chambers*, whose name derived from the cloud chamber, a detector of invisible particles frequently employed in experimental physics before more elaborate and powerful particle colliders were invented.[49] With *On Another Work*, the text's refrain, "Like an anti-proton as opposed to a proton," unambiguously points to Matsuzawa's study of particle physics, which hypothesized the existence of anti-matter and anti-particles.

On Another Work represents a great step forward in Matsuzawa's nascent conceptualism. By making the viewer's mind the central focus, he for the first time made "text" as such the work itself. With the text serving as an "operation manual" for the mind, a gallery and a physical work became secondary and a diagram supplementary. Since the pairing of proton/anti-proton signifies that which is present/absent, this work constituted a more direct way to introduce the invisible than his previous works. Still, his text, accompanied by the mandala-based diagram, was far too complicated. It challenges the regular coordinates of space-time, demanding the viewer to think in "past/present/future" tenses, in "real, imaginary, and opposite" spaces as well as their border areas. The complexity might have immensely perplexed his viewers, overloading their capacities of "sense mind."

* * *

By the end of 1963, Matsuzawa made Psi into his calling card—earning him the moniker of Mr. Psi.[50] Having mustered an array of intellectual and theoretical sources, old and new, East and West—ranging from general semantics to cybernetics, parapsychology to Esoteric Buddhism, particle physics to quantum physics—he formulated his theory of Psi and devised a few conceptualist strategies. Yet in reality, complexity and maximalism hobbled his theory and practice of Psi. He desperately needed an escape route to go forward. In this context, his infamous Revelation took place on June 1, 1964.

MATSUZAWA'S RADICAL RECONSTRUCTION OF ART

Legend (De)constructed: The Beginning of "Art of *Kannen*"

By 1964, close to two decades after he had first articulated his desire for the "invisible," "formless," "soul," Matsuzawa managed to achieve his goal of expressing the invisible in art by devising complex apparatuses and activating the viewer's mind. Yet his solutions were far from elegant. Conversant in mathematics and physics, he must have been keenly aware that a theorem or a truth can be described in deceptively simple terms, while the path it takes to arrive at it may be long and winding.

What is known as Matsuzawa's "Revelation" broke this impasse on June 1, 1964. The legend has it that on that day, in the very early morning, still in his *futon* bed in a half-awake state, he heard a voice commanding "Vanish *objets*!" As he would later narrate it, he immediately knew the enigmatic voice was commanding him to deploy language and language alone in making art, which constituted the beginning of his art of *kannen* (*kannen bijutsu*).[51] With the memorable catchphrase "Vanish *objets*!" this mythologized version of the episode has been recounted so many times by the artist and others since the early 1970s that it feels by now like the most important thing there is to know about his conceptualism, far more important than any of his actual works.

Yet the first work he produced after the episode tells a different story. A handwritten flier dated June 4, 1964 with his text arranged in a 3-by-3 mandala grid, *A Brief Report on the Discovery of the Beginning of Non-Sensory Painting* reveals not confidence but trepidation (figure 2.14) (see appendix for translation). Its mood was the complete opposite of the boastful 1961 flier headlined *Nil novi sub sole* (figure 2.10).

> [T]his past [June] 1st, before dawn, I had a sudden revelation, and since then I have been deliberating on it. Now I finally have reached a state where I am confident [about what it meant]. Thus, I am making a brief report on the above-titled issue. This struck me so violently like Nil that I felt half of my body paralyzed. This is such a horrifying thought. I beg you not to use common sense in criticizing it.

The "horrifying thought" concerned Non-Sensory Painting that cannot be perceived by the senses but is nonetheless present, analogous to the way branches of contemporary physics, such as astrophysics and particle physics, construct new cosmic and subatomic pictures through mathematics and language. As such, Non-Sensory Painting can only exist and be perceived in a meditating brain. In contrast to his past enigmatic maximalism, "once the discovery is made, I myself am so surprised to see how simple and clear its truth can be." However, the proposed new form of art would bring about "discommunication" and the "final state of humanity," or Nirvana, which he defined as "The state of no difference in energy levels. The state of complete stasis."

(Unlike the popular understanding of Nirvana that primarily refers to the ultimate state of enlightenment and happiness, Matsuzawa adapted the fundamental Buddhist interpretation of [Buddha's] death, as the Buddhist iconography of Nirvana, or *nehan*, represents. In his Psi lexicon, Nil, or *Niru*, always rendered in *katakana*, refers to both Nil, contracted from *Nihil*, Latin for nothing, and Nir, his abbreviation of Nirvana.)

Matsuzawa made blueprint (diazotype) copies of *A Brief Report* which he folded and mailed to seven trusted associates, including the poet-critic Takiguchi Shūzō in Tokyo. The secret communication was quickly followed by a public announcement,

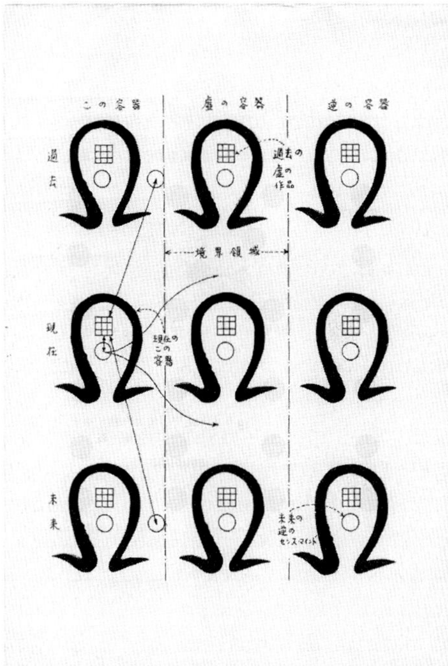

FIGURE 2.13
Matsuzawa Yutaka, *On Another Work in Another Container, or On Cutting* (diagram), 1963. Reproduced from *On Another Work in Another Container, or On Cutting* (brochure). Takiguchi Shūzō Papers, c. 1945–1979, Keiō University Art Center, Tokyo.

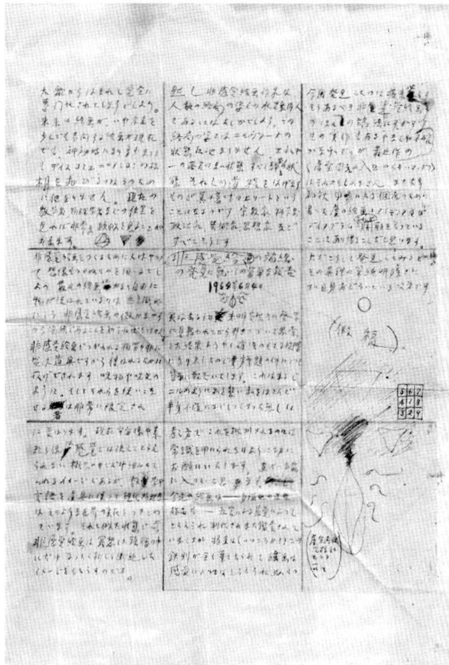

FIGURE 2.14
Matsuzawa Yutaka, *A Brief Report on the Discovery of the Beginning of Non-Sensory Painting*, 1964. Blueprint (diazotype). Takiguchi Shūzō Papers, c. 1945–1979, Keiō University Art Center, Tokyo.

Psi Corpse, at the *Independent '64* exhibition, the first post-Yomiuri independent exhibition, which opened on June 20 at the Tokyo Metropolitan Art Museum (figure 2.15, plate 5) (see appendix for translation). This flier officially launched a new phase of his conceptualism and his active involvement with the independent-exhibition movement, which provided him with his central site of operation (see table 2.1; its history will be further discussed in chapter 3). At the exhibition he distributed 10,000 copies of *Psi Corpse*, a flier printed in red on gray paper. To keep his most sympathetic supporter abreast of his progress, he folded and mailed the flier to Takiguchi. The new work shed his initial trepidation but remained elusive about exactly what Non-Sensory Painting was like, beyond the analogy to contemporary physics. Still, the impact of his Revelation was felt with its title: with this flier, he symbolically put to death his all-important though complicated theory of Psi.

Though the precise words of his dreamlike mystical experience may never be known, what was the gist of the Revelation? One idea that appears prominently in some of his post-Revelation works and texts concerns "vanishing of matter" (*busshitsu shōmetsu*). It first appeared with another key concept, that of Anti-Civilization, in the flier *Vanishing of Matter: Seeing Anti-Civilization Exhibition*, presented at the *All Japan Independent Exhibition*, held at Yokohama Civic Art Gallery in May 1965 (figure 2.16). A brief explanation of the two new concepts was then prepared in August 1965 in "Vanishing of Matter," the abstract of a talk he planned to give at the symposium held in conjunction with *Independent Art Festival* in Gifu, the pinnacle of the independent-exhibition movement. In this short text, he described "vanishing of matter" as a "new principle," one that was informed by an "oscillation of [his] consciousness" caused by the 1957 WOR panel discussions, and which would be the cornerstone of Anti-Civilization that would counter contemporary civilization which "is nothing but a mistake."[52] This sentiment resonated with the admonition he included in the ad for *Independent '64 in the Wilderness*: "Don't believe matter / Don't believe senses / Don't believe the eye" (figure 0.1). In other words, by heightening Matsuzawa's awareness of the invisible that was irrational, his 1957 WOR experience prepared him for the 1964 Revelation, which finally carried him beyond the point of no return and prompted him to forever rid his practice of materiality. It was then logical for him to tackle painting and vanish materiality from this privileged practice of modern art. The result was Non-Sensory Painting, although it would take him three more years to figure out its invisible morphology.

During the 1960s, Matsuzawa's conceptualism remained a work in progress, as he incorporated one new idea after another to support and bolster his new art at every turn. Surely he was painfully aware that his theory and practice of Psi was utterly weird for some who would not take him seriously, and at best daunting for some others who would try to understand him. This must have been one of the reasons for his constant effort to revise and improve his theory. But judging from what he eventually established, he evidently exercised his transdisciplinary mind to its fullest capacity. Psi was too important for him to keep in the coffin, and he quickly resurrected it and subsequently remodeled it with a simpler definition: "human psyche."[53] By March 1965, he updated his use of "persistent meditation" (*shūnen*), which first appeared in the 1963 *On Another Work in Another Container, or On Cutting*, by introducing the more formal term *kannen*, as in "*kannen* painting" and "*kannen* exhibition."[54] Taken from Pure Land Buddhism, the term refers to its basic training of "meditative visualization," through which devotees would be able to see Amida (Sanskrit: Amitābha), or "Buddha of Infinite Light," and his abode, Western Paradise. Matsuzawa used this idea to revamp the theory of Psi and established the practice of *kannen bijutsu*, that is, the art of *kannen*.

In retrospect, it was an exquisite moment when a Japanese artist came up with his own word, that is, in his native tongue, to name his conceptualism that stood outside

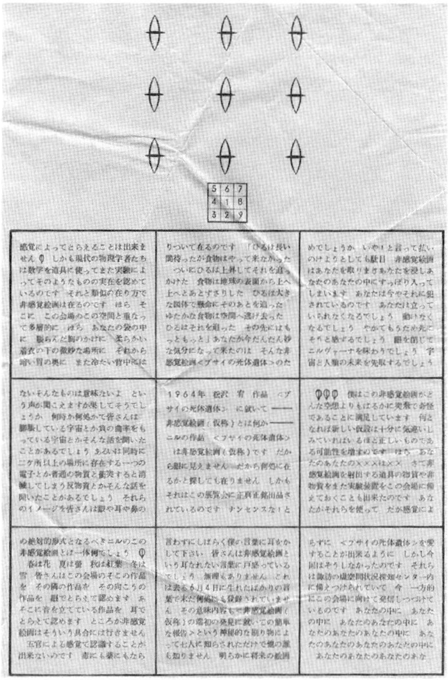

FIGURE 2.15
Matsuzawa Yutaka, *Psi Corpse*, 1964. Offset lithograph; 38.4 × 26 cm. Takiguchi Shūzō Papers, c. 1945–1979, Keiō University Art Center, Tokyo. (Also plate 5.)

TABLE 2.1
Matsuzawa Yutaka in Artist-Organized Independent Exhibitions, 1964–1966

1964 *Independent '64*, Tokyo Metropolitan Art Museum, Tokyo
Presented *Psi Corpse*

Independent '64 in the Wilderness, Nanashima Yashima Highland, Nagano Prefecture
Organizer; presented "future death"

1965 *All Japan Independent Exhibition*, Yokohama Civic Art Gallery, Yokohama
Presented *Vanishing of Matter: Seeing Anti-Civilization Exhibition*

Independent Art Festival, City Civic Center, Gifu, Gifu Prefecture
Presented *Void: Collective Participation of "Anti-Civilization" School*

1966 *Contemporary Art Festival*, Kanaoka Park and Gymwnasium, Sakai, Osaka Prefecture
Presented *Humans, Let's Vanish, Let's Go, Let's Go, Gate, Gate, Anti-Civilization Committee*

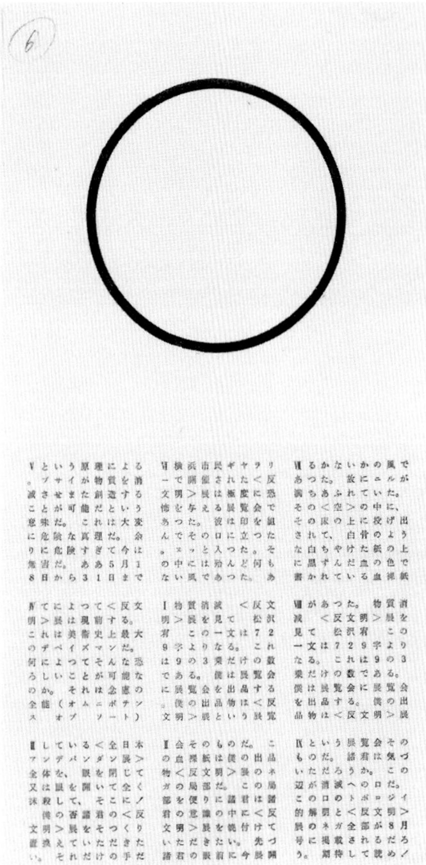

FIGURE 2.16
Matsuzawa Yutaka, *Vanishing of Matter: Seeing Anti-Civilization Exhibition*, 1965. Letterpress; 34.8 × 17.6 cm. Collection of Reiko Tomii.

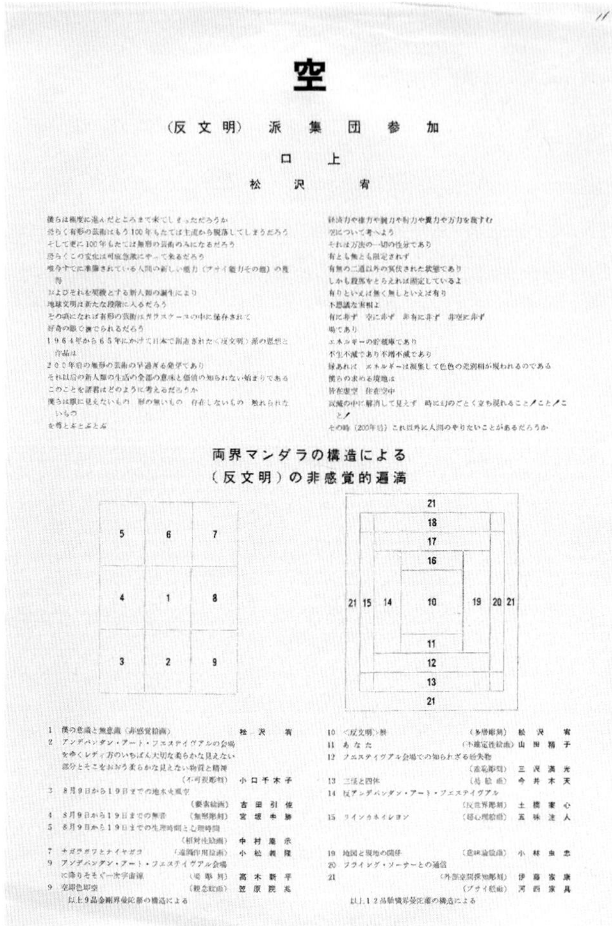

FIGURE 2.17
Matsuzawa Yutaka, *Void: Collective Participation of "Anti-Civilization" School*, 1965. Letterpress; 39.1 × 26.5 cm. 1 of 71 items in *The Whole Works, 1961–1971*. The Museum of Modern Art, New York, Art & Project/Depot VBVR Gift, 2007. Digital Image © The Museum of Modern Art/Licensed by SCALA / Art Resource, NY.

of Euro-American Conceptual Art. Still, the more modern meaning of *kannen*, "idea," complicated his discursive effort, as will be discussed in chapter 5, in the age of international contemporaneity.

In deconstructing Matsuzawa's Revelation myth, we cannot avoid the issue of *objets*, for a question still persists: Why did he shift from vanishing *busshitsu* to vanishing *objets* in narrating his 1964 experience? It is imprecise, if not outright erroneous, to say that what he did was to stop making *objets*, which in Japanese art terminology are two- or three-dimensional works that incorporate readymade everyday images or objects.[55] Certainly, *busshitsu* better describes it. With its standard philosophical pairing with "mind" (*seishin*), the use of "matter" reinforced the choice he made—that is, mind over matter. *Busshitsu* was also integral to Japanese art discourse. It was not an exaggeration to say that one's stated position in relation to *busshitsu* defined his or her art in postwar Japan. We have only to look at Yoshihara Jirō's "Gutai Art Manifesto" of 1956, in which he famously declared, "In Gutai Art, the human spirit (*ningen seishin*) and matter (*busshitsu*) shake hands with each other."[56] In this local tradition, Matsuzawa proposed in principle to eliminate matter altogether from his art. This was a radical contribution to 1960s art in Japan. Yet as he worked in relative isolation, very few paid attention to the profound implication of his work. By the early 1970s, things changed. Gone was the fervor of Anti-Art, which was characterized by *objets* and the accompanying obsession with everyday things. Dominant instead was the sober detachment of Non-Art, to which he made ample contribution. At the same time, his conceptualism began to attract wider attention, thanks to the introduction of Euro-American Conceptual Art. In this atmosphere, he needed to recalibrate and cement his position. In the course of a few public interviews in the early 1970s, we can see his discussion shift from "vanishing of matter" to "vanishing of *objets*."[57]

Vanishing Acts as "Anti-Civilization"

In the post-Yomiuri wilderness, Matsuzawa quietly thrived with his newly expanded conceptualist arsenal of *kannen*, proactively participating in the self-organized independent exhibitions. Especially significant were his inventive "exhibition activities" to which he applied the principle of vanishing, which proved to be quite versatile. The objects of vanishing ranged from materiality of the artwork itself to an entire exhibition to the whole of humankind.

After presenting his first public post-Revelation work at *Independent '64* in June, held at the Tokyo Metropolitan Art Museum, he borrowed its title and offered his own independent exhibition, *Independent '64 in the Wilderness*, in December (figure 0.1). The only tangible form of this exhibition visible to the public eye was a small call-for-entries ad placed in an art magazine, which could be read as an ad for the artist's new art, complete with a strong admonition against matter and the senses. It embodied his radical reduction of materiality both in terms of the work of art and the exhibition. In the local context, with this exhibition Matsuzawa manifested his sympathy and camaraderie with regional artists who were working to bring the independent-exhibition movement to their areas. At the same time, he may have been responding to the critic Takiguchi's desire to see art in the most improbable places, as expressed in his essay for Matsuzawa's solo exhibition catalog at Aoki Gallery in the previous year: "I would rather imagine paintings hanging not on a museum wall but on a remote abandoned rock or under stars silently fluttering in ciphers, [...] or hope to find them lying around in a dry desert."[58] Although Nanashima Yashima Highland, the site of Matsuzawa's exhibition, was a short drive from the artist's residence, its location in central Japan made it a remote place for most people, making the site practically inaccessible, especially in the winter when the exhibition took place. At the same time, a kind of freedom, and thus the possibilities, that came with the deployment of mind was all the more immense.

In the following year, he "organized" as many as three group exhibitions: *Anti-Civilization*, *Void*, and *Anti-Japan*. The most drastic of the three was *Anti-Civilization Exhibition*. Presented at the *All Japan Independent Exhibition* held at Yokohama Civic Art Gallery in May, it was an exhibition within an exhibition (figure 2.16).[59] As declared in the flier, "printed in the color of blackened blood on paper," each viewer was first tasked to vanish the whole exhibition by using the power of Psi. Once the independent exhibition was mentally cleared, there would then appear his *Anti-Civilization Exhibition*. With this work he introduced a new idea, "omnipotence of thought" or *nenryo no zennō*, to underscore his art of *kannen*. In light of his avid research, he likely took it from Freud's psychoanalytic treatise *Totem and Taboo*, where it is identified as "the principle which controls magic, and the technique of the animistic method of thought,"[60] thus corroborating his method of *kannen* with yet another scientific source.

The flier for *Anti-Civilization Exhibition*, contrary to its subtitle, *Seeing Anti-Civilization Exhibition*, only prepares the viewer to clear the galleries of their present contents but gives no alternative exhibition to see, as he ran out of space to do so in his 3-by-3 grid form. For further detail, he referred the viewer to the August issue of an art magazine (he failed to name it), which turned out to be *Gendai bijutsu* (Contemporary art).[61] In light of diverse works in *Anti-Civilization Exhibition*,[62] it can be understood as a group rather than a solo exhibition. Collectivism was more explicitly orchestrated in *Void*, his next project, presented at the landmark *Independent Art Festival* in Gifu in August. Subtitled *Collective Participation of "Anti-Civilization" School*, this is another exhibition within an exhibition (figure 2.17) (see appendix for translation). The flier includes a checklist with a total of 21 works to be mentally arranged to "permeate"—or to be mentally overlaid upon—the exhibition site in the formation of the Two-World Mandalas, as diagramed on it. Most likely, the checklist was a mock-collective scheme Matsuzawa concocted. Sly wordplays abound, with most names apparently made up. For example, with Miyasaka Chūshō (contributor of Work 4), one Chinese character is changed from his priest-friend's name Miyasaka Yūshō; and Yamada Seishi combines the most common Japanese surname with *seishi*, which means "sperm." Still, it is significant that Matsuzawa himself claimed the top billing, with *My Consciousness and Unconsciousness* (Non-Sensory Painting) and *"Anti-Civilization" Exhibition* (Multi-layered Sculpture); other works were also parenthetically accompanied by such improbable medium types as "Outer Space Research Sculpture" and "Bashful Sculpture," implying a wide range of application possibilities for the principle of his *kannen* conceptualism that vanished matter.

Although the artist invoked the Freudian principle of "omnipotence of thought" for the foundation of the "vanishing act," it would have been a tall order for a novice or skeptical viewer to accept the idea, let alone perform the act. How serious was the artist with his proposition? Granted, as a conceptual exercise his proposition was a drastic, even brilliant, form of institutional critique, calling into question the whole range of activities surrounding art and art making. Yet it should be noted that Matsuzawa was not just aiming at institutional critique in abstraction; he was dead serious about offering an alternative to the object-based convention of art making. No wonder he went on to devise a training program for vanishing in 1966. The first of the kind was *Matsuzawa Yutaka's Ritual for Vanishing of Matter 1966* at Modern Art Center of Japan (MACJ), an alternative space in Tokyo that the critic Yoshida Yoshie hosted for a short time. It was a yearlong program to be held on the 28th of each month, beginning in January. The first session consisted of a chair placed in front of a canvas, each edge of which is as long as infinity. The viewer would sit on the chair, relaxed, and meditate the "anti-projection of the real world behind [the canvas]." The size of the canvas would be reduced each month and eventually become zero in December. Unfortunately, the center was closed after three sessions, but the program was presented with modification at his solo exhibition *V.1010* (wherein V. stands for "version" as in "v.1.0") at Azuma Gallery in Kyoto in January 1967 with a lengthy explanatory subtitle: *With Nine Canvases of Nil, Nine Psi Chairs, and Nine Ultra-Futuristic Methods.*

As important as it was to master the method of vanishing, "vanishing" was no more than a means, not a goal in and of itself in Matsuzawa's *kannen* conceptualism. By vanishing materiality, whether from the work of art or the exhibition, what he wanted was to propose alternatives to material-based art making. Likewise, when he used the prefix "anti-" (*han*), he did not merely negate or protest against civilization, but he was intent on offering alternative visions in a manner parallel to "anti-matter," which constitutes the mirror image of "matter" with a negative charge. This is best exemplified by his *Anti-Japan: Today's Art Exhibition*, envisioned in the fall of 1965, which mirrored *Japan: Today's Art Exhibition*, organized by the Art Club and held at Muramatsu Gallery in Tokyo. "Casting shadows on a huge high moor" and "aris[ing] like a phantom in the purple sky," his *Anti-Japan* exhibition was a counterprogramming through *kannen*, sited away from Tokyo at Nanashima Yashima Highland, the same venue as his independent exhibition in the wilderness.

If vanishing was his means, his overarching theme that emerged in these exhibition activities was "Anti-Civilization," the idea whose beginning he dated to January 1965, and which he first declared two months later in the flier-catalog for his solo exhibition, *Ah, Nil, Ah, A Ceremony of Psi's Secret Embodiment Drowning in the Wilderness*, at Naiqua Gallery in Tokyo. In his ever-evolving theory of Psi, he devised Anti-Civilization as an all-encompassing category of his thoughts and acts, as well as his works beginning in 1963 with *Invitation to Psi Zashiki Room* and *On Another Work in Another Container, or On Cutting* and leading to the proposition of Non-Sensory Painting in 1964 and numerous discoveries and creations he would be making in the future. It was in this declaration that he invoked "*kannen* painting," which figured prominently as an unprecedented work of Nil in the category of Anti-Civilization. While his enigmatic maximalism often perplexes us, he succinctly defined Anti-Civilization as an antithesis of civilization in his symposium abstract for *Independent Art Festival* in Gifu that summer:

> My hypothesis is that contemporary civilization is nothing but a mistake. The whole of humankind must sooner comprehend that matter is futile and create "anti-civilization" based on this principle [of vanishing of matter].
>
> I believe that to create Art (*geijutsu*) is to create "anti-civilization." Therefore, in the world of new humanity, there will be no meaningful value system other than Art. And those who aspire to create Art today are progenitors of a new humankind in the future, although they are too early to be understood.[63]

The term "hypothesis" is crucial to understanding his disinterested theoretical stance. With all of his obscure intellectual sources, he was never a fanatical believer but an almost "scientific"[64] student of the illogical, akin to contemporary physicists and mathematicians who hypothesize the improbable with logical language.

It did not take long for him to turn to vanishing of humankind. It was a logical extension of his hypothesis: if the present humankind made a wrong civilization, we might as well vanish and yield space to a new humankind to come. In the summer of 1966, his entry to the independent *Contemporary Art Festival* in Sakai, Osaka, was a 15-meter banner made of pink synthetic fabric bearing his message, *Humans, Let's Vanish, Let's Go, Let's Go, Gate, Gate, Anti-Civilization Committee.* (He took *gate*, a Sanskrit word pronounced *gyatei*, from the Heart Sutra and freely and indeed cheerfully translated it as "let's go.") Beginning in 1970, this *Banner of Vanishing* served as an indispensable prop for his signature recitation performance, which he would continue throughout his life (figure 2.18).

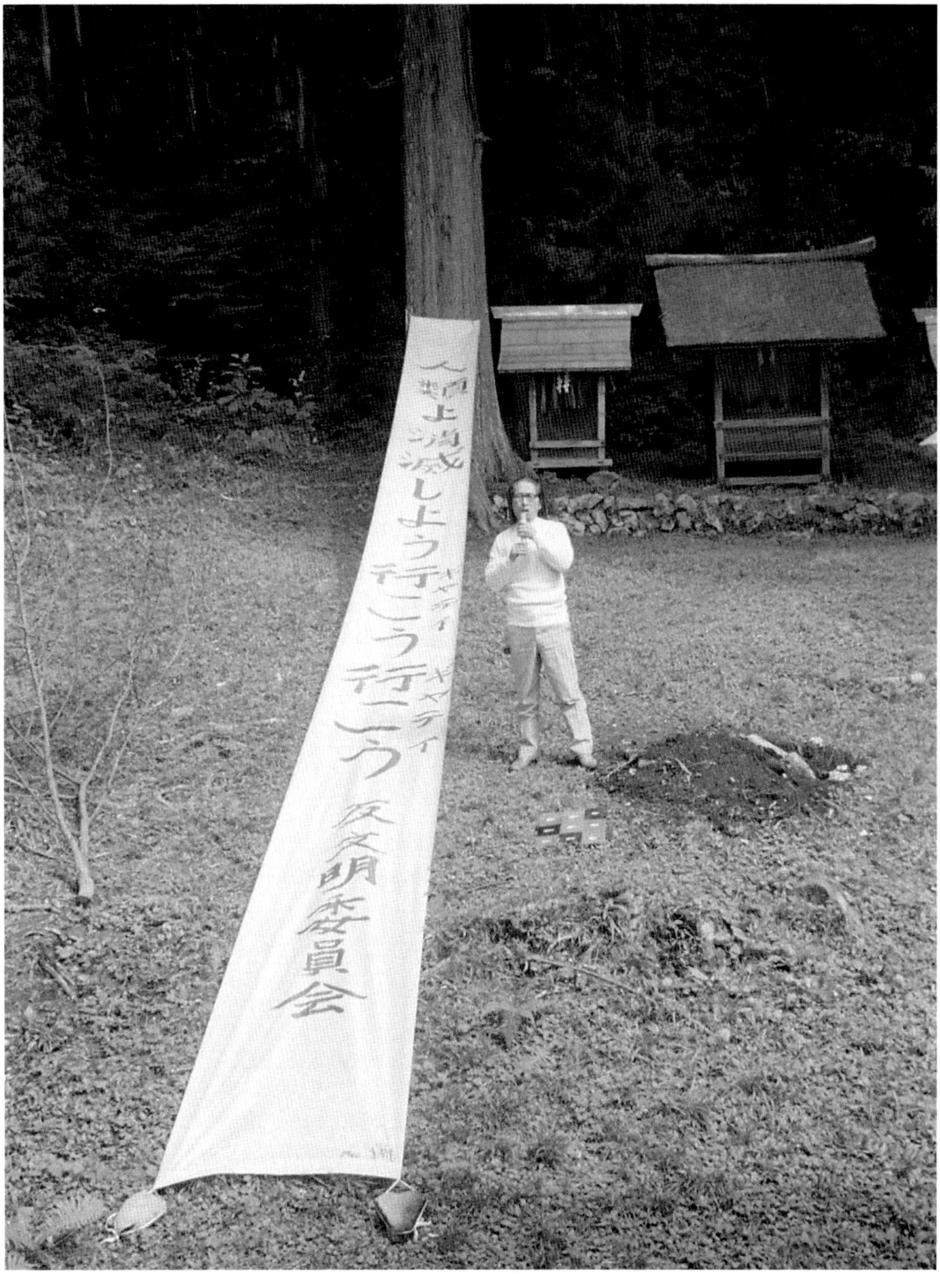

FIGURE 2.18
Matsuzawa Yutaka performing with his 1966 *Banner of Vanishing (Humans, Let's Vanish, Let's Go, Let's Go, Gate, Gate, Anti-Civilization Committee)* at Mount Misa, Shimo Suwa, 1970. Photo © Hanaga Mitsutoshi.

White Circle: An Exercise in Non-Sensory Painting

Matsuzawa's vanishing acts in 1964–1966 constituted a radical reconsideration of the institution of art. As he made progress with his conceptualism, however, he had difficulty in developing a concrete practice for Non-Sensory Painting, his first proposition immediately following his Revelation. It was not until early 1967 that he returned to the issue of painting and devised a set of simple examples for *kannen* painting. A new inspiration to his transdisciplinary mind came from the emerging drug culture—specifically, Henri Michaux's 1957 illustrated book *Infinite Turbulence*, known to have been based on the poet's hallucinogenic experiment with mescaline.[65] Matsuzawa saw the potential of hallucinogenic drugs (from Mexican peyote to the Beatniks' marijuana to the latest LSD) in mind expansion, for drug-induced hallucinations were dissociated from the five senses. He thus surmised that drugs could be part of "direct art" in the future, although he himself did not venture into it. (In Japan, where drugs were, and still are, strictly regulated, it could have been difficult for him to experiment, especially living away from the cultural center of Tokyo. Also with him, theoretical curiosity overrode hands-on experience, as illustrated by his intellectual engagement with parascience.) Instead, he renewed his focus on an area he was most conversant with, Esoteric Buddhism, in which infinity plays a key role in its cosmology and training.

White Infinity 1, published in the October 1967 issue of *Bijutsu Journal*, consists of a spread with an instruction on the left page and a blank page on the right.[66] The instruction was very "precise," so that the reader could "in your consciousness make a white paper [on the right page] extend beyond the top, bottom, right, left edges further and further."

> First you read the instruction by your eyes and see the white paper on the right page. After that, you may want to close your eyes and expand it further and further in your consciousness without thinking anything else. This is a pictorial experience this work offers. All humans can gain the exact same experience.

Matsuzawa's infinity method was most likely adopted from the one employed in the Moon Meditation, which deploys a surprisingly similar procedure.[67] Called in Japanese *gachirinkan*, the "Moon Meditation" was one of the basic meditation methods of Shingon Buddhism, a Japanese branch of Esoteric Buddhism founded by the monk Kūkai in the 9th century. This meditation uses a picture of a white circle (the moon), often in the form of a hanging scroll, to aid the devotee in visualizing the possession, enlargement, and reduction of the moon.[68] The artist was personally familiar with Shingon Buddhism beyond his knowledge of the mandalas (which was more art historical than religious). One of his middle-school friends was the above-mentioned Miyasaka Yūshō (宥勝, 1921–2011), a high-ranking Shingon monk and a respected scholar of

Buddhology, who served as one of the artist's theoretical sources.[69] Not coincidentally, Matsuzawa's parents chose the Chinese character 宥 for his given name Yutaka, which is commonly used for the name of Shingon monks, as in Miyasaka's name.

Matsuzawa labeled *White Infinity* as Precision Painting, because in his formulation it gives the exact same experience to anybody who precisely follows the instruction. It is like a mathematic equation that results in precisely the same answer no matter who solves it so long as he or she precisely follows the logic, as opposed to a conventional painting that induces hundreds of different individual experiences. Precision Painting thus equalizes "pictorial experience."[70] Furthermore, it defies the concept of the "original" work of art because a "multiple" or even "infinite" number of originals can exist for each work, as an unspecified number of people follow its instruction and meditate on it, thereby actively possessing it. As such, Precision Painting disposes the notion of self-expression by "transcending the self" and engendering an "experience of *kannen* through the collective unconscious." In this sense, Matsuzawa's Precision Painting constituted a fundamental critique of the modernist construct of painting involving self-expression, originality, and self-sufficient objecthood.

Of more than 30 Precision Paintings he devised,[71] the most elegant was *White Circle* of 1967. It initially took two forms in his oeuvre. As a "meditation aid," so to speak, he literally offered circles made of white paper.[72] In his art of *kannen*, the more essential was the invisible *White Circle*, which he communicated through a one-year monthly mailing of Postcard Paintings, launched in July 1967. The very first one was *A Blank Painting for All Living and Non-Living Beings*, which reads (figure 2.19, plate 6):

> I show it not only to humans but also to rocks, trees, heavens, birds and animals, music, and self-replicating machines. Gaze at a white circle therein.

As with *White Infinity*, the notion of "white circle" and the use of a physical meditation aid had a likely connection to the Moon Meditation. However, intent gazing on an invisible circle was achieved through pure *kannen*. This had a definite source in Exoteric Buddhism—Pure Land Buddhism, in particular one of its three major sutras, the *Meditation of the Buddha of Infinite Life Sutra* (*Kanmuryōju-kyō*). It advocates 13 progressively difficult meditations to visualize Amida's Western Paradise. The very first entry-level meditation concerns the sun setting in the western sky. Initially the devotee should look at the setting sun, but after practice he would eventually be able to visualize it with his eyes closed.[73] When interviewed by the poet Katō Ikuya for *Bijutsu techō* in 1969, Matsuzawa referenced this exercise as a precedent to his proposed training for seeing the invisible.[74] That is to say, with Matsuzawa's *White Circle*, the viewer should be able to progress from looking at its physical form to gazing at it in its invisible state (figure 2.20).[75]

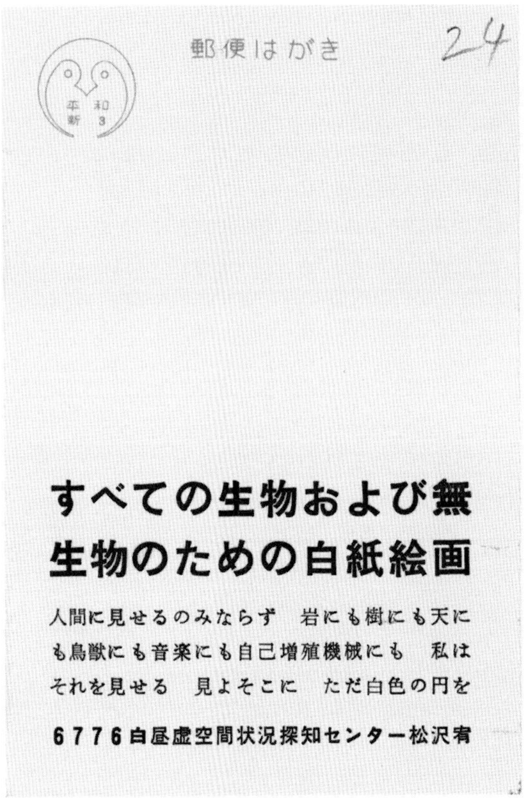

FIGURE 2.19
Matsuzawa Yutaka, *A Blank Painting for All Living and Non-Living Beings (Postcard Painting I-01)*, 1967. Letterpress on preprinted paper; 14.8 × 10 cm. 1 of 40 items in *Psi Box* (1969). Private collection, on long-term loan to The Museum of Modern Art, Gunma. (Also plate 6.)

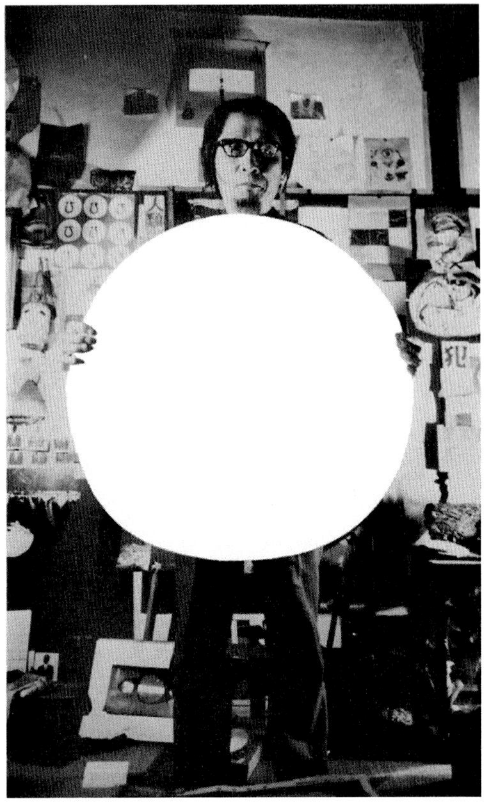

FIGURE 2.20
Matsuzawa Yutaka holding *White Circle*, 1968. Photo © Nakajima Kō. Reproduced from *Y. Matsuzawa* (Tokyo: Aoki Gallery, 1969). Takiguchi Shūzō Papers, c. 1945–1979, Keiō University Art Center, Tokyo.

By 1967, the independent-exhibition movement had waned and Matsuzawa's exhibition activities quieted down. His turn to Precision Painting and mail art resulted from a timely and necessary retreat to his experimental laboratory. Mail art helped to close the distance from his associates and keep his presence known among the Tokyo art world. Unlike the previous mailings in 1963–1964, in which he folded his oversized fliers to place them in regular letter envelopes, the postcard made an excellent all-in-one vehicle. He could have a text printed in color (red in the first one) on the bottom half of the address side and kept the reverse blank so that it would function as a "blank canvas." In the limited space of the postcard, the instruction had to be concise, but the observant recipient would know that the word "therein" (in the instruction of the first postcard) referred to the back side, where the willing recipient could undertake an exercise of meditating on a white circle—improbably together with all sentient and non-sentient beings.

Despite Matsuzawa's heavy reliance on Exoteric and Esoteric Buddhism, his conceptualism was universalist. Aiming to reach out to all humans in a nonsectarian language, he standardized the Eastern wisdom and used the sharable and communicative form of art. Moreover his sources were not just Eastern and ancient; he scoured the peaks and valleys of knowledge to identify ways to see the invisible in its invisible states and codified the method as *kannen*. He did not so much represent the invisible (as did Surrealists or Symbolists) as offer the viewer the means to experience the invisible, sometimes through physical apparatuses (such as paper circles) and other times through immaterial methodologies (such as his commands and instructions). This strongly resonates with Yves Klein's interest in the immaterial, which will be discussed in chapter 6. *White Circle* was in this sense the least enigmatic and most accessible of his oeuvre. As such, he designated it as Fundamental Painting (*konpon kaiga*) in the second postcard dated August 1967. Embracing its universal nature, he declared in the ninth postcard, dated March 1968, that *This Is a Painting That Can Be Owned by All Humans*. It reads:

> All we need is a blank sheet of paper. We don't even need it. On a blank paper, or on a void that can be deemed a blank paper, you will possess a Fundamental Painting that is white and circular. It is shameful to sell and buy painting. Not just painting. Be it a car, a color TV, bread [*pan*], a *panpan* [prostitute], a book [*hon*], or a HON, it should be shared by the entire humanity. If you want it, just fetch it for free.

To reiterate the radically altruistic and egalitarian proposition, he issued a postcard-size silver-lettered owner's certificate from the Void/Imaginary Space Situation Research Center (his quasi-collectivist tag), titled *Certificate of Ownership: Matsuzawa Yutaka's Immaterial Collection of Fundamental Painting* (figure 2.21). Needless

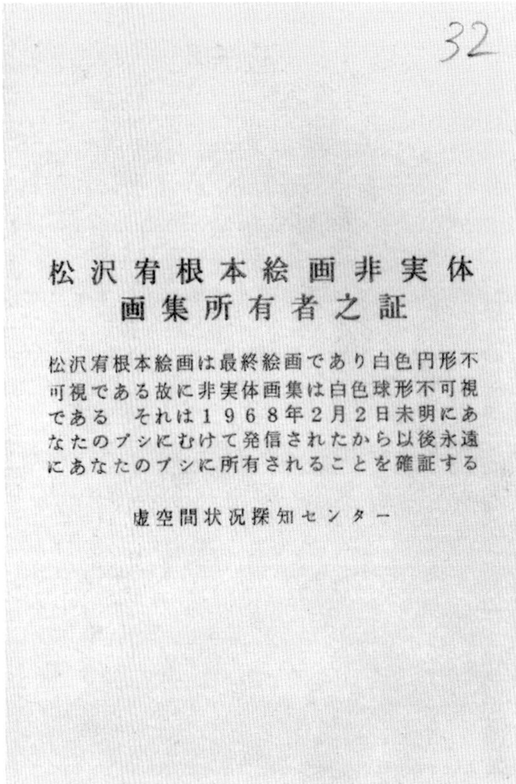

32

松沢宥根本絵画非実体
画集所有者之証

松沢宥根本絵画は最終絵画であり白色円形不
可視である故に非実体画集は白色球形不可視
である　それは１９６８年２月２日未明にあ
なたのプシにむけて発信されたから以後永遠
にあなたのプシに所有されることを確証する

虚空間状況探知センター

FIGURE 2.21
Matsuzawa Yutaka, *Certificate of Ownership: Matsuzawa Yutaka's Immaterial Collection of Fundamental Painting*, 1968. Letterpress on preprinted paper; 14.8 × 10 cm. 1 of 40 items in *Psi Box* (1969). Private collection, on long-term loan to The Museum of Modern Art, Gunma.

to say, one's ownership becomes inalienable only when one accepts the artist's proposition and masters the way to see the invisible circle at will. If any, that was the price of his painting.

White Circle visualized on white paper is not unlike Malevich's Suprematist composition *White on White*. Their material forms are different: Malevich's oil on canvas is material and sensory, whereas Matsuzawa's "White on White," is immaterial and non-sensory. Yet both artists engaged the realms outside modern rationalism in their search for the invisible. After half a century, Matsuzawa updated his predecessor's aspiration for "the supremacy of pure feeling in creative art"[76] through his immaterialist art of *kannen*. Although *White Circle* is a superb example of Matsuzawa's conceptualism, it was no more than a foundational exercise[77] to develop a skill necessary in achieving the ultimate and final art form of Anti-Civilization, which would serve as a counterproposal to material civilization, the peril of which continued to threaten humanity at the brink of extinction with the ongoing Cold War and attendant nuclear crises. From 1970 onward, with his conceptualist arsenal well stocked, Matsuzawa went on to make an ambitious leap into the international.

* * *

It took almost 20 years for Matsuzawa Yutaka to develop his conceptualism from the time he decided to pursue the invisible in art. As he probed his way toward his goal, his trajectory locally intersected with the early interest in intermedia in the 1950s, Anti-Art in the early 1960s, and the independent-exhibition movement in the mid-1960s, before his practice stood prominently in Non-Art in the late 1960s. Unbeknownst to him, by the time he formulated a gamut of conceptualist strategies, he had a number of global peers who likewise questioned and challenged the modernist institution of art and dismantled the object-based conception of the work of art. In this sense, he contributed to generating the state of international contemporaneity. In global conceptualism, his art of *kannen* is unique in that his work actively engages the viewer's mind so that she or he can visualize the invisible—under the concepts of Non-Sensory Painting and Anti-Civilization—without recourse to material objects. In this sense, he at once materially and immaterially dematerialized art. Enigmatic as his theory and practice may appear at first glance, his vast body of work reveals a set of connections and resonances with work by his peers. As part of connection studies, in chapter 5 we will examine his international interfaces, which began in earnest in 1970. On an institutional level, he was invited to *Tokyo Biennale 1970*, which itself offers many narrative tangents to explore. On an individual level, he envisioned engendering an international commune of mail-art conceptualism beginning with *World Uprising* in 1971. In chapter 6, resonances centering on Matsuzawa will be examined in two sets of comparisons. One involves "immateriality" that occupied such conceptualists as Yves Klein and Robert Barry, with a particular focus on their shared interest in the empty gallery. The other concerns Japanese pioneers of conceptualism, Yoko Ono and On Kawara, who developed their version of conceptualism around the same time as Matsuzawa. By identifying and examining these contact points, those chapters will help us further understand the rich possibilities of conceptualism that Matsuzawa contributed to the global 1960s.

3 THE PLAY'S COLLECTIVE VOYAGES INTO THE WILDERNESS

A group of "Happeners" (*hapunā*)[1] founded in Osaka in 1967, The Play emerged in the years following the suspension of the Yomiuri Independent Exhibition in January 1964 and grew into exemplary inhabitants of the wilderness. The group's prehistory was linked to the short-lived artist-organized independent-exhibition movement, which most fundamentally defined the wilderness from 1964 to 1967. Through this movement, Ikemizu Keiichi, a future lead member of the group, transitioned from an *objet*-maker to an *objet*-based Happener, began to lay the strategic foundation for the group, and absorbed the meaning of independence from institutional strictures. Beginning with *Voyage: Happening in an Egg* of 1968 (figure 0.2), their first collective act, The Play decisively "went *out of* the institution of art,"[2] bringing their projects to decentered sites of wilderness. In the tumultuous late 1960s, such collectives as Bikyōtō and Expo '70 Destruction Joint-Struggle Group advocated the idea of "destruction" as a primary method for institutional critique. In contrast, at The Play, "those who acutely sensed the strain of material civilization gathered together to send a message from humans to humans,"[3] representing the flip side of the radical 1960s. The message they produced was constructive, not destructive, as their major concern was to take a "voyage" away from everyday consciousness trapped in familiar space and time. As they observed in 1981,

> The Play went outside the institutions of art, which meant going outdoors. [...]
>
> It is important to do so, like farmers do, daily, empirically, and persistently.
>
> The Play's actions constitute a return to man's essential being. It can be called "art" in that we plow around it.[4]

In so doing, they developed a mode of collectivism which prioritized discussion and collaboration. In this mode, not only did they depart from the body-conscious orientation of performance art in 1960s Japan to merge Happenings and land art; they also thoroughly dismantled the notion of singular authorship and the construct of the work of art as a self-contained object. During the group's most consistently active period, beginning in 1970, they undertook a large-scale annual summer project, which culminated in a 10-year engagement with *Thunder* (1977–1986).

PREHISTORIES IN THE POST-YOMIURI YEARS

Independent Art Festival in Gifu

One may say that the prehistory of The Play began with the announcement by Yomiuri in January 1964 that it was terminating its independent exhibition. In particular, the key player linking The Play to the post-Yomiuri years was Ikemizu Keiichi, who jumpstarted his own career as an artist following the Yomiuri announcement. The termination understandably sent shockwaves among critics and artists alike, but they quickly picked up the pieces. The termination prompted two things. One was the Anti-Art debate centering on Tōno Yoshiaki, one of the Big Three critics, and Miyakawa Atsushi, a new voice of art criticism. The other was a movement of self-organized independent exhibitions, put together by participating artists themselves with little institutional support, that spread nationwide (table 3.1), which significantly involved the discussion of the nature of the independent system and how to extend it.

Few questioned the validity of equating the ideal of "independence" with vanguardism itself. This point was made by the organizers of *Independent '64*, the first independent exhibition put together by artists in response to the Yomiuri termination. Under the stewardship of the critic Haryū Ichirō, it opened in June, three months after the customary opening of the Yomiuri Independent Exhibition in the spring, at none other than the coveted Tokyo Metropolitan Art Museum. In an opening statement in its exhibition brochure, the organizers loftily declared:

> "Independent" means a creative fire burning in an artist and a free forum of experimentation tied to this fire. Its flame may seem faint, its site still small. Our departure point is our resolve to set ablaze all the authorities and constraints and

> illuminate the future. [...] We hope that those who kindle unextinguishable flames inside themselves will proactively explore their creative energies and make this exhibition the first step toward a truly self-reliant independent exhibition.[5]

Yet the same statement also acknowledged the problem: Yomiuri artists had made their "new art" and waged their "resistance" in a "hothouse" environment enabled by the exhibition system created by a newspaper company. Bluntly put, it had been an "independence" sheltered by corporate capitalism. Admittedly, *Independent '64* just took "the first step" toward a genuine form of independent exhibition. To truly ignite a fire of independence, Tokyo was not always a suitable venue, and artists had to go outside the capital. In this regard, Matsuzawa Yutaka's call for *Independent '64 in the Wilderness* (figure 0.1), planned six months later, conceptually rebuked the Tokyo-based affair, for he sited his immaterial exhibition in a remote place which few would physically visit, be they artists or viewers.

The problem of Tokyo-centrism was articulated by Vava, a vanguard collective in Gifu in central Japan, which organized *Independent Art Festival* at their hometown in August 1965. Vava's leader, Nishio Ichizō, wrote in their call for participation:

> We rally all lone wolves biding their time in all corners of Japan to [*Independent Art Festival*]. Howling against the phony authority, we command all artists self-aware of ambition to gather together.
>
> 1. Our "new independent exhibition" begins where the old one ended.
> 2. We must liberate ourselves from the museum, which has become the hermetic site for elitists.
> 3. Let us make our festival as big as the annual National Athletic Meet. [...] Where shall we meet the next year?[6]

What Nishio meant by "the hermetic site for elitists" was what regional artists' perceived as Tokyo artists' bad behavior, including willful rule-breaking. In their first preparatory meeting, he alluded to the example of Kudō Tetsumi occupying an entire room at the Yomiuri Independent. In his conception, a "new independent exhibition" must not be a site exclusive to a select few.[7] His characterization is not completely accurate: Kudō Tetsumi, a Neo Dada associate who mounted his landmark *Distribution Map of Impotence and the Rise of Protection Dome at the Saturation Point* in 1962, merely exploited a loophole in the exhibition rules, which stated that a participant could have a length of wall commensurate with the fees he paid. Kudō paid the fees for all the walls of the room in question.[8] Still, such a ploy was possible only because Kudō was a Tokyo resident perfectly situated to execute this flagrant maneuvering in person. The underlying problem was thus distance, which was a significant if not insurmountable hindrance for many regional artists, as they incurred expenses of time and money that Tokyo artists did not have to worry about. (With a regional exhibition, most participants would equally lack such home advantage.)

Kudō's whole-room installation was but one example. On-site presence was varyingly necessary for many radical experiments of Anti-Art in both installation and performance art. Some regional artists, such as Kyūshū-ha of Fukuoka, Zero Dimension (Zero Jigen) of Nagoya, and Hamaguchi Tomiharu of Kōchi, were willing to travel to Tokyo for the occasions but at considerable personal expense. It is little surprise, then, that seen from outside Tokyo, Anti-Art's off-the-wall adventures—which had practically brought down the Yomiuri Independent—appeared "elitist." Certainly, in the aftermath of the Yomiuri's announcement, criticisms were heard even in Tokyo that the Yomiuri Independent had been academicized or the label "independent artists" had become a cliché.[9] Hardly surprising, as well, that artists' motivation to create their own forum anew was far stronger in the periphery than in the capital. Nishio's reference to the National Athletic Meet (Kokutai) was apt, for Kokutai highlighted all regions in Japan (and still does) by holding prefecture-versus-prefecture competitions and rotating its venue every year from one prefecture to another. Thus Nishio alluded to the possibility of a national networking of hitherto isolated regional artists by serializing an independent exhibition annually in different regional centers.

Among the newly instituted independent exhibitions (table 3.1), Nishio and Vava's *Independent Art Festival* in Gifu excelled in its scale and in the critical attention it received. It had three venues: the city's civic center, the outdoor areas around it, and a vast dry riverbed of the Nagara. Well connected in his hometown, Nishio managed to secure these venues as well as the sponsorship and cooperation of the city hall, a local newspaper company, and other businesses. *Independent Art Festival* attracted more than 100 artists and collectives from all over the country. Especially important were vanguard collectives hailing mostly from regional cities. In addition to Vava, present in Gifu were Okayama Young Artists Collective (Okayama Seinen Bijutsuka Shūdan) from Okayama Prefecture; Nomo Group of Maebashi, Gunma Prefecture; Gaga Contemporary Art (Gaga Gendai Bijutsu) of Ōmiya and Saitama Avant-Garde Artists Collective (Saitama Zen'ei Bijutsuka Shūdan) of Urawa, both from Saitama Prefecture; Zero Dimension of Nagoya; Group "I" of Kobe; two unnamed groups from Osaka; and Jack Society (Jakku no Kai) of Tokyo. These regional vanguard collectives played a central role in advocating contemporary practices of art in their home areas, prompting the term "regional avant-garde" (*chihō no zen'ei*) in the late 1960s.[10] Above all, their participation demonstrated their commitment to overcoming distance and forging a nationwide network that Nishio had proposed. These collectives were a major force that enlivened the riverbed site, which proved to be a success, attracting 21 individuals and collectives, including Nishio himself and his group Vava.

TABLE 3.1
Independent Exhibitions in the Post-Yomiuri Years

1964	
February–March	*17th Japan Independent Exhibition* Tokyo, organized by Japan Art Society (Nihon Bijutsu-kai) since 1947
March	*8th Kyoto Independent Exhibition* Since 1955
June	*5th Himeji Independent Exhibition* 1961–1965
June–July	*Independent '64* Tokyo; one time only
July	*1st All Japan Independent Exhibition* Yokohama; ended 1965
September–October	*Sendai Independent Exhibition* One time only
December	*Independent '64 in the Wilderness* Nagano Prefecture; one time only
December	*Film Independent* Tokyo; one time only
1965	
March	*24th Hokkaidō Independent Exhibition* Asahikawa; since 1946, but not held in 1964
June	*1st Gunma Independent Exhibition* One time only
August	*Independent Art Festival* aka *Gifu Independent Exhibition*; one time only
1966	
March	*Contemporary Art Festival* aka *Sakai Independent Exhibition*; one time only

Source: KuroDalaiJee, *Anarchy of the Body*, 189

An opening-day symposium was an ingenious way to bring in visitors from outside, especially from Tokyo. Among the luminaries on the symposium roster,[11] debating the theme "Is Art Possible in Contemporary Times?," were the artist Ikeda Tatsuo and the critic Tōno Yoshiaki, both from Tokyo, as well as the Osaka critic Akane Kazuo. Since these three also would review the festival for *Bijutsu techō* and *Geijutsu Shinchō*, two art journals of record, the organizers' publicity scheme was very effective. Their reports were favorable, all varyingly noting works on the riverbed site, especially *Hole* by the Kobe-based Group "I" (figure 6.9) and *Homo Sapiens* by Ikemizu Keiichi (figure 3.1).[12] If "Body Art," as it was termed by the internationalist Tōno, was a focal point of the outdoor exhibits, the conceptualism of Matsuzawa Yutaka's immaterial contribution *Void* (figure 2.17), a mere printed sheet of paper, critically stood out, catching the eye of Ikeda and Akane in the eclectic indoor exhibition.

Ikemizu Keiichi Was *Homo Sapiens*

In 1965, the caged presence of Ikemizu Keiichi on a dry riverbed of the Nagara River earned him critical attention, merely one year after he dove into his artistic career (figure 3.1). Born in 1937, Ikemizu graduated in 1960 from Osaka Gakugei Daigaku, a teachers' college now known as Osaka Kyōiku University, and became a middle-school art teacher. He was politically active in a union movement in the midst of the anti-*Anpo* protest and its aftermath, although by 1964 he felt he had hit a dead end. Since politics had long occupied him, he had little interest in participating in any vanguard art movement, unaware of what was going on at the famed Yomiuri Independent Exhibition.[13] On learning of Haryū's effort to organize an alternative independent exhibition in Tokyo, however, he became fired up. The year 1964 saw him participating in a local Kyoto Independent Exhibition in March for the first time as a dry run, showing in Haryū's *Independent '64* in June, and being selected by the Kyoto-based critic Nakamura Keiji to show in *Anti-Art Three-Person Exhibition* at galerie 16 in July. In this succession of exhibition activities, Ikemizu created the series *Cage*, consisting of a grid of multiple boxes with grilled fronts, each containing a different object (a death mask, bread, or a clock with a second hand only, among others). For the outdoor setting of Gifu, he expanded the encasement concept into *Homo Sapiens*, in which he himself was presented as a sample specimen in a 2-by-2-meter cage.

His work, which bore a multilingual label, "*Jinrui*, *Homo sapiens*, *Ningen*, Man, ♂," drew comparisons with another human-in-cage work by Akiyama Yūtokutaishi, a Tokyo-based Happener. In their reviews, the artist Ikeda Tatsuo and the critic Akane Kazuo equally favored Ikemizu's work over Akiyama's indoor piece, *Mr. H's Elegant Life*, which they considered vulgar and cluttered. In contrast, they saw in Ikemizu's work the artist's attempt to confront the human condition confined in the cage of civilization.[14] In his cage, Ikemizu created a situation in which not only the viewer looked at Ikemizu but also the artist looked back at the viewer. After Gifu, Ikemizu transferred

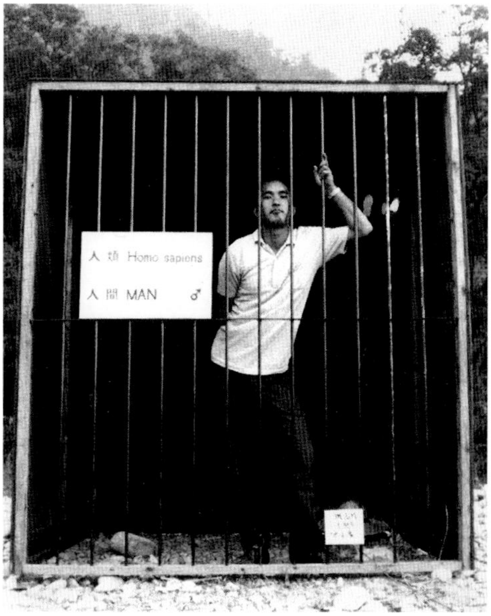

FIGURE 3.1
Ikemizu Keiichi, *Homo Sapiens*, 1965. Installation view on the dry riverbed of the Nagara River at *Independent Art Festival* in Gifu. Photo courtesy of Ikemizu Keiichi.

this confrontational situation to urban settings as a further complication. In November 1965, he had a more compact metal cage fabricated with vertical bars all around and brought it to Osaka's Tennōji Zoo and Shinsaibashi shopping district. In doing so, he highlighted the nature of humankind, at once part of the animal kingdom and in civilization. His decision to explicitly call these acts "Happenings" in his announcement signaled his growing interest in the new art form.[15]

As important for Ikemizu in this formative year was his involvement with Gifu's organizing committee. Inspired by the manifesto of *Independent '64* and Nishio's call for national networking, he, together with his schoolmate Ōta Ryūzō, decided to organize another independent festival in his hometown to extend the spirit and energy of independence.[16] Their *Contemporary Art Festival* was held one year later, in August 1966, in Sakai, a satellite city south of Osaka. The venue was Kanaoka Park and a gymnasium in the park, which their local artist friend Fukuoka Michio helped secure.[17] Some 180 artists and collectives participated. The presence of such familiar names as Gaga Contemporary Art, Jack Society, Gunma Nomo Group, and Group "I," as well as Matsuzawa Yutaka and Nishio Ichizō, shows continuity from Gifu. Camaraderie was palpably being forged among regional independent artists.

While giving favorable mentions to Ikemizu, Gaga, and Group "I," reviewers pointed out the visible waning of the independent energy.[18] No critical attention was given to the innovations the festival organizers devised: an "on paper" exhibition and the first ever Happenings division instituted in Japan. (In retrospect, the former can today be reevaluated as a multiple-edition commemorative portfolio of works on paper and the latter as a nascent form of relational aesthetics.) These negative reviews partly reflected the artist-organizers' limitations. Enthusiasm alone was not enough to plan and execute a nationwide project for which they had to orchestrate the support and cooperation of the local government, businesses, and media. The success of Gifu, under the leadership of Nishio, was rather unusual. Ikemizu and his fellow organizers were burdened by Sakai's location on the southern edge of the greater Keihanshin (Kyoto-Osaka-Kobe) metropolitan area. With the precedent of Gutai in the region, expectations were high, and local journalism was aware that contemporary art was getting traction at the museum level. As the knowledgeable reviewer of *All Kwansai*, a local general-interest monthly, pointed out, the locus of experimentalism was not limited to independent exhibitions, with the Kyoto Modern's annual *Trends in Contemporary Japanese Art* cited as but one example.[19] This was true, yet the museum surveys were built on the lively scenes of experimentalism at the regional independent exhibitions and rental galleries, where artists took operational initiatives and younger artists found opportunities to enter an arena of contemporary art.

Exhibitions that served local vanguard artists outside the two centers of Tokyo and Kyoto were still few. Two such locally centered, artist-organized (but not independent) exhibitions were *All Setouchi Contemporary Art Exhibition* in Okayama (1966) and *South Japan Contemporary Art Exhibition* in Kōchi (1967). Led respectively by Okayama Young Artists Collective (which participated in the independent festivals in Gifu and Sakai) and Avant-Garde Tosa School (Zen'ei Tosa-ha), both exhibitions were supported by local governments, and the former survived for three decades through 1996.[20] Ikemizu was part of this development, being invited to the second Setouchi exhibition in 1968.

* * *

For Ikemizu, the experiences he had gained through the artist-organized exhibition movement were invaluable. He learned to work with other artists to produce a large-scale project in an unconventional venue while laying the foundation for his art, which was shifting from an object-based practice to a more performative direction. By 1968, he was ready to take a bigger stride.

EARLY YEARS: A GATHERING OF HAPPENERS

The Play first took form with its first exhibition of Happenings, held in Kobe in 1967 (figure 3.2, plate 7). In addition to the two strands of its prehistory examined in the previous sections, one more local narrative flowed into the group's formation: a distinct culture of performance art in Kansai (the greater Kobe-Osaka-Kyoto region

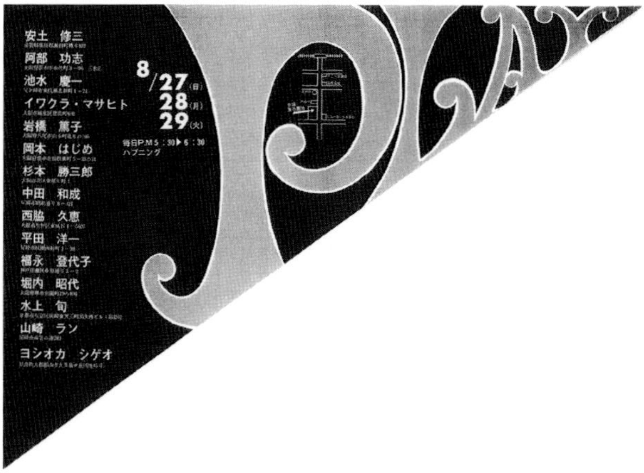

FIGURE 3.2
First Play Exhibition, 1967. Poster. © The Play. (Also plate 7.)

within seven Kinki prefectures; see figure 3.6). Although Kansai was the home of Gutai, by the mid-1960s their performative legacy had been largely forgotten, even among local artists. Gutai by then was regarded less as an experimental pioneer than as an elite establishment, not unlike many other *dantai* (salon-based artists' organizations) which would consolidate their power base through membership expansion.[21] Rather, the local culture in question was post-Gutai *and* post-Yomiuri, a time when performative-minded artists increasingly went into the streets in the heavily body-based mode of "Anti-Art performance."[22] In Tokyo, the Ritualist School (Gishiki-ha) flourished around Zero Dimension, which moved its base from Nagoya to Tokyo. Their visceral, sometimes exhibitionist uses of the body, anti-modern strategies, and longings for the indigenous past characterized this Tokyo strain. In contrast, the Kansai artists were more cerebral in their approach to the body, as amply demonstrated by Ikemizu's cage Happenings.

Another important Kansai performer at mid-decade was Mizukami Jun, one year junior to Ikemizu, who studied law at Kyoto University and began his creative endeavor as a poet while at school. His immediate inspiration was the anti-*Anpo* protest of 1960, in particular the martyrdom of the female student Kanba Michiko, who was crushed by riot police. He commemorated her death with a simple ritual involving hemp rope and pebbles at the site where the incident occurred, near the Diet.[23] By 1964, he had developed a distinct style of acts that featured language and sound, sometimes working with other performers. His early work can be understood from *Round Tape Poem*, presented in Nagoya at *Japan Ultra-Art Fair* organized in August 1964 by Zero Dimension as a post-Yomiuri initiative for performance artists.[24] Words he inscribed on a fabric tape were read by performers seated on the floor as they passed the tape among them.[25] In March 1967, he encountered two fellow performers, Iwakura Masahito and Azuchi Shūzō (aka Gulliver), at the Kyoto Independent Exhibition, and they formed the group Remandaran.[26] Nakata Kazushige, known for using condoms in his work, also joined the group.[27] Through the summer, they presented a few programs together, each showing different elements: Mizukami began to reveal a fascination with the occult and mysticism, while Gulliver, who had been experimenting with performance art since high school, devoted himself to the idea of measurement.[28] In August of that year, Remandaran along with Ikemizu Keiichi and others in Kansai held a three-day exhibition of Happenings at a public playground in Sannomiya, the major downtown district of Kobe. The exhibition title *Play* was subsequently adopted as the name of this new group.

The Play at this point was an eclectic mix of 13 Happeners.[29] The only collective act of the exhibition was *Prologue*, in which the members made one circumambulation of the park, each with his or her eye covered by a white eyepatch. Some smoke candles were lit to attract the attention of park visitors.[30] Ikemizu set up a 4-meter-high wood platform painted in blue, red, and white; those willing could climb a ladder and jump off from the top. (For safety, cushioning was placed below the platform.) Gulliver's "dive" from the platform was particularly photogenic and memorable (figure 3.3). Yoshioka Shigeo set up a dining set, painted white, with a few dental molds on a table; he sat on a chair and kept brushing his teeth, accompanied by a "mother" doll seated on another chair. Among Remandaran's members, Gulliver took measurements of the ground beneath a cagelike jungle gym structure. Iwakura Masahito reprised his charcoal-powered toy train, which had been popular with the crowd and the press at Sakai's *Contemporary Art Festival.* Nakata circled in a pond riding on a gigantic 4-meter-long condom-shaped balloon. He also rushed around on land, clad all in white and with smoke candles attached on his hip. (The candles were so hot that he had to jump into the pond; he was burnt badly and received medical attention at a hospital.)[31] In contrast, Mizukami, with his partner Suzukida Asako, staged a quiet but bizarre ritual, each dressed in black, complete with a black cape. Standing in front of a modern office building near the Sannomiya station, he wound and unwound a red cord around himself in order to stimulate "reactions" from the audience.[32] Local and national media enthusiastically covered the exhibition, with *Asahi Graph* giving them a photographic report, under the title of "Outdoor Exhibition of 'Action Art.'"[33]

Of the 13 artists who participated in what is today known as the "first (and only) *Play* exhibition," six went on to form the core of The Play in its early years through 1969, beginning with *Voyage: Happening in an Egg.* After *Voyage* (figure 0.2), four who had not participated in the first exhibition joined. The most important of them was Miki Tetsuo, an associate of Mizukami born in 1944, who had begun experimenting with performance art in high school and would eventually become a designer.[34] He showed a three-dimensional "square tower" in the outdoor section of Sakai's *Contemporary Art*

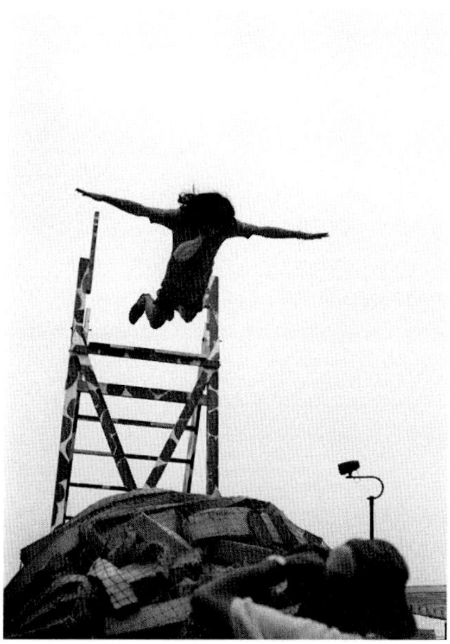

FIGURE 3.3
Azuchi Shūzō (aka Gulliver) jumping off Ikemizu Keiichi's *Skydiving* at *First Play Exhibition*, 1967. © The Play.

Festival in 1966, where he first met Ikemizu. For the first *Play* exhibition in the following year, he assisted Iwakura with his miniature train. While associated with Buzoku (Tribe), a commune movement launched around May 1967 and led by the Beat poet-thinker Yamao Sansei,[35] Miki led a wanderer's life for three years. After his first involvement with The Play in *Reaction in Summer*, the group's stage presentation at SAB Hall in Osaka in August 1968, he often collaborated with Mizukami outside the group. For example, in May 1969, he accompanied Mizukami to Kitakyūshū to perform in *'70 Destruction Convention in Kyūshū*, along with other Play members Okamoto Hajime and Murata Keiichi.[36]

In this early period, diverse activities of The Play unfolded at a brisk pace, broadly ranging from indoor stage presentations to outdoor romping (table 3.2). Two large-scale collective projects stand out: *Voyage: Happening in an Egg* in 1968 and *Current of Contemporary Art*, a journey from Kyoto to Osaka in 1969. Both involved an object—a gigantic fiberglass egg in the former and a Styrofoam raft in the latter; both brought the members out of urban spaces and into larger landscapes; both were planned over a long stretch of time, with assistance sought from outside specialists and government offices in the process of preparation; and both created a distinct sense of communal experience. In fact, these two projects set a pattern for The Play's annual summer projects in the years to come, which can be characterized as collective Happenings with a land-art dimension.

This development centered around Ikemizu, who was the master of eggs and the chief architect of *Voyage*. The egg was originally shown at Gifu's *Independent Art*

TABLE 3.2
The Play's Early Years (1967–1969)

1967	
August 27–29	*Play* The first and only namesake exhibition; Happenings at Sannomiya Higashi Playground, Kobe
1968	
August 1	*Voyage: Happening in an Egg* Collective project; two ships departing from Kushimoto, Wakayama Prefecture, and traveling to and from the Pacific Ocean
August 28	*Reaction in Summer: An Evening of Art Collectives That Aim to Shock* Joint interdisciplinary program with others; SAB Hall, Shin Asahi Building, Osaka
November 8, 14, 19	*Time Zone: We Are Standing Here—And?* The Play's Happening, plus other programs by participants from various disciplines; Mainichi Newspapers Hall, Kyoto
1969	
April 1	*Hospital: April Fool Happenings* Rituals at an abandoned hospital, Osaka
April 10	*The Play* Broadsheet newspaper, no. 1
April 28	*Marshmallows & Hot Air* Happenings and exhibits; Gallery Iteza, Kyoto
May 11–12, June 21–22, July 5–6	*Breakfast of Messrs. Play (at Eggs in Orange)* Participation in *9th Contemporary Art Exhibition of Japan* in collaboration with Ikemizu who presented a room-size installation of *Eggs in Orange*; Tokyo Metropolitan Art Museum and Kyoto Municipal Museum of Art; Matsuzawa Yutaka joins them in Tokyo; they stage outdoor Happenings involving gymnastics and a tug-of-war in Kyoto
June 30	*The Play* Broadsheet newspaper, no. 2
July 20	*Current of Contemporary Art* Collective project to travel from Kyoto to Osaka via a river
August 1	*Cross-Meetin': Mr. Play's Another Voyage* Collective project to meet at Mount Aso, Kyūshū
August 19– September 23	*7 Dimensions* Official exhibit for *Trends in Contemporary Japanese Art*, The National Museum of Modern Art, Kyoto; seven Happenings using three cross-shaped pieces of white cloth over seven Sundays
December 12	*The Play* Broadsheet newspaper, no. 3

Festival as a riverbed exhibit of one of the two "Osaka groups" of which he was part. His *Homo Sapiens* cage there (a 2-meter wooden cube) and this 2-by-3-meter egg made of fiberglass were ingenious exhibits in the outdoors: they were big enough to stand out against a vast and flat open space, but hollow and thus light enough to quickly remove from the venue in case of a flood warning—a prerequisite for this outdoor exhibition, lest large objects carried by a sudden severe flood damage neighboring houses and other property. He went on to use eggs twice more: in an installation for *2nd All Setouchi Contemporary Art Exhibition* in 1968 and in *Eggs in Orange*, a room-size environment for the 1969 Mainichi Contemporary.

Ikemizu's object-based approach markedly differed from Mizukami's more body-centered approach. The latter was vividly demonstrated by Mizukami's participation in *Expo '70 Destruction Black Festival* of June 10, 1969, organized by the Expo '70 Destruction Joint-Struggle Group at Kyoto University (figure 3.4). Assisted by Suzukida Asako, he staged *Rope Dynamics Directional Ritual*, while the anti-Expo group members stood atop the undergraduate lecture building, practically buck naked except for their winged helmets, and struck their signature pose with their right hands raised. Wearing leather gloves and using a primitive anchor, Mizukami struggled to slide down from the rooftop on a rope stretched to the ground, but he fell midway

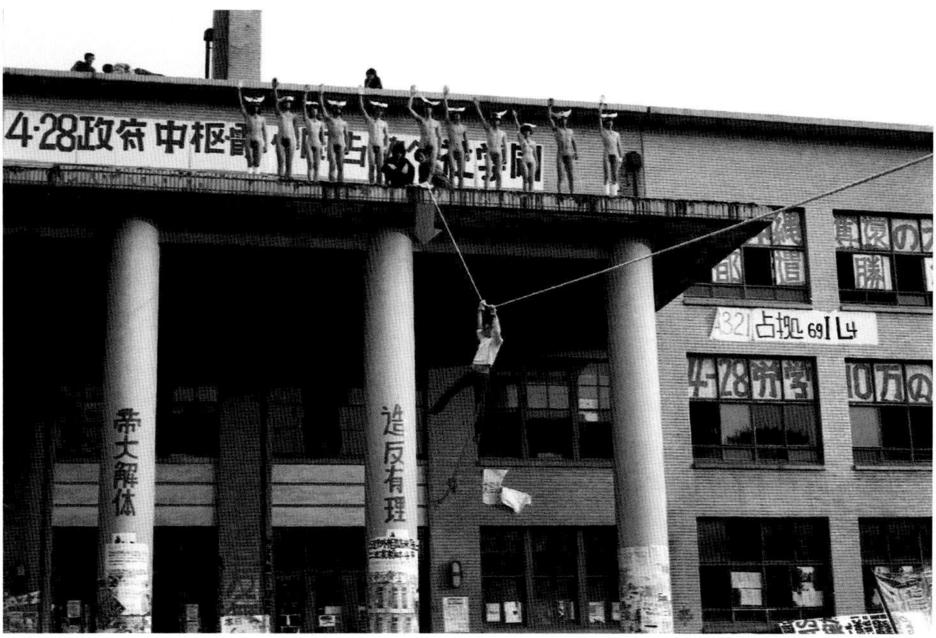

FIGURE 3.4
Mizukami Jun staging *Rope Dynamics Directional Ritual* at Kyoto University, with Expo '70 Destruction Joint-Struggle Group performing a naked ritual on the rooftop of the General Education Building, June 10 1969. Documentary photograph of performances. © Hirata Minoru.

through and was badly hurt.[37] He fluidly networked with Happeners in Tokyo and Kansai. One such example in Kyoto was *Time Zone: We Are Standing Here—And?*, a stage performance program, to which The Play contributed stage Happenings. In contrast, Ikemizu excelled in orchestrating long-term projects as with *Voyage* and *Current of Contemporary Art*.

It turned out to be impossible for two minds embracing two diverging directions to coexist in a single group. In November 1969, Mizukami left the group, feeling that the display of objects would contradict act-based expressions. His deepening interest in religion and mysticism was also dissonant with the group's sometimes whimsical emphasis on the everyday. Vocal about liberating the group's activities from objects and transcending the parameters of art, he was apparently unable to shift its direction. At the time of his departure, as he would later recall, he asked Miki to come with him, but Miki demurred, and his desire to "destroy The Play," too, was unfulfilled.[38] Mizukami's departure concluded the early period of The Play. The group as a whole found its compass and embarked on a series of annual summer voyages into the wilderness, leaving urban spaces. Mizukami moved on to became an important member of Matsuzawa's Nirvana School, while Ikemizu led The Play and developed a zoologically inspired conceptualism in his individual practice. Miki became a project manager of The Play working closely with Ikemizu.

INTO THE WILDERNESS

Launching *Voyage*

Voyage: Happening in an Egg in 1968 marked the very beginning of The Play as a unique collective distinguished by their expressive goal of voyage, which was inseparably entwined with their open and fluid mode of collaborative operation (figure 0.2). Their foray into the wilderness—in the dual sense of going out of the institutional space and traveling into landscapes—was extensive and expansive. The chronology of their large-scale annual summer projects alone eloquently bespeaks the scope of their adventure through their destinations in nature near and far (table 3.3).

The most ambitious project, both in scale and distance traveled, was *Voyage*, which dates back to an outdoor installation at the 1965 *Independent Art Festival* on the dry riverbed of the Nagara River in Gifu.[39] To demonstrate solidarity with the ambition of the self-organized independent-exhibition movement, Ikemizu Keiichi and his colleague Ōta Ryūzō formed a nameless group in Osaka and brought a 2-by-3-meter fiberglass egg there. It was constructed in the backyard of Ikemizu's residence under the direction of his artist neighbor Hirata Yōichi. To pay for the materials—a large amount of clay and resin—he applied his research fund at school. Once transported to Gifu, the egg prompted Ikemizu and other members to fantasize about its

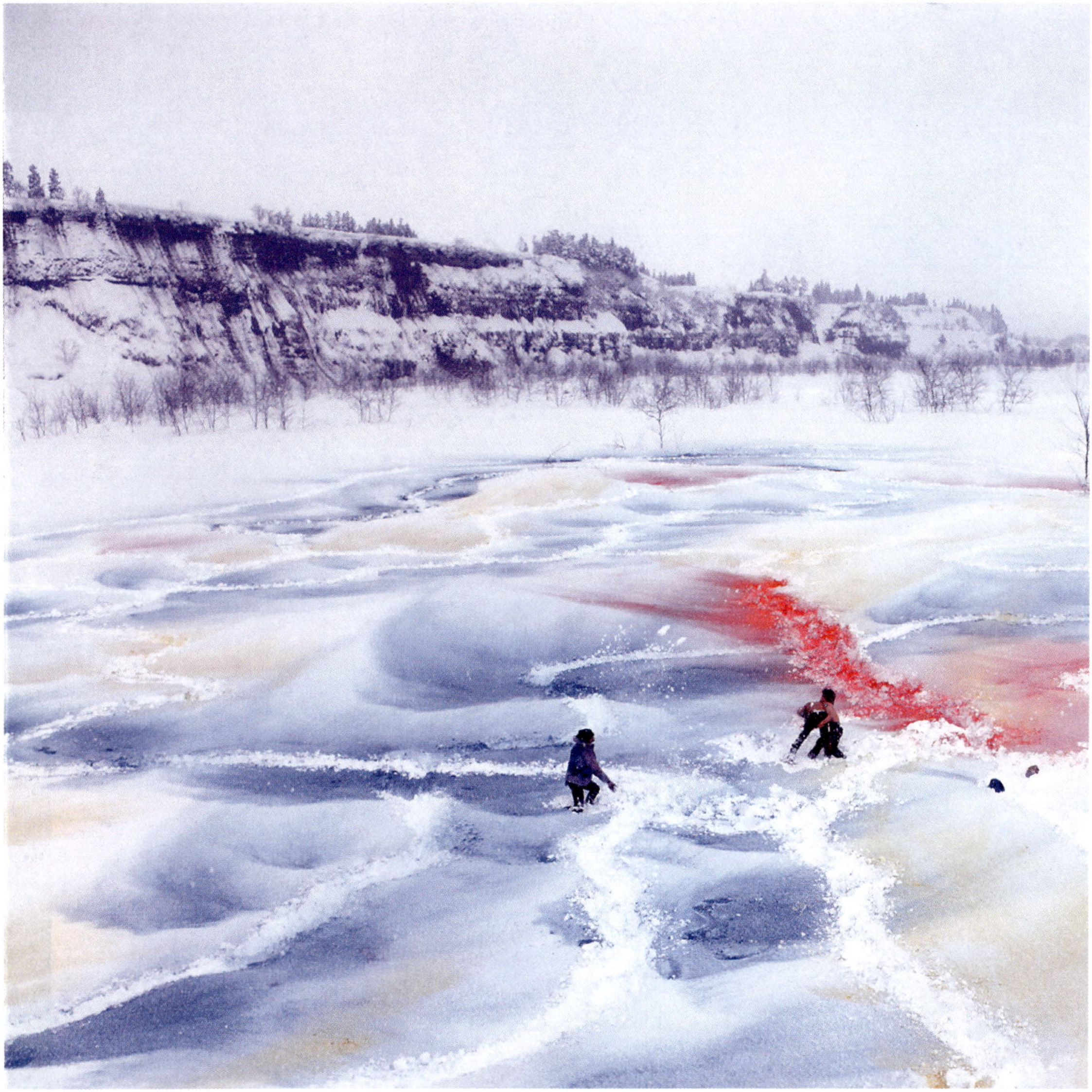

PLATE 1
GUN, *Event to Change the Image of Snow*, 1970. Documentary photograph of performance art. Photo © Hanaga Mitsutoshi.

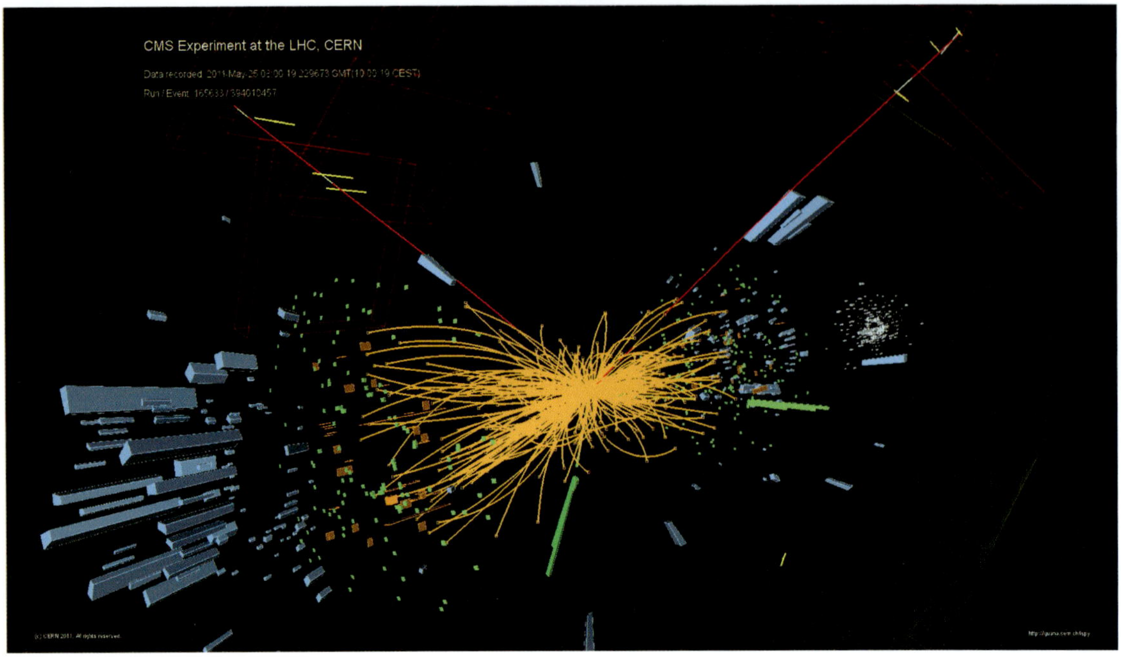

PLATE 2
A typical candidate event in the CMS Standard Model Higgs Search, with two high-energy protons (in red towers) and tracks of other particles produced in the collision (yellow). © 2011 CERN.

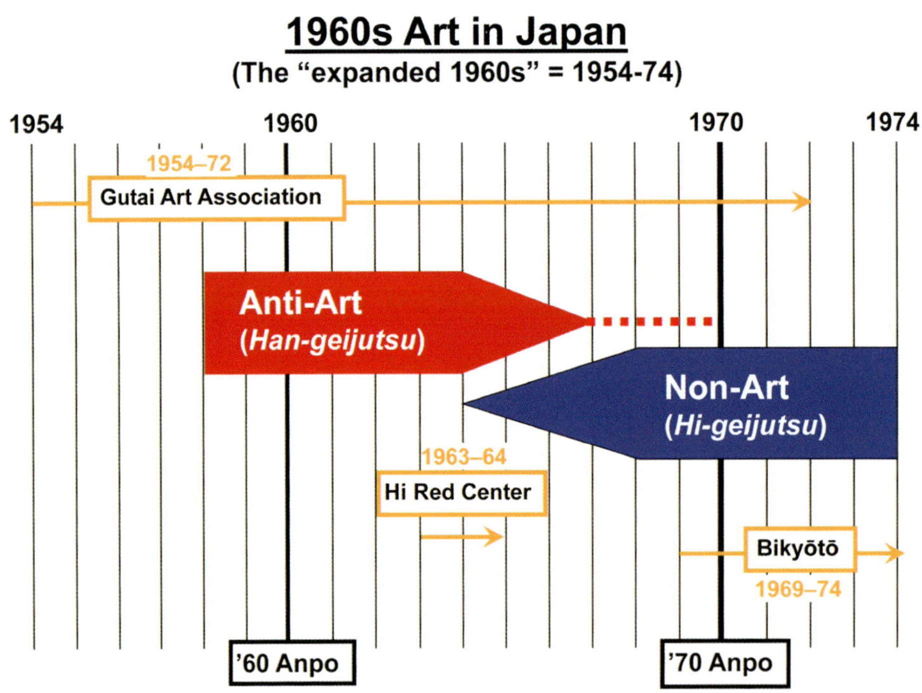

PLATE 3
Chronology of Japanese art in the expanded 1960s. © Reiko Tomii.

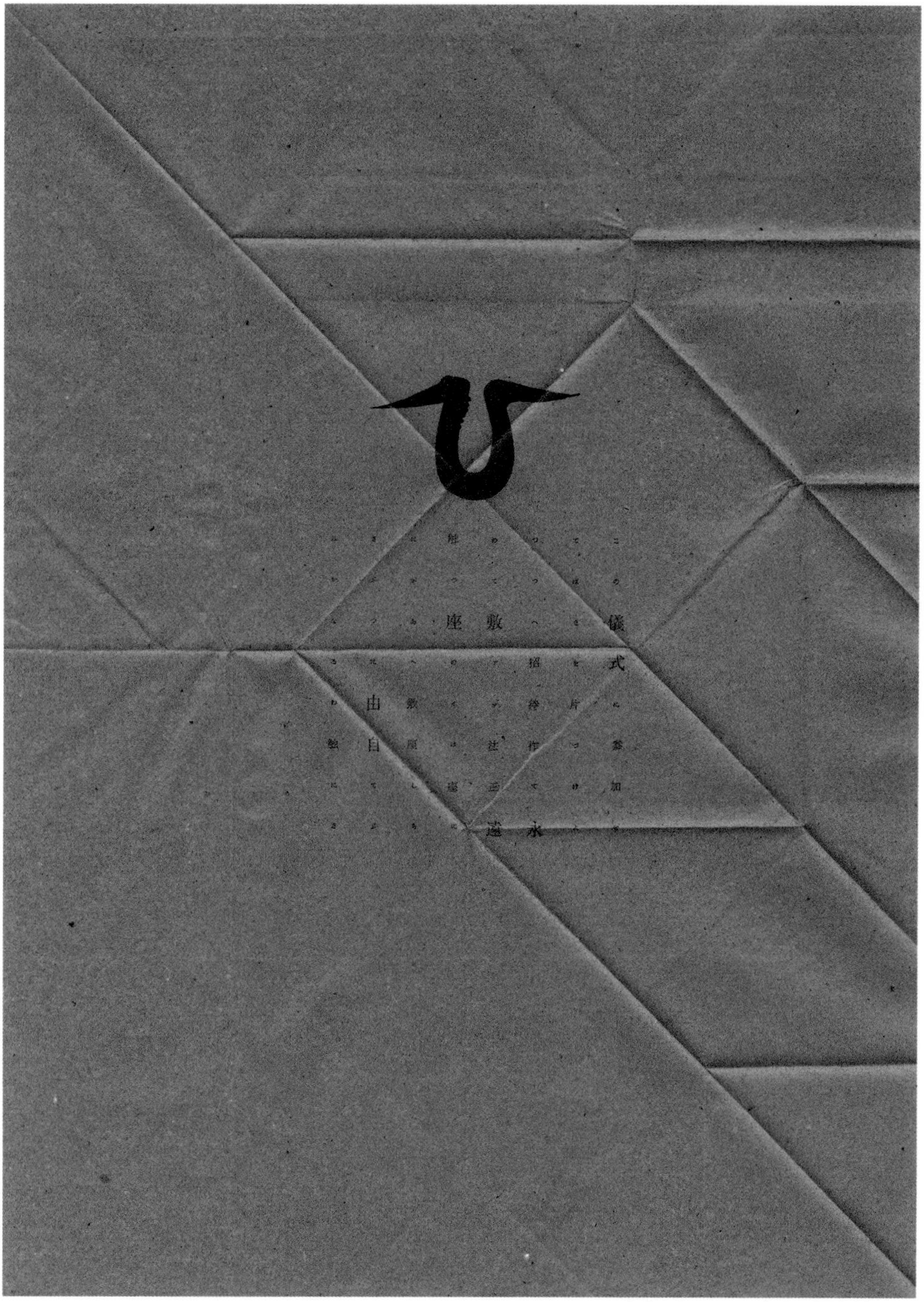

PLATE 4

Matsuzawa Yutaka, *Invitation to Psi Zashiki Room*, 1963. Letterpress; 35 × 25.6 cm. Takiguchi Shūzō Papers, c. 1945–1979, Keiō University Art Center, Tokyo.

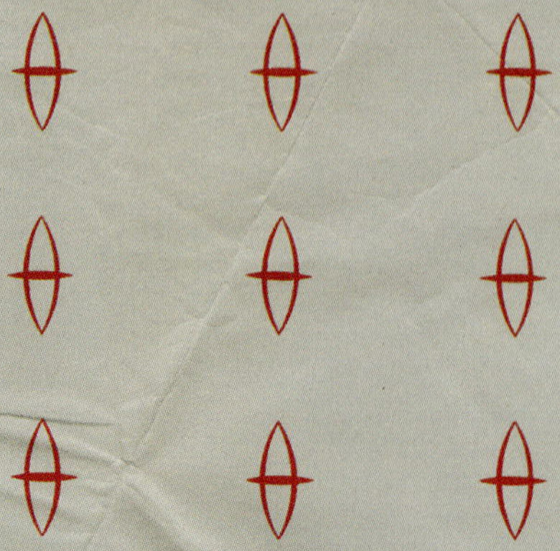

5	6	7
4	1	8
3	2	9

１９６４年　松沢　宥　作品　<プサイの死体遺体>　に就いて ――
非感覚絵画（仮称）とは何か ――
ニルの作品　<プサイの死体遺体>　は非感覚絵画（仮称）です　だから眼に見えません　だから何処に在るかと探しても在りません　しかもそれはこの展覧会に正真正銘出品されているのです　ナンセンスな！と言わずにしばらく僕の言葉に耳をかして下さい　皆さんは非感覚絵画という耳なれない言葉に戸惑っているでしょう　無理もありません　これは去る６月４日に生れたばかりの言葉で未だ何処にも登録されていません　その意味内容も<非感覚絵画（仮称）の端初の発見に就いての簡単な報告>という神秘的な刷り物によって七人に知らされただけで他の誰も知りません　明らかに将来の絵画の絶対的形式となるべきニルのこの非感覚絵画とは一体何でしょう

　春は花　夏は螢　秋は紅葉　冬は雪　皆さんはこの会場のそこの作品を　その隣の作品を　その向こうの作品を　眼でとらえて認めます　あそこに音を立てている作品を　耳でとらえて認めます　ところが非感覚絵画はそういう具合には行きません　五官による感覚で認識することが出来ないのです　毒にも薬にもならないそんなものは意味ないよ　という声が聞こえますが果してそうでしょうか　何時か何処かで皆さんは膨脹している宇宙とか負の曲率をもっている宇宙とかそんな話を聞いたことがあるでしょう　あるいは同時に二ケ所以上の場所に存在する一つの電子とか普通の物質と衝突すると消滅してしまう反物質とかそんな話を聞いたことがあるでしょう　それらのイメージを皆さんは眼や耳や鼻の感覚によってとらえることは出来ません　しかも現代の物理学者たちは数学を道具に使ってまた実験によってそのようなものの実在を認めているのです　それと類似の在り方で非感覚絵画は在るのです　ほら　そこに　この会場のこの空間と重なって多層的に　ほら　あなたの袋の中に　脹らんだ胸のかげに　柔らかい着衣の下の微妙な場所に　それから暗い胃の奥に　また冷たい背中にはりついて在るのです　「ひるは長い間待ったが食物はやって来なかった　ついにひるは上昇してそれを追っかけた　食物は地球の表面から上へ上へとあとずさりした　ひるは大きな図体で懸命にそのあとを追った　ゆたかな食物は空間へ逃げ去った　ひるはそれを追った　その先にはもっともっと」あなたが今だんだん妙な気分になって来たのは　そんな非感覚絵画<プサイの死体遺体>のためでしょうか　いや！と言って払いのけようとしても駄目　非感覚絵画はあなたを取りまきあなたを浸しあなたのあなたの中にすっぽり入ってしまいます　あなたは今やそれに犯されているのです　あなたは立っていられなくなるでしょう　動けなくなるでしょう　やがてもうだめ死にそうと感ずるでしょう　眼を閉じてニルヴァーナを味わうでしょう　宇宙と人類の未来を先取するでしょう

　僕はこの非感覚絵画がどんな空想よりもはるかに突飛で奇怪であることに満足しています　何となれば新しい仮設は十分に気違いじみていればいるほど正しいものである可能性を増すのです　ほら　あなたのあなたの×××は××　さて非感覚絵画を射出する道具の物質や非物質をまた実験装置をこの会場に備えておくことも出来たのです　あなたがそれらを使って　だが感覚によらずに　<プサイの死体遺体>を愛することが出来るように　しかし今回はそうしなかったのです　それらは諏訪の虚空間状況探知センター内に備えつけられていて　今　一方的にこの会場に向けて発信しつづけているのです　あなたの中に　あなたの中に　あなたのあなたの中に　あなたのあなたのあなたの中に　あなたのあなたのあなたのあなたの中に
あなたのあなたのあなたのあな

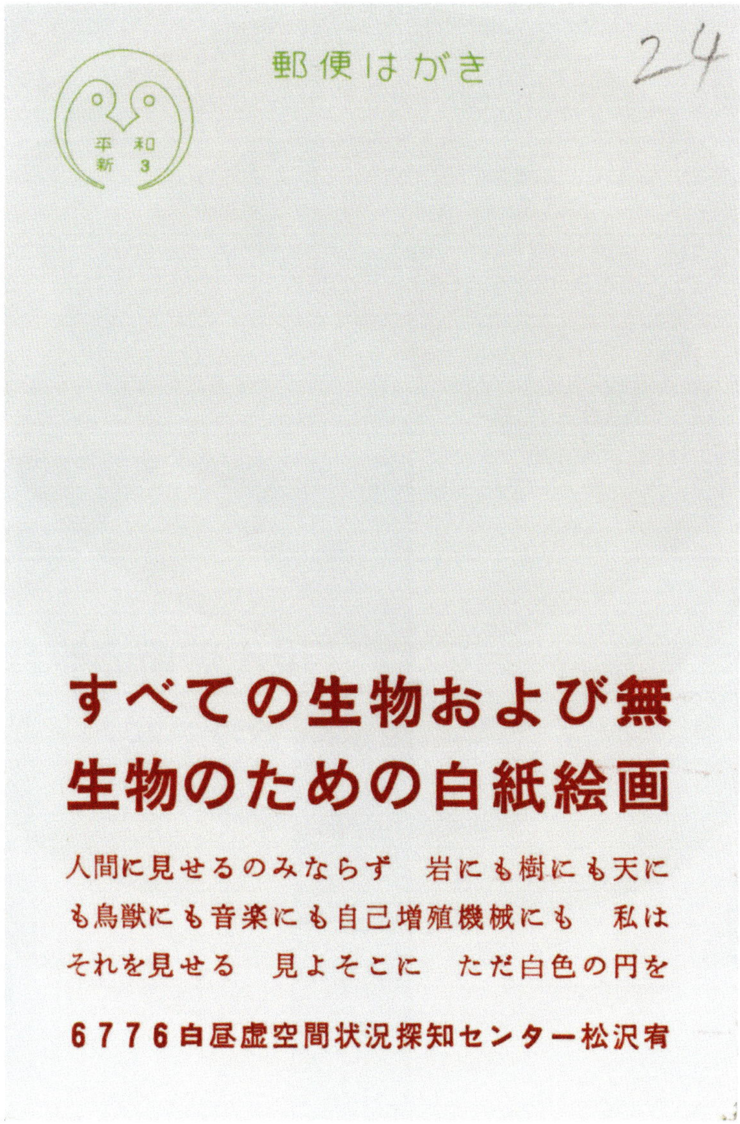

PLATE 5 (facing)
Matsuzawa Yutaka, *Psi Corpse*, 1964. Offset lithograph; 38.4 × 26 cm. Takiguchi Shūzō Papers, c. 1945–1979, Keiō University Art Center, Tokyo.

PLATE 6
Matsuzawa Yutaka, *A Blank Painting for All Living and Non-Living Beings (Postcard Painting I-01)*, 1967. Letterpress on preprinted paper; 14.8 × 10 cm. 1 of 40 items in *Psi Box* (1969). Private collection, on long-term loan to The Museum of Modern Art, Gunma.

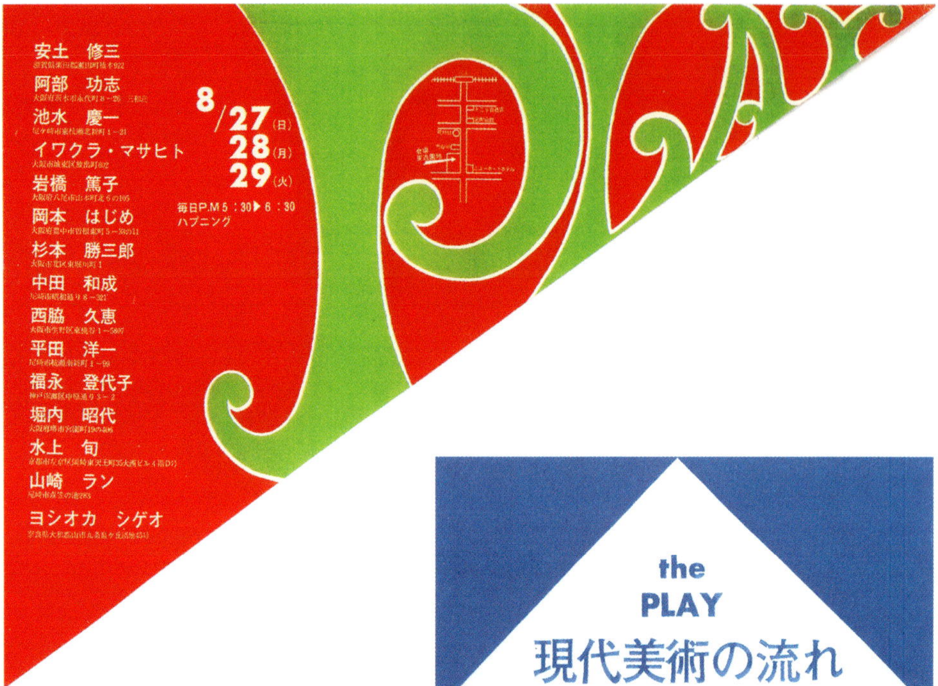

PLATE 7
First Play Exhibition, 1967. Poster. © The Play.

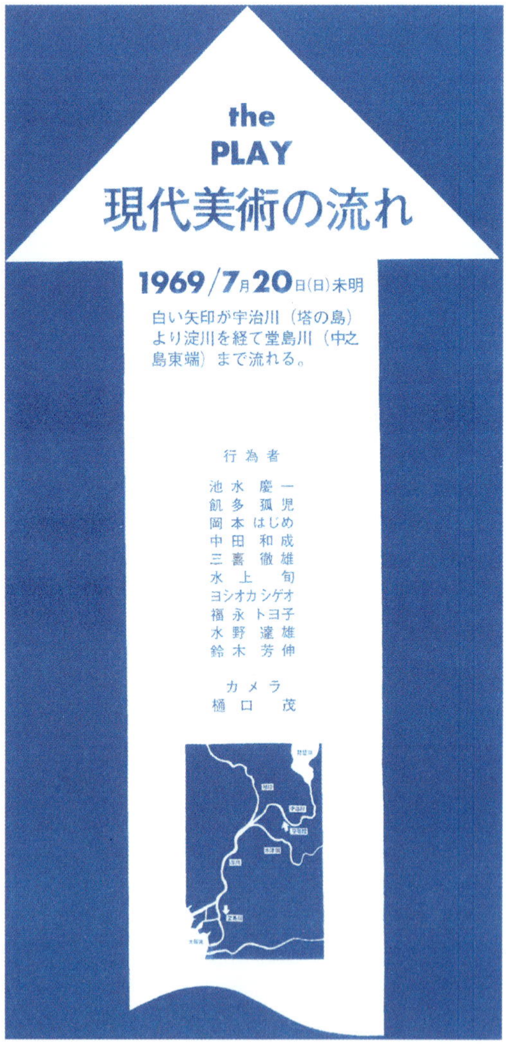

PLATE 9
The Play, *Current of Contemporary Art*, 1969.
Poster. © The Play.

PLATE 8 (facing)
The Play, *White Cross Manifesto*, 1970.
Installation view (close to the mountaintop),
as seen from the foot of Kinchōzan in Kobe.
© The Play.

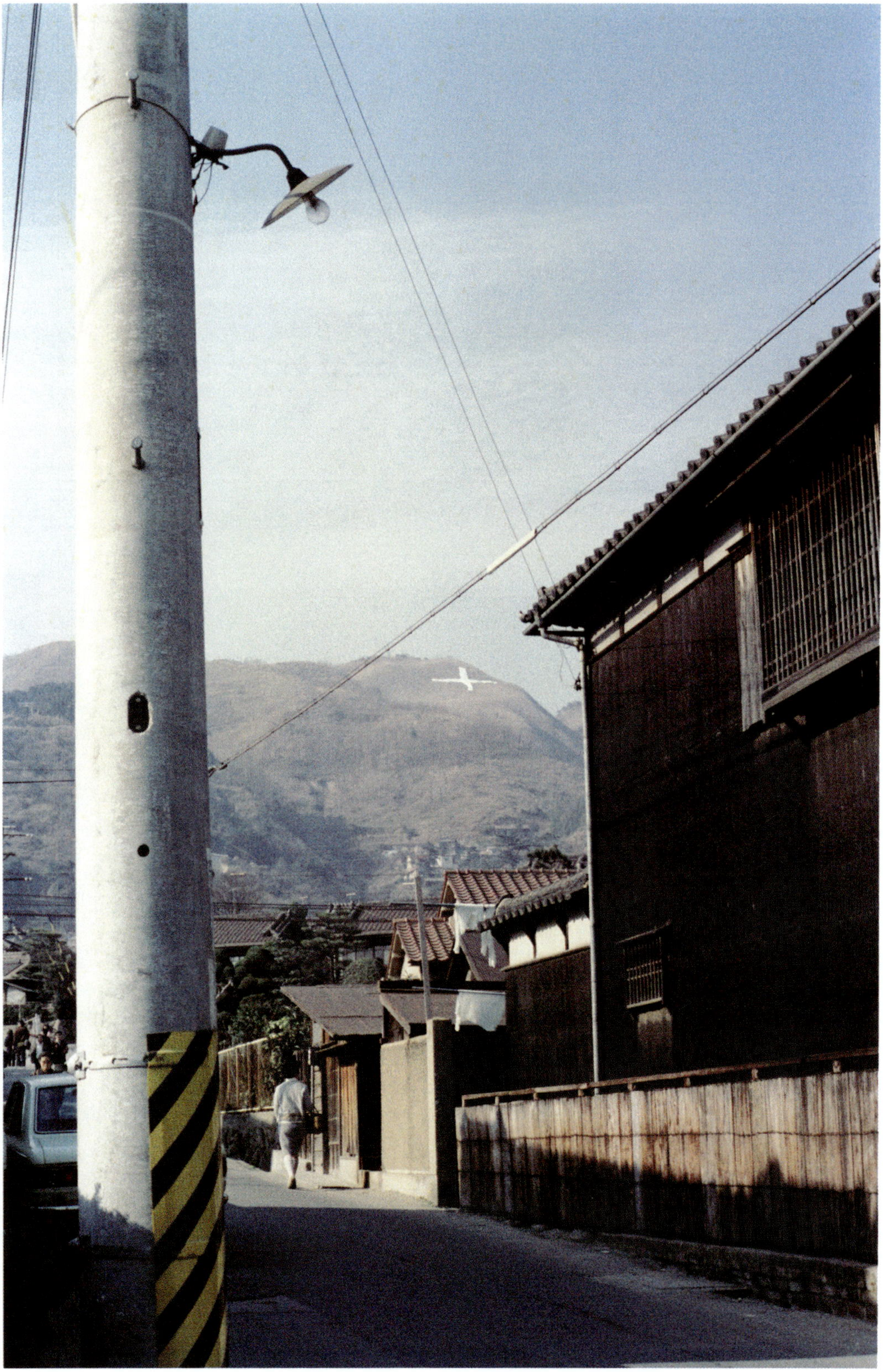

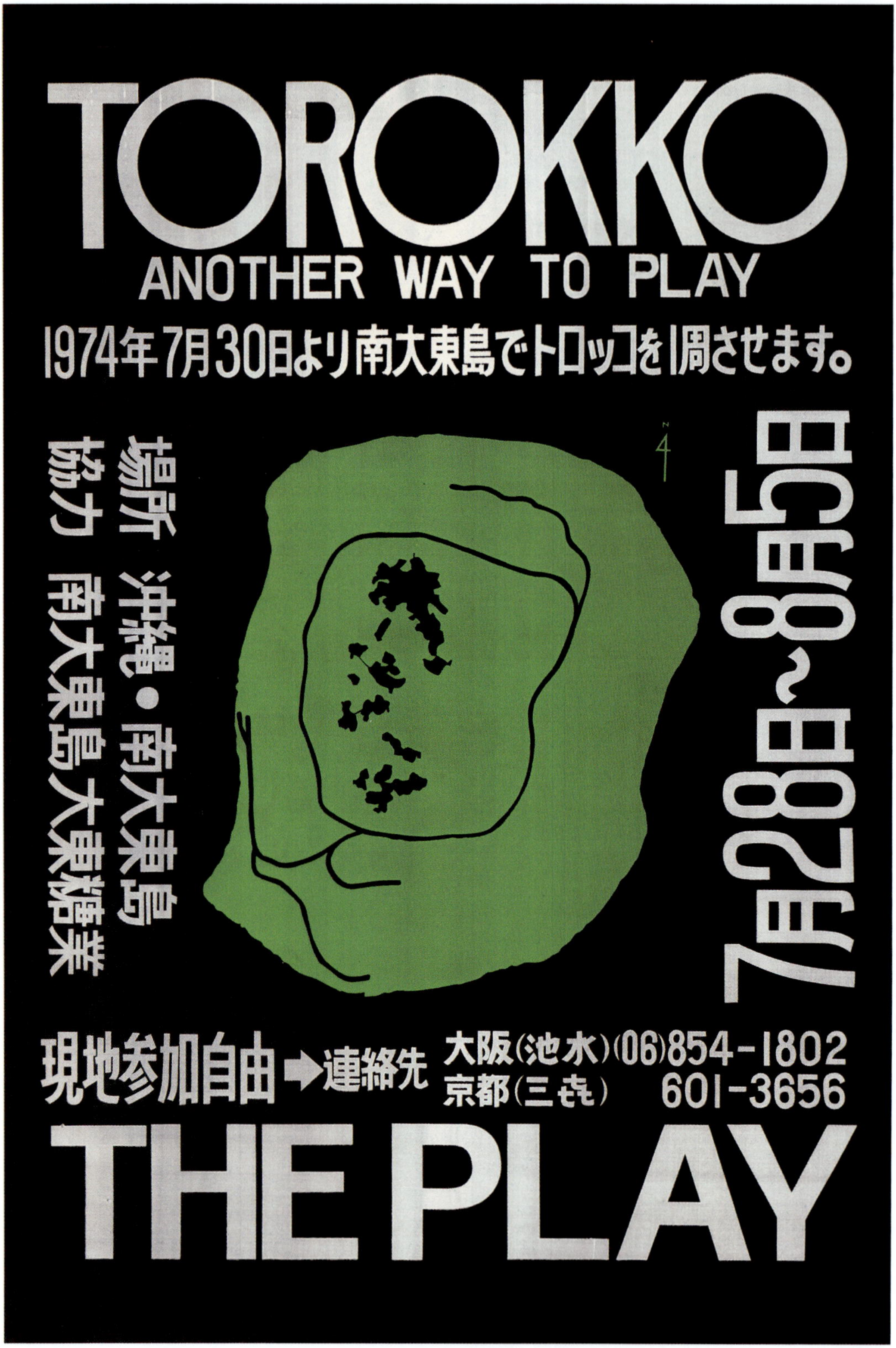

TOROKKO
ANOTHER WAY TO PLAY
1974年7月30日より南大東島でトロッコを1周させます。
7月28日~8月5日
場所 沖縄・南大東島
協力 南大東島大東糖業
現地参加自由→連絡先
大阪(池水)(06)854-1802
京都(三むら) 601-3656
THE PLAY

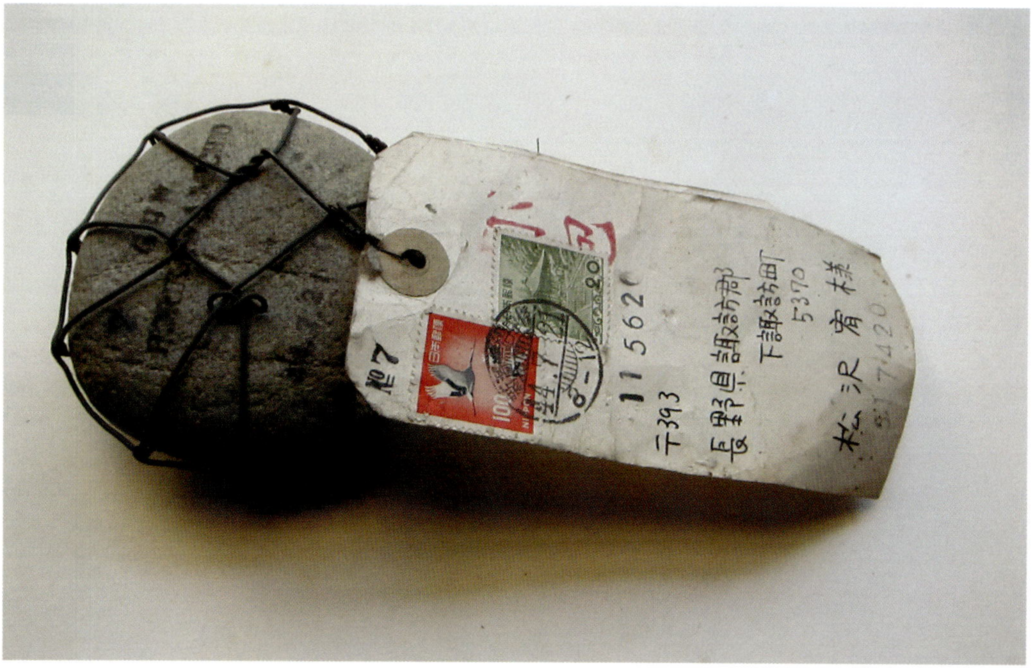

PLATE 10 (facing)
The Play, *Torokko*, 1974. Poster. © The Play.

PLATE 11
Horikawa Michio, *The Shinano River Plan: 11*, 1969. From the series *Mail Art by Sending Stones*. Stone, wire, mail tags (mailed to Matsuzawa Yutaka). Collection of Matsuzawa Kumiko. Photo by Reiko Tomii.

PLATE 12
GUN, *Event to Change the Image of Snow*, 1970. Documentary photograph of performance art. Photo © Hanaga Mitsutoshi.

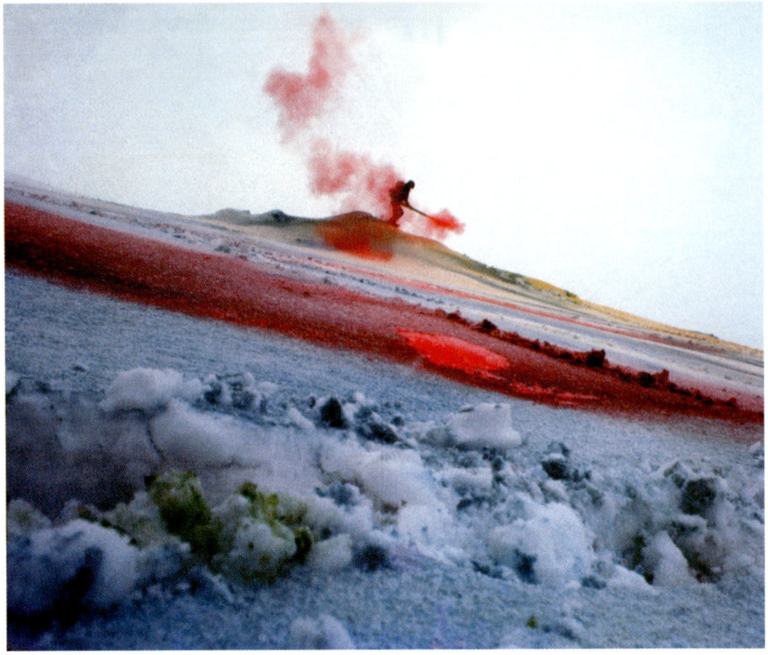

PLATE 13
Maeyama Tadashi, *Event to Change the Image of Snow (Trajectory of Steps)*, 1970. Documentary photograph of performance art. Photo by Horikawa Michio.

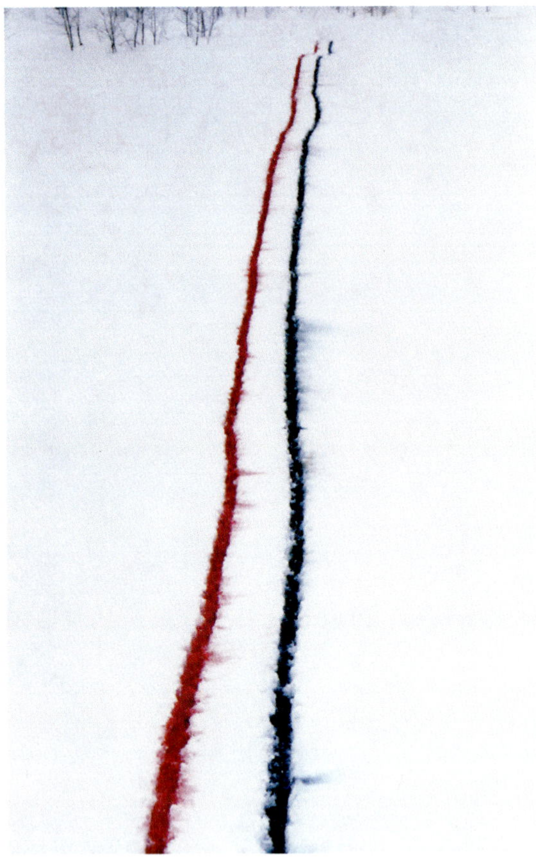

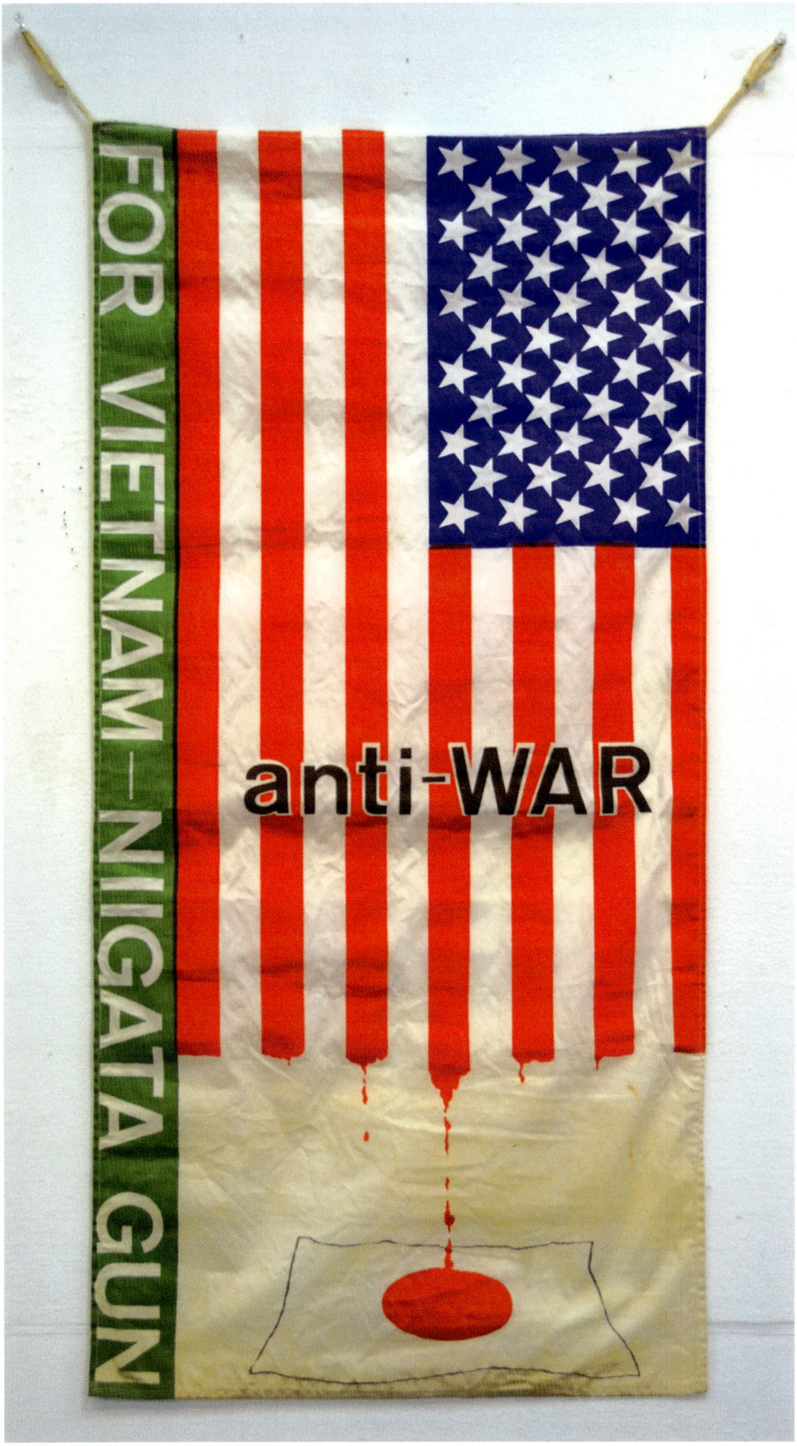

PLATE 14
Maeyama Tadashi, *Antiwar Flag*, 1970. Fabric; 98 × 48 cm. Collection of the artist.

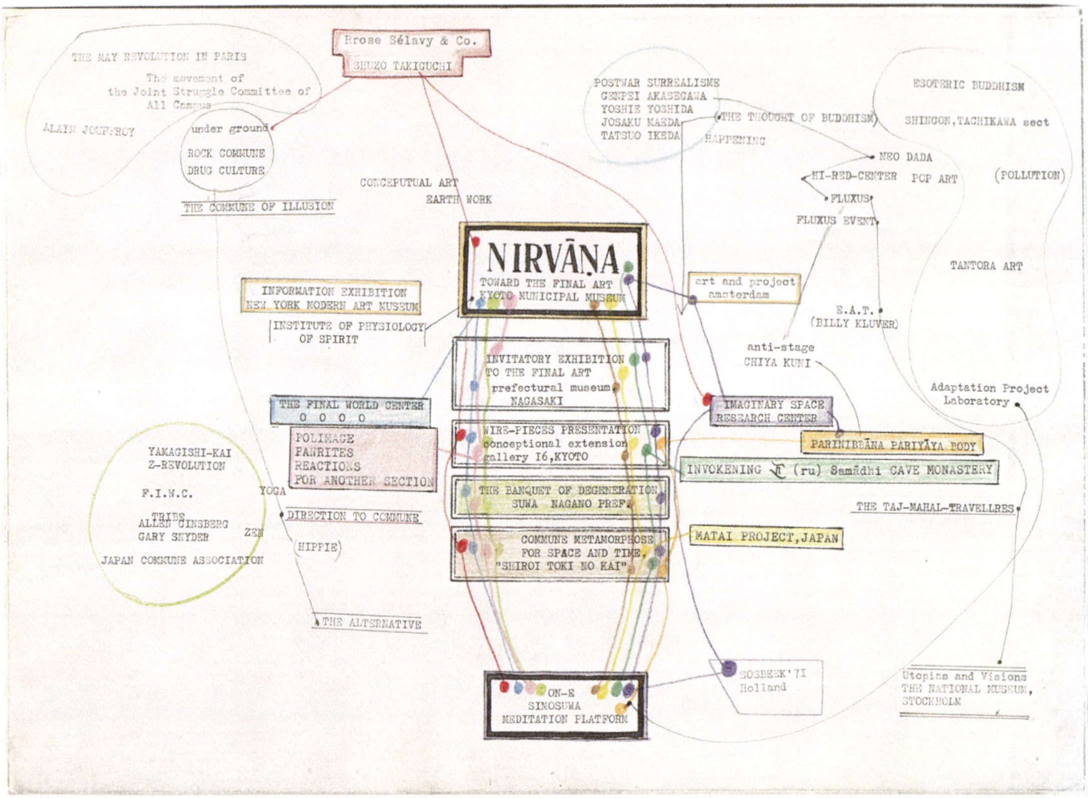

PLATE 15

Matsuzawa Yutaka, untitled document (diagram of Nirvana School), ca. 1971. Photocopy (electrostatic print) with colored pencil additions; 29.7 × 21.1 cm. 1 of 3 documents in *Post Nirvāna: Our Commune*. The Museum of Modern Art, New York, Art & Project/Depot VBVR Gift 1063.2007. Digital Image © The Museum of Modern Art/Licensed by SCALA / Art Resource, NY.

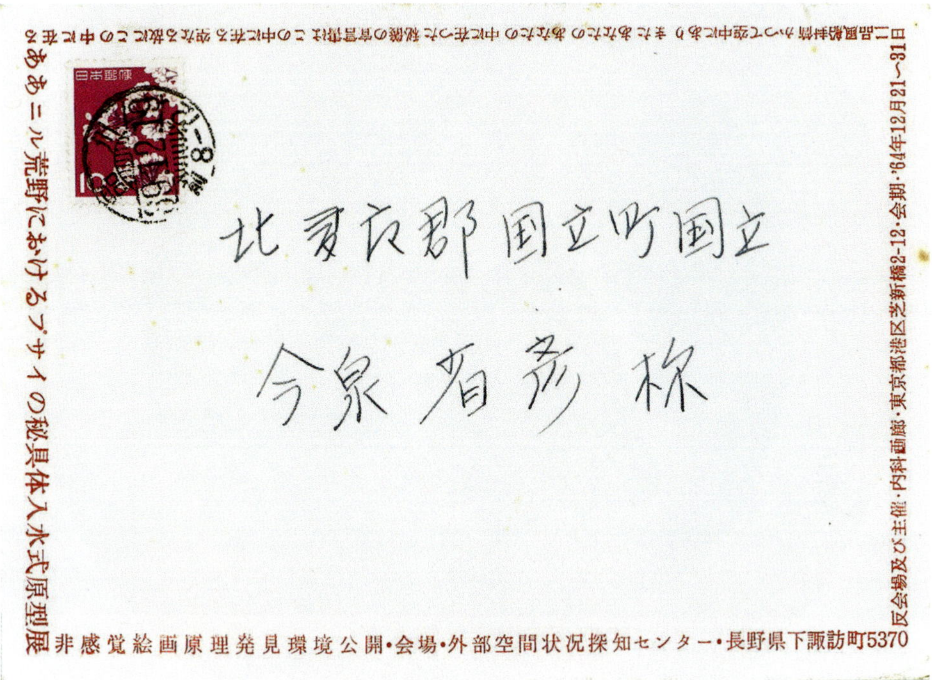

PLATE 16
Matsuzawa Yutaka, *Ah, Nil, Ah, A Ceremony of Psi's Secret Embodiment Drowning in the Wilderness: Prototype Exhibition*, 1964. Envelope addressed to and received by Imaizumi Yoshihiko. Private collection.

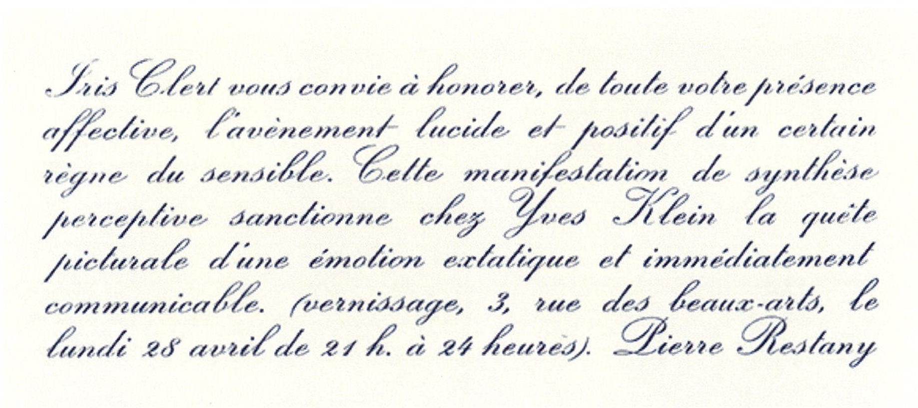
Iris Clert vous convie à honorer, de toute votre présence affective, l'avènement lucide et positif d'un certain règne du sensible. Cette manifestation de synthèse perceptive sanctionne chez Yves Klein la quête picturale d'une émotion extatique et immédiatement communicable. (vernissage, 3, rue des beaux-arts, le lundi 28 avril de 21 h. à 24 heures). Pierre Restany

PLATE 17
Yves Klein, invitation to the vernissage of the exhibition *La spécialisation de la sensibilité à l'état de matière première en sensibilité picturale stabilisée*, later known as *Void*, on April 28, 1958, Galerie Iris Clert, Paris. © Yves Klein/Artists Rights Society (ARS), New York/ADAGP, Paris, 2015.

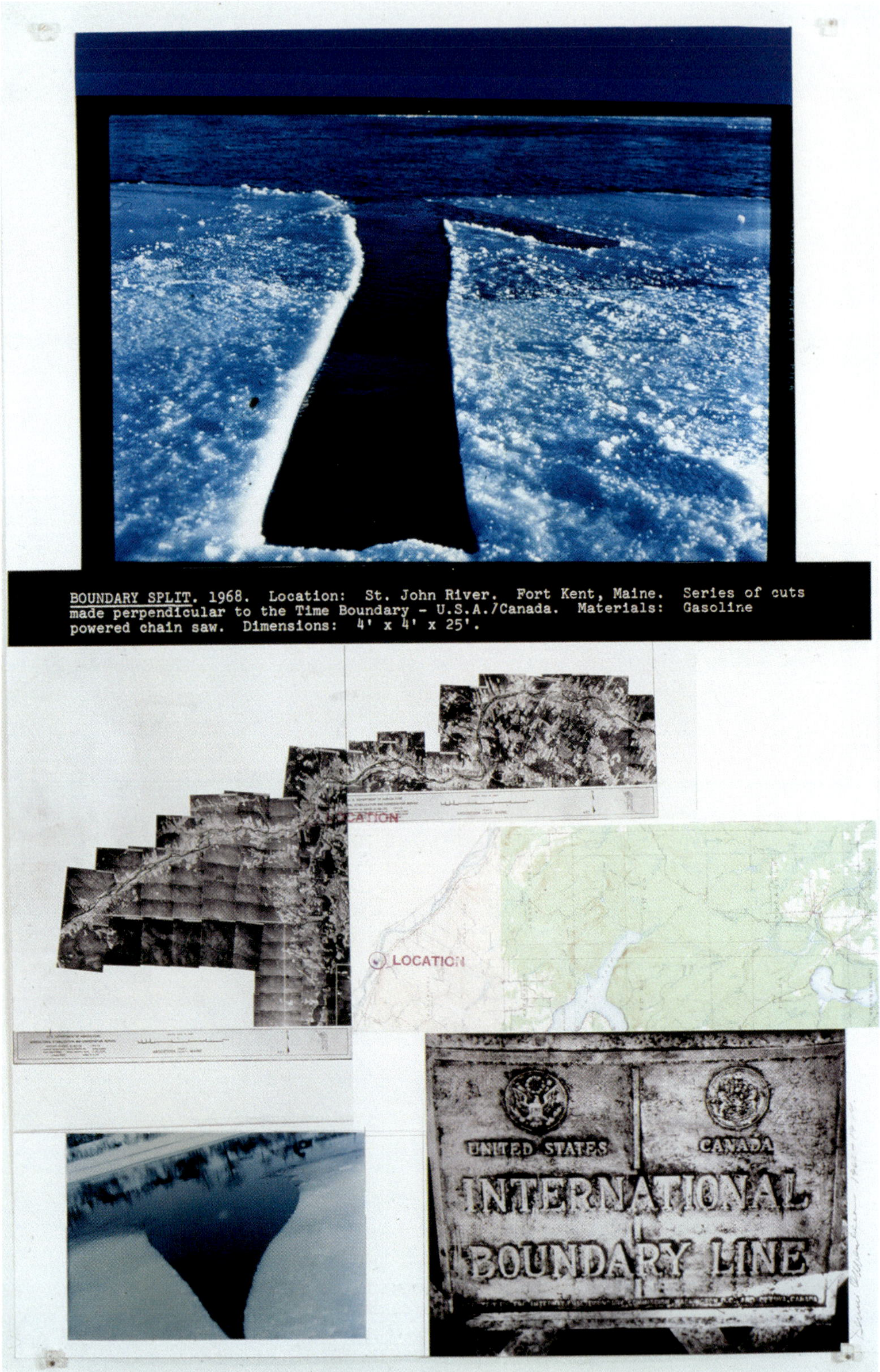
BOUNDARY SPLIT. 1968. Location: St. John River. Fort Kent, Maine. Series of cuts made perpendicular to the Time Boundary - U.S.A./Canada. Materials: Gasoline powered chain saw. Dimensions: 4' x 4' x 25'.
LOCATION
LOCATION
UNITED STATES
CANADA
INTERNATIONAL
BOUNDARY LINE

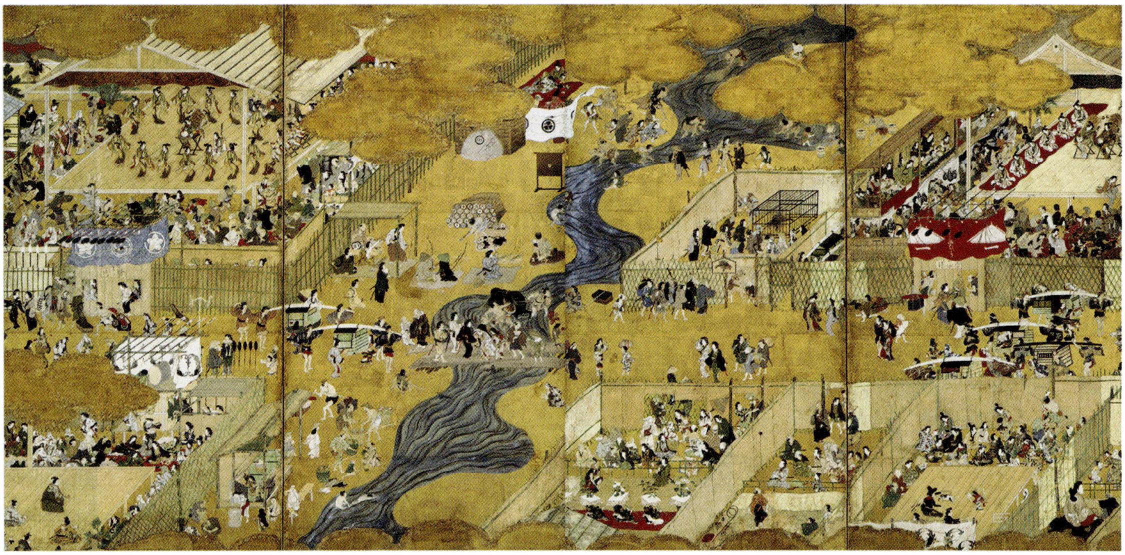

PLATE 18 (facing)
Dennis Oppenheim, *Boundary Split*, 1968. "Location: St. John's River, Fort Kent, Maine. Series of cuts perpendicular to the Time Boundary U.S.A./Canada. Gasoline powered chain saw. Dimensions: 4 × 4 × 25 feet." Black and white and color photography, hand-stamped topographic map, aerial map, text on rag board; 60 × 40 inches. © Dennis Oppenheim. Courtesy Dennis Oppenheim Estate.

PLATE 19
Entertainment on the Riverbed at Shijō, unknown artist, 17th century, Japan. Pair of two-panel screens, color on paper with gold leaf; 164.4 × 172.8 cm each. Collection of Seikadō Bunko Art Museum, Tokyo. Photo courtesy of Seikadō Bunko Art Museum Image Archives/DNPartcom.

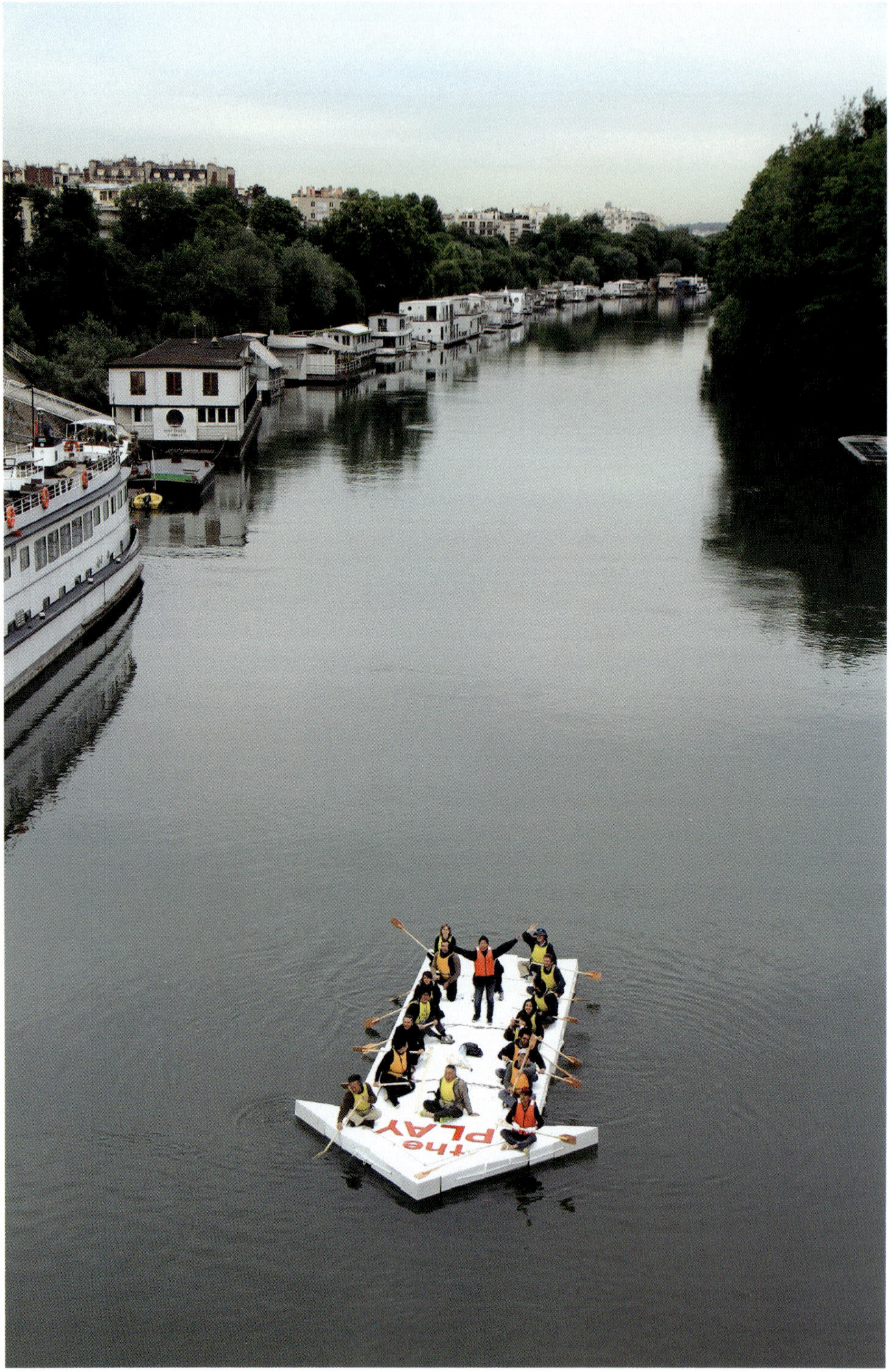

PLATE 20
The Play, *La Seine: Current of Contemporary Art*, 2012. Documentary photograph of performance art. Photo by Minami Takao. © The Play.

TABLE 3.3
The Play's Annual Summer Projects (1968–1986)

1968	
August 1	*Voyage: Happening in an Egg* Travel between Kushimoto, Wakayama Prefecture, and the Pacific Ocean. 7 members participated*
1969	
July 20	*Current of Contemporary Art* Travel from Kyoto to Osaka via the Uji River to the Yodo River to the Ōkawa River. 10 members participated
1970	
August 23–26	*Sheep* Travel from Kyoto to Osaka along the Kamo River to the Katsura River to the Yodo River. 11 members participated
1971	
May and June	*Bench* Installation for *10th Contemporary Art Exhibition of Japan*, at Tokyo Metropolitan Art Museum and Kyoto Municipal Museum of Art. 7 members participated
1972	
August 5–10	*Ie: The Play Have a House* Travel from Kyoto to Osaka via the Kizu River to the Yodo River. 5 crewpersons plus 13 members participated
1973	
August 10–19 and 20–22	*The Bridge* A structure installed for the Kyoto Biennale at Kyoto Municipal Museum of Art and transferred to the Kizu River after the exhibition. 12 members participated
1974	
July 28–August 5	*Torokko* Travel to Minami Daitōjima, an island 400 kilometers east of Okinawa. 11 members participated
1975	
December 8, 1974; July 19–August 10	*Canoe* Travel to Lake Biwa; three-part project: (1) cutting down a tree at Mount Ibuki (December 8, 1974); (2) making a canoe from the tree; (3) bringing the canoe through the Tsuchikawa River to Nagahama and floating it on Lake Biwa. 11 members participated
1976	
August 8–16	*Wind: Wandering in the Wind* Travel to Sarobetsu plain in Hokkaidō. 10 members participated
1977–1986	Summer months *Thunder 1–Thunder 10* Travel to Mount Jūbu and Mount Ōmine (*Thunder 5* and *6*) in Kyoto. Members participated (*Thunder 1*: 16, *2*: 15, *3*: 12, *4*: 10, *5*: 9, *6*: 9, *7*: 9, *8*: 13, *9*: 13, *10*: 12)

*The number of participants in each project is based on *Play* (Paris: Bat; Osaka: The Play, 2014). Recent oral-history research by Hashimoto Azusa has indicated some oversights in the compiled rosters of participants.

possible deployments—including floating or releasing it on the river before their very eyes—while they spent 10 days on site under the summer sun. In 1966, after the exhausting experience of putting up *Contemporary Art Festival* in Sakai, he began to give serious thought to "releasing the egg to a body of water." Floating it in the sea, even having it travel across the Pacific Ocean, was not as far-fetched as it might appear. One major precedent was the 1947 voyage of the *Kon-Tiki*, well known through the Norwegian ethnographer Thor Heyerdahl's book and documentary film. More recently and closer to heart was the 1962 venture of Horie Ken'ichi, native of Osaka, who sailed solo across the Pacific Ocean—a feat that fascinated the whole nation. In the spring of 1967, Ikemizu sought advice from Nakamura Akikazu, associate professor of oceanography at his alma mater Osaka Kyōiku University (renamed from Osaka Gakugei University), with whom he had taken a course and who had recommended he read Heyerdahl's account. He learned from the oceanographer that the plan would require releasing the egg to the Japan Current, running south of Japan's main island, which in Japan is evocatively called Kuroshio, or "Black Current," due to its dark blue color. An artist's idle daydream was about to turn into a plan for adventure (figure 3.5).

Ikemizu was quick to move. The ideal departure point was the port of Kushimoto in Wakayama Prefecture, near Shionomisaki, a cape at the southernmost point of the main island; it was accessible from Osaka by rail and by car. When he looked for a boathouse catering to anglers in order to transport the egg to the open sea, he was told to contact the local fishermen's union. Asked by the union president why he would do such a thing, his honest artist's answer—he just wanted to see it—was supplemented by a more strategic response, suggested by Professor Nakamura: this would be a viable study of the current. With the union president's informal agreement to help him, he waited until after the first *Play* exhibition to broach the idea to the other participants. By October 1967, six of them agreed to work together to form what would become known as The Play. In July 1968, they were busy preparing for the big day planned for August 1. Among other things, they had to improve the structural strength of the egg by reinforcing the interior surface and placing weight at the bottom. It so happened that the Black Current was farther south than usual that summer and they needed more than a small fishing boat, customarily 5 tons or so in size, to reach it. The union president took the matter into his hands and negotiated with the Kushimoto station of the Prefectural Fisheries Experimental Department to borrow its training ship *Kii* (the ancient name for Wakayama). In addition to this 35-ton boat with 180 horsepower, the group had to hire another 30-ton vessel, *Tatsu* (Dragon), with 200 horsepower, to accommodate all seven members. (Having two ships proved to be advantageous in photographing the proceedings.)

Toward the end of July, the news of *Happening in an Egg* excited the mass media. However, a sensationalized appearance with the egg on the local Kansai Television

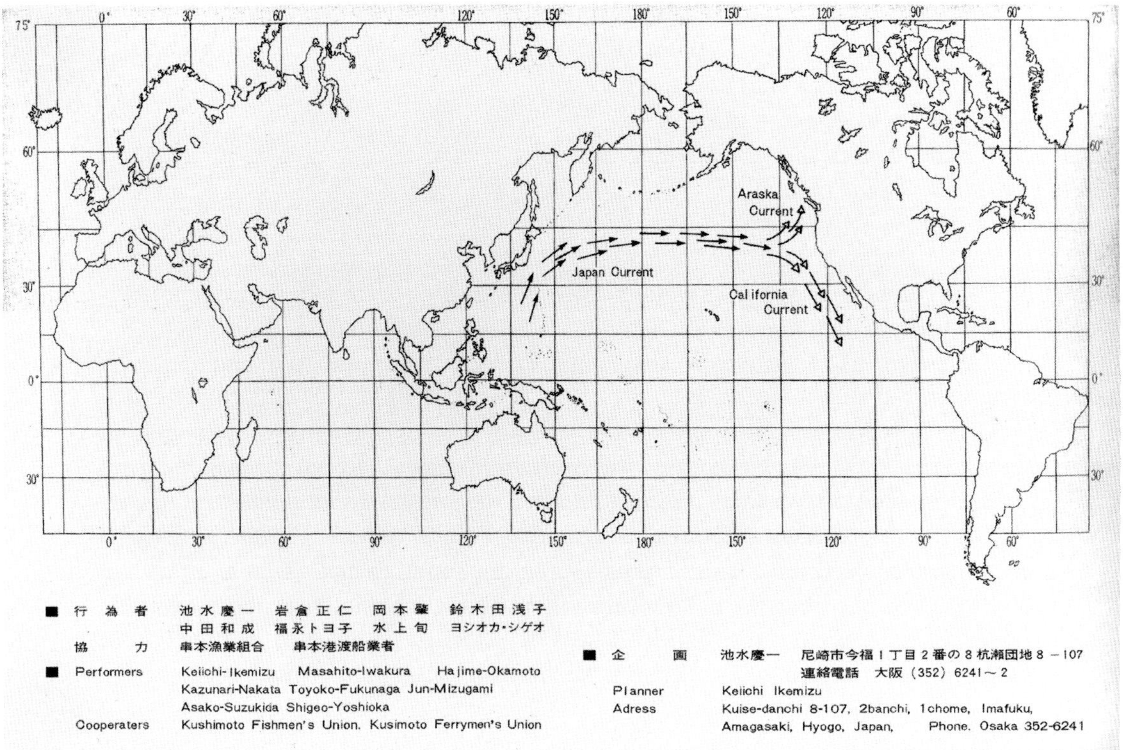

FIGURE 3.5
The Play, *Voyage: Happening in an Egg*, 1968. Back of poster (map and project summary). © The Play.

stirred suspicion in the minds of the prefectural fisheries department that the project was not truly scientific but publicity-mongering. Ikemizu immediately asked the assistance of Professor Nakamura, who wrote a letter of recommendation to the department head emphasizing the project's "oceanographic and aesthetic significance" and its potential to raise awareness about oceanography among the public. Express-mailed from Osaka to Kushimoto along with a copy of the professor's dissertation to prove his bona fides, the letter mollified the prefectural department, but the participants became mindful about having too much publicity. They allowed a reporter of *Asahi Graph* to come on board but declined an on-site interview for Yomiuri Television's notorious late-night talk show, *11 P.M.* To clear one last, regulatory, hurdle, they filed an application to release the egg into the ocean with Kushimoto's Marine Safety Department. As part of the "scientific study," they had to paint in red an English sign reading:

> VOYAGE
> We released at 33°N off Shionomisaki
> Would you please report us the place
> and date, when you found this egg.
> Osaka Kyoiku College art course
> Ikeda Osaka Japan
> 潮流調査中　大阪教育大学[40]

The sign ruined the egg's pure white surface, but the group had to leave aside aesthetics and back up their avowals of scientific purpose in order to realize the project.

The whole trip in choppy waters from the port to the release point and back took seven hours. The egg was released at 14:00 (2 pm) at 33°05′N, 135°41′E. In early September, a Canadian cargo ship near 155°10′E saw a huge egg drifting and contacted the university.[41] Thereafter, nothing was heard of the egg at sea, but it generated news on land. In addition to a small notice in *Bijutsu techō*, the newspapers ran short reports on the project, including a few local newspapers (the local pages of *Yomiuri* and *Asahi*) and a national magazine (*Weekly Asahi*). As for the monthly *Asahi Graph*, which had given major coverage to the first *Play* exhibition and sent a photographer to cover the launch of the egg, no article appeared because priority was given to the invasion of Czechoslovakia by the Soviet Union later that August. Although news reports were generally favorable, if half mocking, one intellectual saw it otherwise. In a column in the daily *Osaka shinbun*, Aida Yūji, a conservative historian at Kyoto University, accused The Play of an "imitation Happening" blindly following the Euro-American trend, based on the understanding that *hapuningu* should negate absolute rationalism by emphasizing an abrupt occurrence.[42] The Play's theory of Happenings will be further discussed in chapter 5; but in response to this Japanese attitude of reverse chauvinism, Ikemizu wrote in *Violet Mail*, a newsletter published by the member Miki Tetsuo:

> *Voyage* need not happen suddenly.
>
> People may know about it in advance. They may know about it afterward. They may not know about it at all.
>
> When we released the egg, our act ended and *Voyage* began.[43]

Now that the newly formed group had completed their first project, their collective voyage, too, began.

The Play's Collectivism

Even though *Voyage: Happening in an Egg* was initiated by Ikemizu as its chief architect, collaboration among the seven artists was essential to its success. *Voyage* served as a veritable blueprint for The Play's future projects. Each project would be planned and executed through a mixture of the members' taking certain initiatives and holding discussions to build consensus. On many levels, indeed, *Voyage* anticipated the way the group would operate.

As saliently demonstrated by their project the following year, *Current of Contemporary Art*, their acts would often take the form of travel that would transport them away from mundane reality while allowing them to share a communal time of living together. In their travels, The Play typically eschewed urban spaces and staged their acts outdoors, favoring especially landscape settings. Their preference for landscapes imbued their activities with a land-art dimension, both in scale and spirit, incorporating natural elements. Their love of nature was at once informed by the easy access to nature afforded even city dwellers in Japan and an "infinite time and space" they found in nature.[44] This set them apart from the urban- and street-oriented Anti-Art performances earlier in the decade.[45] In another difference from Anti-Art performers, who were sometimes overtly political, The Play tended toward latent politics of the everyday—through which, in their words, they aspired to "plow people's everyday life" with "farmer-like" persistence.[46] In a way, The Play engaged the flip side of 1960s Japan, where high economic growth enabled the mass modernization of everyday life and comfort bred complacency. Rejecting a strategy of outright destruction, they sought to offer a positive alternative, which in retrospect can be placed between the two opposites of radical politics and the Hippies/commune movement, the latter of which was understood in Japan as apolitical. Their seeming apoliticality was once attacked by a few militant students who physically interrupted the proceedings of *7 Dimensions* to rebuke their Happenings as "bourgeois art," on an occasion when The Play atypically participated in a museum show, the Kyoto Modern's *Trends in Contemporary Japanese Art* in September 1969.[47] At the height of the antiwar and antiestablishment protests, the cliché thrown at The Play was nonetheless beside the point (again based on a wrong assumption, as was Aida's criticism); indeed with their farmer-like persistence The Play outlived student radicalism, which would begin to collapse that autumn under the strong hand of the state and utterly lose legitimacy in 1972 in the wake of the murderous United Red Army incident.

Furthermore, unlike the artists producing subversive Anti-Art performances, The Play was in principle law-abiding, if only on the surface. It should be remembered that even indoors, Anti-Art practitioners routinely took advantage of and broke the museum's display guidelines, and their unruly antics in effect led to the termination of the Yomiuri Independent Exhibition. Outdoors, most Anti-Art street performances were staged without police-issued permits. Undertaking clandestine acts in broad daylight was the point of their intervention, to begin with. Accordingly, to promptly run away from the site of action lest they be caught by the police was part of their routine, whether in Hi Red Center's *Cleaning Event* (figure 1.8) or Zero Dimension's naked parades or Collective Kumo's sex ritual. A new attitude was formed with the 1965 *Independent Art Festival* in Gifu, for which the organizers had to devise their own exhibition guidelines for the riverbed venue in light of the strict river laws, duly followed by the participants.

When Ikemizu and others mounted the first *Play* exhibition, they simply told the city's parks department that they would display some outdoor artworks. Indeed they did show some conventional artworks, but the main focus of the exhibition was on Happenings. The park was located right next to the city hall building, and the parks department must have noticed the racket they were making in the park, but the group got away with it. Ikemizu later recalled that some "stretching" (*damashi*)[48] had also happened in subsequent projects. Calling *Voyage* a scientific experiment was but one example; taking advantage of Ikemizu's social standing as a middle-school teacher was perhaps another. In Japan, school teachers command high respect from the general public, and his profession gave credibility to The Play's often nonsensical projects. However, The Play never aimed at deception. To the contrary, they were sincere in working with people outside the art world, as demonstrated by *Voyage*. Beyond that, we need only look at their long-term project *Thunder*, which would not have been possible without building trust with landowners, lumber suppliers, and others who helped them over 10 summers. It presciently anticipated a public dimension of socially aware, community-based art that would emerge in 21st-century Japan and elsewhere.

Their conception of what constituted the circle of The Play was accordingly expansive. In *Play: 1967–1980*, a self-published book compiling their activity records that commemorated their 15th anniversary, their membership is listed as 11 as of 1981, but

> Since the founding in 1967, our membership has always been fluid, overlapped, and chaotic. The Play at present exists by encompassing all of them. Therefore, the list below includes the present members of The Play, the former members of The Play, and those around The Play.[49]

This larger circle of The Play encompassed 61 former members along with 12 institutions and businesses "around The Play," plus two translators of the book.[50] With the open form of their collectivism, a sizable number of non-artists were included in the membership: in 1985, their professions encompassed the areas of education (school teachers/students), design, architecture and construction, computer engineering, and clockmaking, among others.[51] It was such a wide range of skill sets that would enable a mega project, *Thunder*, in 1977–1986. In retrospect, for each project the group called for participants (members), and the membership roster was thus constantly renewed and expanded. This fluidity and the fact that their projects were fun to experience likely made possible their unusual longevity as a contemporary-art collective.

Their avid self-documentation, which resulted in three artist's books (1974, 1981, and 1991), distinguishes The Play from Anti-Art performers in 1960s Japan, when the importance of turning documentation of action-based works into something more tangible than the media's coverage rarely entered the mind of artists often so preoccupied with the thrill of action itself (more on this in chapter 6). For *Voyage*, The Play created a double-sided poster to announce the project. The front side bears the title of the project and its action plan, while the reverse shows a world map with a chain of currents, from the Japan Current to the California or Alaska Current, which could theoretically bring their egg to the continental U.S. (figure 3.5). The roster of the Play crew and the outside collaborators are duly listed on this side, declaring their collective and collaborative endeavor. This poster, which encapsulated the essence of The Play as outlined above, was accompanied by a report in the form of a flier offering the hard data of their boat trip, including the times of departure and return, the day's weather conditions, and a map to show the release point complete with the water's color at key points before the release. In addition to these two kinds of document—the announcement and the project report—future projects would often include a "schedule for members" that outlined the necessary preparation and the intended timeline. For *Voyage*, Ikemizu wrote an account chronicling the whole project from its inception for *Violet Mail*, a newsletter published by Miki. In 1969, a broadsheet newspaper became part of The Play's discursive repertoire, under the editorship of Mizukami Jun, and three issues were published. (The last issue was published under Miki's supervision after Mizukami's departure from the group.) Their newspaper became a forum for the members to articulate their divergent conceptions of Happenings, some of which were also printed in their announcements and reports.

All in all, The Play's Happenings, as understood from *Voyage*, were imbued with the spirit of independence from the institution of art, all self-organized and collectively executed. The sense of communal experience was of paramount importance, while both aesthetic and discursive aspects were embraced. A new form of performativity that the group had developed through collectivism was soon applied to their voyages to other destinations.

DESTINATIONS IN NATURE NEAR AND FAR

Based in the larger metropolitan area of Keihanshin (Kyoto-Osaka-Kobe), The Play took full advantage of the rich diversity of the natural environments in the Kansai area. Blessed with a temperate climate and a complex geography enlivened by numerous small to middle-sized mountains, large rivers and their tributaries, and other bodies of water (falls, lakes, and seas), Kansai's nature had been celebrated in literature since ancient times. Most of their summer projects had destinations within Kansai close to The Play's home base (figure 3.6). At the same time, the group strategically selected a few remote places to expand their formative repertoire beyond Kansai.

Although not part of their annual summer projects, *White Cross Manifesto,* a modest venture of March 1970, illustrates the proximity of nature to Keihanshin residents (figure 3.7, plate 8). The project was sited on a side of Kinchōzan, a mountain just over 300 meters high. It is located slightly over 2 kilometers from the nearby Okamoto station, east of Kobe. Placed "as a matter of sight and thought,"[52] a 50-by-50-meter white fabric cross cut a brilliant figure against the green mountainside, which was readily visible from areas between Ashiya and eastern Kobe. Eight members spent three days, one day each for installation, display, and deinstallation. The Play staged this project when the American filmmakers brothers Christian and Michael Blackwood visited them with an introduction from the critic Haryū Ichirō.[53] It was also the first project after Mizukami's departure, which represented their continuing engagement with object-based Happenings. In the poster, they declared: "We do not intend to convey a specific thought to people through our Happening but we expect something will happen in their consciousness when they come to know about our act."[54]

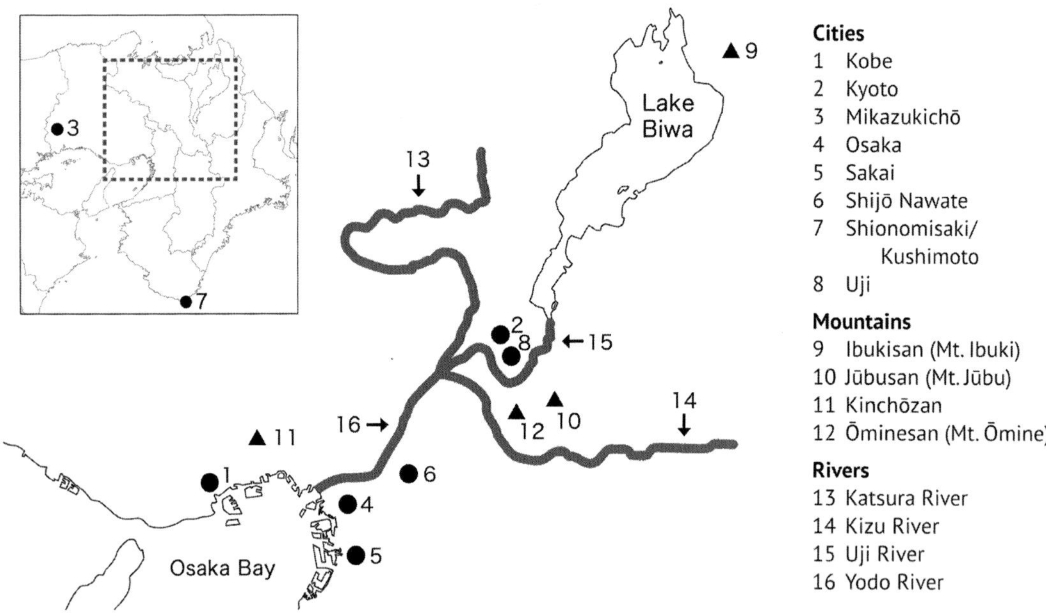

FIGURE 3.6
Destinations of The Play's Voyages in Kansai region and seven Kinki prefectures (in inset). Map designed by Takako Oishi-Marks.

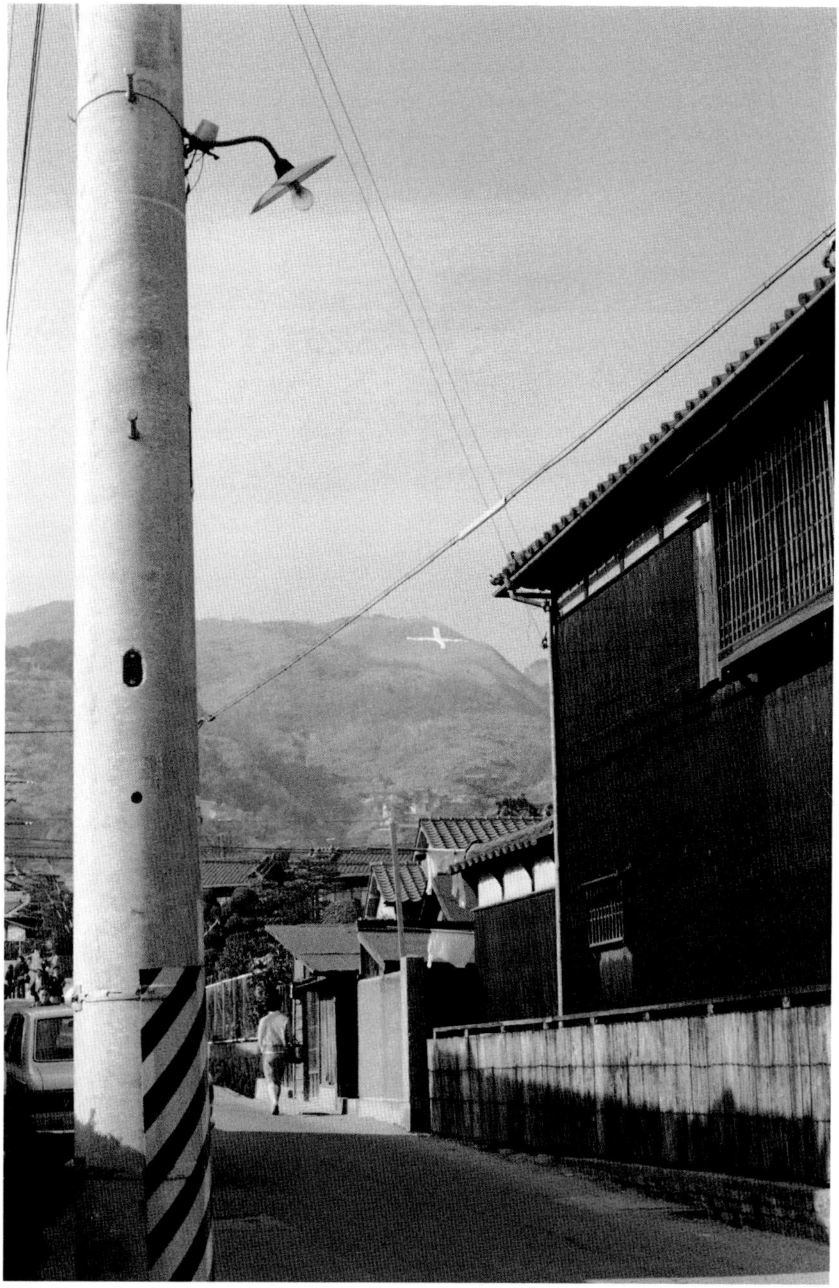

FIGURE 3.7
The Play, *White Cross Manifesto*, 1970. Installation view (close to the mountaintop), as seen from the foot of Kinchōzan in Kobe. © The Play. (Also plate 8.)

Compared with this whimsical undertaking, their annual summer projects were more involved. The planning customarily began in the spring, although possible ideas might be broached at the time of the previous year's project. This was the case for *Voyage* (figure 0.2), whose core idea to float the egg on water was hatched on the dry riverbed of Nagara when it was displayed there in August 1965. At the time of *Voyage*, three summers later, some members began to talk about using another type of body of water. This led to the River Trilogy, beginning with *Current of Contemporary Art* in July 1969 (figure 3.8). Once called the Capital of Water, Osaka was historically known for its rivers and canals, which crisscrossed the city. The main waterway, with numerous tributaries and feeders, is the Yodo River, which connected it with Kyoto, another ancient capital.

With *Current of Contemporary Art*, the group used the route of the Uji River to the Yodo River to the Ōkawa (the Yodo's historical main stream), as shown in the map on its poster (figure 3.9, plate 9). The departure point was set at Tōnoshima, an island of

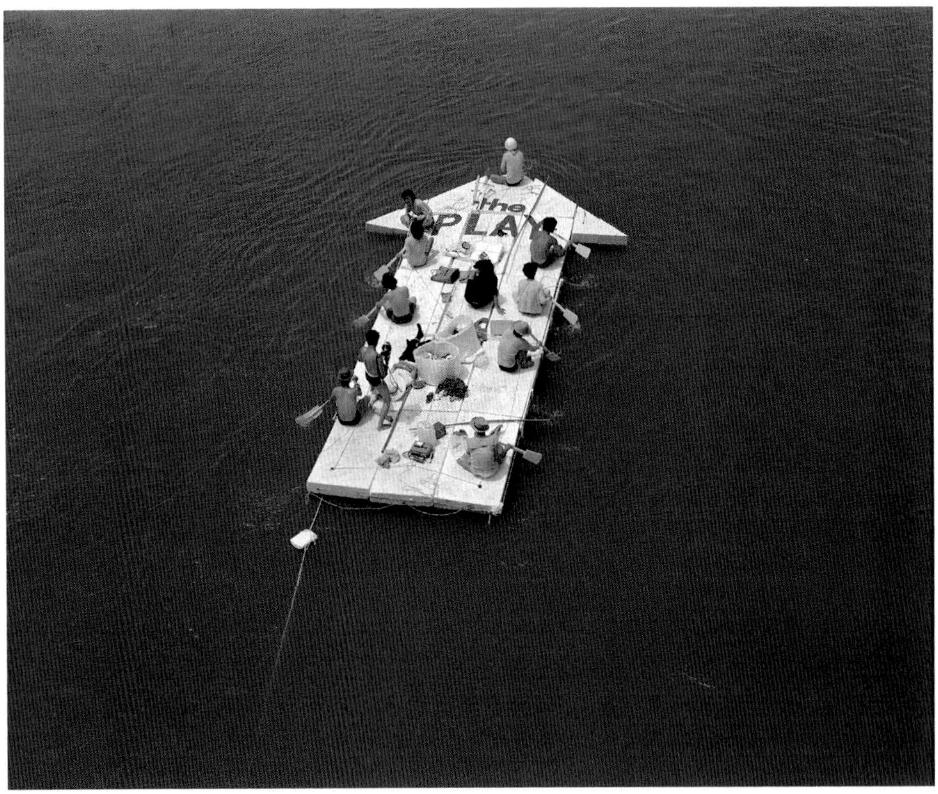

FIGURE 3.8
The Play, *Current of Contemporary Art*, 1969. Documentary photograph of performance art. Photo by Higuchi Shigeru. © The Play.

the Uji River, located south of the city of Kyoto and near the famed 11th-century Phoenix Hall. A key feature of *Current* was a stunning arrow-shaped raft the crew created with Styrofoam blocks. The idea of the "arrow" was contributed by Mizukami, who frequently used red arrows in his rituals. The idea of Styrofoam was put on the table during their preparatory meetings. It was a novel petro-based synthetic material invented in Germany in 1950 and introduced to Japan in 1959 for various construction applications.[55] Styrofoam was a very expensive material at the time, and The Play decided to rent the *tatami*-sized 20-centimeter-thick slabs to create their 8-meter-long raft. Most blocks were minimally modified, with a pike inserted into each block to thread ropes through to bind them into the final shape. Such modification did not undermine the material's commercial value and later uses, since these large blocks would normally be carved into appropriate shapes for different practical uses. Renting various materials became one of The Play's strategies to keep expenses as low as possible.

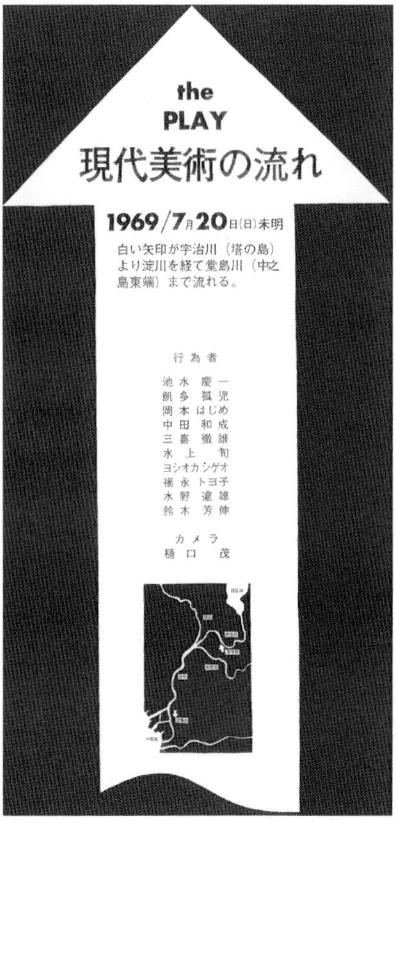

FIGURE 3.9
The Play, *Current of Contemporary Art*, 1969. Poster. © The Play. (Also plate 9.)

Based on Ikemizu's rough design, the raft was fabricated by a company he had found through his school connections in Shijō Nawate, between Osaka and Kyoto. The "arrowhead" was successfully tested at a pond on Mount Ikoma, some 30 minutes by car from the company (figure 3.10).[56] Then, on the appointed date of July 20, the group gathered at Tōnoshima, assembled the 12-part raft, and embarked on their journey at 8:40 in the morning. Propelled by handmade oars, the raft progressed mostly smoothly. Lifejackets were duly prepared, for the flow at Tōnoshima can be brisk and violent, especially when massive discharges are made from the upstream Amagase Dam after the June-July rainy season. The group typically contacted the dam's management office and succeeded in having the discharge reduced that morning.[57] One mishap took place and was filmed: the raft bumped into a bridge pillar and was slightly damaged and quickly repaired. As their report describes, after 12 hours, close to 9 at night, they safely arrived at the east end of Nakanoshima island, in the central part of downtown Osaka.[58]

Their second river travel was *Sheep* in August 1970 (figure 3.11). More precisely, it was a walking trip along the Kamo River to the Katsura River to the Yodo River. A flock of a dozen sheep was loaned by Mihara Ranch in Mikazukichō of Sayō Province, Hyōgo Prefecture, which is located some 100 kilometers west of Kobe. They were transported from the ranch to Kyoto near the Shimogamo Shrine, close to the Kamo River. In the initial plan, the members, serving as shepherds, would bring the flock from Kyoto to Kobe in eight days from August 23 to 30. Along the way, they would take advantage of empty fields and riverbeds to camp out and have the flock rest (figure 3.12). In reality, the sheep often refused to move during the day, accustomed to their quiet pastoral life and unnerved by the crowd and the traffic. Eventually, their journey ended on the final day just beyond Tennōzan, which historically demarcates Kyoto from Osaka, far short of Sannomiya in Kobe.[59]

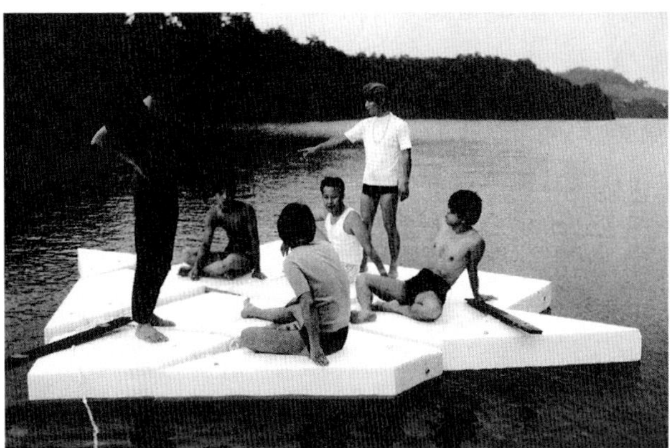

FIGURE 3.10
The Play members testing a raft for *Current of Contemporary Art*, 1969. © The Play.

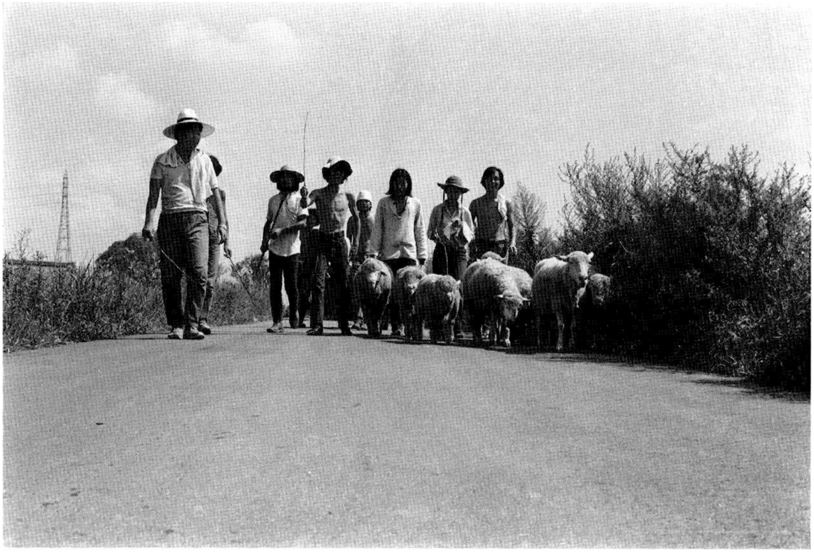

FIGURE 3.11
The Play, *Sheep*, 1970. Documentary photograph of performance art. © The Play.

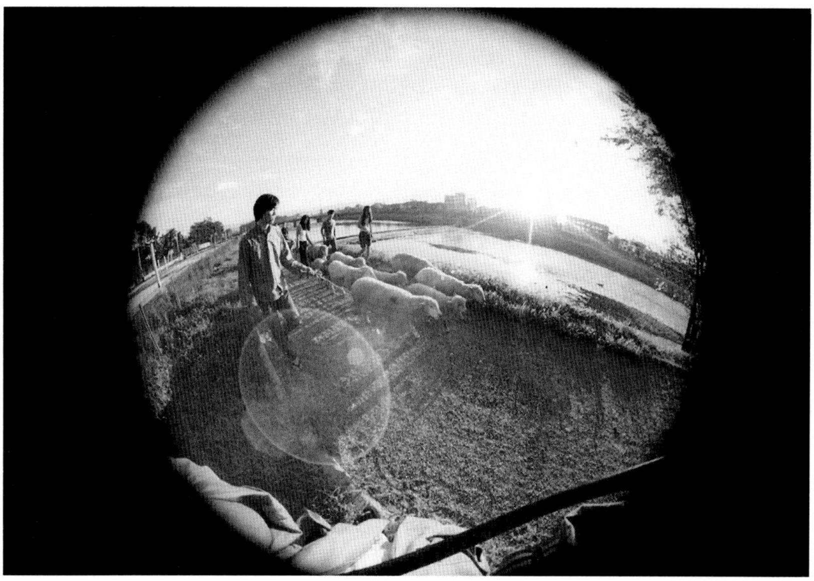

FIGURE 3.12
The Play, *Sheep*, 1970. Sheep resting on a dry riverbed. © The Play.

Sheep marked another important turning point for The Play. Above all, up until then the group had been conscious of challenging the established forms of art, and their 1969 projects were full of provocation. Even *Current*, a leisurely trip downstream, contained irony, in that the institutionalized notion of "contemporary art" was taken out of the museum to drift in unsteady waves. In contrast, *Sheep* was an explicit act of "removing the boundary of everyday life."[60] Needless to say, this idea had been latent in their past projects but remained rather abstract. Thanks to an increasing number of non-artists who joined the group's projects, their perspective on the everyday evolved. The goal of rallying "those who acutely sensed the strain of material civilization"[61] began to shift to reflections on human existence. In going out into landscape, for a brief moment they went out of their daily routines: artist-members departed from their studios, while salaryman-members and others with regular jobs took a break from their offices and other places of work. In *Sheep*, they gathered together to share an experience as modern-day shepherds "traveling to the most fundamental part of humankind."[62]

It was then apt that the last of the River Trilogy was *Ie: The Play Have a House*, in which they traveled downstream in a small floating house (*ie*) (figure 3.13). By giving their house a distinctly Western look with a red roof and white walls, they perhaps made their *ie* closer to "my home" (*mai hōmu*), the postwar ideology grounded in me-ism, modernization, and material affluence, than to the more traditional connotation of the family system of *ie*. Like the drifting contemporary art in *Current*, The Play's communal "my home" nonetheless rambled downstream over six eventful and difficult days, from August 5 to 10. Their report outlines damages their house-shaped vessel suffered and repairs they made to it.[63] These problems thwarted their initial plan to eventually enter the Gulf of Osaka, and the journey was terminated at the Toyosato Bridge, some 10 kilometers upstream of downtown Osaka. The ending was unusually violent for The Play, who destroyed and burned the house before disbanding and going home.[64] What linked the three projects symbolically was the rivers' flow—the "flow" that embodies the flow of their consciousness. When the art monthly *Bijutsu techō* featured *Ie* in its November 1972 issue, the group wrote:

> *Ie* flowed at the speed of the river's flow. At some moments, [we realized] our consciousness flowed at the same speed.
>
> By flowing in one river, each one of us flowed in the stream of his or her consciousness. When a new landscape opened up before *Ie*, a new and different landscape opened up in the consciousness of each of us.[65]

After the River Trilogy, The Play extended the idea of voyage to a remote island near Okinawa (*Torokko*, 1974) (figure 3.14, plate 10), a lake (*Canoe*, 1975), and a plain

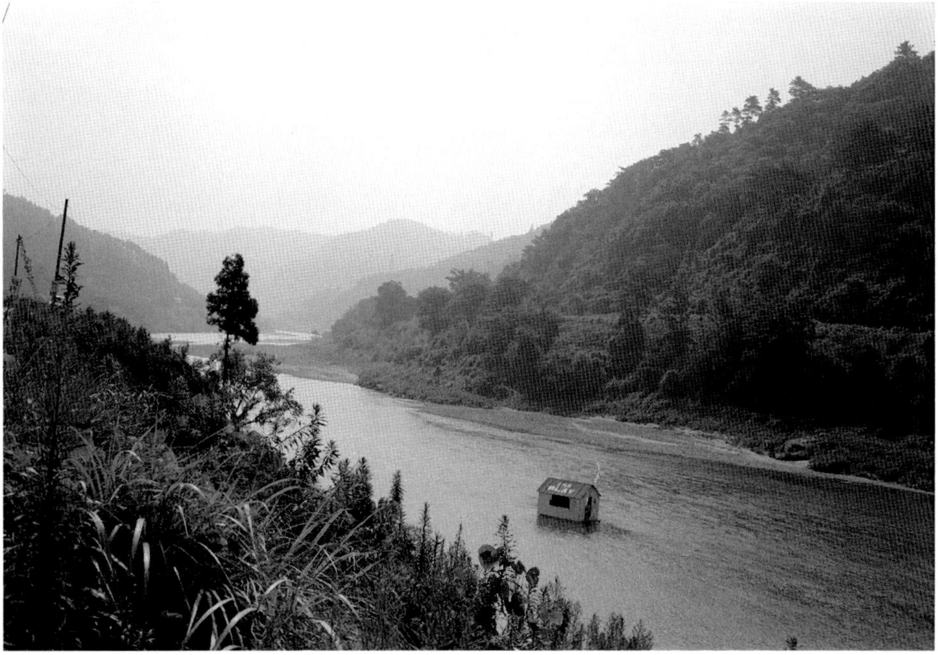

FIGURE 3.13
The Play, *Ie: The Play Have a House*, 1972. Documentary photograph of performance art. © The Play.

in Hokkaidō (*Wind*, 1976) (figure 3.15), before coming back to nature nearby in 1977 to stage *Thunder* near Kyoto (figure 6.13). At the same time, the group began an effort to expand its membership by staging *Tent*, a series of small events. The first *Tent* was erected on April 29, 1974, on the dry riverbed of the Kizu River, near the Keihan commuter rail's Hachiman-shi station. The basic idea was to have fun at a "clinic picnic," with anybody interested invited, to "concretize the idea for The Play in the summer of 1974."[66] Some members later commented that the infusion of new non-artist members that year made the project different.[67] One development of the *Tent* series was *Wind: Wandering in the Wind* of 1976, which was an anomaly of sorts, not centering on a prop-object but purely concept-driven. Furthermore, the idea of going "against the wind" was contrary to the previous river projects, in which the group had traveled along a flow. An idea for *Wind* was brought to the table by a newcomer, Kawasaki Masayuki, who was then a college student. After research on the wind conditions in various places, they selected Sarobetsu Plain close to the northern tip of Hokkaidō. In their imagination, "Only the wind exists in Sarobetsu Plain. There must blow the wind par excellence that is extracted from the whole universe."[68] Some even harbored a romantic vision of taking a solitary walk in a vast open field, while blown in the wind.[69]

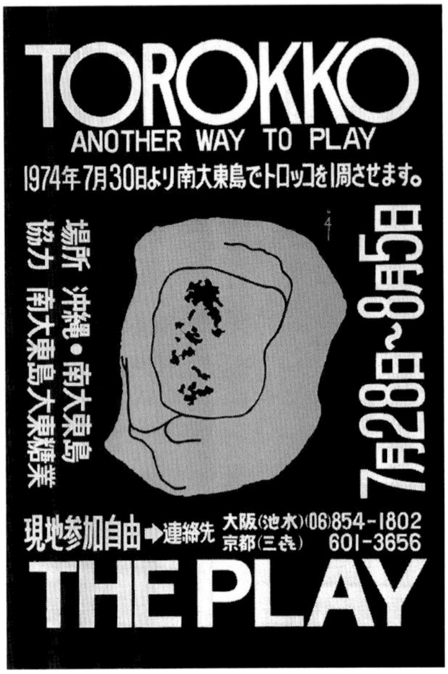

FIGURE 3.14
The Play, *Torokko*, 1974. Poster. © The Play. (Also plate 10.)

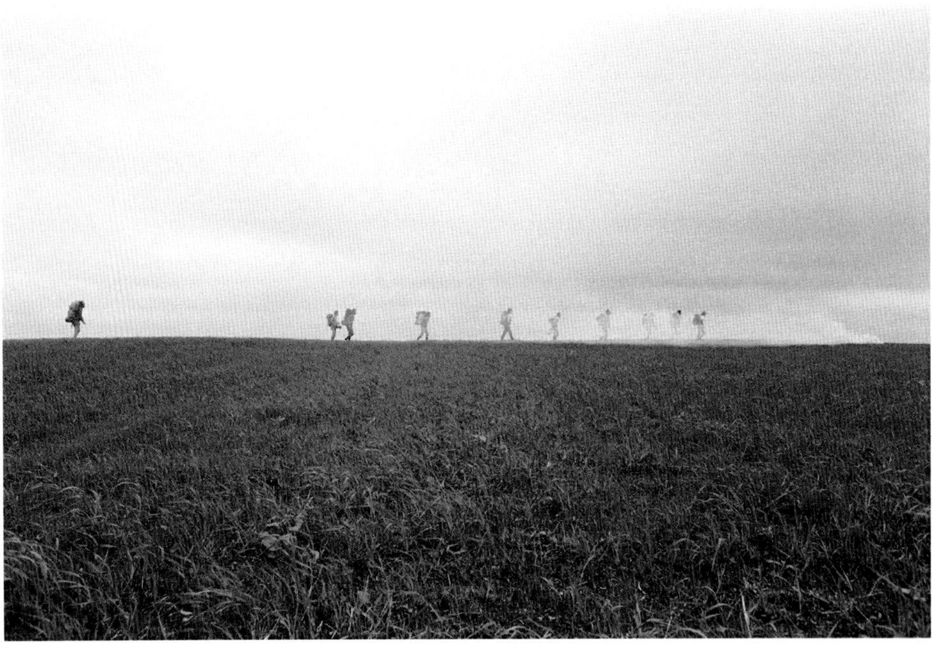

FIGURE 3.15
The Play, *Wind: Wandering in the Wind*, 1976. Documentary photograph of performance art. © The Play.

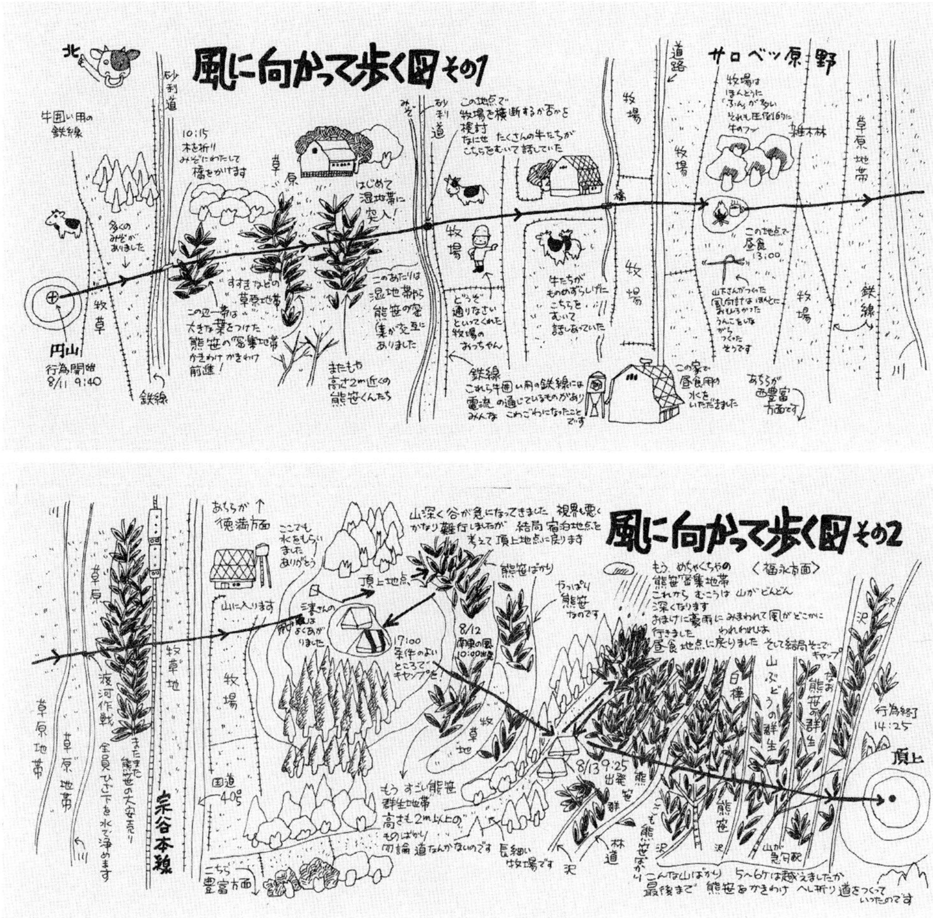

FIGURE 3.16
The Play, "Walking against the Wind, 1 and 2," 1976. 2 cards from the report for *Wind: Wandering in the Wind*. © The Play.

The reality of three days in that August in the northern field was far from what they had anticipated. They managed to stage a few romantic shots, with smoke candles showing the direction of the wind and creating a foggy mood. However, since the wind blew from the top of a small hill, they had to climb up the hill, cutting an arduous path through dense bushes of striped bamboo as tall as them and at one point wading into shrubs of poison ivy. The report they made for *Wind*, in a mail-art style, consists of eighteen cards, which included recollections by nine members vividly demonstrating nine different thoughts coexisting in the shared time and space (figure 3.16).

* * *

The Play emerged from the local independent-exhibition movement that constituted a major aspect of the post-Yomiuri years. They adapted Happenings as their organizing principle, while responding to the local tradition of performative practices. In doing so, they developed a unique form of collectivism, at once collaborative and communal, in a locale where collectivism had functioned as a driving force of modernism. Their Happenings, imbued with a land-art dimension, fascinated both the art world and the mass media alike, the evidence of which fills their artist's books documenting their unconventional projects. At the same time, their contribution to the global history of land art and performance art is distinct, with any one of their annual summer projects embodying a sense of space-time at once ordinary (everyday) and extraordinary. In fact, The Play offers an excellent case study in understanding how international contemporaneity was lived through consciously and unconsciously in 1960s Japan. As will be discussed in chapter 5, their practice came hand in hand with theory, as they articulated their own discourse on Happenings in order to repossess the imported idea. This was one way to consciously live through international contemporaneity. In chapter 6, a rare instance of pure resonance between The Play and Walter De Maria in their respective uses of thunder and lightning provides a starting point. In this case of unconscious realization of international contemporaneity, the two works will be briefly compared in order to delve into the study of the relationship of Japanese contemporary artists with landscape and nature.

4 GUN'S ASPIRATIONS FROM THE WILDERNESS

GUN, short for Group Ultra Niigata, was the youngest among the three practitioners studied in this book and the last to emerge from the wilderness. Founded in 1967, GUN was the first vanguard collective hailing from Niigata Prefecture, long pejoratively called the "backside" of Japan. As such, they were burdened by their geography, and due to their young age—with two central members, Maeyama Tadashi and Horikawa Michio, having just graduated from Niigata University in 1967 and 1968—they missed the chance to experience any of the newly self-organized independent exhibitions in the post-Yomiuri years. Their opportunities as contemporary artists were indeed limited; by getting together as GUN, they had a clear intention of generating an avant-garde movement and closing their gap from the center. Yet they exhausted their resources after presenting six exhibitions in Tokyo and Niigata in the short space of one year. No longer able to continue as an exhibition society, in the conventional manner of group activity, they decided to mount individual efforts under the banner of GUN. From 1969 onward, Horikawa and Maeyama began to look more closely at their locale and found concrete realities to work with, while adopting the repertoire of contemporary-art strategies—mail art, land art, and political art.

TOKYO AS A DISTANT CENTER: GUN'S EARLY YEARS

Among the three practitioners studied in this volume, GUN was the remotest in location from Tokyo, the center for contemporary art in Japan (figure 4.1). The Play was headquartered in Kansai, the center of ancient Japan, which continued to be an economic and cultural center throughout history second only to Tokyo. As for Matsuzawa Yutaka's hometown of Shimo Suwa, it was historically a minor center though remote from Tokyo. It hosted a key station on a primary highway, Nakasendō, that ran through central Japan to connect Edo (the old name for Tokyo) and Kyoto. Surrounded by the scenic Japan Alps, the small town was blessed with the Suwa Shrine, one of the oldest Shintō institutions and the headquarters of a nationwide network of subshrines. Thanks to its clean mountain air, modern Suwa and its environs enjoyed a thriving clock and watch industry and later a precision machine industry. In contrast, Niigata was a typical area in the "backside" of Japan—mostly rural, with a primary-sector economy (depending on agriculture, forestry, fishing, and mining). When Niigata-born Tanaka Kakuei became Prime Minister in 1972, his notoriously grandiose plan to "Improve the Japanese Archipelago" (*Nihon kaizō-ron*) encompassed a bullet train and highways to Niigata (and other remote areas nationwide) to close their distance from Tokyo.

Distance was acutely felt in the snow country separated by mountains from Tokyo. For Maeyama Tadashi,[1] who would become the de facto leader of GUN, moving to Tokyo was not an option, given his family obligations. The eldest son of a farming family in a rural area, Maeyama was expected to inherit the family property. Yet, since the family land was not large enough to generate a sustainable income in modern society, he had to seek employment. Being an art teacher was his best option for making a living and continuing his art making. To pursue this goal, he studied at the Takada branch of the teachers' college of Niigata University, which was located within commuting distance of his home and had a renowned arts division.

In his sophomore year, Maeyama began to frequent Tokyo to understand the capital's vanguard circles. These formed a small world consisting of a handful of commercial galleries specializing in contemporary art (e.g., Tokyo, Minami, Nantenshi, and Aoki) and a number of rental galleries promoting vanguard experiments (e.g., Akiyama, Lunami, Mudo, Muramatsu, Ogikubo, and Shirota). It was an enormous thrill and an education to see firsthand what he had known from small monochrome reproductions in such art magazines as *Bijutsu techō*. He quickly expanded his network in Tokyo, enjoying impromptu discussions at these galleries, where he encountered, for example, the theory-minded low-talking critic Miyakawa Atsushi, whose interest in French theory confirmed the importance of certain ideas the budding artist had contemplated. He visited some of his new acquaintances at their homes, including the critics Ishiko Junzō and Akatsuka Yukio and the painter Maeda Jōsaku. Visiting Tokyo

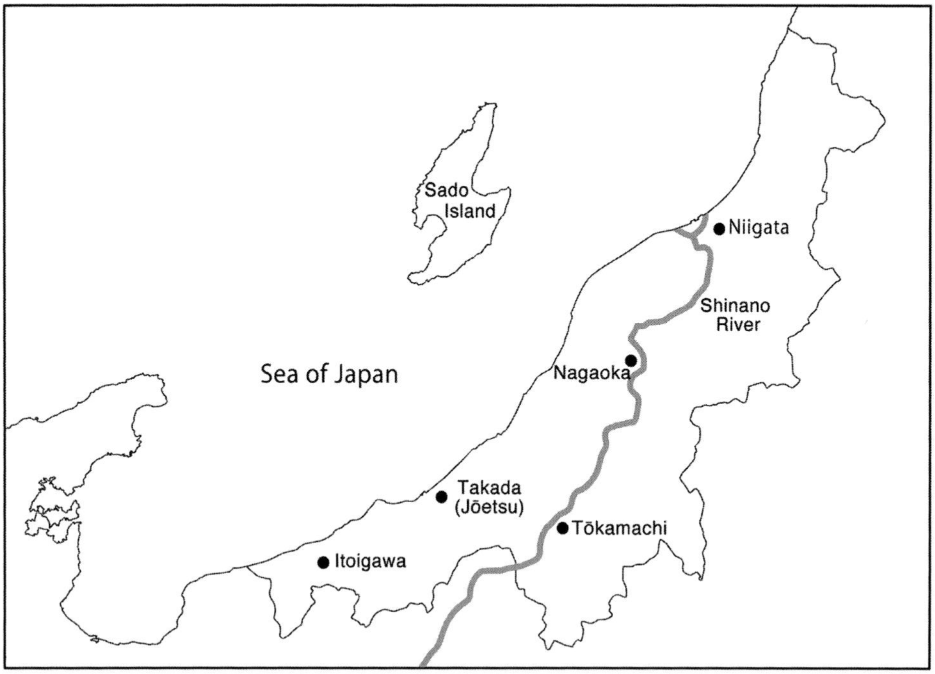

FIGURE 4.1
Map of Niigata Prefecture. Designed by Takako Oishi-Marks.

above all helped him learn the ropes of Tokyo's art world. In particular, he learned that no qualifications were required to show at a rental gallery (except for paying weekly rental fees). In 1966, his senior year, he decided to have his first solo exhibition at Lunami Gallery, which he felt came closest to his aesthetic sensitivity. This was succeeded by a second show in 1967 at Lunami and yet another at Shirota in 1968.

The most important contact he forged in Tokyo was with Ishiko Junzō, a young critic known for his unwavering critique of modernity, who would later turn to the topic of kitsch and *manga*. Ishiko supported Genshoku (meaning "tactile hallucination"), a collective established in 1966 in Shizuoka.[2] In their individual works, Genshoku members explored the ambiguity of seeing, sometimes using such natural objects as stones and a tree with minimal artificial treatment, in parallel to the Mono-ha artists (figure 5.4).[3] Encouraged by Ishiko, Maeyama moved to form GUN, which included Horikawa Michio, a friend from his high-school art club and one year behind him at the teachers' college.

Maeyama also developed a network in Niigata, a large prefecture stretching over 300 kilometers from northeast to southwest, by participating in local open-call exhibitions. In postwar Japan, the open-call prefecture salons (*kenten*) expanded exhibition opportunities for regional artists, with practically every prefecture organizing a salon.[4]

These prefectural exhibitions largely replicated the juried salon system of *dantai* (artists' organizations), complete with the evils of favoritism and sectionalism. As such, the prefecture salons, along with the local *dantai* chapters, constituted the establishment for local vanguards to rebel against. Although not as ubiquitous as *kenten*, *shiten* or open-call city salons were also instituted in postwar years and, depending on the locale, could be progressive forums. The most famous example is Ashiya's city exhibition, founded by the influential Gutai leader Yoshihara Jirō.[5] As a member of its jury panel, he made every effort to promote unconventional and experimental works. Notable in Niigata was the Itoigawa city exhibition at the prefecture's southwestern end, established in 1959. In the mid-1960s, it began to invite progressive judges from Tokyo. In 1965, it invited Ōoka Makoto, a poet-critic close to the critic Takiguchi Shūzō and the artist Sam Francis. In that year, Maeyama presented canvases of gestural abstraction at Itoigawa, one of which received the top Mayor's Prize. The recognition by a Tokyo critic certainly boosted Maekawa's confidence. In 1968, Ōoka returned as a judge, along with artist Maeda Jōsaku, born in neighboring Toyama Prefecture and known for his mandala theme, and the poet-critic Okada Takahiko, who founded the vanguard photography collective Provoke in that year. Itoigawa's exhibition also distinguished itself by making its jury process open to the public, contrary to the customarily secretive and thus murky salon-style judging methods. Those dissatisfied with the establishment aesthetics flocked to Itoigawa from around the prefecture every August. Both Maeyama and Horikawa did well there through the later 1960s.[6]

By October 1967, Maeyama and Horikawa were ready to launch a movement of *gendai bijutsu*, initially calling their group Niigata Contemporary Art Collective GUN (Niigata Gendai Bijutsu Shūdan GUN). The word GUN derived from their desire to make a "big impact," as expressed by a modern onomatopoeia, *gān*, which sounds like the English *gun*. (In Japanese, *gān* sonically signifies the state of a great emotional shock.) The photographer-collaborator Hanaga Mitsutoshi later interpreted it as an acronym for "Group Ultra Niigata," which the group happily adopted. The members frequently met at the lobby café in a building that housed the Nagaoka Museum of Contemporary Art on the first floor. Their shared dream was to someday show their works at the museum, which was a bright symbol of international contemporaneity with its collection of Euro-American contemporary art. Short of showing there, they presented their first exhibition on a floor above—at the rental Nagaoka Culture Hall (Nagaoka Bunka Kaikan) in December 1967. Altogether 14 artists gathered to make a mixed team of vanguard aspirants and salon hopefuls. Bringing together six critics and practitioners—five from Tokyo and its environs, including Ishiko and the Genshoku member Suzuki Yoshinori—they held a symposium and staged ritual-like street Happenings.

From the beginning, GUN had a two-pronged plan to create a Niigata-Tokyo axis by holding exhibitions in two locales in succession. Their manifesto flier was handed out to dozens of people in Niigata, but more importantly they managed to have its

TABLE 4.1
GUN: First Three Years

1967	
October 6	Meeting by some 15 artists to establish GUN
December 9–10	*GUN* (1st exhibition) Exhibition of 14 artists, held at Nagaoka Culture Hall. Street demonstration and Happenings. Symposium "How an Art Movement Should Be" with panelists Ishiko Junzō (critic), Kimura Tsunehisa (designer-critic), Yasunao Tone (musician-critic), Matsumoto Momoji (painter), Suzuki Yoshinori (Genshoku), Maruyama Shōzō (local painter), Maeyama Tadashi (GUN)
December 21	*GUN*, no. 1 (journal)
December 21–28	*GUN* Exhibition of 7 artists, held at Gallery Shinjuku, Tokyo
1968	
January 15	Street Happening by 6 or so artists, at Niigata
January 18	Happening show by 13 artists aired by BSM Television
April 13–14	*GUN* Exhibition of 13 artists, held at Ōshima Gallery, Takada. Happening at Takada Park. Discussion "Contemporary Art: Today's Situation" with Akatsuka Yukio (critic)
August 1	*GUN*, no. 2
August 8	*GUN*, no. 3
August 8–11	*Thoughts on Being* Exhibition of 8 artists with 4 special participants from Tokyo (Sekine Nobuo, Kojima Nobuaki, Tanaka Shintarō, and Nonaka Yuri), held at Nagaoka Culture Hall. Film screenings by Kanesaka Kenji and Miyai Rikurō. Happening by GUN. Symposium "What Is Possible: Approaches to Being" with panelists Okada Takahiko, Kojima Nobuaki, Sekine Nobuo, Tanaka Shintarō, and Miyai Rikurō
September 7–12	*GUN* Exhibition of 8 artists, held at Tsubaki Kindai Gallery, Tokyo
1969	
April	Appeal to Open the Jury Panel of the Contemporary Japanese Exhibition of Japan to the Public

densely written text (mainly by Maeyama) published in *Me* (Eye), a monthly newsletter of Ogikubo Gallery in Tokyo, in the same month, making their presence known in the capital.[7] Their second exhibition, later in December, was held at Gallery Shinjuku in Tokyo with seven artists. At a brisk pace, they presented a total of five exhibitions in their first 10 months: two in Tokyo and three in various sites in Niigata (see table 4.1). GUN's membership was fluid, as Maeyama and Horikawa, two constant members, recruited whomever they could for each exhibition. The salon hopefuls would inevitably leave the group, as their participation in GUN added almost nothing to their standing in the local art establishment. It was not until after *Event to Change the Image of Snow* (figure 0.3) that GUN would have a meaningful infusion of new members (e.g., Satō Hideharu and Sekine Tetsuo).

After September 1968, their push to hold exhibitions ground to a halt. Maeyama and Horikawa, as well as others, had literally exhausted their financial resources. Their monthly salary as middle-school art teachers was around 20,000 to 30,000 yen, which would evaporate with each exhibition, and they could only ask for a loan of a month's salary from their schools. On the aesthetic front, Maeyama made steady progress with his first signature work using a mirror and Pop-like female iconography through which he interrogated the trickery of vision, a theme in the air among Japanese artists in the mid-1960s (figure 4.2). In contrast, Horikawa stagnated in his development, unable to move beyond his Pop experiment with fabrications of everyday objects, such as a gigantic necktie made of shiny sheet metal and fabricated at a factory. Under these circumstances, with no real strategy to extend their collective life, GUN decided to focus on individual activities under the group's banner. Ironically, this strategy of non-strategy proved to be successful. In a sense, the real life of GUN began where the customary group activities ended.

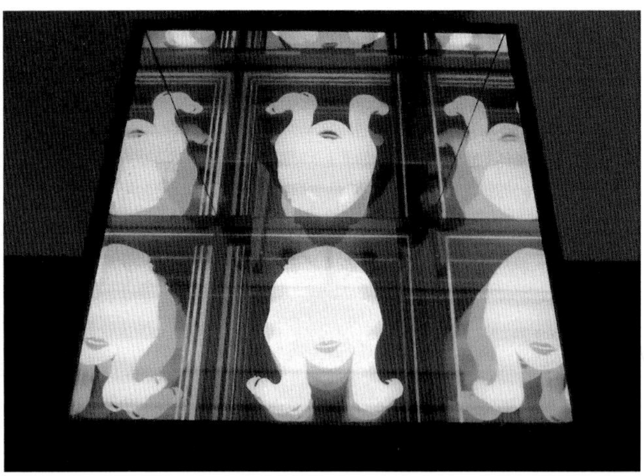

FIGURE 4.2
Maeyama Tadashi, *Breaching an Idea*, 1967/2012. Mirror; 40 × 40 × 65 cm. Collection of the artist.

WILDERNESS POTENTIAL: CLOSING THE DISTANCE AND ENGAGING THE SOCIAL

GUN's second beginning in 1969 inevitably made them latecomers to 1960s art. With one new tendency emerging after another, they were keenly aware of what had come before them in the immediate past and what was happening in the present. In a sense, distance, whether temporal or spatial, was greatly reduced by the late 1960s, primarily due to the print media. Domestically, for example, the studious Horikawa avidly read a serialized essay by Ushio Shinohara in *Bijutsu techō*, which ran in 11 parts from February to December 1966 and historicized his group Neo Dada and his wide-ranging exploits afterward.[8] The same magazine increased its coverage of international art beginning in January 1968 under the new editorship of Miyazawa Takeyoshi,[9] and became a must-read for contemporary artists. It not only featured the latest trends in art and culture (see table 4.2)[10] but also carried serious essays and substantial reviews by a host of art critics, both veterans (e.g., the Big Three and Miyakawa Atsushi) and new faces (e.g., Fujieda Teruo, Ishiko Junzō, and Lee Ufan).

In this sense, GUN consciously lived through the state of international contemporaneity—much more so than Matsuzawa and The Play—as they learned from their immediate predecessors and aspired to contribute something new to ongoing developments. It should be noted that their relationship to their contemporaries was in spirit less "imitational" than "interpoetic," the model of transmission in art proposed by Ming Tiampo wherein an artist creatively borrows from and builds upon a predecessor's work while adding his or her own creativity.[11] Especially Horikawa, who emerged as a new driving force of the group in this phase, has been very frank about his inspirations and sources, revealing healthy respect for and genuine interest in his predecessors' achievements[12]—perhaps because he knew that his and GUN's additions or twists were original, intimately grounded in their lived reality and the environment of Niigata. By channeling the international to the local, GUN effectively closed the distance from Tokyo and, indeed, from the international, while opening new ways of engaging the social by exploring their own local conditions.

Stones of the Shinano River: Horikawa Michio's Mail Art

In the second phase of GUN, the first to break out was Horikawa Michio, who tapped into the new local tradition of mail art while responding to the developing international news story of the Apollo space missions. His idea was expansive: he wanted to create a situation on Earth parallel to the astronauts' on the moon and share the experience with others, be they ordinary people or art world denizens. Thus born was a unique series, *Mail Art by Sending Stones*.

On July 20, 1969, at 10:56:15 p.m. EDT, Neil Armstrong, mission commander of Apollo 11, made the first ever footprint on the barren surface of the moon.[13] At the same moment, Horikawa Michio was on a dry riverbed of the Shinano River with a

TABLE 4.2
Bijutsu techō: Special Features and Supplementary Issues (1968–1969)

1968	
January, no. 293	Pollock; Art of the Electronic Age; Odilon Redon
February, no. 294	Robert Rauschenberg; Another Image Culture
March, no. 295	Changing *Objets*; Marcel Duchamp
April, no. 296	Pierre Bonnard; Regional Avant-Garde; Jean Dubuffet
May, no. 297	Arshile Gorky; Art Education in Chaos; LSD, Art, Creativity
June, no. 299	Jean Tinguely; Crisis in U.S. and Its New Art; Amedeo Modigliani
July, no. 300	Road to the World: Contemporary Art in Japan; Transitional Time for *Contemporary Art Exhibition of Japan*; Jasper Johns
August, no. 301	Happenings; Light Art as Environment; Willem De Kooning
September, no. 302	Mystery, Ecstasy, and Contemporary Art; Venice Biennale; Jean Fautrier
October, no. 303	Contemporary Art and Its Theories; Documenta and Triennale; Wols
November, no. 304	The Collapse of *Gadan*; Surrealist Fantasy; Yves Klein
December, no. 305	Contemporary Art and Human Image; Suma Contemporary Sculpture Exhibition; Death of Marcel Duchamp; Nicolas Schöffer
December, no. 306	Photography: Here, Now (supplementary issue)
1969	
January, no. 307	Changing Art; In Order to Understand Art of Tomorrow
February, no. 309	Contemporary Art and Technology; Andy Warhol
March, no. 310	The Era of Artists Is Over?; Robert Morris
April, no. 311	What Is Intermedia?; George Segal; Winners of 20th Anniversary Art Criticism Competition
May, no. 312	New Image of Eros; Phillip King
May, no. 313	Humankind of Technology (supplementary issue)
June, no. 314	New Nature (1): Air Art; Dan Flavin
July, no. 315	New Nature (2): Elementalism "Earthworks"; *Contemporary Art Exhibition of Japan*
August, no. 316	Invitation to the Art of Klee; *Contemporary Art: Dialogue between the East and the West*
September, no. 317	Language and Image; Iannis Xenakis
October, no. 318	Development of Contemporary Sculpture: From Henry Moore to Anti-Form
November, no. 319	Marcel Duchamp; Claes Oldenburg
December, no. 320	Destruction for Creation

morning class of seventh graders from Nakajō Middle School in the city of Tōkamachi in Niigata Prefecture.[14] (In local time, it was close to noon on July 21.) Listening to the radio reporting on the unfolding historic event in outer space, the art teacher and his charges undertook an art assignment of "picking a stone on the earth weighing 300 grams," as Armstrong and his fellow astronaut Buzz Aldrin executed one of their EVA tasks, gathering a total of 21.7 kilograms of rocks on the moon. That afternoon, Horikawa, now alone at his desk, selected 11 stones to echo Apollo's mission number and prepared them for mailing by post. He tied each of them with wire and attached a paper mailing tag (figure 4.3, plate 11). Accompanied by a few of his students, he went to a local post office which duly accepted and processed them, at 120 yen (about 33 cents at the time) per piece. Eleven addressees included nine figures of the art world, plus himself and his fellow GUN member Maeyama Tadashi. A data card he created for this project summarized the very first mailing in the series, *The Shinano River Plan: 11* (figure 4.4).

The list of 11 recipients is telling. The first three are the Big Three critics (Nakahara Yūsuke, Haryū Ichirō, and Tōno Yoshiaki), followed by Ishiko Junzō, the previously mentioned Tokyo critic who was close to GUN. A group of artists is headed by fellow member Maeyama, with five senior and established artists: four in Tokyo (Sekine Nobuo, Maeda Jōsaku, Takamatsu Jirō, and Quac Insik) and Matsuzawa Yutaka in Shimo Suwa. A desire to connect with the art world in Tokyo is evident—not surprisingly because mail art was perhaps the most cost-effective and most direct strategy to close the distance. At the same time, it is also evident that Horikawa was not uncritically participating in the historical event of the moon landing. In his statement, "69721115620" (signifying the precise Japanese time of Armstrong's first footstep, July 21, 1969, 11:56:20 am), which is pasted in his data card, he wrote:

> I am not interested in rocks on the moon. Let us have a thought that will transcend this event. And from there let us newly look at ourselves. Let us change the foundation of our thinking. Let us think of a world that envelops Earth, the Moon, Mercury. No, the whole solar system. No, let us think of a world that envelops the whole universe. And let us think of the moon rocks. The world is infinitely vast. Let us be aware of this absolute vastness. And let us look at this world from the outside. Nothing has changed in the universe even if humans stand on the moon and bring back moon rocks. What changes are humans, and their thinking. And let us think about the physical existence of humankind. A human called Horikawa also represents a certain combination of elements within the universe. Yet I am not a stone. I am a human. Full of emotion and passion. Let us be moved like a child, let us question like a child. That proves that Horikawa is Horikawa and Horikawa is a human.[15]

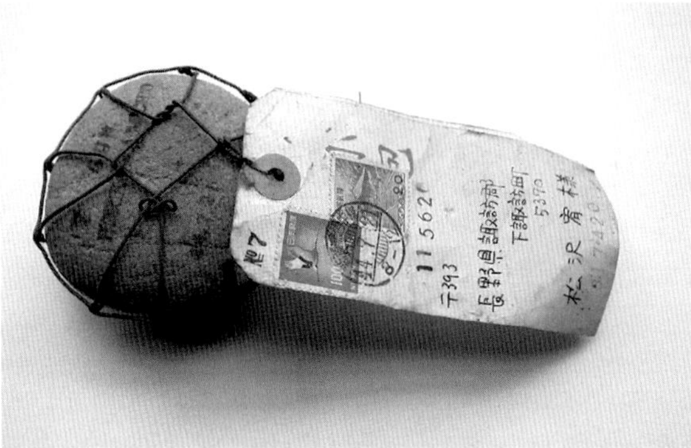

FIGURE 4.3
Horikawa Michio, *The Shinano River Plan: 11*, 1969. From the series *Mail Art by Sending Stones*. Stone, wire, mail tags (mailed to Matsuzawa Yutaka). Collection of Matsuzawa Kumiko. Photo by Reiko Tomii. (Also plate 11.)

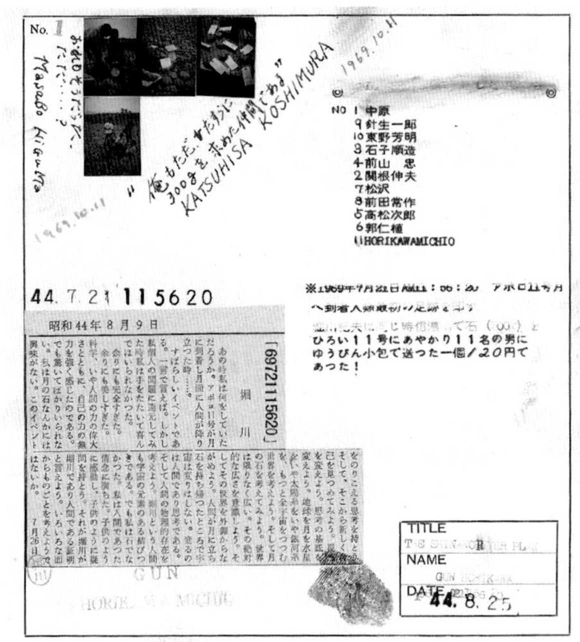

FIGURE 4.4
Horikawa Michio, *The Shinano River Plan: 11*, 21 July 1969. Document card with stamp, clipping, pencil, and type on paper; 20 × 20 cm. Collection of the artist. Numbers correspond to those on the mailing tags.

As though to demonstrate his alliance with his pupils, he included in the data card four thumbnails documenting the gathering of stones on that day, and two comments, dated October 11, from his students.

While the Apollo 11 mission was a catalyst for his series *Mail Art by Sending Stones*, the core inspiration came from the practice of mail art, then increasingly prevalent in Japan. The example of Fluxus (but not Ray Johnson's) was known to Horikawa, but more relevant to him were the precedents of Matsuzawa Yutaka, who "elegantly communicates" with Tokyo "while staying in Shimo Suwa" with his Postcard Painting series (figure 2.19),[16] and On Kawara, whose postcard series *I Got Up* had been shown at the Mainichi Contemporary earlier that May (more on his work in chapter 6). Crucial, however, were two models for mailing three-dimensional objects. One was what Horikawa long thought of as a mail-art package by Niwa Katsuji, hanging on a wall of Ishiko Junzō's apartment, which he had visited in one of several forays to Tokyo. (It turned out to be a misplaced memory: in reality, this was a two-dimensional representation of a mailed parcel, in which the artist typically thematized the deceptive relationship between the real and the visually represented.)[17] The other was "*kokeshi* mail," which was—and still is—promoted as novelty mail by the makers in Tōhoku of the local *kokeshi* wood dolls characterized by a spherical head and a tubular body.[18] A piece of paper can be rolled and inserted in a doll's body cavity and the whole thing can be mailed by post for the basic package rate, without wrapping.

The idea of using stones came in part from Takamatsu Jirō, whose "empty gallery" show at Tokyo Gallery in February 1969 was reviewed by Ishiko in the April 1969 issue of *Bijutsu techō*.[19] If the visitor followed a note in the gallery that stated that "works can be found on the street here and there," she or he would find "washed natural stones" at the foot of a street tree, for example, as illustrated in a black-and-white photo accompanying the review. Takamatsu reportedly prepared 120 stones, each bearing such decimal numbers as "0.02" and "0.97." (He first laid out 80 of them, and when some were removed by passersby he replaced them during one week of his exhibition.) Ishiko's review of Takamatsu's work and a photo of another of the artist's stone projects at the Tama River in the July 1969 issue of *Bijutsu techō*[20] (figure 4.5) together prompted Horikawa to think of using stones that were abundantly available on a nearby dry riverbed of the Shinano River. At the time, he was assigned to teach in Tōkamachi, some 50 kilometers inland from his hometown of Takada (the present Jōetsu) and located at the midpoint of the longest river in Japan, which originates in the Japan Alps and flows into the Sea of Japan. Indeed, he was ideally located for his project: around Tōkamachi he could easily pick up a variety of stones, from fist-sized ones of a few hundred grams to larger rocks weighing a few kilograms.[21] The collection point was a playground for his students, just a few minutes' walk from his school.

A positive feedback ("It's interesting!"), which Maeyama had brought back from one of his outings to Tokyo, encouraged Horikawa to continue the series. Toward the

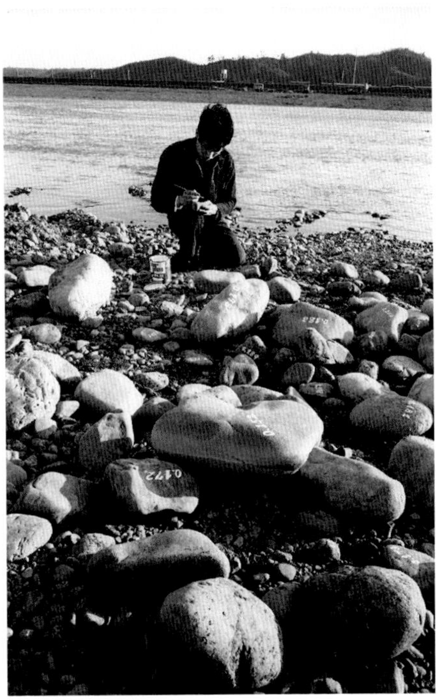

FIGURE 4.5
Takamatsu Jirō, *Stone and Numeral*, 1969. Documentary photograph of performance art. Photo by Aihara Akira. © The Estate of Jirō Takamatsu. Courtesy of Yumiko Chiba Associates.

end of August, he made another set of mailings to Tokyo, this time of 10 stones, targeting other critics and galleries, both commercial and rental.[22] They were (in the order of the list):

Namikawa Emiko (Lunami Gallery)
Kawashima Yoshiko (Muramatsu Gallery)
Shirota Sadao (Shirota Gallery)
Yamamoto Takashi (Tokyo Gallery)
Shimizu Kusuo (Minami Gallery)
Akatsuka Yukio (critic)
Miki Tamon (curator of the Tokyo Modern)
Miyakawa Atsushi (critic)
Miyazawa Takeyoshi (chief editor of *Bijutsu techō*)
Minemura Toshiaki (Mainichi Newspaper's exhibition staff)

This round brought three significant responses. Shimizu acknowledged the reception of an "artwork titled *Stone*" by sending him a postcard. Akatsuka sent him two playful "conceptual receipts," using a commercially available form. One was issued to Horikawa acknowledging his receipt of a river stone, while the other was addressed to the river itself for a "*kannen* of … ," which can be interpreted as "an idea of something unidentifiable" (figure 4.6). Horikawa created data cards with these "receipts" pasted on them, turning the recipients into tangible elements of his project. The third response came from Lee Ufan, then emerging as a critic with intellectual acumen, in his article "Is an Art of Idea Possible?" in the November 1969 issue of *Bijutsu techō*.[23] In this article the artist-critic questioned the pervasive "conceptualism," by which he meant "focus on *kannen* (idea)," in contemporary art. Having learned that Miyazawa, the magazine's editor, had received one of Horikawa's stones, Lee began his article by a fictionalized episode of a stone "I received," declaring that this stone is "a mere 'stone,' nothing more or nothing less, just a 'predetermined stone.'"[24] Which is to say, Lee saw in the mailed stone the "coagulation of [the sender's] idea," thereby equating "idea" with a readymade object.[25] Horikawa's stone is given a place of distinction as the only work illustrated in the essay, which critiqued a wide swath of contemporary art for presenting nothing but idea-cum-object, ranging from Takamatsu's stones (mentioned immediately after Horikawa's) to Joseph Kosuth's dictionary definition pieces, as well as examples of Euro-American Minimal Art and Earthworks. Needless to say, Lee's goal was to support what would be known as "Mono-ha," embodied by Sekine Nobuo, who in Lee's view endeavored to transcend the modernist objectification of the world and open up new horizons of the "world as it is" (*arino mama no sekai*).[26] Negative publicity is better than no publicity, however. For a nameless rookie like Horikawa, Lee's harsh words were the best response to his humble attempt—that is, until the critic Nakahara Yūsuke invited him to *Tokyo Biennale 1970* a few months later. (More on *kannen* as "idea" in chapter 5.)

As a token of appreciation, Horikawa sent a stone to Lee Ufan in the next round of mailings in conjunction with Apollo 12 in November 1969 (figure 4.7). In this mailing, he made full use of data cards.[27] Adapting Akatsuka's receipt idea, Horikawa requested his stone-cutter (who cut 12 stones into halves for mailing) and the post office to issue receipts for each of the 12 stones, and created 24 data cards. Later, in his outings to Tokyo, he asked the recipients of his stones to countersign and acknowledge their receipt, thus elevating the remote mail relationship into a more direct interpersonal connection. (He managed to collect five countersignatures, including Lee's.)

The level of collaboration, participation, and interaction Horikawa orchestrated with his *Mail Art by Sending Stones* made his stones more than "mere stones," while taking his stones outside the modern construct of the object-based work of art. If his project took his art out of the confines of the museum, it delivered the wilderness to one's home. And that was just a starting point: each of his stones had the potential to become a node in a human network of actions and reactions, thoughts and counterthoughts, opening up the world not as it is but as it can be many times over, since responses to his stones were far from monotonous, varying from individual to individual. The most prized interaction Horikawa achieved was with U.S. president

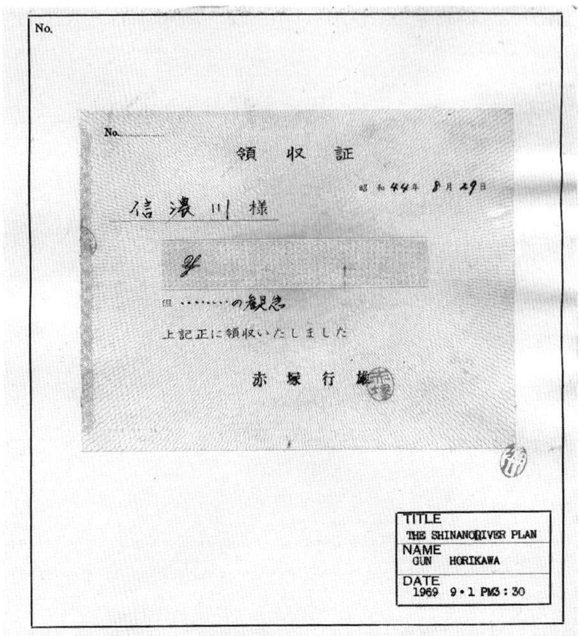

FIGURE 4.6
Horikawa Michio, *The Shinano River Plan*, 1969. Document card with receipt from Akatsuka Yukio, stamp, and type on paper; 20 × 20 cm. Collection of the artist.

FIGURE 4.7
Horikawa Michio, *The Shinano River Plan: 12*, November 1969. Document card with two photographs pasted on paper; 20 × 20 cm. Collection of the artist.

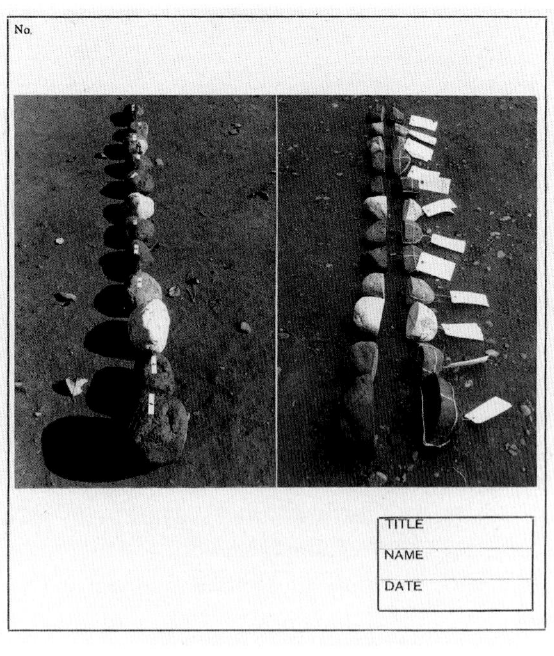

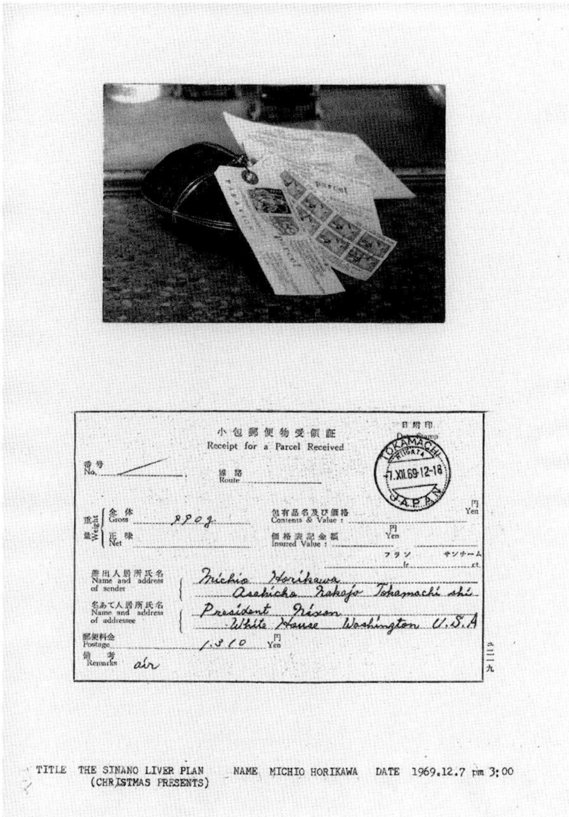

FIGURE 4.8
Horikawa Michio, *The Shinano River Plan (Christmas Present)*, 1969. From *Psychophysiology Research Institute* (1969–1970). Printed matter; 29.7 × 21 cm. Collection of the artist.

Richard Nixon (figure 4.8). As one of his seven contributions to the mail-art collective Psychophysiology Research Institute (Seishin Seirigaku Kenkyūjo) in 1969–1970,[28] he sent a black stone, weighing about one kilogram, to Nixon at the White House as a "Christmas present" (so inscribed on two of the four mailing tags attached to it). The American embassy in Tokyo sent an official thank-you letter conveying the president's "great appreciation for your thoughtfulness in sending him a most unusual Christmas gift."[29] Most unusual, certainly, but the artist's intention was no benign season's greeting. This particular stone had three meanings. First, it represented a message to Nixon that he should think more about the problems on Earth than on the moon, as the Apollo missions advanced. Second, the color black was emblematic of death (in the Vietnam War) and race problems, pointing to his earthbound concerns. And third but not least, the mailed stone was tantamount to throwing a stone at Nixon, when "stone throwing" was a means of political activism among the antiwar and antiestablishment protesters on the streets of Tokyo and other major cities. Partly because of his position as a school teacher in rural Japan, he abstained from overt political acts; thus, the mailed stone was a symbolic substitute of his protest.[30] He subsequently sent another stone on May 3, 1970, also a contribution to the mail-art collective, in the hope that it would reach Prime Minister Satō Eisaku, with an unequivocal slogan, "For Peace of World" [*sic*]. No response came from Satō's office.

As the Apollo mission slowed down, so did Horikawa's stone mailing. His mailings to *Tokyo Biennale 1970* coincided with the ill-fated Apollo 13 mission in April. It became increasingly difficult for him to maintain the motivation to send the stones. With the final Apollo 17 mission in December 1972, he concluded his mail-art project by sending five stones—one to himself, three to his fellow GUN members, and one to Hikosaka Naoyoshi, the artist-theorist who led the radical group Bikyōtō in its post-1970 phase.[31]

Snow in Niigata: GUN's Land Art

Horikawa's *Mail Art by Sending Stones* was crucial to GUN's development. Above all, the scheme of individualism under the collectivist banner of GUN was yielding results. As Maeyama pushed forward with his individual career by actively entering his new works in large-scale institutional exhibitions, Horikawa found a wilderness solution to his art making. His embrace of the group identity is unmistakable in the double signature of "GUN / HORIKAWA MICHIO" that he rubber-stamped on each of his stones and mailing tags (figure 4.3). Furthermore, his stone series led to a reunion project, *Event to Change the Image of Snow* in February 1970, which revitalized the group's collective aspirations and put GUN on the national map of contemporary art (figure 0.3). The two projects shared the location of Tōkamachi and the evocative local nature, proving their potential to reach out to the audience outside the art world at a time when *gendai bijutsu* was becoming increasingly incomprehensible to the general public.

With his *Mail Art by Sending Stones*, the early idea of calling the project a "Mail Happening"[32] was in line with the Japanized meaning of Happening: "unexpected occurrence in daily life" (see more in chapter 5). The incongruous combination of an inanimate stone and the social medium of postal mail at once perplexed and amused the recipients. Journalism took notice (figure 6.11). In December 1969, one day before he sent a stone to President Nixon, the artist happened to see Hanaga Mitsutoshi, a Tokyo-based photojournalist with whom Horikawa had been acquainted since GUN's first Tokyo exhibition in December 1967. He was in Tōkamachi on an assignment with a local company. Immediately intrigued by Horikawa's project, he documented the scenes of mailing the stone and managed to arrange an article on the project in the Yomiuri newspaper. The article called the artist a "Mail Art Teacher" and dubbed the whole stone mailing project a "Playful Happening."[33] This encounter led to a Happening with snow in the following February.

Doing something with snow was a topic among the members of GUN from the summer of 1969.[34] Thanks to the special feature on Earthworks in the July 1969 issue of *Bijutsu techō*,[35] they were aware of a variety of land-art projects in the U.S. The feature included two of Dennis Oppenheim's snow-related works, *One Hour Run* (1968) and *Annual Rings* (1969), in which the American artist cut paths into fields of snow as his pictorial ground.[36] For residents of Niigata, snow is a gloomy proposition. Indeed it is a "White Devil."[37] According to the records compiled by the Japan Metrological Agency, among the ten greatest snowfalls in Japanese history are seven in Niigata locations, the sixth (391 cm deep, 1981) and seventh (377 cm deep, 1945) being at Tōkamachi, where Horikawa then taught, and at Takada, his and Maeyama's hometown.[38] There, snow represents a potentially fatal danger due to its sheer weight, and it must be promptly and diligently removed from rooftops. Even though the accumulated snow is a valuable resource when thawed (beneficial for farming and generating electricity and drinking water), it is a menace to everyday life during the nearly six-month-long winter.[39]

To "change the image of snow," therefore, was more than a conceptual or formal exercise. The members entertained but quickly dismissed a few fantastic ideas. One was to make a geometric abstraction in the manner of the Nazca Lines (a set of prehistoric geoglyphs in the desert of Peru), which would require aerial views. Another was to cover a large swath of ground with yellow or red pigment from a helicopter at 4 a.m. so that nearby residents would wake up to "a changed earth."[40] This idea, which would have directly engaged an audience outside the art world, proved too costly: the budget for pigment alone was enormous and they would have had to hire a helicopter, another expensive item. Altogether several million yen was needed, while their monthly salaries averaged 20,000 to 30,000 yen. The photographer Hanaga joined their discussion in Tokyo when Maeyama and Horikawa came to stay with him. Having personally witnessed Anti-Art scenes of the early decade, Hanaga was conversant with contemporary art and became a "big brother"[41] to the inexperienced GUN members. Apart from Maeyama and Horikawa, he discussed the snow project with another member, Ichihashi Tetsuo, during his research on the mercury poisoning of the Agano River. Finally, in December 1969, while he photographed Horikawa's mailing of Nixon's stone, he hatched a feasible plan together with the artist.

The plan was a streamlined combination of the two fantasies: the members would spray pigment from the ground to make a color-field abstraction on the snow, with the aim of challenging snow's depressing image. The group soon got together in Nagaoka to further refine the plan. They decided to time the project close to Tōkamachi's annual snow festival in February, partly because snow was generally in good condition then. The location of Tōkamachi was advantageous on two counts: there was a vast graveled dry riverbed of the Shinano River, and the Tōkamachi Bridge offered a strategic vantage point for viewing. In executing the various preparations, three GUN members, Maeyama, Horikawa, and Ichihashi (then a resident of Tōkamachi), were the core of the team. They worked closely with Hanaga, who served as a producer behind the scenes and took full advantage of his residency in Tokyo. Aided by Ichihashi and the artist's surveyor friend Yashima Tsutomu, Hanaga spearheaded the effort to obtain permission to use the riverbed from the Ministry of Construction, just as the organizers of *Independent Art Festival* in Gifu had done. The requirements were the same: to restore the riverbed to its original state after the performance. Group "I" had complied with the regulation by filling in a hole they had dug; GUN's application claimed that the pigments, similar to food colorants, would be harmless and flushed away with melting snow.[42] Hanaga was also instrumental in obtaining a donation of pigments from the Color Planning Center in Tokyo, through the company's executive Unagami Masaomi. Known today as the owner of Unac Tokyo, a contemporary art gallery, Unagami then occasionally produced art publications, including a lavishly illustrated 1969 monograph of Yagi Kazuo, an avant-garde ceramicist, with photographs by the renowned photographer Narahara Ikkō.[43] Sympathetic to an experimental use of pigments, he donated 120 kilograms of pigment to the project in four colors, at an estimated value of 450,000 yen.[44] To apply the pigment, Ichihashi and Horikawa borrowed a fertilizer sprayer from a neighboring farmer.

On February 11, 1970, the first painting was executed by Ichihashi and Horikawa, with two others. (Residing away from Tōkamachi, Maeyama was unable to come that day.) Two photographers were on hand: Hanaga and Iso Toshikazu (who would later be known for his work with the popular photo weekly *Focus*). Using the four colors of pigment, they painted over an area of some 100 meters square (figure 4.9, plate 12). The result was phenomenal. The Tōkamachi Bridge provided a perfect bird's-eye viewpoint for the two photographers to shoot the iridescent landscape, before the falling snow erased their masterpiece within 30 minutes (figure 0.3). Additionally, upon request from Hanaga, Horikawa did a performance wearing a loincloth alone, thrashing in a red-stained snow field (figure 4.10). He also made imprints of his body on a pile of snow higher than his head, which he would later develop as *Snow Performance* in the 1980s. For the second execution, on February 15, Maeyama and another member joined to repeat the feat, for Hanaga and about 10 viewers, including Unagami, watching from the bridge. As his solo act, Maeyama recruited a high-school student in the audience to help him draw two seemingly infinite lines in red and blue, expanding on one of his ongoing engagements with measurement of nothingness (figure 4.11, plate 13).

Hanaga was an agile promoter. After the first execution, he enticed *Asahi Graph* to send its reporter to the second execution and managed to get the project featured in the March 6 issue of *Asahi Graph*, which put it on the cover and ran a three-page opening article.[45] The national exposure was followed by a four-page article in the April issue of *Geijutsu seikatsu* (Art life), for which he also provided an uncredited

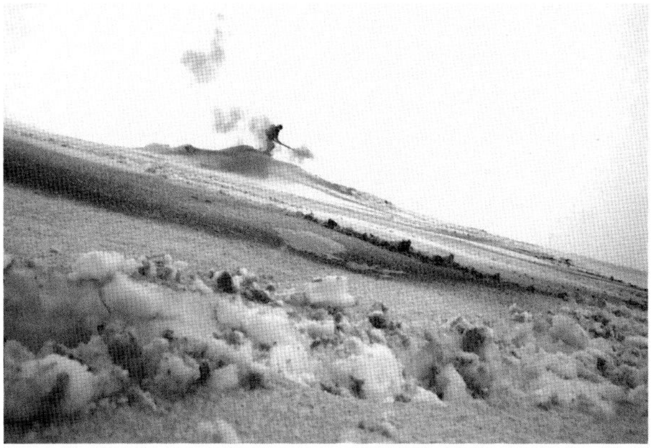

FIGURE 4.9
GUN, *Event to Change the Image of Snow*, 1970. Documentary photograph of performance art. Photo © Hanaga Mitsutoshi. (Also plate 12.)

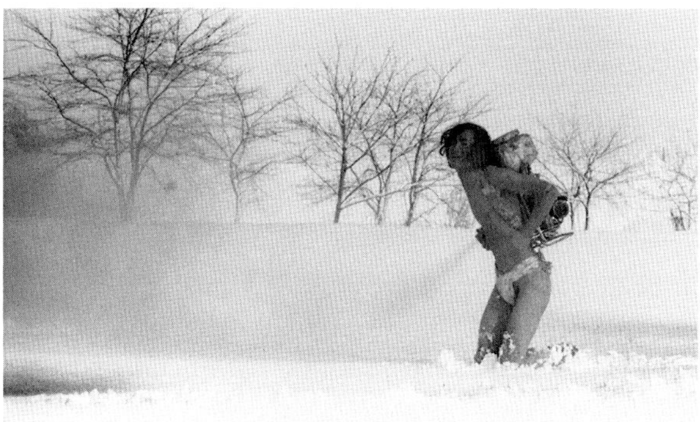

FIGURE 4.10
Horikawa Michio spraying on the snow for *Event to Change the Image of Snow*, 1970. Documentary photograph of performance art. Photo © Hanaga Mitsutoshi.

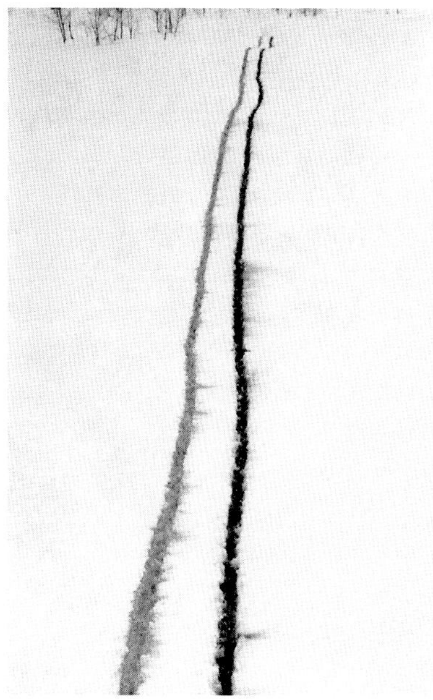

FIGURE 4.11
Maeyama Tadashi, *Event to Change the Image of Snow (Trajectory of Steps)*, 1970. Documentary photograph of performance art. Photo by Horikawa Michio. (Also plate 13.)

text to accompany Iso's photographs.[46] Among the frequent hazards of publicity in the mass media were overt sensationalism and misrepresentation. In this respect, having a photojournalist on the team was a real asset in GUN's publicity campaign. Most significantly, in both articles their sentiment as snow-country habitants—involving "fear of white"[47] and the "heavy weight of white"[48]—was accurately communicated to the nationwide audience of readers, so that they could understand the meaning of a color abstraction on the white ground. This publicity, especially the work's spectacular visuality, landed GUN's *Event to Change the Image of Snow* on the back cover of *Art as Action and Concept*, the 11th volume of the publisher Kōdansha's 13-volume series *Art Now*, in 1972. Its striking image was paired with another visually and conceptually stunning work, Charlotte Moorman playing Nam June Paik's *TV Cello* of 1971, on the front cover. However, most telling was the pairing of GUN's project and Robert Smithson's magnificent *Spiral Jetty* on the volume's advertising flier, with its front bearing works by GUN and three other practitioners and the back devoted to Smithson's.[49] GUN's path from the very local material (snow) to an accolade in the international context was glorious. Still, GUN's problem was what to do next, away from the center.

An Anti-Military Soldier in Sado: GUN's Political Turns

The realization of *Event to Change the Image of Snow* in February 1970 revitalized GUN with a few new faces joining the group, although it fatally accelerated the departure of the more conventionally minded members. The group was as good as nonexistent except that Maeyama and Horikawa were in close contact, and together with a new member, Satō Hideharu, they communicated with each other through mail art. By early 1971, GUN took a decisive political turn. In search of a viable mode of collectivism, they proposed a "Postal Mailing Front" (Yūsō Sensen), seeking nationwide alliance with antiwar teachers and activists by issuing a newsletter modeled after political tabloids. Their political efficacy may have been minimal, but the Postal Mailing Front served as a vehicle to disseminate their conceptualist works. This shift was spurred on by an incident involving a local post of the Self-Defense Forces on Sado Island in Niigata Prefecture.

In Japan as elsewhere, all politics is local. In the postwar decades, the nation's self-defense and its military alliance with the U.S. were constantly contested in light of its postwar Constitution, which has earned the nickname of "Peace Constitution" due to its Article 9 that unambiguously renounces warfare. The two nationwide *Anpo* struggles in 1960 and 1970 highlighted the popular aspiration for peace in the 1960s against the backdrop of the intensifying Cold War and Vietnam War, in which the country became an implicit collaborator under the U.S.-Japan Security Treaty. In addition, the protest movements played out at several incendiary local spots in the 1950s and 1960s, including Okinawa. Closely related to ordinary people's lives, local politics offered more concrete rallying points, which frequently gained a national profile as they spilled into the courtroom. One of them was the incident on Sado, which was unique because the protest came from within the Self-Defense Forces (SDF). The so-called "Konishi Anti-Military Struggle" began in the turbulent days of 1969 leading up to the contested extension of *Anpo* in June 1970, as the state geared up to deploy every means possible to suppress opposition forces. So intent was the state that it contemplated the mobilization of SDF under the pretext of maintaining public safety and began the training for such deployment. The incident on Sado centered on Konishi Makoto, a 21-year-old defense-force airman specialized in radar surveillance.[50] The location of Sado's radar facility in the midst of the Sea of Japan made it a strategic outpost against the Soviet Union in the context of the Cold War. Fully conversant with the SDF ideology, Konishi began to have doubts about the state-controlled military forces in the late 1960s, as his correspondence study of law at Hōsei University in Tokyo advanced. Though not averse to warfare and military forces per se, he developed the idea of a militia as a people's military, based on his understanding of the Second Amendment to the American Constitution. He thus opposed the state mobilization of SDF against the anti-*Anpo* and antiwar demonstrations, which he considered expressions of popular will. (This is why his struggle is called "anti-military," or *hangun*, not "antiwar.") He authored and clandestinely distributed fliers titled "Anti-*Anpo*," and eventually refused to participate in the mobilization training in the fall of 1969.

To make a long story short, Konishi was quickly arrested and tried for the crime of sabotage under the SDF Law at the Niigata Regional Court. (Article 76 of the Japanese Constitution prohibits a special court from trying a certain category of people, such as SDF members. There is thus no court-martial in Japan.) His trial, which began in July 1970, became a major leftwing cause and the first test case to contest the very constitutionality of SDF. A series of protests were waged in Niigata in support of the rebelling soldier, with many activists traveling from outside the prefecture (figure 4.12). The trial concluded with a verdict of not guilty in 1975, although the court predictably avoided deciding on SDF's constitutionality. With this partial victory, Konishi went on to become a widely published military critic.

Hoping to partake in the avant-garde spirit in a political arena, Maeyama and Horikawa joined the demonstrations in support of Konishi in 1970–1971.[51] These two artists had made a modest attempt at political art, but the experience with the Konishi Anti-Military Struggle decisively radicalized them. The ground was laid for their Postal Mailing Front by their mail-art exchanges in 1969–1970, which took the form of anti-authority intervention into the postal system. When Horikawa began his stone mailing project, his act was unconventional and unexpected yet completely lawful, as he followed the postal regulations to the letter. The priority was to lawfully insert stones into the postal circuit so as to achieve a larger goal of stirring up everyday consciousness in their recipients. In their mail-art exchange, Maeyama, Horikawa, and

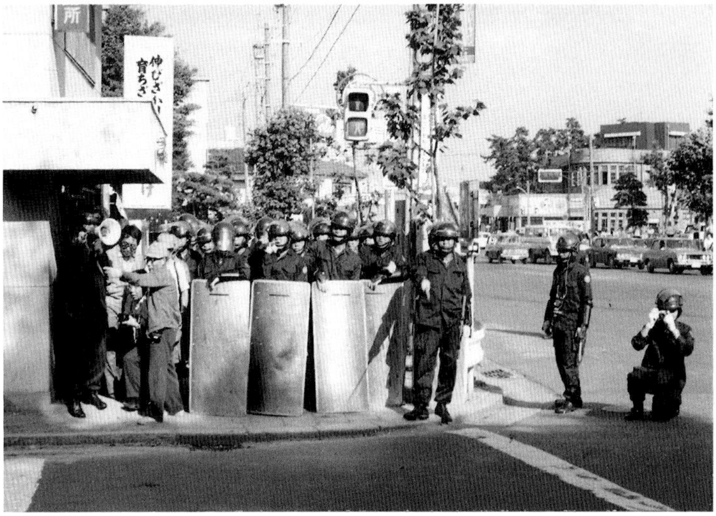

FIGURE 4.12
Horikawa Michio, *Niigata, 1971.7.5 (Armored Police at a Konishi Anti-Military Struggle Demonstration)*. From *Photo Postcard Series* (set of 14), 1970–1972. Collection of the artist.

Satō began to explore ways to push the postal regulations to their limits and beyond using the post office's prepaid postcard, which was a ubiquitous communication tool in postwar Japan when the telephone was still costly. The three artists developed four basic strategies: (1) to physically alter the prepaid postcard; (2) to affix no or insufficient postage; (3) to inscribe a bogus sender and/or recipient; and (4) to create other kinds of confusion. The post office is generally good at spotting irregularity, but some may elude the sharp eye of bureaucracy. When irregularity is discovered, the postcard may be returned to the sender; if not, the recipient is required to pay the additional postage incurred by the irregularity in order to receive it. Thus, whether discovered or not, the mailing constitutes a successful intervention.[52]

Among intriguing examples created by GUN members, Maeyama's "double-sided New Year's postcard," dating from December 1969, is a masterpiece of "confusion," exemplifying the fourth strategy (figure 4.13). In this mailing, he reproduced the address side of an already mailed 1969 postcard on the text side of a 1970 postcard, which was filled out with the same name and address on its address side. Thanks to the consistent design scheme the post office uses on the prepaid New Year's postcards year after year, both sides look very much alike, except that the text side bears a postmark from the previous year. One may write or draw anything on the text side according to the postal regulations, and at least one postcard reached its recipient, Yoshimura Masunobu (a former Neo Dada member). But the post office seized one addressed to

Horikawa and returned it to Maeyama with an official notice warning him not to do it again, for it was indeed confusing. Maeyama made the whole thing—the returned postcard and the official notice (bottom two sheets in figure 4.13)—into his March 1970 contribution to the publication *Psychophysiology Research Institute*. Instead of communication, Maeyama's postcard engendered disturbance within the postal system, challenging this state-run institution in the conformist society of Japan. He forced the post office to perform extra work, with his double New Year's postcard reaching the Postal Inspection Bureau in Tokyo for deliberation. It was another way to reach the distant center of Tokyo from remote Niigata.[53]

Following their radicalization with the Konishi Anti-Military Struggle, GUN applied this mail-art experience to a newsletter operation, which they revived after long hiatus following their early years. In the new format, they combined political sloganeering and conceptualist art works. The inaugural issue, dated March 10, 1971, set the tone, proclaiming: "Stand Up, All Fighting Workers, Students, and Citizens, for

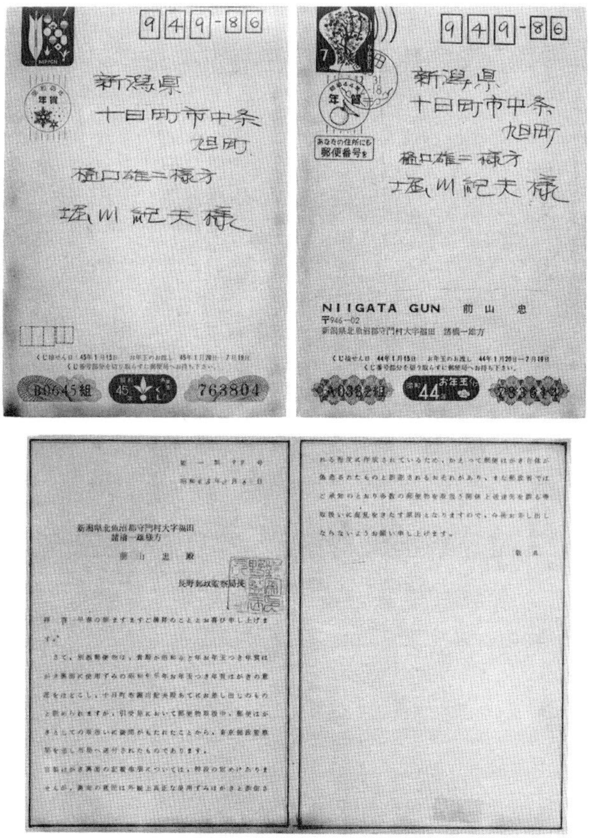

FIGURE 4.13
Maeyama Tadashi, *Double-Sided Nengajō and Notice from Nagano Postal Inspection Office*, 1970. From *Psychophysiology Research Institute* (1969–1970). Printed matter; 29.7 × 21 cm. Collection of the artist.

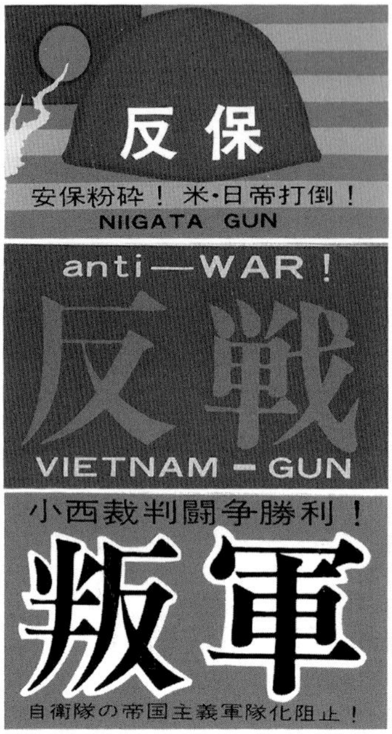

FIGURE 4.14
Maeyama Tadashi, *Antiwar Stickers*, 1971. Decals; 4.7 × 8.2 cm each. Collection of the artist.

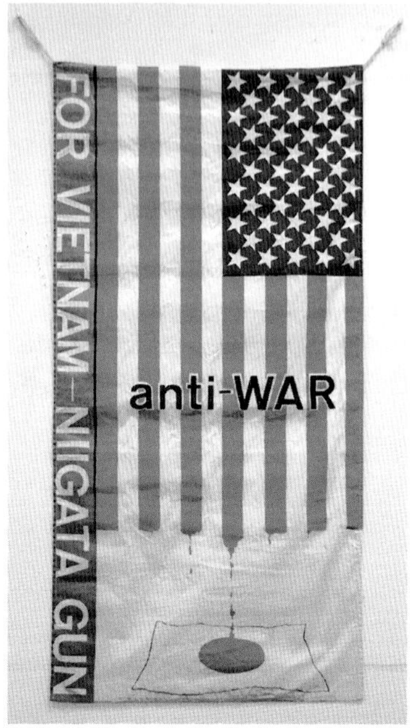

FIGURE 4.15
Maeyama Tadashi, *Antiwar Flag*, 1970. Fabric; 98 × 48 cm. Collection of the artist. (Also plate 14.)

the Anti-Imperialism Struggle!"[54] It carried an obligatory amount of ideological speech and a number of slogans of the day, topped by the one dear to their heart, "Win the Konishi Anti-Military Struggle!" But the essence of their operation concerned three stickers Maeyama designed with the logos "Anti-Military" (in support of Konishi), "Antiwar" (*hansen*), and "Anti-*Anpo*" (*hanpo*) (figure 4.14). Those interested could acquire a set by donating 100 yen and show solidarity by putting them "on every doorway, on every room, on every bag!," as the slogan suggested.[55] The most political by temperament among GUN's members, Maeyama must have understood it was no time for aesthetics. Compared with his previous political work from 1970, *Antiwar Flag*, the stickers were more straightforward, with typography holding the design together. Gone was the graphic ingenuity of the earlier work's flag indicting the U.S. (the Stars and Stripes on top) for the "blood" it shed in the Vietnam War, and Japan (the *hinomaru* flag at bottom) for willingly accepting this blood to preserve its national polity (represented by the red circle of the rising sun) (figure 4.15, plate 14). GUN's newsletter was in contrast dead serious, perhaps too serious, both in its political speechifying and graphic design.

It was in the newsletter's second issue, dated 10 days later, that GUN announced the "Postal Mailing Front," proposing to "nationwide postal activists" that they should "Gather together at the Postal Mailing Front!" and "Rise for Zero-Yen Mailing, a Tactic Proposed by GUN!" Continuing the stern tone from the first issue, they included a disclaimer with their proposal:

> This tactic has nothing to do with chain letters of happiness or unhappiness, one-off rogue mails, or the child's play of so-called "mail art," all of which abound in our society.
>
> We must deploy all necessary means to strengthen people's solidarity, and our Postal Mailing Front must be a surefire component of this effort.[56]

The Front implored "postal mailing guerrillas" to undertake Zero-Yen Mailing as a way to "shoot bullets at targets." Specifically, a suggestion was made for postal activists to send at least nine mailings (bullets) each to Prime Minister Satō Eisaku; their mailings should bear a message of protest but no postage. To facilitate "daily guerrilla acts," GUN issued a *Zero-Yen Stamp.*

Zero-Yen Stamp was Horikawa's contribution (figure 4.16). The work was a tribute to Akasegawa Genpei, his conceptualist predecessor who had bravely and humorously combated state power through his *Greater Japan Zero-Yen Note* of 1967.[57] Building on this example, Horikawa devised a series of unusable postage stamps featuring politicians in power from 1971 onward. The first was Satō, who was an "incompetent imperialist," as he noted in the top of the stamp.

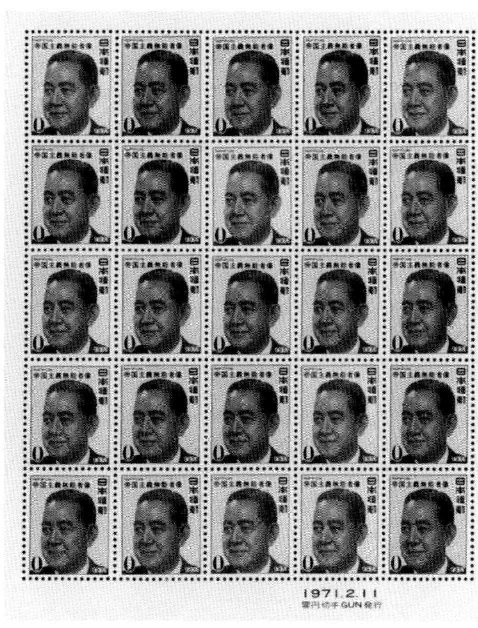

FIGURE 4.16
Horikawa Michio, *Zero-Yen Stamp*, 1971. Printed sheet. Collection of the artist.

By the time the third newsletter issue was published on May 5, 1971, carrying member Satō Hideharu's proposal for *Peaceful Japan Prize*, at least one group, On-Off in Nagoya, had joined the Postal Mailing Front. But the fourth issue, dated May 6 and carrying no art project, marked the last of GUN's political sloganeering. On the art world front, that same May, Maeyama was invited by the critic Haryū Ichirō to show his *Antiwar* ensemble (the set of stickers and similarly slogan-bearing flags) at that year's Mainichi Contemporary (figure 4.17). Here, too, his political effort was thwarted: a donation box he had placed as part of his work for those willing to obtain his stickers was removed by the organizer immediately after the opening under the excuse of the museum's display regulations. In protest, Maeyama withdrew the whole work within a week. After 1972, GUN returned to the more conventional activities of exhibitions and outdoor performances. As a postscript to their political turn, in 1977, one year after the semicentennial of Emperor Shōwa's reign, Maeyama and Horikawa made their statements for the occasion: Horikawa's sheet of *Zero-Yen Stamps* commemorating His Majesty's 51-year reign (figure 4.18) and Maeyama's artist's book, *Anti-Emperor System*, critically tracing the history of Japan that included Japan's aggression into Asia under the emperor's name.[58]

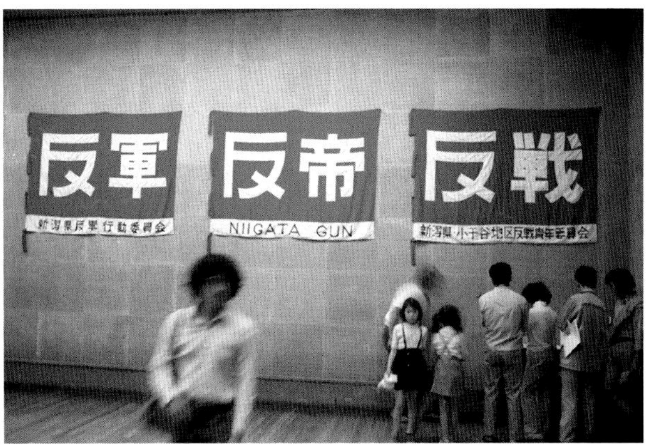

FIGURE 4.17
Maeyama Tadashi, *Antiwar Flags*, 1971. Installation view with a table bearing a donation box, *Antiwar Stickers*, and *GUN* newsletter, at *Contemporary Art Exhibition of Japan* at Tokyo Metropolitan Art Museum. Photo by Horikawa Michio.

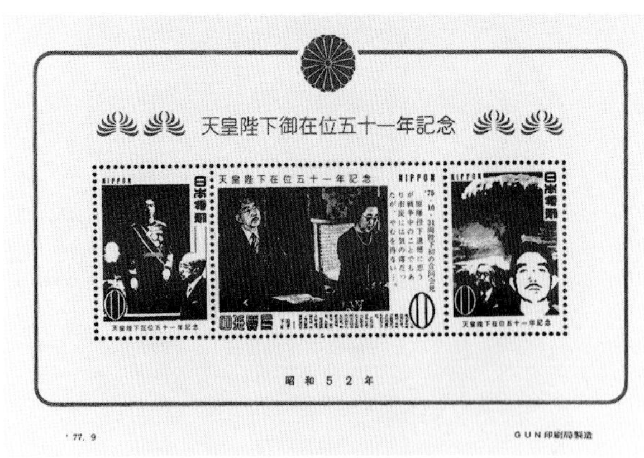

FIGURE 4.18
Horikawa Michio, *Zero-Yen Commemorative Stamp for 51st Anniversary of Emperor Shōwa's Reign*, 1977. Printed sheet. Collection of the artist.

* * *

Latecomers to contemporary art from a remote province, GUN made its first task to learn the mechanisms of Tokyo's art world. In retrospect, their true work began when they lost momentum as a group in late 1968 after their forays into the capital. From 1969 onward, focusing on their own locale, they managed to develop do-it-yourself solutions in order to participate in the rapidly evolving scenes of contemporary art in Tokyo. While closing up the distance, they realized a state of contemporaneity with Tokyo. Just as 1960s artists in Japan caught up with their counterparts in Euro-America and even sometimes went ahead of them, so GUN in Niigata caught up with their Tokyo counterparts and even went ahead of them—producing internationally relevant works. In other words, they realized "contemporaneity" on two levels, international and national, through their performative land art and mail art. To achieve this feat, they learned well from their contemporaries, both inside and outside Japan.

In the strict sense of definitions given in chapter 1, their keen awareness of their contemporaries makes a case for connection; but at a time when artists had a growing sense of international contemporaneity, the nature of this "connection" varied from that of Yoshihara Jirō, for example, when he first encountered Pollock's canvases almost 20 years earlier. In 1951, Yoshihara exercised his power of eye to discern the American painter's "true discovery, true originality" in his drip method that he pursued "persistently and profoundly"[59]—despite the almost total lack of regard for Abstract Expressionism among Japanese critics at the time. In contrast, the news of Earthworks that intrigued GUN in the late 1960s was part of the ready-to-take information flow provided by the art media. Furthermore, it was widely shared not just in Japan but in many other regions in the world, among other new practices known and available to GUN. The heightened perception of international contemporaneity in Japan around 1970 engendered a situation in which the significance of connection (knowledge of, say, Earthworks) must be weighed against that of local situations (a postwar evolution of land-based practices). The distinction between connection and resonance is less than clear-cut, with the two overlapping inextricably, especially when artists—such as GUN and to some extent The Play—consciously deployed interpoetic strategies with a resonating spirit and within a local tradition. This hybrid situation may be called "connected resonance." With this understanding, chapter 6 will examine the nature of GUN's land art as part of resonance studies by looking closely at what I call the "culture of showing" in 1960s Japan, in which showing was given the ultimate priority over all other concerns at a time when the market for contemporary art barely existed.

5 CONNECTION STUDIES

FOLLOWING NARRATIVE TANGENTS

Toward the end of the 1960s, Japanese artists and critics were widely aware of international contemporaneity, whether they embraced it or not and whether they belonged to the mainstream or in the wilderness. This might seem to resemble the sense of contemporaneity pervasive in the early 21st century, but the context was rather different. In the early 21st century, the state of contemporaneity has become so widespread that "being global" almost feels self-evident, even though the gap between global and local is still vast. Back in the 1960s, the state of contemporaneity was sporadic, and "being international" was not a given. Certainly, actual connections were more frequently made than during the immediate postwar years. Still, connectedness was hard-earned. It had to be consciously created, while opportunities to connect either institutionally or individually remained occasional and limited.

The first section of this chapter seeks out two sets of narrative tangents and related comparisons by studying direct interfaces, both incoming to Japan and outgoing. The first centers on *Tokyo Biennale '70: Between Man and Matter*. A major event that almost single-handedly made visible the state of international contemporaneity for a

Japanese audience, the exhibition serves as a valuable contact point from which local and international narrative tangents can be drawn and through which a number of comparisons can be formulated. I identify two narrative arcs, international and domestic, in terms of exhibition innovations. For comparative studies, of particular note is the presence of the wilderness in this exhibition, especially of Matsuzawa Yutaka, as an acknowledgment of its immense relevance in an international arena. His work is compared with that of On Kawara, also in the exhibition and also from the diasporic wilderness, so to speak.

If the wilderness fared well in this "incoming interface" of international contemporaneity, it showed its vitality in an "outgoing interface," too. The second set of narrative tangents stems from Matsuzawa's attempts at international networking through mail art under various eschatological guises. Though his success was limited due to what may be called "discursive malfunction,"[1] his effort was heroic, all the more because the reality of international contemporaneity felt indirect for most Japanese artists, whose international experiences were limited to the incoming flow of information through art journalism. In this sense, Matsuzawa was a rare instance of international contemporaneity during the 1970s as a whole, for far less active effort was made institutionally than in the 1960s to develop outgoing interfaces.

Following some methodological notes on discourse, the second section of chapter 5 will focus on discourse and "internalized interfaces," which involve indirect relationships with the international and "repossession" of imported ideas.

Tokyo Biennale 1970 as a Contact Point

A milestone in the annals of postwar Japanese art, *Tokyo Biennale 1970: Between Man and Matter* was organized by the Mainichi newspaper company and held at the Tokyo Metropolitan Art Museum in May 1970. Curated by the art critic Nakahara Yūsuke, the exhibition gathered 40 artists who attempted to focus on "relationships between man and matter that contain endless contradictions,"[2] which Nakahara believed exemplified the most salient characteristic of new art that looked like neither painting nor sculpture in the conventional sense. Mostly young, in their twenties and thirties, the artists hailed from 25 cities (including 10 Japanese municipalities) and demonstrated the most recent trends, ranging from minimalism to conceptualism, land art to performance art (see table 5.1). As such, the exhibition represented by far the most tangible display of international contemporaneity yet realized in Japan. Its internationalism was immediately recognized outside Japan, as indicated by its entry in Lucy Lippard's seminal publication *Six Years,* with all the participants' names listed.[3]

Tokyo Biennale 1970 was, however, more than a sum of these artists' works. Including such well-known names as Christo and Sol LeWitt as well as such local figures as Matsuzawa Yutaka and Horikawa Michio, the roster of participants tells only a fraction of the story. What distinguished *Tokyo Biennale 1970* was Nakahara's proposal for the

TABLE 5.1

Artists in *Tokyo Biennale 1970* (ordered by age, then by surname)

Name	Residence	Age
Penone, Giuseppe	Turin	23
Horikawa Michio*	Niigata Prefecture	24
Nomura Hitoshi	Kyoto	25
Schnyder, Jean-Frédéric	Bern	25
Albrecht, Dietrich	Stuttgart	26
Koshimizu Susumu	Yokohama	26
Narita Katsuhiko	Tokyo	26
Zorio, Gilberto	Turin	26
Enokura Kōji*	Tokyo	27
Inumaki Kenji	Osaka	27
Dibbets, Jan	Amsterdam	29
Flanagan, Barry	London	29
Nauman, Bruce	Pasadena	29
Raetz, Markus	Amsterdam	29
Sonnier, Keith	New York	29
van Elk, Ger	Amsterdam	29
Kaltenbach, Stephen J.	New York	30
Kawaguchi Tatsuo	Kobe	30
Koike Kazushige	Shizuoka	30
Panamarenko	Antwerp	30
Tanaka Shintarō	Hitachi	30
Rinke, Klaus	Düsseldorf	31
Serra, Richard	New York	31
Shōji Satoru	Nagoya	31
Buren, Daniel	Paris	32
Ruthenbeck, Reiner	Düsseldorf	33
Fabro, Luciano	Milan	34
Haacke, Hans	New York	34
Kounellis, Jannis	Rome	34
Takamatsu Jirō	Tokyo	34
Andre, Carl	New York	35
Christo	New York	35
Louw, Roelof	London	35
Boezem, Marinus	Gorinchem, Holland	36
Kawara, On	New York	37
LeWitt, Sol	New York	42
Kolibal, Stanislav	Prague	45
Krasinski, Edward	Warsaw	45
Merz, Mario	Turin	45
Matsuzawa Yutaka	Shimo Suwa	48

Note: Asterisks (*) indicate Japanese artists who did not participate in the Mainichi Contemporary in 1969.

exhibition's organizing principle: *rinjō-shugi*, which can be translated as "on-site-ism," or "in-situ-ism."[4] A crucial element in his curatorial vision, the idea of site specificity encouraged the participating artists to deal directly with the site (the city, the museum, or the exhibition itself). To give them the full benefit of "on-site-ism," he assigned only one or two artists to each of the museum's spacious galleries. This decision made it an unusually sparse exhibition for Japan, where large-scale international exhibitions were routinely conceived on a scale of hundreds.[5]

The result in 1970 was aesthetically diverse and critically profound. Floors were as important as walls: Whereas Enokura Kōji covered his floor with sheets of paper soaked with machine oil, Hans Haacke spread a network of plastic water pipes on his (which extended to the outside). Emptying out the space was as fundamental as filling it up: two artists, Matsuzawa Yutaka and Jannis Kounellis, presented the empty galleries as their works (figure 5.1). Outside the museum was as relevant as inside: Daniel Buren pasted his signature stripes in downtown locations, while Richard Serra, among other things, planted a Japanese cedar tree in Ueno Park, where the museum was located. Instead of going outside, some brought the outside in, as with Horikawa Michio's *Mail Art by Sending Stones*. And time was as elemental as space: if photography helped Nomura Hitoshi and Jan Dibbets to document time, video delivered Bruce Nauman's performances from New York (figure 5.2). These non-paintings and non-sculptures represented an increasingly dematerialized state of vanguard practices contemporaneously progressing both in Japan and across Euro-America.

Making it all happen was a feat in itself. Yet that was not all. Nakahara's call for site specificity prompted many foreign artists to visit Tokyo for advance site inspection or on-site production and installation, helping reduce the psychological distance from the international practically to zero. It was a thrill for the young Horikawa, a GUN member based in Niigata and an invited artist, to witness Richard Serra digging into the ground in front of the museum to produce *To Encircle: Base Plate (Hexagram)*, Carl Andre scattering metal scraps on the floor as *Rust Garden* (figure 5.3), and Klaus Rinke performing *Masculine-Feminine* with Monika Baumgartl in his room, as much as it was to see Takamatsu Jirō chiseling his logs of *Oneness* on site and Koike Kazushige piling up *Stones* sliced into halves (figure 5.4). Even though most exhibition-goers could not see what Horikawa had witnessed on the day of installation, the lively stories about their preparations, some of which were avidly reported by art journalism and the general press (in which Mainichi naturally played a central role), became an integral part of their exhibition experiences. In a rare case of real-world politics entering the museum, the news of the Kent State shootings on May 4 prompted Andre and Serra to create an impromptu protest piece, *The Pig Will Eat Its Children*, in time for the May 10 opening.[6] This would not have happened without their presence in Tokyo. In sum, Nakahara enabled a dynamic interplay of international contemporaneity to materialize in Tokyo, rather than being content with a static display of resonant works.

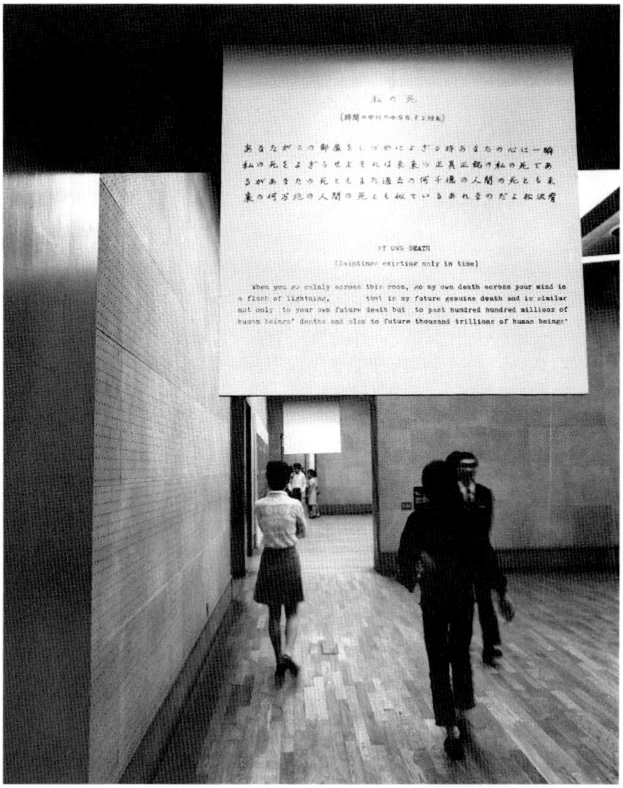

FIGURE 5.1
Matsuzawa Yutaka, *My Own Death*, 1970. Installation view at *Tokyo Biennale 1970* at Tokyo Metropolitan Art Museum. Minemura Toshiaki Papers, on loan to Keiō University Art Center, Tokyo. © Hara Eizaburō.

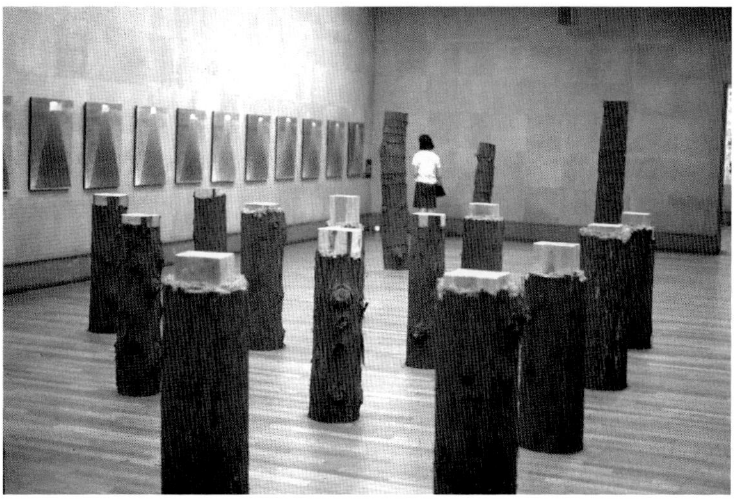

FIGURE 5.2
Nomura Hitoshi's *Dry Ice* on the wall and Takamatsu Jirō's *Thirty-Seven Onenesses* on the floor. Installation view at *Tokyo Biennale 1970* at Tokyo Metropolitan Art Museum. Photo by Horikawa Michio.

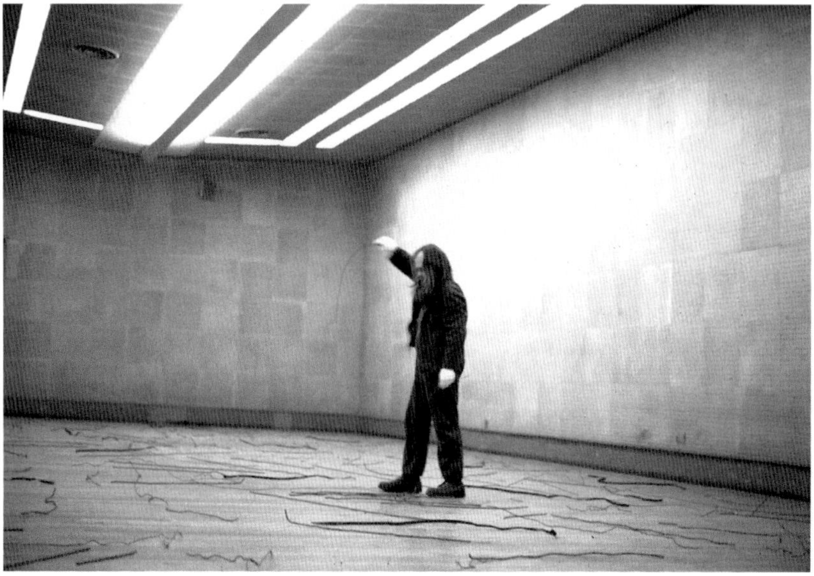

FIGURE 5.3
Carl Andre creating *Rust Garden*, at *Tokyo Biennale 1970* at Tokyo Metropolitan Art Museum. Photo by Horikawa Michio.

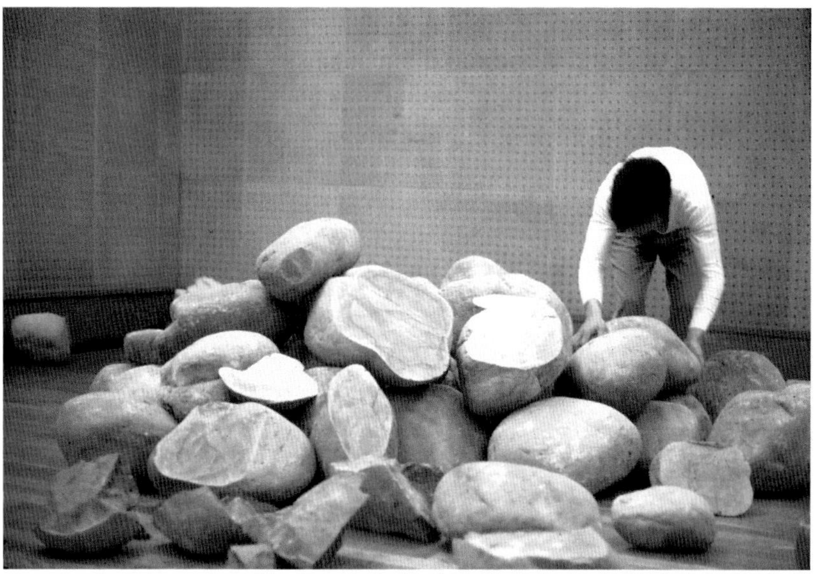

FIGURE 5.4
Koike Kazushige creating *Stones*, at *Tokyo Biennale 1970* at Tokyo Metropolitan Art Museum. Photo by Horikawa Michio.

In terms of exhibition innovations, *Tokyo Biennale 1970* belongs to a historic lineage of experimental exhibitions that captured the changing nature of new art around 1970. It followed three 1969 exhibitions, *Square Pegs in Round Holes* at the Stedelijk Museum, Amsterdam; *When Attitudes Become Form* at Kunsthalle Bern; and *Anti-Illusion: Procedures/Materials* at the Whitney Museum of American Art, New York, while preceding the legendary *Documenta 5* organized by Harald Szeemann in 1972. A clear line of connection existed between the 1969 predecessors and Nakahara's 1970 exhibition, for he conducted extensive research, which included studies of these three exhibitions,[7] to realize an unprecedented enterprise in Mainichi's exhibition history. Indeed, *Tokyo Biennale 1970* boasted many firsts.[8] It was the first time that a single "commissioner" (that is, artistic director) was charged to select all the artists based on his aesthetic and critical judgment, rather than a jury-based or committee-based selection process. The appointment of the single commissioner meant another organizational first: the artist selections were not based on Venice-style national representation. It was also the first large-scale exhibition to do away with awards, at a time when the award system was a prerequisite of large-scale exhibitions organized by Mainichi or other entities (such as the outdoor exhibitions at Suma and Hakone). Taken together, *Tokyo Biennale 1970* was more a Documenta than a Venice Biennale. In this sense the narrative line from the exhibitions of 1969 continued through Nakahara's exhibition in 1970 to Szeemann's *Documenta 5* in 1972, which captured the continuing strength of conceptualism that emphasized site specificity, duration of time, performativity, and phenomenological viewership.

These firsts of *Tokyo Biennale 1970* were orchestrated by Minemura Toshiaki, the de facto exhibition manager for the Mainichi newspaper company, who selected Nakahara for the commissioner's position. Minemura was also instrumental in reengineering the biannual Mainichi Contemporary which the company sponsored alternately with the Mainichi International (the latter renamed as "Tokyo Biennale" in 1961). At the time of the 1968 Mainichi Contemporary, Nakahara had made the provocative observation, "The goal of an exhibition should not be to sort out works [that artists made] after the fact, but to proactively assist creative acts."[9] Intent on revamping the contemporary biannual, Minemura took a cue from Nakahara and introduced a few innovations for the 1969 Contemporary. One was a curated section, "Frontiers of Contemporary Art," the organization of which he entrusted to Nakahara's fellow Big Three critic, Haryū Ichirō. The 86 artists invited to this section were mostly in their twenties and thirties. They were divided into seven themes, such as "Reproduction and Originals" and "Eros and Humor." These themes were intended as a test to see whether Japan's contemporary art had "reached a stage wherein its practices can be examined not through imported ideas but its own ideas,"[10] in Minemura's words. That is to say, Minemura saw a stake in nurturing "our own art" (*jimae bijutsu*) through the Frontiers section. Particularly important was the theme of "Labyrinthine

Room," for which nine artists were invited to work in "rooms," or partitioned spaces of their own. (Among them was Ikemizu Keiichi, who won the Frontier Grand Prize with his *Eggs in Orange: Breakfast for Mr. Play.*) A seed of "on-site-ism" was sown in the "Labyrinthine Room" of 1969. Thus, two developments in exhibition practice, international and domestic, converged in *Tokyo Biennale 1970*. This emphasis on commissioning new works of living artists for an exhibition was radical at the time, establishing the Tokyo Biennale as an early example of an exhibition-as-event project in the international world of contemporary art. Moreover, the resulting site specificity pointed to a global shift from studio-made painting and sculpture to on-site installations.

At *Tokyo Biennale 1970*, Nakahara's selections from Japan included a sizable number of regional artists, though not all of them hailed from the wilderness (see table 5.1 for the participants' regional distribution). Of 12 Japanese-born artists, only four were from the Tokyo-Yokohama metropolitan areas. The continuity from Mainichi's 1969 contemporary biannual, which included 10 of these 12, either by invitation or through open calls, indicates the acknowledged importance of those regional or wilderness artists for the overall evolution of *gendai bijutsu*. Their presence was particularly prominent in the critic's selection of conceptualists. A former graduate student in physics and the most analytical and coolest-minded of the Big Three critics, Nakahara presented such prominent Euro-American conceptualists as Sol LeWitt, Daniel Buren, and Jan Dibbets alongside two generations of Japanese conceptualists. The younger conceptualists were generally analytical and systemic in their strategies and varyingly engaged the external world.[11] Among the very first Japanese artists to adopt photography as a primary means of inquiry, Nomura Hitoshi of Kyoto "sculpted time" by recording the disappearance of such volatile matter as dry ice and iodine (figure 5.2).[12] A member of the land-minded Group "I," Kawaguchi Tatsuo applied his concern with cognition and existence to a new series of photo-based work, which he staged on the beach of Suma near his home in Kobe.[13] The material of choice for Shōji Satoru, from Nagoya, was newspaper. Two works he presented are self-explanatory from their titles: *30 Newspapers Painted Out with Red Except a Square Part* and *52 Copied Newspapers on a Part of Which the Real Newspapers Are Stuck Mar. 31st–May 1st*. The youngest among the set was Horikawa Michio, who sent 13 stones to the exhibition in reference to the Apollo 13 mission launched in April.

It was memorable to see two veterans, On Kawara and Matsuzawa Yutaka, share the stage with their new achievements in conceptualism. A rising star of 1950s art in Japan, On Kawara had been missing in action since his move to Mexico in 1959. A nomad of the diasporic wilderness, away from the attention of his homeland, he resurfaced in Tokyo with his *I Got Up* series in the 1969 Mainichi Contemporary (a year after he had begun it). This work, listed in the checklist as *Pictorial Diary*, won a prize sponsored by the Museum of Contemporary Art, Nagaoka. For this set, he sent a postcard every day for the entire month of April. Interestingly, Kawara selected 15 × 23 cm postcards of New York City, much larger than his usual ones (approximately 10 × 15 cm), probably conscious of their display effect. He chose three images that typified the city—the Empire State Building, the UN building, and the city's skyline—and sent 10 of each in a minimalist serialism.[14] Kawara's contribution to *Tokyo Biennale 1970* was what he would later call *Everyday Meditation*. In a gallery he shared with Tanaka Shintarō, who created a shiny black skin of urethane that carpeted the floor, 97 freshly painted canvases of *Today* from January 1 to March 31 lined the walls in a single row (figure 5.5).[15] The large quantity of Kawara's "date paintings" were countered by Matsuzawa Yutaka's "empty gallery," titled *My Own Death*, with two panels hanging at the entranceway on either side of his room (figure 5.1).

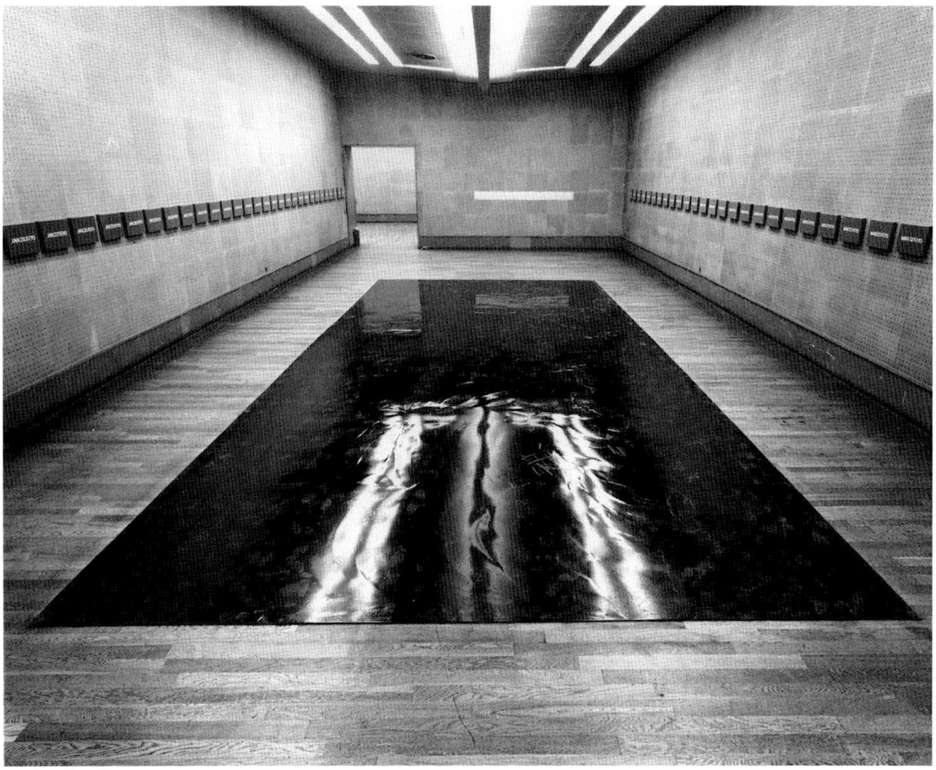

FIGURE 5.5
Tanaka Shintarō's *Congelation* on the floor and On Kawara's *Today* on the walls. Installation view at *Tokyo Biennale 1970* at Tokyo Metropolitan Art Museum. Minemura Toshiaki Papers, on loan to Keiō University Art Center, Tokyo. © Hara Eizaburō.

As it was for Kawara, 1969 was a banner year for Matsuzawa. He was invited to the Mainichi Contemporary's Frontiers section and the Kyoto Modern's *Trends* exhibition, for which he conceived two "empty gallery" situations. For the Mainichi Contemporary, he was asked to participate in the "Labyrinthine Room" section. Rather ominously titled *Ψ Gas Chamber*, his contribution merely consisted of an "immaterial (*hi-jittai*) space of 360 × 360 × 360 centimeters," according to the catalog checklist, which was duly delineated on the floor with red chalk.[16] In the physical manifestation, his room was empty except for a chair and a white square canvas in one corner and a double-sided flier, *Showing This to Light, Sound, and Time? / Yet Another Painting*, on the floor. In his continuing exploration of the gallery as an apparatus, he demanded a great deal from the viewer in his typically enigmatic maximalism: to vanish the whole Mainichi exhibition, visualize a *White Circle*, and devise his or her own *Fundamental Painting* all in one sitting. For the ensuing *Trends* exhibition, he went to the other extreme and presented a very simple exercise of vanishing in *From This Corner: For a Change*.[17] Its flier reads:

> Vanish all that lies in this direction, starting from here, even though what will emerge afterward has not yet known.

Despite the inscrutability of his work, many took note of his utter seriousness in proposing to vanish matter and eschew the five senses.[18] And Nakahara invited him to *Tokyo Biennale 1970*.

For Matsuzawa, *Tokyo Biennale 1970* was practically his first international exposure as a major figure. (His stay in the U.S. in 1955–1957 constituted the exploratory phase of a budding artist.) For an artist long concerned with the issue of communication, it was evident that he had to go bilingual, in Japanese and English. That was an easy part. A difficult part ultimately was deciding what his message would be. How to bring his message of Anti-Civilization to an international audience without being too simplistic or too cryptic? After much deliberation, he decided to present "future," as he proudly reported to his confidant, the critic Takiguchi Shūzō.[19] Two panels placed at either entranceway to the gallery assigned to him bore his message, whose English text reads:

> When you go calmly across this room, [let] go my own death across your mind in a flash of lightning, that is my future genuine death and is similar not only to your own future death but to past hundred hundred millions of human beings' deaths and also to future thousand trillions of human beings'

His "future" death was, however, only nominally a subject of the work, as it in effect made the past, present, and future of the entire human race into the object of reflection. The gallery space he kept empty served as a blank canvas in which the viewer might meditate on a *memento mori* of the post-atomic age.[20] It constituted an understated yet successful marriage of his theory ("Vanishing of Humankind," which he had articulated in 1966) and practice (his radical reconfiguration of what art could be, on which he had worked throughout the decade). Its grandiose sense of time resonated with On Kawara's laborious *One Million Years* (see chapter 6).

A major occasion of international contemporaneity, the exhibition allows us to identify a number of resonances. To name just a few, Dibbets and van Elk, as well as Nomura and Kawaguchi, deployed photography to record time in seriality, while Andre, Christo, and Haacke, as well as Enokura and Tanaka (figure 5.5), used the floor less as a support than as a defining or signifying element of their works. The most striking were the empty galleries presented by Kounellis and Matsuzawa. Matsuzawa's empty gallery operations will be further discussed in chapter 6, but here it is instructive to compare his and Kounellis's materials as listed in the checklist.[21] Above all, the Greek artist needed material objects: ideally he wanted to close the entranceway to his gallery by stacking up rocks, but since this would damage the museum's floor, he instead nominally blocked "a whole room" by inserting an "iron pole" stabilized by "springs" into the opening. In contrast, the materials the Japanese artist gave to the organizer for listing were "consciousness" and "duration of time," which would have to be provided by the viewer, not the artist, whose job was to supply two panels as an operation manual. Although Matsuzawa brilliantly capitalized on the empty space as a container, his intention contradicted the site specificity envisioned by Nakahara's "on-site-ism," because "This room can be that room or that garden or that city or that sea or that sky. It can be non-being or void," as he explained in "Some Exegesis on *My Own Death*."[22] Instead, he orchestrated site specificity by staging a performance, also titled *My Own Death*, in his assigned gallery. Under the watchful gaze of the intermedia artist Yamaguchi Katsuhiro, serving as a witness to the whole rite, Matsuzawa had the female Butoh dancer Tsujimura Kazuko touch his chest through an opening in his shirt and feel his heartbeats until she could visualize his death (figure 5.6). (A longtime collaborator of the artist, Tsujimura had telepathically entrusted three parts of her body to the milky mist at Matsuzawa's *Independent '64 in the Wilderness*.)[23] The use of the artist's body within a museum context had a local tradition heralded by such Anti-Art practitioners as Zero Dimension and Hi Red Center. However, Matsuzawa's body, presented as an emblematic locus of life and death rather than a vehicle of actions, foreshadowed the singular meditation on the body and the artist's presence crystalized by Marina Abramović, for instance, in her *The Artist Is Present* of 2010.

Ultimately, the site specificity that mattered to Matsuzawa was that of the wilderness. Later that year, when he sent a variation of *My Own Death* to *Japan Art Festival*, held at the Guggenheim Museum in New York, he incorporated a highland near his home into his work. The panel reads:

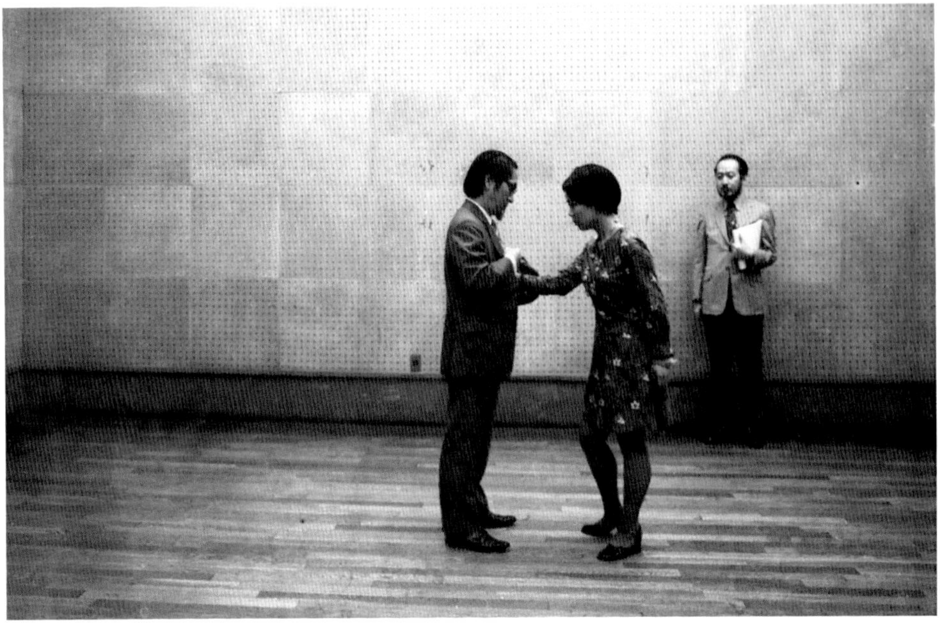

FIGURE 5.6
Matsuzawa Yutaka performing *My Own Death* with Tsujimura Kazuko touching his chest and Yamaguchi Katsuhiro as a witness, at *Tokyo Biennale 1970* at Tokyo Metropolitan Art Museum. Photo © Hanaga Mitsutoshi.

> Now I hand my future death over to you who are passing here by. At the exact same time in a cavern in a central high land in Japan I extract your two hearts from under your breasts and let 'em fly into the milk white mist that is characteristic around here.[24]

Always a man of his word, he trekked to Geiroppara (literally "frog's field") on Kirigamine ("misty peak") Highland, clad in all black—a black mask, black gloves, and a black cloth—and "let his two hearts fly into the sky's window."[25] This was one of his private performances witnessed only by his family members or friends.

* * *

A historic exhibition for 1960s Japan, *Tokyo Biennale 1970* proved to be a one-off experiment, followed by no similar endeavor. Mainichi's international biannual went back to being a more staid affair, having failed to gain poplar support in 1970.[26] In the domestic context, it indeed marked the beginning of the end to an era in which newspaper companies played a leading role in mainstreaming *gendai bijutsu* and exercising internationalism. Thereafter, a primary institutional force that propelled contemporary art was the museums. Two national museums of modern art, in Tokyo and Kyoto, continued to study domestic practices, while prefectures and municipalities began to build art museums to feature modern and contemporary artists of national and regional significance. The year 1970, in fact, marked the beginning of the regional museum construction boom, with the first two regional museums inaugurated in Wakayama and Hyōgo prefectures, with "modern art" in their official names.[27] These museums have prioritized the local; the international frequently meant bringing in modern and contemporary art mainly from Euro-America as special imports. The kind of internationalism that *Tokyo Biennale 1970* represented in sync with international contemporaneity far exceeded public museums' resources and purview. Newspaper companies offered financial and logistical support to the museums, but their roles were mostly limited to behind-the-scenes operations. It was not until 1999 that Japan resumed its international exhibition activities, at a time of exponential growth of global biennales and triennales.[28]

Matsuzwa Yutaka's Communal Internationalism

In 1960s Japan, the state of international contemporaneity was fragile, and direct connections were not so easy to generate, let alone sustain, without will and vision. Even the corporation-backed *Tokyo Biennale 1970* had to be a one-off affair. The vision and will were, however, found in the wilderness—more specifically, in Matsuzawa Yutaka. His leap into the international began auspiciously in 1970, around the same time as *Tokyo Biennale 1970*, through an individual channel. By stepping into an international arena, Matsuzawa entered the second phase of his conceptualism and developed a communicative and communal mode of internationalism. In an era when homebound Japanese artists mostly relied on institutional entities (such as newspaper companies and art magazines) to gain international interfaces, his efforts at international networking were ambitious and exceptional.

The initial contact point was simple enough: an encounter with Adriaan van Ravesteijn, a director of the Art & Project gallery in Amsterdam, who traveled to Japan that spring.[29] Ravesteijn had originally planned to publish and mail out one issue of the gallery's *Bulletin* in Tokyo, featuring Gilbert & George.[30] However, in mid-February, having visited Matsuzawa, he immediately offered to publish the Japanese conceptualist's work. He thus produced not one but two issues (nos. 20 and 21) in March 1970 (figure 5.7). Matsuzawa's bilingual contribution was elegant and poetic, with a 3 × 3 grid accompanied by a command which reads:

> Fill the frame of the diamond-world mandala with water and drink to satisfy your thirst.

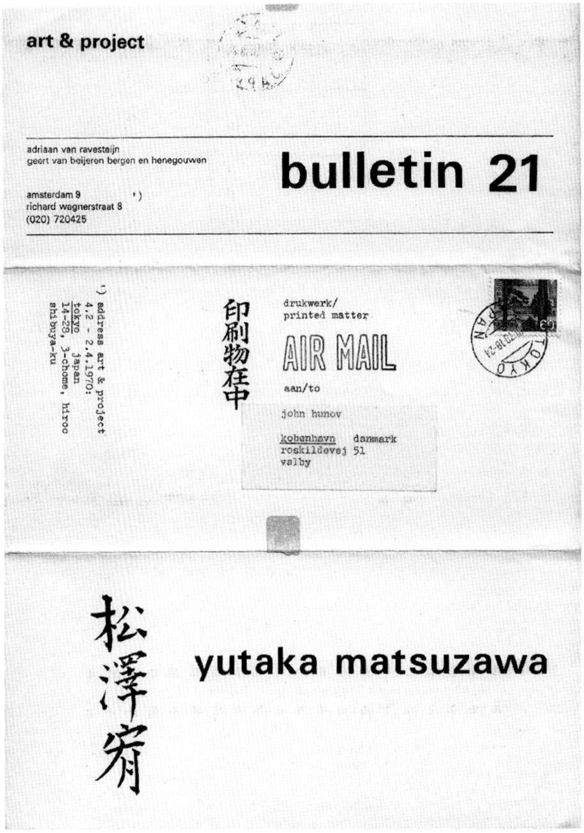

FIGURE 5.7
Matsuzawa Yutaka, *Bulletin 21* (Art & Project, 1970). Letterpress. Collection of Reiko Tomii.

The artist's association with the gallery strengthened upon a second encounter in late March. Earlier that month, Ravesteijn placed a classified ad in newspapers on behalf of Stanley Brouwn for "Land Wanted." The search for an area of one square meter utterly perplexed Japanese realtors, who wanted to know why anybody wanted one square meter of land, but it intrigued Matsuzawa. With the mediation of the critic Nakahara Yūsuke, Matsuzawa offered the required area of land from his mountain property for the sum of Psi yen (figure 5.8). The transaction was duly witnessed by Nakahara, who accompanied Ravesteijn to Shimo Suwa.[31] Thanks to these two interactions, the artist gained a European gallery's representation and thus a viable channel to reach his international peers. His affiliation had an immediate effect in connection with *Information*, an exhibition of conceptualism at the Museum of Modern Art, New

York, later that summer. Although his name does not appear in the exhibition's checklist (thus he was not an official participant), his issue of *Bulletin* was prominently illustrated to represent Art & Project's work in the catalog.[32] More positive results followed. Matsuzawa would subsequently contribute nos. 42 and 84 of *Bulletin* and publish the small booklet *Catechism Art* with Art & Project. To mount a solo exhibition at the gallery in August 1971, he made a monthlong trip during his school's summer recess, traversing the Eurasian continent from Niigata to Moscow to Italy to London. Along the way, he dropped by Stockholm to present *Banner of Vanishing* in a dome set up by the musician Kosugi Takehisa for the *Utopia and Vision* exhibition at Moderna Museet;[33] and visited *Sonsbeek 71*, an outdoor exhibition in Arnhem, where he gave a performance of *Banner of Vanishing* by extending his 15-meter pink banner on the lawn of the Sonsbeek Park. This constituted the first European presentation of the performance, following the first private performance in October 1970[34] at Mount Misa in Shimo Suwa (figure 2.18) and the first public presentation at the Tokyo Metropolitan Art Museum for the 1971 Mainichi Contemporary. In Amsterdam, he accompanied Stanley Brouwn's "walk," visited Lawrence Weiner at a scrapped boat that the American artist had turned into his residence, and "enjoyed listening to his beautiful English" in "a low, quiet voice."[35] He then had a "swell time"[36] with Gilbert & George, a "sculpture worth visiting in London"[37] (figure 5.9).

From the beginning of his international interface, he was intent on promoting his work as well as his recently formed group, Nirvana School. This was a loose-knit assembly of those who embraced his ideas of vanishing and *kannen*. The membership encompassed such like-minded colleagues as Mizukami Jun, a former member of The Play, and such younger conceptualists as Horikawa Michio and Maeyama Tadashi of GUN. The group began to form with his 1969 call for *Psi Art Gathering*, in which interested artists were asked to consider the guidelines, as specified in the flier of the same title:

1. Minimize the material trace as much as possible in accordance with anti-materialism
2. Invisible, immaterial, or imaginary [*kyo*] expressions are desired
3. Search for expression of non-*bhava* (being), non-*śūnya* (void), non-non-*bhava*, and non-non-*śūnya*
4. I await crazy enough methods[38]

The call attracted young sympathizers and led to *End of an Illusion That Is Art*, an exhibition at the Nagano Prefectural Shinano Art Museum. This was, in Matsuzawa's words, the first exhibition of the art of *kannen* in Japan.[39] Mizukami Jun visited him in Shimo Suwa after seeing the exhibition, and went on to plan with the elder artist the second *kannen* exhibition, *Nirvana: For Final Art*. Based in Kyoto, Mizukami

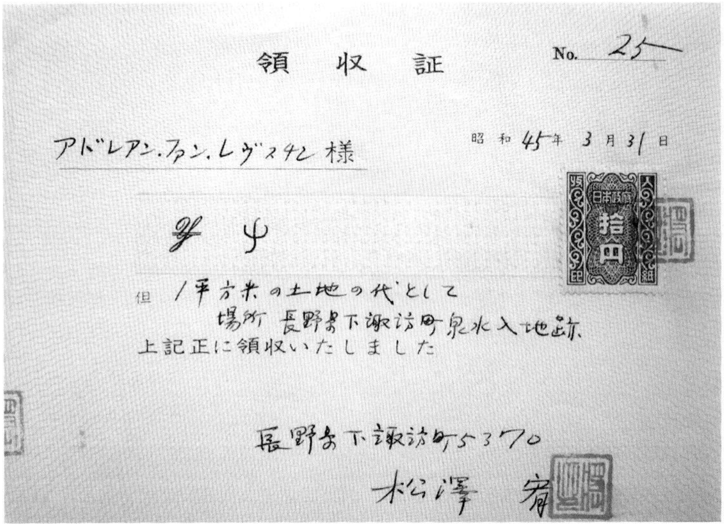

領　収　証　No. 25

アドレアン.ファン.レヴスタイン 様　昭和45年3月31日

日本政府 拾円

但 1平方米の土地の代として
場所 長野県下諏訪町泉水入地跡
上記正に領収いたしました

長野県下諏訪町5370
松澤宥

FIGURE 5.8
Matsuzawa Yutaka, *Receipt to Adriaan van Ravesteijn*, 1970. Ink, revenue stamp, and seals on commercially printed paper. Collection of Matsuzawa Kumiko.

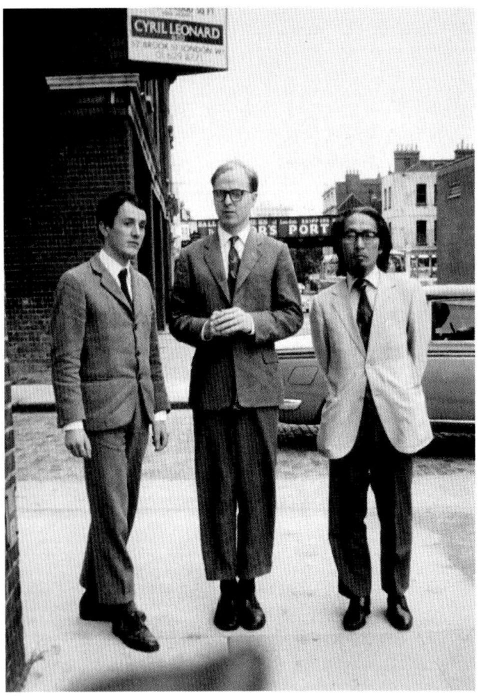

FIGURE 5.9
Matsuzawa with Gilbert & George in London, August 1971. Photo by Matsuzawa Kumiko.

managed to secure an exhibition slot in the rental schedule of the Kyoto Municipal Museum of Art in 1970. The Nirvana movement climaxed in July 1971 with *On'e* (literally "sound gathering") that inaugurated Matsuzawa's Sensuiiri Meditation Platform—a shed on a tree he and a few of his followers built on the one-square-meter plot now owned by Stanley Brouwn.[40] More than 30 artists, poets, musicians, and other cultural practitioners gathered to participate in an informal concert of sound art and performance.[41] Their gathering was informed by the spirit of "commune,"[42] the idea of which had entered the Japanese popular imagination with the news of the anti-establishment Hippie movement in the late 1960s.

On his 1971 summer trip, he brought with him a number of his works and other materials to consign with Art & Project. They included five sets of *The Whole Works 1961–1971*, each consisting of 71 works on paper as well as numerous mandala and "white circle" collages, among other items.[43] Notably, Matsuzawa's consignment encompassed three works by Nirvana artists (Kawatsu Hiroshi, Kobayashi Kiichi, and Kaneko Shōji) and a pair of diagrams of Nirvana School in Japanese and English (figure 5.10, plate 15), which place the group in an international context. It puts the group's exhibitions in the center and maps around it a broad constellation of aesthetic, cultural, and social ideas, figures, and events.[44] The May Revolution and Japan's Zenkyōtō (All-Campus Joint Struggle Committees) movement are found at top left, while Esoteric Buddhism with its fringe manifestations in Japan, placed in the top right corner, are countered with alternative kinds (e.g., of American Beat poet Allen Ginsberg and the Zen enthusiast Gary Snyder) placed in the bottom left corner. It suggests artistic kinships with E.A.T., Pop Art, Conceptual Art, and Earthworks, as well as postwar Surrealists (e.g., Akasegawa Genpei and Ikeda Tatsuo), Duchamp (by way of Takiguchi Shūzō), and such 1960s vanguard collectives as Hi Red Center and Neo Dada. In terms of Conceptual Art, there are additional references to Fluxus, MoMA's *Information* exhibition, and, of course, Art & Project.

With his sense of international contemporaneity amplified by the 1971 trip, Matsuzawa was determined to continue his international networking. In a typically wilderness and do-it-yourself move, he envisioned organizing an international commune through an annual mail-art campaign. In December 1971, he mailed out a call for work under the banner of *World Uprising*:

> I hope this communication finds you well with your vanishing. In order to realize *World Uprisings*—the final form of expression that represents our bond and lives together in this Final Era and signals the first form of expression through which we share our minds—I would like to invite you to participate [in this project]. This is the very first of numerous *World Uprisings* that will take place for the next 250 years until the time of Vanishing of Humankind.[45]

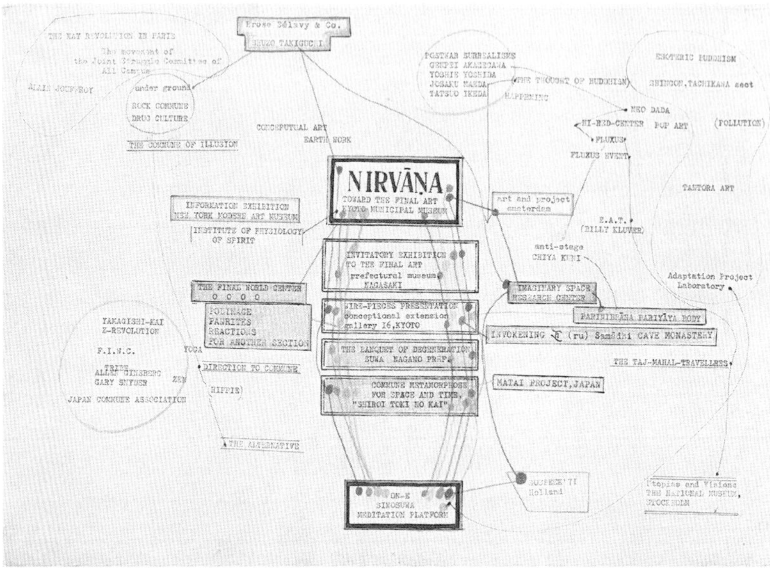

FIGURE 5.10
Matsuzawa Yutaka, untitled document (diagram of Nirvana School), ca. 1971. Photocopy (electrostatic print) with colored pencil additions; 29.7 × 21.1 cm. 1 of 3 documents in *Post Nirvāna: Our Commune*. The Museum of Modern Art, New York, Art & Project/Depot VBVR Gift 1063.2007. Digital Image © The Museum of Modern Art/Licensed by SCALA / Art Resource, NY. (Also plate 15.)

The plan was to organize this mail-art assembly annually for 250 years, which would make 2222 the project's last year and a hypothetical date for Vanishing of Humankind. Matsuzawa came up with this date by his numerological calculus, setting it 300 years after his birth, February 2, 1922, or "22/2/2."[46] (It should be noted the date was *hypothetical* because his theory of Vanishing of Humankind was hypothetical, for in his mind art guaranteed a total freedom of thought, unlike science that requires proof one way or another.)

This type of collective mail art was not rare. A Fluxus member based in Japan, Shiomi Chieko, organized a *Spatial Poem* series among her international colleagues beginning in 1965 and compiled the responses to each mailing as her work. Similarly, in Japan, when Ina Ken'ichirō and Takeda Kiyoshi organized a mail-art collective, Psychophysiology Research Institute (Seishin Seirigaku Kenkyūjo), in 1969–1970, they published a portfolio for a wider dissemination beyond the group members. (The membership encompassed Matsuzwa Yutaka, as well as GUN's Maeyama Tadashi and Horikawa Michio.) In the case of *World Uprising*, thanks to the growing attention to conceptualism in general and his practice in particular, Matsuzawa was able to publish the results of three years' worth of work in two magazines. The first *World*

Uprising was published in the November 1972 issue of *Bijutsu techō* as part of a special feature, "Toward Commune."[47] Among 18 artists reproduced, three were non-Japanese. Daniel Buren sent a signed statement "Daniel Buren make [*sic.*] a special work for this show, in Paris with no record." Douglas Huebler contributed *Duration Piece #31* with 10 photographs of icicles. Lawrence Weiner sent a data sheet of his Public Freehold works for *Undertown and/or Overtown*. A selection from the combined 1972 and 1973 mail-ins was published in the April 1974 issue of the art magazine *Geijutsu kurabu*, which devoted the whole issue to Conceptual Art (*Gainen geijutsu*).[48] Of 78 "World Uprisers," 32 were non-Japanese hailing from many places both familiar and unfamiliar: Stanley Brouwn of Holland, Ben Vautier of France, Terry Reid of Australia, Peter Stembera of Czechoslovakia, László Lakner of Hungary, Gilbert & George of the U.K., and John Baldessari of the U.S.

Alternatively to *World Uprising* (which ended after three calls), Matsuzawa also conceived a campaign for "art before the catastrophic end of humankind" under the rubric of Catastrophe Art, partly inspired by catastrophe theory, a new idea in mathematics that had first emerged in 1969.[49] He envisioned this project as mostly for Japanese artists, but one unrealized plan prepared for the poetry journal *Galant* was international in scope. For this plan, 14 out of 42 expected participants were non-Japanese, including three new names in Matsuzawa's international network, one of which was Robert Barry.[50] A label of "Catastrophe Art" (which in Japanese was rendered in *katakana* syllabary as *Katasutorofī āto*) was more universal than "*Kannen* Art." It also felt less ominous and final than "Final Art" (*Saishū bijutsu*). In 1972–1973, Matsuzawa frequently discussed his art under the label of Catastrophe Art,[51] and he contributed a selection of Catastrophe works by 23 artists as a semifeature in the March 1973 issue of *Bijutsu techō*.[52] Indeed, his Catastrophe Art found an international audience as well. In 1972, he organized *Catastrophe Art from the East*, an exhibition of 21 artists, many of them regulars of *World Uprising*.[53] He was then asked to organize another show by CAYC (Centro de Arte y Comunicación) in Buenos Aires, which was realized in 1974, with assistance from the critic Yoshida Yoshie.[54] Ultimately, the São Paulo Biennale in 1977 had a section of Catastrophe Art and invited Matsuzawa as its originator.[55] He made the installation *Nine Thoughts* by placing nine sheets of white paper on the floor, while showing documentary photographs of actions by 21 Catastrophe artists.[56]

* * *

Throughout the 1970s, Matsuzawa was also individually active in the international arena. He was invited to large and small group shows, including the Venice Biennale and the Sydney Biennale (both 1976); and had solo exhibitions at such far-flung places as Lausanne (1974), Poznań, Poland (1975), and Buenos Aires (1977). This continued to some extent into the 1980s. In other words, for a wilderness practitioner, he built an impressive international resume over two decades. The scope and effort of his internationalism may be compared with the internationalism of Gutai. While both were practitioners of do-it-yourself collectivism, Matsuzawa varied from Gutai in many respects. Above all, Matsuzawa's focus was anti-materialism, while Gutai embraced "the handshake between the human spirit and matter," as their leader Yoshihara Jirō proclaimed in the 1957 "Gutai Art Manifesto,"[57] and even though they reached the threshold of conceptualism, this tendency remained more latent than fully explored.[58] Gutai, under Yoshihara, and Matsuzawa operated in two different times and thus two different international environments. Gutai's internationalism began as an outreach effort partly from deep conviction and partly from idealism, but subsequently received valuable support from Michel Tapié, an ardent critic of gestural abstraction under the rubric of Art Informel who actively offered market opportunities to the group. Matsuzawa's internationalism first arose as his abiding concern with humankind but did not take a concrete shape until he gained assistance from the innovative but alternative Art & Project, whose most valuable contribution to art history was its mail-art publication, *Bulletin*.

A crucial difference was discursive support in the international arena. In addition to that of Tapié, Gutai enjoyed critical support into the 1960s, which included a critical assessment of Shiraga's painting by the Italian feminist art critic Carla Lonzi in 1962[59] and a magazine feature by the French critic Jean Clay in *Robho* in 1971.[60] The group also enjoyed the discursive and exhibition support of fellow artists such as Allan Kaprow and Henk Peeters. In contrast, Matsuzawa had little discursive support internationally. Although Art & Project's *Bulletin* was a powerful strategic vehicle of conceptualist works, it carried little critical discourse that would articulate the stakes of conceptualism. Vocal in performing this task were English-speaking artists (especially Sol LeWitt, Joseph Kosuth, and Art & Language) whose theory and practice were analytical and linguistic. Partly due to its discursive nature, this strain of conceptualism was more exclusive and localized than, say, the internationalized and all-inclusive conceptualism of Fluxus. (Matsuzawa had at best a cursory connection to Fluxus.) Yet by the power of being in the putative center, New York, Conceptual Art became the foundational and internationally accepted discourse of conceptualism. The politics of the art world aside, its influence was far-reaching also thanks to the lingua franca of contemporary art, English. As a case study, how the term and idea of Conceptual Art came to dominate art discourse in Japan will be examined later in this chapter.

Matsuzawa's international outreach was thus mired by language, not so much because he used Japanese in his work as because he lacked discursive power. His practice was certainly Japan's "own art" (*jimae bijutsu*), to borrow Minemura Toshiaki's term; but the core of his claim, *kannen*, was too local and too specific. Granted, he tried to universalize his idea by a string of terms, such as *World Uprising*, Catastrophe Art, and Final Art. Yet they came short of fully encapsulating the spirit of Psi and his theory and practice of *kannen*, through which he aspired to express the invisible and critique material civilization; his articulation of "vanishing of matter," which was at once obscure yet alluring, was somehow lost in translation. It was not until 1988 that he advanced his thinking to a more recognizable and less macabre form, by declaring *Quantum Art* (*Ryōshi geijutsu*), which effectively appropriated a sense of uncertain and invisible reality from quantum mechanics.

LANGUAGE MATTERS

Language and the discourse it generates were a thorny issue for 1960s Japan. The problem did not affect just Japan, however. As Allan Kaprow commented on his contact with Gutai, modern communications could malfunction.[61] Indeed, communication malfunctions were not as "rare" as Kaprow defensively characterized them. Still, they were not just about translation. Languages mattered in communication, certainly, but the timing and methods of communication mattered too, even before politics was brought into equation. Transnational communication, and for that matter, cross-boundary transmission of information, was not as simple as connecting one dot to another with a straight line.

In this respect, language and discourse are more like a living organism than an impersonal analytical tool. A transplanted word, and an accompanying idea, can take on its own life in its new home, sometimes dissociated from its original meaning but gaining new layers of signification. Or a transplanted word may receive a corrective to realign it to the original, sometimes due to an unavoidable intervention of art world politics. Such an evolution takes place after an incoming interface (contact) inserts the word (idea) into a certain locale. This process happens within the locale but the place of origin is always present, albeit latently. I call it an "internalized interface." It is a continuation of interface (vis-à-vis the origin) that will result in either assimilation or dissimilation. Internalized interfaces apply to both practice and discourse. They frequently take the form of "response" in practice and "repossession" in discourse when undertaken in proactive and thinking manners. Bluntly put, when done in passive and unthinking ways, they tend to yield "imitation" in practice and "submission" in discourse.[62]

A good example of "repossession" is the "Anti-Art" discourse that evolved in 1960s Japan from an art-historical concept of "anti-art." Another is Environment Art (*Kankyō geijutsu*), which was not unrelated to Environments in Kaprow's sense but had an intermedia and technological dimension in its Japanese incarnation.[63] In examining these cases, it is dangerous to assume the familiar meanings (e.g., prewar Dada's and American Neo-Dada's "anti-art" and Kaprow's "Environment"). Instead, we need to defamiliarize them by deciphering the words in their transplanted and incarnated lives. The distance of time helps us to perform such deciphering.

The first study in this section concerns repossession on an individual level: The Play's Happening discourse. The word "Happening" entered Japanese art discourse in two stages, first in the early 1960s through the Cagean circle, and after 1967 through Kaprow's 1966 publication *Assemblage, Environments & Happenings*. The Play's Happening exploration began with Ikemizu's 1965 *Homo Sapiens* and continued as the group devised a collaborative mode of voyage. By 1969, they began to articulate what Happening meant to them, intently setting apart their practice from Kaprow's as much as from the popular parlance, thereby "repossessing" the idea of Happening as their own.

The second study concerns "submission" to the central discourse. This happens after a transplant when an assumption is made of the "correctness" of the original terminology, which was constructed at the center (West) in dominant languages (English, French, and German), thereby forcing realignment to the center. The state of international contemporaneity can complicate the situation if a locale in question is in the process of developing its own word (idea) or discourse for a parallel practice, concurrently with but separately from the presumed center. An extraordinary example is the clash between the Euro-American label of Conceptual Art and Matsuzawa Yutaka's terminology of *kannen* which continued from the late 1960s to the mid-1970s. We will trace a complex unfolding of the conflicting and confusing deployment of *gainen* (concept) and *kannen* (idea/meditative visualization).

The Play's Happenings Discourse

Performance art was one of the major developments of 1960s art in Japan, beginning with Gutai's performative experiments especially in outdoor and onstage situations in the mid-1950s. In art discourse, the Japanese term of choice to discuss them was *kōi* (行為, "act" or "action"). For example, Gutai member Shiraga Kazuo discussed his action-based work as *kōi* in 1955.[64] In 1971–1972, when the publisher Kōdansha issued a 13-volume series on international contemporary art, volume 11 was titled *Kōi ni kakeru* (Staking on action), featuring performance and land art.[65] The word *pafōmansu* (パフォーマンス, "performance") did not appear in art until 1969 and was not widely used until the early 1980s.[66] In between the two, several other rubrics were applied to performative works in the 1960s; notably, each term has its own history and specific associations.[67] Simply put, *akushon* (action) was linked to "action painting," as exemplified by Ushio Shinohara's bravado actions inspired directly by the French Informel painter Georges Mathieu's public demonstration at the Shirokiya Department Store in Tokyo in 1957 (figure 6.10).[68] *Ivento* (イヴェント, "event") had dual roots in Fluxus and the experimental music of Group Ongaku (figure 1.8). The Japanese term *gishiki* (ritual) derived from the esotericism of the Marquis de Sade, which entered Japan via the writer Shibusawa Tatsuhiko on the one hand and the premodern body espoused by Zero Dimension on the other (figure 6.18). Like "action" and "event," the word *hapuningu* (ハプニング, "Happening"), which prominently figured in the oeuvre of The Play, was an English import. In 1961, two years after Allan Kaprow's initial use of it in art, the composer Ichiyanagi Toshi, who had just come back from New York, presented his *IBM for Happenings and Concrete Music* (1960) in his solo concert in Tokyo. When Yoko Ono, then married to Ichiyanagi, returned from New York and gave a solo concert at the Sōgetsu Art Center in May 1962, her work was generally understood as Happenings, despite her distaste for the term.[69] Then John Cage, whose famous composition course Ichiyanagi took at the New School, and David Tudor visited Japan five months later and gave a series of concerts in Tokyo and elsewhere. Their visit, which caused the so-called "Cage Shock" in Japan, solidified the generic link between the term Happening and performative works in general. This was the first stage of introduction of Happenings to Japan mainly through John Cage's circle.

The second stage began in earnest with Kaprow's *Assemblage, Environments & Happenings*, published in 1966. In its May 1967 issue, the art magazine *Bijutsu techō* published a special essay on his practice of Happenings, along with his book.[70] One year later, the magazine followed it up with a special feature on Happenings in the August 1968 issue.[71] These two introductions primarily outlined Kaprow's conception and method of Happenings, including his use of scripts and his assertion of the Happening as a new form of art unrelated to the unfortunate everyday usage of the term. They also introduced the new term "Happener" (*hapunā*)[72] to the Japanese readership. While the unsigned special essay of 1967 acknowledged Japan as an advance site of Happenings, ranging from Gutai to Zero Dimension, its main purpose was to offer a corrective to vague and willful misunderstandings, especially by "young Japanese artists and students who think anything chaotic is a Happening."[73] The timing of the 1968 special feature is curious, as the Kijima Norio Happening Show, a notorious television program on Nippon TV, ran from May to October that year. Although not mentioned by the two contributors, the art critic Nakahara Yūsuke and the music critic Akiyama Kuniharu, the special feature might have been a corrective to the vulgarization of *hapuningu*, which entered the vernacular lexicon to mean "unexpected occurrences [that are not so auspicious]."[74] Taken together, these *Bijutsu techō* articles in effect elevated Kaprow to the status of the standard bearer of a new art form, while casting a wide net to capture other Happeners "worldwide," from Cage to Fluxus, Al Hansen to Wolf Vostell. Thus, the introduction of Euro-American Happenings to Japan took place in two stages.

Significantly, The Play's Happenings discourse as the organizing principle of their practice evolved from the gap between these two stages. It dates back to the dry riverbed of Gifu in 1965, when Ikemizu Keiichi, a future member, staged *Homo Sapiens* under the summer sun (figure 3.1). One day that fall, he reprised the work as *Cage* twice in downtown Osaka, first at the Tennōji Zoo and then on the busy shopping thoroughfare of Shinsaibashi (comparable to Ginza in Tokyo). A turning point came at this last undertaking in the streets.[75] His philosophical observation of the human condition—humans were imprisoned in a cage that is civilization—continued from the previous two iterations. But in the typically urban setting, some curious passersby were bound to ask him: "Why are you doing this?" It was the first time that he realized that his act stirred the consciousness of some ordinary people. Indeed, the experience was so intense that he characterized the second performance of *Cage* as his very first Happening.

With this reckoning, he went on to institute a "Happenings" section in the independent *Contemporary Art Festival* in Osaka, which he co-organized in August 1966. This constituted the first purely domestic usage of the term in art, derived from the word as understood in its first phase. In 1967, he co-organized *The First Play Exhibition*, expressly billing it on the poster as a program of Happenings (figure 3.2). He then produced *Voyage: Happening in an Egg* in 1968 (figure 0.2), which formally launched The Play as a group of Happeners. In retrospect, Kaprow's attitude as an "un-artist"[76] who detested the traditional forums of the art world resonates with The Play's voyage into the wilderness outside the confines of museum and gallery and their stanch anti-commodity stance. Still, The Play's notion of Happenings was nominally borrowed from Kaprow. Rather than conforming to the newly introduced understanding of Kaprow's theory, they developed their own discourse through their practice. In fact, the prevalence of the term, both in the art world and in the mass media, compelled them to articulate their position clearly. In a sense, without knowing it, Ikemizu and other members of The Play heeded Kaprow's command to "declare what sort of phenomenon they are referring to," as he expressed in his essay "Pinpointing Happenings" of 1967.[77] Or, in member Miki Tetsuo's words, "You have to by and large take apart Happenings for cleaning," even though "Happenings may have arisen as a cool thing thanks to Uncle Kaprow."[78]

The acclimation of the term Happenings in the late 1960s in Japan can be understood from the use of the term by Sekine Nobuo, who explained in 1969 that "I am making my work as a Happening through which I come to grips with the world."[79] In light of the well-known engagement with materiality by this Mono-ha artist, his usage may at first sound unexpected, but it echoes the frequent use of the related term "Happener" by Lee Ufan in his Mono-ha theory, typically when he discussed Sekine as one. Among his texts that employ "Happener" is "Self-Awareness toward the Non-Objective World," published in the September 1969 issue of *Miru* (Seeing), a monthly newsletter of the National Museum of Modern Art, Kyoto.[80] More compact than his better-known treatise "World and Structure" of June 1969, it saliently lays out his basic position by critiquing the "revisionist modernism" of Earthworks and Conceptual Art and embracing the work of "new-face Happeners" who were "aware that [what they produced] reveal the structure of a world that transcends objecthood."[81] Although the term did not survive in Lee's theorization on Sekine's work, eventually replaced by *shigusa-sha*, or "he who engages in an act [*shigusa*],"[82] his use of "Happener" points to the latent performative nature of Mono-ha works.[83] In the same text, Lee faulted the "groundless and false fashion of international contemporaneity" and criticized some critics for relying on "foreign yardsticks" to examine Mono-ha works. Given his cautious attitude toward Euro-American terminologies, his very use of the foreign word "Happening" and its derivative "Happener" implies the normalization of the terms in Japanese art discourse.

Interestingly, Lee's text shares space in the Kyoto Modern's four-page newsletter with "What Happenings Mean to Me," authored by Ikemizu Keiichi.[84] The two texts were published in conjunction with the museum's annual *Trends in Contemporary Japanese Art* exhibition, which included The Play and Mono-ha artists (Koshimizu Susumu, Yoshida Katsurō, and Lee himself) that August. If Lee was a sympathetic theorist-artist who himself had begun to produce his version of Mono-ha works, Ikemizu was a practitioner par excellence whose theory was inextricably informed by his practice and experience. In his essay, proudly identifying himself as a "Happener,"[85] Ikemizu recounted his experiences from *Cage* onward. By the time he participated in *2nd All Setouchi Contemporary Art Exhibition* in October 1968 (three months after *Voyage*), his engagement with Happenings was firm. In his comment to the catalog, he wrote: "Happening to me is not a matter of accident or bodily engagement. It concerns the experience of he who acts and those who see it. It is about the expansion of image, the transformation of an environment."[86] In his 1969 essay in the Kyoto Modern's newsletter, he forcefully rejected the conventional understanding that Happenings were a new form of aesthetic expression. He declared that Happenings should transcend mere aesthetics. Granted, this generally echoes Kaprow. Still, it was not a borrowed idea but a conviction that Ikemizu derived from his own practices. He wanted to see more than "art" as such in Happenings, something that can "address a much larger question inside us." He continued:

> To me, Happening as a freedom of expression is over. It is neither a form of expression nor a genre of art. Happening in and of itself is the whole that is at once the purpose, the content, and the means. Therefore, those who see [my] Happening should stop making an effort to read from it what I am trying to express. Instead, upon seeing my Happening, they should gaze at that which arises within them, construct it, react to it, enlarge it. [...] Happening allows us, regardless of time, space, and method, to relate to people who firmly believe that art has no place in their lives. By deploying any and every expressive method available offered by art and science, Happening can be communicated to people, not only in museums and galleries but also in plazas, on the streets, in nature, via the news media, or by word of mouth. Regardless of whether or not it is recognized as "art" as such, Happening can expand consciousness by making people feel something.[87]

In such an expansive and optimistic view, Ikemizu conceived Happenings as a communicative act that engages not just art audiences but ordinary people outside the art world, with an express goal to affect their consciousness.

His theorization was part of the collective discursive effort made by The Play which filled the pages of their broadsheet newsletter, three issues of which were published in 1969.[88] The first of these was published in April 1969, with seven members contributing. Among them was Mizukami Jun, another lead member, who composed "9 Basic Statements on Happenings," which prominently headlined the front side. In an analytical style, Mizukami point by point outlined the theoretical characteristics of Happenings. Some statements sound like Kaprow: in Statement 5, notably, he declared that Happenings "are an interpenetration of the realm of life and the realm of art." Yet it is dangerous to attribute Kaprow-esque ideas to Kaprow alone at the late date of 1969, since the idea of "the everyday" had been in Japanese art discourse since 1964, when the critic Miyakawa Atsushi formulated the notion of "descent to the everyday" in the context of Anti-Art. In tune with his fellow member Ikemizu, three out of Mizukami's nine statements concern "consciousness":

> 3. [...] What matters is the movement of consciousness during the process of the act.
>
> 4. Happenings expand the realm of form and consciousness.
>
> [...]
>
> 9. Happenings are a pursuit of consciousness and act in a demarcated segment of everyday time.[89]

However, when Mizukami spoke of "consciousness," he seems to have meant not that of the audience but the Happeners' own, diverging from Ikemizu's conception. (Indeed, Statement 9 may sound closer to Kaprow's idea.) Still, "communication," too, enters Mizukami's formulation in Statement 8:

> 8. Happenings stimulate thought. Communication is established when a new thought is prompted by them.

Although Mizukami did not specify the type of audience, he put the issues of consciousness and communication at the center of his theorization. In his case, the term Happening was incorrect; instead he proposed "Reaction" to amplify his communicative intention.[90]

The Play's desire to communicate with ordinary people contrasts with Kaprow's conceptualization of the Happening as "a code without a message," as observed by art historian Judith Rodenbeck.[91] The Play's willingness to engage a broader audience was most saliently demonstrated by *Bench* of 1971, one of their rare contributions to institutional exhibitions (figure 5.11). This was produced for that year's Mainichi

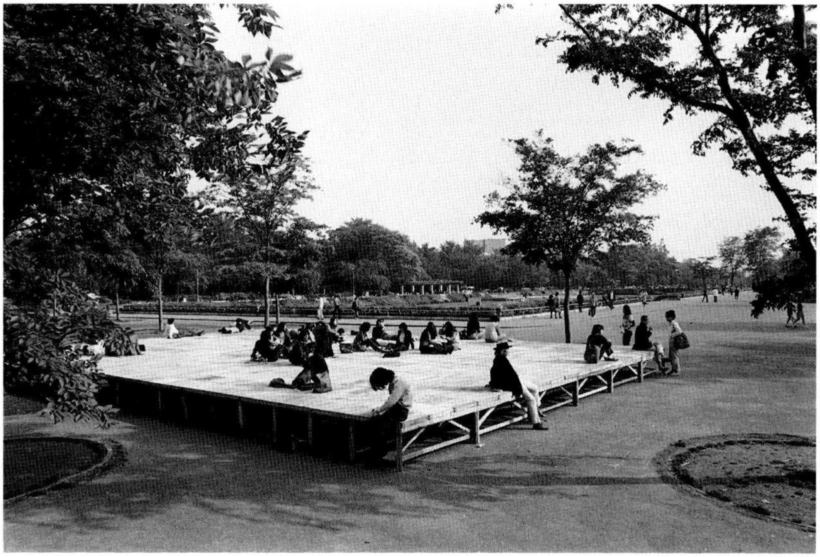

FIGURE 5.11
The Play, *Bench*, 1971. Installation view at *Contemporary Art Exhibition of Japan*, outside Tokyo Metropolitan Art Museum in Ueno Park. © The Play.

Contemporary. On this occasion, the group decided to take advantage of the locations of the exhibition's two venues, because the Tokyo Metropolitan Art Museum and the Kyoto Municipal Museum of Art were both located in large public parks. In an open space in front of either museum, they installed a low 18 × 13-meter platform, calling it *Bench*. It served as a resting spot and a gathering place not just for exhibition visitors but for anybody visiting the park. The platform itself was nondescript and insignificant, constructed with standard wood materials, all rented as usual. They used them in such a way that the platform could later be easily disassembled and the materials reused. In Tokyo, this communal space was visited by Matsuzawa Yutaka with his class at the school Bigakkō one day in May. In Kyoto, The Play organized a concert one Sunday in June for which they brought their instruments and equipment, including drum sets and speakers, to entertain themselves and passersby.

* * *

A vital part of their activities, The Play's theorization was a rare instance among Japanese artists working in performative veins. It is notable that theory and practice were inseparable in their theorization, as evident in the first issue of their newsletter. Its front side was devoted to the members' texts and the back to a chronology of "Play

Happenings," listing their performative works undertaken as a group and as individuals since 1962. Most significantly, they were intent on extending their compilation beyond their group. The front side bears a small notice at the bottom, calling for information on Happeners and Happenings in Osaka and its environs with an express goal of creating a Happeners map in the region. The call was printed in the second issue, but nothing concrete appeared to have come of it. Even so, their active effort to generate a context of their own typified the do-it-yourself spirit of the wilderness which they made their habitat.

Gainen (Concept) versus *Kannen* (Idea)

It is no small irony that conceptualism, the most language-driven practice of 1960s art, was mired in language troubles. Or, perhaps, because it was language-driven, language had to become an issue. In Euro-America, the label "Conceptual Art" was disavowed by some supposedly Conceptual artists, just as "Minimal Art" was rejected by the canonical Minimal artists. Meanwhile, in Japan, two words were competing for use: *gainen* and *kannen.*

Matsuzawa Yutaka first introduced the term *kannen* in his conceptualism in 1965 to signify "meditative visualization" in the Buddhist sense, with an additional modern connotation of "idea." By 1969, the world of *gendai bijutsu* caught up with Matsuzawa Yutaka and his practice of *kannen.* That year, he was invited to two mainstream exhibitions, the Mainichi Contemporary and the Kyoto Modern's *Trends in Contemporary Japanese Art.* They in effect acknowledged his idea of "vanishing matter" by gathering vanguard practices that revealed a decisive departure from the convention of painting and sculpture and a growing dematerializing tendency. This shift toward Non-Art (*Hi-geijutsu*) was captured through the discourse of *kannen.* In this, *kannen* was informed partly by Matsuzawa's use of the term[92] and partly by the English term "Conceptual Art,"[93] which by then had gained currency in Euro-America and was initially translated into Japanese as *Kannen bijutsu.*[94] This proved to be an intriguing confluence of local and international discourses in world art history—indeed a collision that Japanese critics would resolve primarily in favor of the New York discourse under the new label *Gainen geijutsu.*

On the surface, it was a translation issue, involving two close synonyms, *gainen* and *kannen,* and their different etymologies and connotations. As discussed in chapter 2 on Matsuzawa, *kannen* originated in Buddhism. In modern Japan, Nishi Amane, a philosopher known for laying the linguistic foundation of modern thought, assigned a new meaning to *kannen* by linking it to the English "idea" in 1873. A year later, Nishi coined *gainen* and assigned it to the English "concept" and the German "Begriff." According to *Daijirin,* an authoritative Japanese dictionary, the former concerns the content of subjective consciousness when one thinks of something, while the latter refers to the content expressed by language common to things with the same nature.[95]

Notably, in 1972, the artist-theorist Lee Ufan advocated *gainen* as a better translation for "concept" by acknowledging a broader signification of *kannen* that encompassed "a vast realm of imagination."[96]

(To avoid confusion, in this book, "Conceptual Art" refers to the Euro-American trend, while "conceptualism" signifies a broader range of practices that strategically called into question the institutions of art.[97] Both *kannen* and *gainen* and its derivatives, such as *Gainen geijutsu*, correspond to the original Japanese usages.)

In 1960s Japan, the term *kannen* was commonly deployed in its modern sense of "idea" to deal with the ongoing development of Non-Art, object-based or otherwise. The most notable example was one of the seven themes devised for the 1969 Mainichi Contemporary's "Frontiers of Contemporary Art" section: *Rittai* (three dimensions) and *Kannen* (ideas). Matsuzawa's distinct Buddhist-derived use was thus unfortunately obscured, although the extremism of his theory and practice attracted due attention as an example of the modern sense of *kannen*. (Matsuzawa was not included in this section but assigned to the "Labyrinthine Room," as discussed in the section on *Tokyo Biennale 1970*.) What complicates the matter is that in a rare state of international contemporaneity, the word "Conceptual Art" arrived in Japan much earlier than its substance and *kannen* was given as its translation. Devoid of the concrete referent, the idea of Conceptual Art took on its own life in a developing local context tied to *kannen*. It should be remembered that at the time of 1969, there was barely a consensus on what Conceptual Art was in Euro-America, either. A broad and institutional recognition in the art world was signaled by *Conceptual Art, Conceptual Aspects*, a 1970 exhibition curated by Donald Karshan at the New York Cultural Center, followed by such publications as Ursula Meyer's *Conceptual Art* (1972) and Gregory Battcock's critical anthology *Idea Art* (1973).[98] Thus, Japanese critics and artists alike had to probe their discursive way through the art of *kannen*/Conceptual Art.

A mainstream indicator of the domestic situation, the Kyoto Modern's *Trends* exhibition offers a quick and useful discursive synopsis from 1966 onward. In 1966, the museum recognized "new *objet*-like works that cannot be called painting or sculpture,"[99] which evolved out of Anti-Art with certain technological or optical components. (Those works are today understood as part of Environment Art.) With this reckoning, the Kyoto Modern that year simplified the whole title as *Trends in Contemporary Japanese Art* (*Gendai bijutsu no dōkō*), doing away with the reference to "Painting and Sculpture."[100] The 1967 edition made a big impression by presenting trends similar to Primary Structures as well as Environment Art in the vein of Light and Kinetic Art, the latter of which would continue into 1968. A sudden turn to dematerialization took place in 1969, with a distinct "tendency to pursue the self-sufficiency of *kannen* (ideas) by presenting the elementary state of *mono* (things) and eliminating as much materiality and presence as possible."[101] In the 1970 iteration, which concluded the annual survey, these aspects intensified to the extent of attempting to "explore and define the essence of art on the border of Art and Non-Art."[102] In this context, *kannen* signified the prioritization of "ideation"—or more broadly "thinking"—over "making," and a tendency to the ephemeral was observed beyond the emerging practice of Mono-ha.[103] In other words, the Kyoto Modern used the term *kannen* in a primarily local manner.

Regardless of its partial origin in Euro-America and the frequent terminological confusion,[104] what was at stake with *kannen* can be well understood within the domestic context: the departure from the modern convention of painting and sculpture, which was framed as part of "transcending the modern"[105] and informed by the supremacy of *kannen* over the materiality of art and the act of making. For example, among the works in the 1969 Mainichi Contemporary, the critic Haryū Ichirō singled out three works, On Kawara's *Pictorial Diary*, Matsuzawa's *Ψ Gas Chamber*, and Takamatsu Jirō's *Slack of Cloth*, as the "clear and extreme pursuit of *kannen*"; in contrast, Haryū berated Ikemizu Keiichi's *Eggs in Orange*, which won the grand prize, for being more emotive and eerie than inherently *kannen*-based.[106] When critics sought parallels to the self-sufficiency of *kannen* in Western art, Duchamp's readymades offered a major historical precedent,[107] and such contemporary manifestations as Earthworks and Air Art were considered part of the "expansion of the realm of *kannen*."[108] That is to say, *kannen* was a convenient catchword that could capture multiple characteristics of Non-Art that became evident in 1969. That was why Lee Ufan, who was then forging his theory of Mono-ha as a singular practice that truly transcended the modern paradigm of representation, could use *kannen* as a blanket term to critique all other contemporary practices in "Is an Art of *Kannen* Possible?,"[109] published in the November 1969 issue of *Bijutsu techō* (see chapter 4).

Unlike *kannen*, which was only partially (and mistakenly) international, *gainen* definitely derived from Conceptual Art, and critics in discussing it increasingly looked toward the New York discourse of Conceptual Art as their reference. The actual examples of Euro-American Conceptual Art shown at *Tokyo Biennale 1970* played a role in prompting this turn, but more importantly the exhibition offered opportunities for a new crop of art critics to assert themselves. Two in particular stand out: Fujieda Teruo and Minemura Toshiaki. Having studied at the University of Pennsylvania in the mid-1960s, Fujieda wrote a master's thesis on Pop Art at Kyoto University before turning to art criticism.[110] Not content with being a mere observer of the changing trends, he identified the issue of *gainen* (concept) as an unavoidable aspect of contemporary art within a few tendencies appearing in the biennale, thereby opening an avenue of critical discussion for *Gainen geijutsu* (Conceptual Art).[111] A mastermind behind *Tokyo Biennale 1970*, Minemura left the Mainichi newspaper company after the biennale and launched a prolific career as an art critic. His biennale review demonstrates his intimate knowledge of individual works in his project, and his focus on Daniel Buren and Jan Dibbets, as well as On Kawara and Nomura Hitoshi, points to his growing interest in conceptualism.[112] For these two critics, it was a given that in discussing *Tokyo Biennale 1970* they examined not the local but the international. It was logical, then, for their writing to extensively reference the unfolding international discourse, mainly American. Even though they by no means ignored the local circumstances in which Japanese artists operated, these were more supplementary than essential in their theoretical and intellectual engagement. Into the 1970s, the two went on to become active interlocutors—more precisely, vocal detractors—of Conceptual Art/*Gainen geijutsu*.

By the end of 1973, the contentious discursive arena of *Gainen geijutsu* grew large enough for the young critic Hayami Takashi to take on the daunting task of putting it in perspective.[113] His three-tiered essay "Toward 'Time,'" which combined his analysis, excerpts of critical texts, and a chronology of related exhibitions, makes a valuable starting point to understand the state of art criticism on this subject. Useful in particular for the present examination is his observation that all contemporary tendencies had a conceptual (*gainen-teki*) dimension and were thus to be discussed in conjunction with *Gainen geijutsu*; yet this situation obfuscated what exactly *Gainen geijutsu* was. In an extreme instance, Hayami pointed out, Fujieda saw no contemporary artists, Euro-American or otherwise, as deserving the label of *Gainen geijutsu* in the most authentic sense—as engaging the concept of Art (*geijutsu*)—for their works "did not transform Art or the concept of Art, and thus did not become themselves the concept of Art" but only managed to offer "concepts about the concept of Art."[114]

A decisive moment came in April 1974, when the art magazine *Geijutsu kurabu* (Art club) decided to give a more concrete view of the "infamous yet elusive"[115] tendency that was *Gainen geijutsu*/Conceptual Art. A short-lived art magazine edited by a group of cultural practitioners including the critic Nakahara Yūsuke and intended to generate in-depth discussion outside art journalism, it devoted almost the whole of its eighth issue to *Gainen geijutsu*.[116] As can be seen from its table of contents (table 5.2), the special issue strove to be at once informative and serious, carrying critical essays, artists' words, albums of works, and a detailed chronology that covered both Japanese and international events. Attention paid to New York discourse was hard to miss. Three texts are translated from English into Japanese: Joseph Kosuth's 1969 "Art after Philosophy" from *Studio International*, Willoughby Sharp's 1972 interview "Lawrence Weiner at Amsterdam" conducted for *Avalanche*, and Robert Pincus-Witten's 1973 *Artforum* article "Theater of the Conceptual."

The editorial agenda was put forth by Nakahara, who curated the opening album, "Conceptual Artscape." In his opening remarks, he compared *Gainen geijutsu* to "Western medicine" and characterized it as having two essential components, "account by language" and "manipulation of signs," that engage the "concept of Art."[117] In Japan at the time, Chinese medicine, called *kanpō*, was commonly utilized as an alternative medicine, though it carried a stigma of lesser science than its Western

TABLE 5.2
Geijutsu kurabu, no. 8 (April 1974), Special Feature: *Gainen geijutsu*

Table of Contents

Nakahara Yūsuke, comp.
"Conceptual Artscape" [album]

Joseph Kosuth
"Art after Philosophy" (1969) [trans. Matsuoka Kazuko]

Minemura Toshiaki
"*Gainen Geijutsu* of Who's He?"

Ishizaki Kōichirō
"Reading the Work of Art: From Minimal Art to *Gainen Geijutsu*"

Shiomi Mieko
"Trajectory of Musical Thought That Transcends Sound"

Robert Pincus-Witten
"Theater of the Conceptual" (1973) [trans. Takashima Heigo]

Miyakawa Atsushi, Takamatsu Jirō, and Nakahara Yūsuke
"Things and Language: From Style to Situation" [roundtable discussion]

Terayama Shūji (interviewer), "Exploring the Artist's Concept"
Matsuzawa Yutaka: "Recording Dream, Mail Art, and Mr. Psi's C.V."
Kashihara Etsutomu: "Discussing His Work: *Monroe as Method*"
Kawaguchi Tatsuo: "From Relational Energy to Nullified State"

Void/Imaginary Space Situation Research Center
"The World-Uprising 1972, 73" [album]

Iimura Takahiko
"Film on Paper: 400 Frames"

Willoughby Sharp
"Lawrence Weiner at Amsterdam" (1971) [trans. Matsuzawa Yutaka]

Takashima Heigo, comp.
"Chronology of *Gainen Geijutsu*: 1966–1973"

Editorial Committee: Awazu Kiyoshi, Ishizaki Kōichirō, Konno Tsutomu, Terayama Shūji, Nakahara Yūsuke, Matsumoto Toshio counterpart. His terminologies hence unambiguously signaled his overt Eurocentrism. This was reinforced by his selections for the album, which included no Japanese artists and spoke loudly for his adaptation of the Western criteria that eliminate any consideration of a Japanese iteration of conceptualism. In retrospect, his insight exquisitely encapsulates the contrast between the more analytical aspect of Euro-American Conceptual Art (such as that of Kosuth and LeWitt) and the more mystical strain of Japanese conceptualism (such as by Matsuzawa and his Nirvana group)—not so different from the difference between Western medicine that rigorously "extracts essences alone" and Chinese medicine that empirically emphasizes "synergetic effects." In a few words, Nakahara advocated Euro-America in general and New York in particular as the authentic site of *Gainen geijutsu*, thus contributing to the construction of New York as *the* center. Worse, his readers in 1974 would have readily understood and accepted with little question his medical comparison and the implied supremacy of Euro-American Conceptual Art.

The drastic degree of Nakahara's New York–centric turn can be understood when we compare another special feature that he worked on three years before, "Art of Concept, Concept of Art," for the May 1971 issue of *Bijutsu techō*.[118] Its 60-page coverage consists of two critical essays (Nakahara and Fujieda), separated by one album in between. In his 15-page essay, Nakahara devoted two full pages to Matsuzawa under the heading "A Thought That Art Will Vanish" and wrote at length on the artist's response to Stanley Brouwn's ad and his interaction with Adriaan van Ravesteijn.[119] Furthermore, the critic collaborated with the artist and his Nirvana group to compile a 32-page album, of which 12 pages illustrated the works of such Japanese artists as Akasegawa Genpei, Nomura Hitoshi, and Takamatsu Jirō, among others. Pages excerpted from Kashihara Etsutomu's tautological artist's book, *This Is a Book* (1970), are reproduced at the bottom of the album as a visual footer. Based in New York, On Kawara was the only Japanese artist who appears in the two features with the same work: a telegram he sent to Matsuzawa for the 1970 *Nirvana* exhibition.

The magazine *Geijutsu kurabu* reiterated Nakahara's New York–centered view by placing Kosuth's text immediately after the opening album, thus making it the lead text in the whole issue. Minemura Toshiaki's critical exegesis of the American artist's analytical Conceptual Art was negative in its tenet, yet its placement immediately after Kosuth's translated essay in effect confirmed the place of Kosuth as *the* face of Conceptual Art. The editorial agenda was further supported by an extensive 24-page "Chronology," which was built on Lucy Lippard's 1973 book *Six Years* and extended it by two years. The two-tier format is blatantly Eurocentric. The top tier, which takes up two-thirds of each page, is reserved for Euro-American events (precious exceptions being the New York–based On Kawara and *Tokyo Biennale 1970*, which was duly included in *Six Years*). Japanese events are segregated to the bottom tier, which looks like a footnote area with its size no more than half of the top tier. With such a lopsided treatment, the message was unambiguous: Japanese conceptualism was no more than a sideshow.

Matsuzawa Yutaka managed to keep his prominence in the special issue of *Geijutsu kurabu*: he was interviewed by the poet-dramatist Terayama Shūji, translated the interview of his friend Weiner, and contributed a second album section, "The World-Uprising 1972, 73." Yet his presence was no doubt undercut by the magazine's obvious Eurocentrism. The setback was twofold. First, his conceptualism grounded in the local tradition of *kannen* was completely eclipsed by the magazine's embrace of *gainen*. Second, his kind of internationalism, whereby he sought to create an artists' network with the potential for an open system of communication, was defeated by another kind of internationalism, in which the margin deemed the presumed center as the site of legitimacy, submitted itself to the exclusionary system of canon, and thereby compounded self-marginalization.

It is fair to say that Matsuzawa lost the battle of language. But he likely saw such a discursive skirmish as superfluous to his agenda of Anti-Civilization, a project much larger than art as such. He willingly accepted the definition that "*Gainen geijutsu* is language-based," the lowest possible common denominator of conceptualism, recasting his Revelation as the moment when he launched his "language-based" practice. He called it *kannen bijutsu* (the art of *kannen*), because ultimately *kannen* was his own strategy and his own terminology. At the same time, a slight but real possibility that *kannen* could have played a role in local discourse was completely aborted.

* * *

Connection studies begin by identifying contact points, contact being either direct (personal) or indirect (informational). More importantly, we need to differentiate connections in terms of interfaces in three modalities: incoming, outgoing, and internalized. Narrative tangents can be drawn, either domestically or internationally. Or, as with the case of *Tokyo Biennale 1970*, a pair of domestic and international tangents may intersect.

As four case studies in this chapter demonstrate, the state of international contemporaneity was fluid and unstable in 1960s Japan. Connections were made, certainly. An incoming interface of *Tokyo Biennale 1970* was dynamic and exceptional, but it was never repeated. An outgoing interface of Matsuzawa's international communalism reached far corners of the world, but it remained more or less a wilderness effort, invisible to the mainstream. It must be remembered, however, that international contemporaneity was a new reality in history: artistic practices of a locale in the margin striding forward contemporaneously with the presumed center (Euro-America). Even though Japan was not alone—with similar phenomena occurring in other areas of Asia, as well as in Latin America and Eastern and Central Europe—central sight was not acclimated enough to the developing situation to recognize a crucial shift in the existing paradigm.

Japan was singular in developing a discourse of international contemporaneity, as outlined in chapter 1. Yet there was no owner's manual, so to speak. Peripheral vision helped them to understand their place in the world, but old habits die hard. The entrenched ideology of Eurocentrism and the accompanying reverse chauvinism were persistent in local discourse, as exemplified by the clash between *gainen* and *kannen* which resulted in the internalization of the Euro-American discourse of Conceptual Art. Modest as it might have been, then, The Play's effort to discursively repossess Happenings that emerged in tandem with their practice was noteworthy.

The importance of discursive examination in our study cannot be overstated, because discourse mirrored not so much the state of international contemporaneity as the awareness of it and the speaker's relationship to it. The two discursive cases studied in this chapter reveal a complicated fact of living through international contemporaneity, for discourse customarily lagged behind practice. In other words, degrees of international contemporaneity inevitably varied between what Japanese artists produced and what Japanese critics discoursed on. Furthermore, artists and critics discoursed differently. In general, as with the case of The Play, artists were more empirical, as they often built their discourses by thinking through their practices. Critics were more normative; they were expected more often than not to know and introduce the discourses from abroad to Japan. So much so that, just as critics might fault artists for imitating foreign trends, some artists would chide critics for "wielding foreign-made yardsticks."[120]

It was no coincidence that Lee Ufan, whose words these are, devised Mono-ha discourse to set the Japanese movement apart from Euro-American counterparts of Post-Minimal Art and Arte Povera. Firmly situated in the mainstream part of Japanese contemporary art, the Korean-born Lee nonetheless had a little of the wilderness in him, with an outsider's eye that enabled him to see the status quo in perspective.[121] Working from the wilderness, Matsuzawa and The Play pressed on, pursuing their own innovations. Their individual contributions to international contemporaneity typify the do-it-yourself spirit in which artists take matters into their hands, developing structures they need without relying on the existing institutions. This is precisely the principle of the wilderness that had propelled the evolution of modernism in prewar Japan and now that of contemporary art in postwar Japan.

6 RESONANCE STUDIES

The study of resonances helps us not only decenter the established narrative but also regroup newly drawn narrative tangents. Unlike connections, which signaled lived experiences of international contemporaneity, we often discover resonances after the fact, since resonances might not have been recognized at the time. Through comparison of "similar yet dissimilar" works, we add contact points between different locales and further build local knowledge. There are at least two levels of comparison needed to understand local knowledge: individual differences and larger contextual differences.

MATSUZAWA YUTAKA'S CONCEPTUALISM COMPARED

The first section of this chapter will center on Matsuzawa Yutaka's conceptualism and make two sets of comparisons. One of the innovations that Matsuzawa contributed to 1960s art through his theory and practice of *kannen* (meditative visualization) was immateriality. In the decade when a major direction of new art was dematerialization, which was generally understood as material reduction with an increased conceptual engagement, he proposed commanding the viewer to exercise his or her mental faculties, as opposed to sensory and thus physical perceptions. This contribution put his work in contact with Yves Klein's engagement with the void. Born in 1928, the French artist (d. 1962) was a close contemporary to Matsuzawa, and the pursuit of immateriality was his mission through all his work. The discussion focuses on their shared strategy of emptying the gallery. The empty gallery is to conceptualism what hole digging is to land art. Like hole digging, the empty gallery is an intuitive and simple idea that offers ways to reconceptualize what art could be. Like hole digging, instances of the empty gallery abound.[1] And thus, like hole digging, the empty gallery makes a good case for the futility of arguing who was first, prompting us instead to examine what the artist did with it and why he did it. To expand the comparison and create a spectrum of immateriality, we will add to this mix the younger Robert Barry (b. 1936).

Matsuzawa will then be compared with Japanese pioneers of conceptualism, in particular Yoko Ono and On Kawara, two New York–based practitioners, with some reference to the Japan-based Akasegawa Genpei and another New Yorker, Shūsaku Arakawa. Except for Kawara, they came out of the Anti-Art context and devised their own versions of conceptualism in the early 1960s. Their pioneer status contrasts the second generation of Japanese artists—such as the photo-based Nomura Hitoshi, the analytical Kashihara Etsutomu, and the institutionally critical Bikyōtō—who emerged at the end of the decade to form a wing of the Non-Art tendency. Beyond their generational proximity, Matsuzawa and Ono both engaged with instruction-based conceptualism, while Matsuzawa and Kawara had in common their deep concern with humankind as a whole.

In the second section of this chapter, we will delve into the local contexts that contrast the land art of GUN and The Play with that of their American contemporaries. A discussion of methodological issues opens the second section.

In a Spectrum of Immateriality

In his relentless endeavor to express the invisible in art, Matsuzawa came to work with immateriality by mobilizing the viewer's mind through *kannen* (meditative visualization). While this mind-based method makes him stand out in global conceptualism, his radical reconceptualization of the exhibition and the gallery space allied him and put him in contact with his counterparts who also worked with immateriality in varying degrees.

Matsuzawa paid extensive attention to his exhibition activities as he developed his version of conceptualism (see table 6.1). He conceptualized the gallery as a container in 1963, "organized" an independent exhibition and several imaginary exhibitions from 1964 onward, and even vanished a whole exhibition to replace it with another in 1965. The most reductive and minimalist of his moves was the empty gallery, which he executed twice: in his solo exhibition at Naiqua Gallery, Tokyo in 1964 (figure 6.1, plate 16) and at *Tokyo Biennale 1970* (figure 5.1). In the 1964 Naiqua exhibition, the artist literally closed off the gallery space, offering a contact point with his international peers who performed similar acts.

TABLE 6.1
Matsuzawa Yutaka's Exhibitions by *Kannen*, 1963–1970

1963

Invitation to Psi Zashiki Room
  Presented at Yomiuri Independent Exhibition, Tokyo
  Exhibition display as a sampling of a remote display in Shimo Suwa

On Another Work in Another Container, or On Cutting
  Presented at solo exhibition, Aoki Gallery, Tokyo
  Gallery as a container

1964

Independent '64 in the Wilderness
  Group exhibition presented at Nanashima Yashima Highland, Nagano Prefecture
  Submission through various communication methods including *kannen*

Ah, Nil, Ah, A Ceremony of Psi's Secret Embodiment Drowning in the Wilderness: Prototype Exhibition
  Solo exhibition, Naiqua Gallery, Tokyo
  Empty gallery, closed gallery; "anti-venue" in Tokyo, "venue" in Shimo Suwa

1965

Vanishing of Matter: Seeing Anti-Civilization Exhibition
  Presented at *All Japan Independent Exhibition*, Yokohama Civic Art Gallery
  Voiding an existing exhibition to replace it with a *kannen* exhibition

Void: Collective Participation of "Anti-Civilization" School
  Presented at *Independent Art Festival*, Gifu
  A *kannen* exhibition overlaid on an existing exhibition

Anti-Japan: Today's Art Exhibition
  Group exhibition presented at Nanashima Yashima Highland, Nagano Prefecture
  "Anti-exhibition" to an existing exhibition; "imaginary exhibition"

1967–1968

Postcard Painting series:
  Fundamental Painting Exhibition to Be Shown to the Lake; Painting Exhibition to Be Shown to the Lake and the Spirit; Matsuzawa Yutaka Solo Exhibition to Be Seen by a Painting; Fundamental Painting Exhibition to Be Seen by Death and to See Breasts; Exhibition of Painting You Never See and Painting You Cannot See: Revelation for Anti-Being of Expo '70; Painting Exhibition to Be Shown to Sleeping Energy (The Last Painting Exhibition in the World); "Visiting with a Globe" Exhibition

1969

Psi Art Gathering
  Group exhibition at Void/Imaginary Space Situation Research Center, Shimo Suwa
  First exhibition of *Kannen* Art

Ψ *Gas Chamber*
  Presented at the Mainichi Contemporary
  Empty gallery as apparatus

From This Corner: For a Change
  Presented at *Trends*
  Empty gallery as apparatus

1970

My Own Death
  Presented at *Tokyo Biennale 1970*
  Empty gallery as apparatus

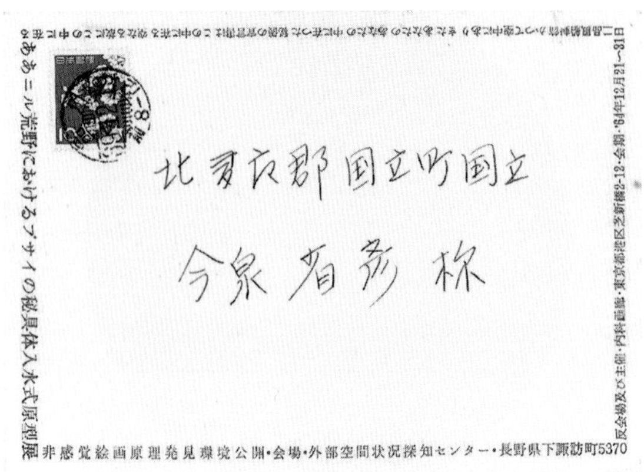

FIGURE 6.1
Matsuzawa Yutaka, *Ah, Nil, Ah, A Ceremony of Psi's Secret Embodiment Drowning in the Wilderness: Prototype Exhibition*, 1964. Envelope addressed to and received by Imaizumi Yoshihiko. Private collection. (Also plate 16.)

In this section, two cardinal works featuring the empty gallery, by Yves Klein and Robert Barry, will be compared with Matsuzawa's in order to map the Japanese artist in a spectrum of immateriality that embodied one of the most salient characteristics of conceptualism in postwar art. Both Klein and Barry had much in common with Matsuzawa: all three pursued the invisible in art, in different manners. Like Matsuzawa, Klein was an early figure of conceptualism whose interest in the invisible arose out of his painting practice. Barry, younger than the other two, shared interests in the ephemeral with Matsuzawa as evident in his *Electromagnetic Energy Field* (1968) and *Telepathic Piece* (1969), respectively engaging modern physics and parapsychology.[2]

Chronologically, Klein's 1958 work, commonly known as *The Void*, inaugurated the global lineage of the empty gallery. For this exhibition, officially titled *The Specialization of Sensibility in the Raw Material State into Stabilized Pictorial Sensibility*, Klein painted white the walls of Iris Clert Gallery in Paris and created an environment that was hermetic (not visible from the street) and elaborately staged. Two uniformed Republican Guards stood at the outside gate, and only a limited number of people could enter at one time after being greeted by the artist.[3] Some two or three thousand visited the gallery without knowing exactly what to expect. Some remarked it as a "void," based on its emptiness, and the artist came to embrace the idea and actively incorporate it into this work, as with that famous photo performance, *Leap into the Void*.

Matsuzawa's 1964 empty gallery was part of his double solo exhibition, the Tokyo portion held at Naiqua Gallery in the last days of December 1964. Not coincidentally, this was the second time that Naiqua was closed for an exhibition. Earlier that year in May, Hi Red Center "closed" the gallery on the opening day of their *Great Panorama Exhibition* and "opened" it on the exhibition's closing day for a party, in which a who's who of Tokyo's vanguard community joined (figure 6.2). Commonly known as *Closing Event*, this physical closure, marked by an X (made of wooden boards) and a sign, was announced by a postcard stating, "Right now, the gallery is being closed by the

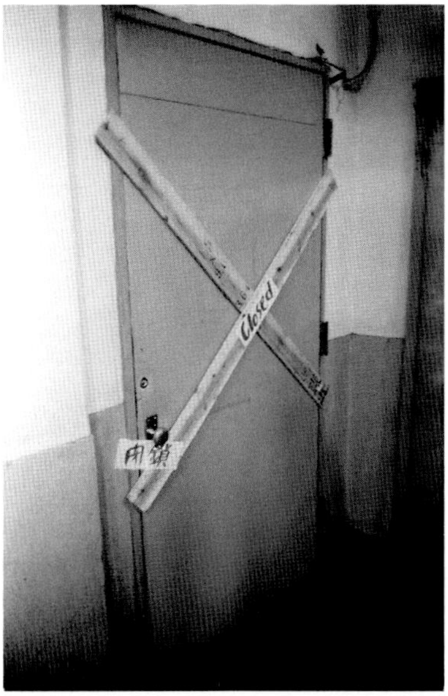

FIGURE 6.2
Hi Red Center, *Great Panorama Exhibition* (aka *Closing Event*) at Naiqua Gallery, Tokyo, May 1964. Documentary photograph of event. © Hirata Minoru.

hand of Hi Red Center. When you have free time, please make sure not to visit it."[4] The clever, tongue-in-cheek inversion of "opening" and "closing" characterizes Hi Red Center's dry humor. At the same time, by the minimal intervention of sealing the gallery, they turned the whole mundane world that existed outside the gallery into a readymade object presented as a "great panorama."

As opposed to Hi Red Center's messy non-show, Matsuzawa's empty Naiqua was a concerted operation dealing with the immaterial itself. During the busiest days of the year before the New Year's celebration, when few would visit art exhibitions, he literally closed the gallery in Tokyo for the duration of his solo show, *Ah, Nil, Ah, A Ceremony of Psi's Secret Embodiment Drowning in the Wilderness: Prototype Exhibition*.[5] (It was called "prototype," because he expected to have another solo show there in the spring of 1965, the title of which was to be exactly the same, minus the subtitle.) The third piece in our comparison, Barry's 1969 work, was literally titled *Closed Gallery*, for which the New York–based artist closed three galleries: Art & Project in Amsterdam, Galleria Sperone in Turin, and Eugenia Butler in Los Angeles.

In all three, an announcement or invitation played a key role. Klein's was an elegantly printed card, in blue letters on white paper, enclosed in an envelope with a fake stamp in the shade of his signature blue (figure 6.3, plate 17). On the card, the gallery announced the occasion as a "demonstration of perceptive synthesis [that] officially sanctions Yves Klein's pictorial quest for ecstatic and immediately communicable emotion."[6] The content of the exhibition was intentionally kept vague to intrigue the recipients. Matsuzawa's announcement was an ingenious work on paper (figure 6.1,

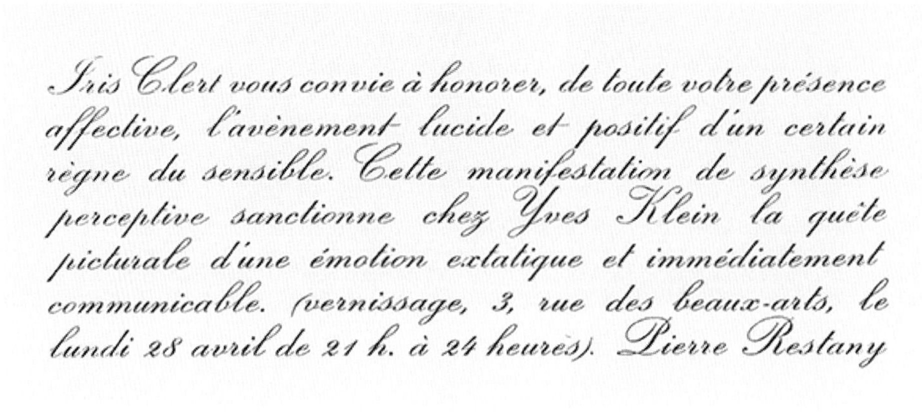
Iris Clert vous convie à honorer, de toute votre présence affective, l'avènement lucide et positif d'un certain règne du sensible. Cette manifestation de synthèse perceptive sanctionne chez Yves Klein la quête picturale d'une émotion extatique et immédiatement communicable. (vernissage, 3, rue des beaux-arts, le lundi 28 avril de 21 h. à 24 heures). Pierre Restany

FIGURE 6.3
Yves Klein, invitation to the vernissage of the exhibition *La spécialisation de la sensibilité à l'état de matière première en sensibilité picturale stabilisée*, later known as *Void*, on April 28, 1958, Galerie Iris Clert, Paris. © Yves Klein/Artists Rights Society (ARS), New York/ADAGP, Paris, 2015. (Also plate 17.)

plate 16). On a white large-format envelope, he had the exhibition data and the artist's concept statement printed in bright red. Beginning at the top left and continuing counterclockwise, it read:

> *Ah, Nil, Ah, A Ceremony of Psi's Secret Embodiment Drowning in the Wilderness: Prototype Exhibition*. The environment in which the principle of *Non-Sensory Painting* was discovered is made public. Venue: Outer Space Situation Research Center • 5370 Shimo Suwa-chō, Nagano Prefecture. Anti-venue and organizer: Naiqua Gallery, 2-12 Shiba Shinbashi, Minato-ku, Tokyo • Period: December 21–31. Nihon's balloon envelope once existed in the air • And the manifesto for a secret rite that existed in you, you is in this • This is empty, therefore it's in this.

Although the announcement did not explicitly state that the gallery would be closed and empty, this could have been inferred from the way the envelope was mailed out: unsealed and empty of content. Barry's announcement cards are the simplest, merely stating "The Gallery will be closed" with the relevant data (the exhibition title "Robert Barry," as well as exhibition venue and dates) (figure 6.4).

One important lesson is that the empty gallery was never empty—never devoid of signification. It was Klein who declared, "Having rejected nothingness, I discovered the void."[7] Klein's view of void was likely informed by his familiarity with Zen Buddhism through his practice of *jūdō*. Matsuzawa more concretely articulated his idea of void based on his intensive ongoing study of Buddhist metaphysics throughout the

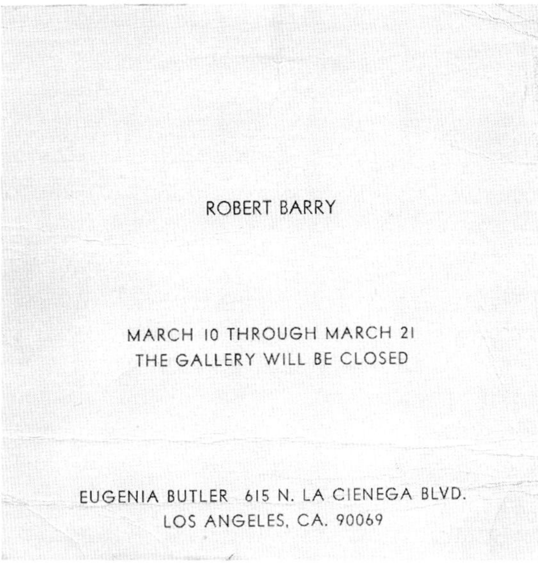

ROBERT BARRY

MARCH 10 THROUGH MARCH 21
THE GALLERY WILL BE CLOSED

EUGENIA BUTLER 615 N. LA CIENEGA BLVD.
LOS ANGELES, CA. 90069

FIGURE 6.4
Robert Barry, *Closed Gallery*, 1969 (detail). 1 of 3 announcement cards, 14 × 14 cm. © Robert Barry.

1960s. In 1965, he put the nature of "void"(*kū*) in the center of his work *Void*, which reads (see appendix for full translation):

> Let us think of *kū* [void]
> That is the whole character of all the laws
> It is not limited as *yū* [existence] or *mu* [nonexistence; also nothingness]
> It is a dormant [*myōbuku*][8] state, neither the path of existence nor that of nonexistence
> [...]
> Not existence, not void, not nonexistence, not non-void
> [...]
> The state we desire is "all being in void," "living in void"
> Dissolve into nirvana [*jakumetsu*] and be invisible, but appear like an apparition at times! times! times!

A likely source that Matsuzawa could have referenced was the Madhyamaka school (Chūgan-ha), one of the major Mahayana schools that taught emptiness to be the "middle path" between existence and nonexistence.[9] The last line of the envelope, "This [envelope] is empty, therefore [the manifesto] is in this," should be read in the spirit of "emptiness is latently full." This formulation helped him to differentiate his void from the one-dimensional and rationalist concept of nonexistence and nothingness, thereby opening a wide horizon of possibilities for his search for the invisible.

In Klein's *The Void*, what was at stake was his investigation of the monochrome (his signature blue), which was part of Klein's larger investigation of pure and stabilized pictorial sensibility that took many material forms, including pure pigment and gold leaf. The long title, *The Specialization of Sensibility in the Raw Material State into Stabilized Pictorial Sensibility*, hence bespoke his desire to offer a tangible sensory experience of an ultimately invisible yet intensified pictorial state of monochrome—that is, the essence of painting, or what he called its "radiance."[10] Although he bravely declared that he had "overcome the problematics of art,"[11] he was still saddled with the materiality of his demonstration of immateriality at Iris Clert. He resolved this problem in two ways. One was a physical solution. In 1961, when he had a retrospective at Museum Haus Lange, Krefeld, he created a room of its own, *Raum der Leere* ("White Room"), to enshrine his "object lesson" of immateriality and preserve it in its absolute material form. The other was a more conceptual approach that arose from the materialist situation of the art market. He claimed he was reluctant to debase his immateriality by monetizing it, while boasting of selling a few immaterial paintings from his 1958 exhibition in his exegesis of the whole affair.[12] Thus was born *Immaterial Pictorial Sensitivity Zones* in 1959. The work consists of a ritual of transferring the right to an immaterial sensitivity from the artist to a collector, and gold pieces from the latter to the former; each ritual was recorded in *Receipts*, a logbook of transactions (figure 6.5). (The artist would throw the gold into a river, while the collector had to burn the receipt to complete the transaction, though few followed the procedure.) By symbolically mimicking mundane sales activities, Klein had to exorcise the evil of the art market in which he operated. In contrast, as discussed in chapter 2, Matsuzawa, whose philosophical foundation had lain in anti-materialism from the outset, conceived a democratic value for his *White Circle*. (The art market in Japan will be further discussed in the context of land art later in this chapter.) In Barry's case, thanks to his teaching position at Hunter College, he was not concerned about benefiting financially from *Closed Gallery* and later worked with all three galleries.[13]

If Klein interrogated a sensory dimension of immateriality, Matsuzawa resolutely sought a non-sensory path to immateriality. For Matsuzawa, the empty gallery was an apparatus through which to solicit non-sensory reactions in the viewer's mental, not perceptual, faculty. While the French artist saw immateriality as closely tied to painting, the Japanese artist saw immateriality as a condition countering materialist civilization. What the latter offered in the form of art was a series of non-sensory exercises. With his 1964 Naiqua exhibition, more important than the fact of closing the gallery was the designation of Naiqua as "anti-venue" in the announcement. In his conception, the "anti-venue" in Tokyo, which was closed and empty, countered the "venue" in Shimo Suwa, where his bedroom was theoretically on display as the environment where "the principle of *Non-Sensory Painting* was discovered." In this regard, the Naiqua closing was an extension of the 1963 *Invitation to Psi Zashiki Room* (figure

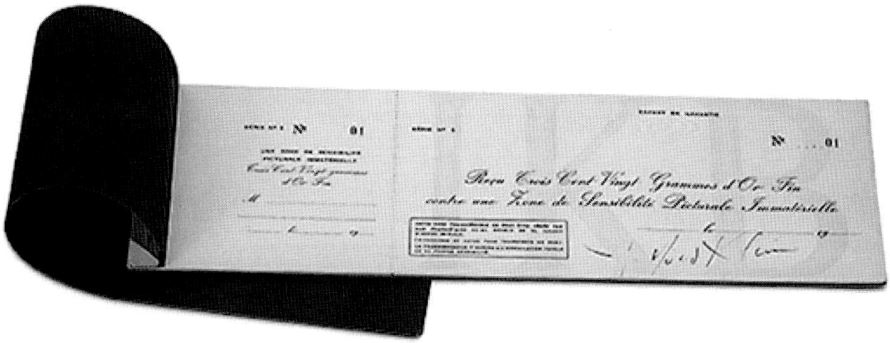

FIGURE 6.5
Yves Klein, *Receipt Book for the Zones of Immaterial Pictorial Sensibility, Series No. 5*, 1959. Printed paper. © Yves Klein/Artists Rights Society (ARS), New York/ADAGP, Paris, 2015.

2.12), which conceptually linked Tokyo and Shimo Suwa, not unlike Smithson's "Site/Non-Site" (see chapter 2). The binary of "venue/anti-venue" works similar to the pairing of "matter /anti-matter" in contemporary physics, which Matsuzawa first invoked in his *On Another Work in Another Container, or On Cutting*, also dating from 1963 (figure 2.13). At the "venue" in Shimo Suwa, the physical "environment" of his Revelation is physically present (as in "matter"), whereas at the "anti-venue," the "anti-environment" *theoretically* exists (as in "anti-matter"). The closing of the gallery, which resulted in the impossibility of entering it, illuminated the theoretical conceit of "anti-venue," and the distance, which signified the unlikelihood of traveling to the "venue," insured the enigma of his Revelation. In sum, *Prototype Exhibition* was an exercise in unknowability.

Although Matsuzawa physically closed the gallery, the literal or material void was not as crucial to his purely meditative operation, because what mattered to him was the activation of the viewer's brain to "think of" void. This is particularly true with his work that commanded the viewer to mentally empty the exhibition (e.g., *Anti-Civilization Exhibition* of 1965). It is instructive to remember that his mantra in 1964, as articulated in the ad for *Independent '64 in the Wilderness* (figure 0.1), was: "Don't believe matter / Don't believe senses / Don't believe the eye."

What, then, was offered by Robert Barry's empty gallery? His simple, deadpan card announcing the closure of a gallery appears too literal to decipher. Helpful in this regard is art historian Liz Kotz's insightful reading of language-based works.[14] In general, the photographic image is uncoded and "appears as a purely indexical sign," and the linguistic sign is "inherently arbitrary, figural, and coded." However, in some works by Conceptual artists, including Barry's *Closed Gallery*, language is "used quasi-photographically, as a straightforward means of inscription and recording." In other words, language serves in lieu of photography to "document" the empty gallery, making it unnecessary to photograph the emptiness. Not unlike Matsuzawa's empty gallery, all Barry needed was the idea of closing, which must be acknowledged by the recipient of his announcement; the physical fact of the empty gallery becomes redundant, though still necessary.

Yet it is tempting to read further into Barry's closing. If we remember that he was then based in New York while the galleries he closed were located in Los Angeles, Turin, and Amsterdam, distance was implicitly built into this work, just as Matsuzawa worked with the distance between Tokyo and Shimo Suwa. (Distance was also an ingredient of Barry's *Invitation Piece* of 1972–1973, a kind of chain-letter operation among galleries, with one gallery announcing the artist's exhibition at another gallery, which then announced the following exhibition at yet another gallery.)

Another implicit element in Barry's *Closed Gallery* is that the three galleries he closed were commercial venues. Like Klein's empty gallery at Iris Clert, where the French artist showed nothing, in shutting the doors of these galleries Barry disabled their economic functions. If not committing outright institutional critique, he was at the time highly conscious of "art world strategies."[15] Thus his closing of commercial galleries can be understood as a subversive intervention in the system. This may appear a truism too obvious to mention. However, when compared with Matsuzawa's closed gallery, it is no insignificant point to consider in mapping out a spectrum of immateriality. Naiqua, the anti-venue of Matsuzawa's *Prototype Exhibition*, was a non-commercial venue called *kashi garō*, or "rental gallery," which was ubiquitous in 1960s Japan, where few market opportunities existed for vanguard artists. Those rental galleries in effect served as alternative spaces, with some doubling in dealing in their back rooms. The short-lived Naiqua, especially, was known for its advocacy of experimentalism, offering space in which artists "can put anything" and "use as [they] wish"—that is, Naiqua was a total freedom zone.[16] In this context, it would hardly have been a radical statement had an artist merely closed a gallery; Japanese artists had to go a step farther to conceptualize what an empty gallery could mean. That was what Matsuzawa did, as did Hi Red Center. In the case of Matsuzawa, the gallery, more than a place of display, was an apparatus for communication with the audience. For him, a closed gallery (Naiqua in 1964) served this purpose as effectively as an open one (solo show at Aoki in 1963) had done in initiating a mental movement in the viewer.

* * *

In the study of resonances, individual differences matter, needless to say. Klein's sensory and thus material investigation of immateriality contrasts with Matsuzawa's non-sensory apparatuses. Klein's viewer is a passive recipient of immaterial experience, while Matsuzawa's is required to be an active generator of his or her own immaterial experience. They form two poles of immateriality—sensory versus non-sensory, and passive versus active viewer—with Barry opening another angle by treating language as indexical, which contrasts the two predecessors' conventional reliance on language. We can map them as a spectrum of immateriality as a way to "regroup" local narrative tangents. In conceptualism, not just the act of art making but the art system that encompassed it were made into objects of interrogation; and artists responded and reacted to the respective art systems they inhabited. Therefore, the structural issue must also be taken into account in resonance studies. The issue of the art market, which varyingly figured in these three artists' practices of immateriality, will be a topic in studying land art later in this chapter. In addition to the systemic dimension, the generational difference must also be factored in. While Klein and Matsuzawa invented their conceptualisms from their respective works in Nouveau Réalisme and Anti-Art, Barry came out of Minimal Art, thus building his conceptualism on his experience in analytical formalism.[17]

In an ideal scenario, the regrouping necessary for world art history may be fed back into local histories, whether on an individual, contextual, or systemic level. A closer look at Barry's background is one such example that can be further pursued, not just in his monograph but in world art history. This is one way to "amplify" the existing knowledge base, decentering the center (New York, in this case) while potentially enriching it as a locale through a comparative perspective.

Japanese Pioneers: Matsuzawa Yutaka, Yoko Ono, and On Kawara

In 1960s art, Matsuzawa Yutaka belongs to the pioneer generation of global conceptualism. In fact, Japan offers a collection of important early practitioners who established their signature practices by the mid-1960s. They were the first generation of Japanese conceptualism, including Akasegawa Genpei (1937–2014), Shūsaku Arakawa (1936–2010), On Kawara (1933–2014), and Yoko Ono (b. 1933). Born in 1922, Matsuzawa was more than a decade older than these four pioneers; they spent their childhood years during World War II, when he was entering adulthood. However, for all five of them, their wartime experiences varyingly informed the core of their mature thinking and their rejection of the status quo. Another similarity was their gradual and singular evolution toward their versions of conceptualism.

Among them, the resonance between Matsuzawa and Ono is particularly strong. Most of all, like Matsuzawa, Ono made the deployment of the viewer's mind a generative element of her art. However, their paths to conceptualism were divergent. Ono's conceptualism was grounded in her early study of music,[18] with her event scores and instructions dating back to *Secret Piece* of 1953, which is the first English work of the Music section of her 1964 bilingual book of instructions, *Grapefruit*. (In the subsequent English-only version, the work opens the Music section.) In this poetic piece, she instructs the viewer to play "one note you want to play" with the accompaniment of "the woods from 5 a.m. to 8 a.m." (as noted in a text) or "the bird's singing at dawn" (as noted in a five-line score). Music gave her the initial freedom to expand the use of language in art. Yet it was not until 1961 that she first used language in a work of art (outside of music or poetry)—the same year Matsuzawa first used language in his work outside poetry. While Matsuzawa struggled for another three years before renouncing materiality and proposing *Non-Sensory Painting* in 1964, Ono took deliberate steps to deconstruct "painting" in her *Instructions for Painting* series between 1961 and 1964, moving from objects (ink-soaked fabrics) to words inscribed on paper (instructions) to language in printed book form (anthologized in *Grapefruit*), all the while making viewer participation an integral part of her operation.[19] Once this process was complete, she was symbolically liberated from the constraints of objecthood and went on to apply her methodology in every area of expression. It may sound improbable that Matsuzawa's and Ono's paths never crossed during Ono's stay in Tokyo in 1962–1964, when she was active in the Tokyo avant-garde circle, giving concerts and staging event-exhibitions in Tokyo and Kyoto. There were a few factors that prevented their meeting. Matsuzawa's distance from Tokyo was a main reason; with his teaching job, he came out to the capital mostly for his exhibition activities. His remoteness also resulted in his detachment from Tokyo's vanguard circles, especially the Fluxus-Cage axis formed around the Sōgetsu Art Center, which encompassed Ono's core associates.[20]

Coincidentally, Matsuzawa had a brief connection with Fluxus in 1974, when the composer-theorist Yasunao Tone, who had by then settled in New York, produced *Communication with Mr. Psi* for Charlotte Moorman's *11th Annual New York Avant-Garde Festival: At Shea Stadium*. For this work, Tone asked Matsuzawa to recite his 1966 mantra *Humans, Let's Vanish* over the phone, which would have been broadcast over the ballpark's PA system, but due to the time difference and technical difficulty the project was unsuccessful.[21]

It is of no small significance that painting was the first object of critique in Matsuzawa's and Ono's practices. In fact, painting was the most contentious issue in Japanese modernism—contentious because it was *the* foremost institution in the transplanted paradigm of modernist art as experienced in Japan. As such, it was one institution that could not be lightly disposed of. Doing so would have been tantamount to denying the whole history of the struggles of Japanese artists who had squarely faced Western modernism and tried to develop their version of modern art. Matsuzawa and Ono might not have consciously thought of history this way, but it is as though they had, for they each early on dismantled and denounced the material foundation of painting in favor of mind over hand. Notably, three other pioneers also made painting a primary medium of investigation in their works. After moving to New York in 1962, the former Anti-Art artist Shūsaku Arakawa developed "diagram paintings," which prefigured *The Mechanism of Meaning* (1971) he subsequently developed with his wife, poet Madeline Gins. On Kawara's "printed painting" (*insatsu kaiga*) in the 1950s was an attempt to democratize painting that predated his attempt to depersonalize painting in his "date painting" (*Today* series) (figure 5.5).[22] Akasegawa Genpei deployed both painting and printed matter as vehicles of Capitalist Realism, calling the 100-times-enlarged ink-on-paper rendition *Morphology of Revenge: Take a Close Look at the Opponent before You Kill Him* (1963–1968) (figure 6.6).

Between Matsuzawa and Ono, the function of ideation is differently mobilized. A telling comparison can be made with their postcard works that prompt the recipient to make a circle: Matsuzawa's postcard version of *White Circle—A Blank Painting for All Living and Non-Living Beings* of 1967 (figure 2.19)—and Ono's *Draw Circle Event*, a postcard dated 1964 and mailed out probably in early 1965 (figure 6.7). Both are communicative and interactive. Matsuzawa's postcard bore his command to meditate on *White Circle* on the back of the postcard (which was left blank), whereas Ono's

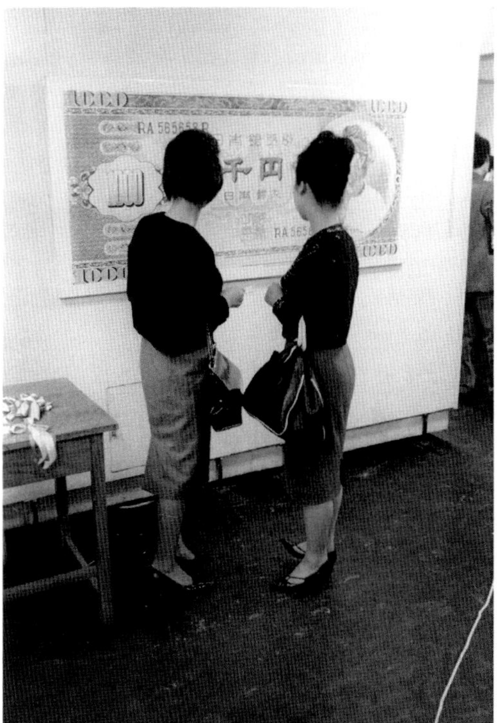

FIGURE 6.6
Hirata Minoru, *Visitors Looking at Akasegawa Genpei's Morphology of Revenge (a.k.a. 1,000-Yen Note Painting),* *at Hi Red Center's 5th Mixer Plan exhibition at Shinjuku Dai-Ichi Gallery,* *Tokyo,* May 1963. Photograph. © Hirata Minoru.

postcard is a friendly invitation to "Draw Circle" in a blank box, fill in a questionnaire, and send the postcard back to the artist. Thanks to this last act requested of the recipient, Ono's archive contains a number of responses that demonstrate free and inventive ways in which her peers drew their circles.[23] The New York–based Japanese artist Ay-O punched holes in lieu of the letter O in his questionnaire answers, while leaving the rectangle blank. The Japanese art critic Takiguchi Shūzō contributed neatly drawn concentric circles, using "the small motor of a table juicer," as he annotated (an operation that in part recalls *Rotorelief* by Duchamp, with whom the critic had a close affiliation). And among several Fluxus associates, George Brecht reported he saw "a wet ring on the table," and declared himself "a circle-drawer now," but drew an up-down arrow (↕) in the box. Their responses to Ono's call for the freedom to make a circle as one wished reveal multiple possibilities that probably went beyond the artist's expectation. It is a hallmark of Ono's conceptualism to keep the possibilities open for interpretation on the viewer's side. Unlike the participants in Ono's postcard piece, we do not know how Matsuzawa's recipients responded. However, what he offered with his postcard was not the freedom to make any circle but the simplest and purest form of idea. The universal shape of *White Circle* can be shared equally by anybody, provided one applies one's mind to it. Their different approaches may partly be explained by the different branches of Buddhism they espoused: the Zen Buddhism Ono referenced in her 1966 talk "To the Wesleyan People"[24] was newer and less prescriptive than the earlier disciplines of Buddhism, such as Amida faith and Esoteric Buddhism, that Matsuzawa intensively studied.

Keeping his sight trained beyond the confines of art is another trait Matsuzawa had in common not only with Ono but also with the other three pioneers. Matsuzawa's declaration of Anti-Civilization in 1965 and Vanishing of Humankind in 1966 was built upon his observation that humankind had produced a misguided civilization that had led to the 20th-century wars. Sharing a similar antiwar belief, Ono turned to antiwar activism with her husband John Lennon and called for peace through their *War Is Over!* project in 1969. Her commitment to world peace resurfaced after 9/11, which prompted her ongoing communal project of *Imagine Peace*. If Matsuzawa gave up on architecture to pursue the invisible in art, Arakawa shifted to architecture in 1987 to extend the philosophical implications of *The Mechanism of Meaning* by founding the Architectural Body Research Foundation, which was recast as the Reversible Destiny Foundation in 2010. In their collaboration of *Reversible Destiny*, Arakawa and Gins aimed to undertake an intervention in human life and awaken the body and consciousness to their hidden potential.[25] Akasegawa was never as grand in his temperament as Matsuzawa, Ono, or Arakawa, but within the domestic context he exercised a unique populism by exploiting the print media to reach out to a broad base of the Japanese populace from the 1980s onward, through his projects of *Ultra-Art Tomason* (1972–1985), *Geriatric Power* (*Rōjinryoku*) and its spinoffs (1998–2001),

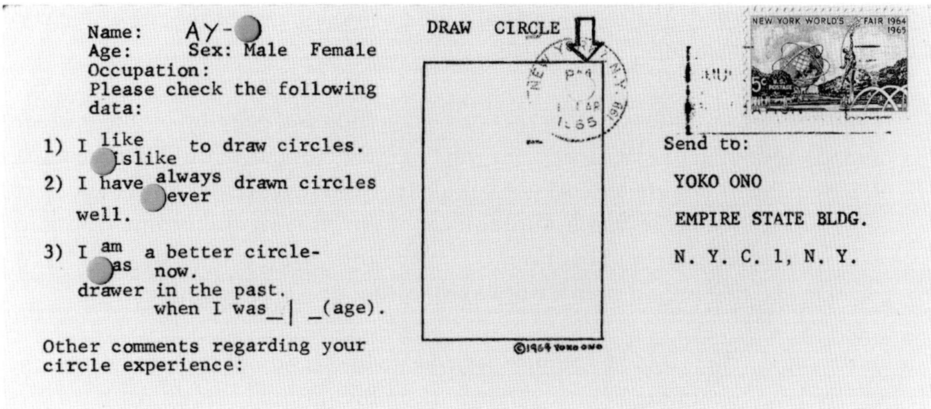

FIGURE 6.7
Yoko Ono, *Draw Circle Event*, 1964–1965. Postcards returned to Yoko Ono from Ay-O. Collection of the artist. © Yoko Ono.

and *Cheerleaders of Japanese Art* and its related projects (2000–2004), among other publications.[26] Taciturn in public concerning his ideas, On Kawara, too, had an overreaching humanist vision: his stated concern was "human consciousness, an individual's heightened awareness of his or her existence in the world."[27]

Although their aesthetic strategies varied greatly, Matsuzawa and Kawara had much in common in their thinking. Communication was their early interest. In the case of Kawara, he identified communication as a paramount goal of art and its primary social function in his essay on "printed painting" in the late 1950s.[28] Especially important for him was a "two-way exchange" between the artist and the viewer. An active viewer's potential, he felt, was hampered by the notion of the "unique original" and by conventional exhibition displays. To counter this situation, he devised "printed painting" that utilized the techniques of commercial printing for wide distribution among the masses, his target audience. In reality, the result was not so successful, amounting to no more than labor-intensive offset posters.[29] Yet his theory of "printed painting," a mixture of Social Realist aspiration and proto-conceptualist critique of the institution of art, paved a way for his future work in New York. The path to the signature *Today* series was rocky still. A serious doubt of his art making struck him while in Paris in 1963, but his visit to Altamira to see the prehistoric cave paintings that year renewed his commitment to art.[30] It should be noted that not masterpieces but a primal origin of painting in human history helped him to reaffirm the enduring value of art. His 1965 text-painting *Composition of Words for a Catalogue*, which he sent from New York to the National Museum of Modern Art, Tokyo, which surveyed

Japanese artists abroad, articulates precious little of what he was thinking at the crucial moment of transition:

> If you seriously wonder whether this printed section is a painting or not, you are, honestly speaking, too far away from what we mean. Because you still hold a definite view that literature and art are completely different artistic media and, perhaps, you still embrace that beautiful ideal of purification and synthesization of each artistic medium. And because you still believe that it is impossible to "read" painting and that even if such a work existed, that's complete nonsense.[31]

The text marked a threshold he had just passed into his version of conceptualism. The idea of "reading" a painting at once refers back to his "printed painting"—his desire for communication, which would require the viewer to "read" his painting—and forward to his "date painting" series, *Today*, which he meant the viewer to "read." That is to say, each "date painting" is a communication made to the viewer. It serves as a daily reproducible, subtly variable, self-fulfilling yet never-ending canvas that either individually or collectively forces the viewer to creatively respond and produce a new meaning. In a sense, with *Today* Kawara created a Barthesian apparatus that could transform the viewer into a "reader" of open-ended text that is painting.

Whether prescriptive or open-ended, Matsuzawa's and Kawara's works equally challenge viewers to reexamine their assumptions of art in particular and the world in general. In comparison with Matsuzawa's vocal interest in alternate realities, Kawara was much subtler but never mute in expressing his concerns about the external world. With the *Today* series, he encased that day's painting with a newspaper clipping of the day and the location he produced it in a cardboard box. The newspaper clipping functions as another kind of "printed painting," reflecting the state of "today's world," which existed beyond the frame of the canvas that he and the viewer alike should be aware of. If so, it is intriguing to examine other hints he left behind concerning his idea of our "existence in the world." Though much later in his life, he had three Japanese texts translated and included in his solo exhibition catalogs. They were the parapsychologist Yamamoto Kajin's *A Philosophical Study of Cosmic Consciousness* (1974),[32] the "consciousness science" specialist Inomata Shūji's *Paradigm of New Science: Principia for the 21st Century* (1987),[33] and the planetary science scholar Matsui Takafumi's *How to Live as Aliens* (2003).[34] These texts show that Kawara's interest in unconventional sciences was as serious as Matsuzawa's.[35] Nonetheless, it must be cautioned that facile reading of these texts in relation to his art is what the artist would have hated most.

A striking resonance is found in two works from 1970: Matsuzawa's *My Own Death* and Kawara's *One Million Years, Past*, made in 1970–1971 (to be followed by *One Million Years, Future* in 1980–1998). Both artists thematized consciousness and time, albeit differently. The former work, shown at *Tokyo Biennale 1970*, commands the viewer to meditate on the artist's death as well as "your own future death," "past hundred hundred millions of human beings' deaths," and "future thousand trillions of human beings." He invoked the entire human history, past, present, and future, through "deaths" that denote "lives" which vanished or will vanish. His sweeping sense of time at once echoes and contrasts Kawara's. On the one hand, as Kawara noted in the works, *One Million Years: Past* is meant "For all those who have lived and died" while *One Million Years: Future* is "For the last one."[36] These works thus reveal the artist's gaze on the entire history of human lives, like Matsuzawa's. On the other hand, Kawara here chose to focus on time, the most abstract aspect of life. It is intriguing, however, that his conception of *One Million Years* was at one point related to "All the Information of Mankind on the Earth," as noted in his page on the catalog of *Information*, a landmark exhibition of conceptualism at the Museum of Modern Art, New York in the summer of 1970.[37] Narrowing down his expression to time from an impossibly vast realm of knowledge (in which he was truly interested) was a typically "self-limiting"[38] and disciplined approach he demonstrated in his body of work after he launched his "date painting" in 1966. Unlike Matsuzawa, who was verbose in his work, Kawara preferred economy of language, deliberately and laboriously marking time one year after another, one column after another, one page after another, to compile into binders. Yet the resulting effects were also opposite: Matsuzawa's time can be meditated by the viewer in the stretch of time required to pass through a gallery, while Kawara's time must be experienced in a prolonged manner through reading it or listening to its recitation.

* * *

Sharing certain historical and cultural backgrounds, Matsuzawa and other Japanese pioneers of conceptualism developed their distinct practices. While Matsuzawa made the whole human civilization his prime concern and developed the concept of Vanishing, Kawara reflected on the entirety of human history through his engagement with time. Both Ono and Matsuzawa endeavored to activate the viewer's mind through their work: in doing so, Ono upheld an optimistic view of human freedom and world peace, whereas Matsuzawa devised his theory of Anti-Civilization as an ultimate Nirvana.

In a broader context, the resonance studies of pioneer Japanese conceptualists point to a set of challenges we face in linking the global and the local. Obviously, it is necessary to continue to identify more contact points and draw narrative tangents to amplify the global history of postwar art, especially with such Japan-based artists as Matsuzawa and Akasegawa Genpei. Yet the reverse is also needed: linking such emigrant artists as Ono, Kawara, and Arakawa into their original locale of Japan. In other words, linking diasporas to a mother country remains a task for historians of postwar Japanese art.[39] As the present study demonstrates, even for On Kawara, whose refusal to use the Japanese language in his *Today* series epitomizes his dissociation from his native country,[40] the study of his conceptualism can be expanded by examining his Japanese connections and resonances. In this sense, local and global inherently inform each other, seldom completely detached from each other.

LAND ART: DIGGING INTO THE LOCAL

The second section of this chapter examines two contextual issues related to land art. Extending the local history of land art that had begun with hole diggings, The Play's "voyages" (chapter 3) and GUN's *Event to Change the Image of Snow* (chapter 4) made major contributions to the global history of land art. In a broad stroke, their ambitious scales and inventive uses of landscape are comparable, for example, to such icons of American Earthworks as Robert Smithson's *Spiral Jetty* (1970) and Michael Heizer's *Double Negative* (1969–1970) from the same time period. Yet the differences cannot be clearer. Set against American artists' single authorship and deployment of heavy construction equipment to produce veritable monuments, the Japanese practitioners stand their ground with their collective and performative strategies to materialize ephemeral outcomes. The monument builders were well financed by their patrons, while the rainbow chasers were practically self-financed, although they managed to secure support from some art world professionals and benevolent laypersons. Furthermore, the American continental landscape was vast and remote, whereas the Japanese archipelago's scenery was intimate and proximate to human habitats. A conundrum of international contemporaneity was that *despite* such differences, resonating practices arose in locales an ocean apart.

Having said this much, we must exercise caution and not overgeneralize. On the one hand, American land art constitutes a larger pool of practitioners. To speak of nothing else, their economic circumstances varied from artist to artist and from project to project. On the other hand, the existence of a functioning market for contemporary art and associated transactional opportunities (e.g., collectors willing to support land projects) afforded U.S. artists multiple options in their art making, ranging from acceptance to circumvention to outright rejection of the market. Their choices are not always visible to the eye of history yet constitute a legitimate topic of study that goes beyond the scope of the present book.[41] However, the absence of a market for their Japanese counterparts is a relevant topic, along with one of its consequences—what I call "the culture of showing." In this respect our comparative study necessarily remains incomplete and one-sided, but offers an important understanding of 1960s Japan.

The first part of the study centers on the culture of showing, which gave top priority to display in exhibitions as well as in the media, with particular reference to photographic recording. An opening comparison is between GUN's snow event and that of Dennis Oppenheim, who was highly photo-conscious. This is followed by an examination of the artists' relationship with nature and landscape. The remoteness of the sites of American Earthworks has been well studied;[42] the Japanese characteristic of using nature nearby requires equal attention. This part of the discussion will open with a comparison of The Play's *Thunder*, a 10-year project to catch lightning that began in 1977, and Walter De Maria's *The Lightning Field*, a permanent installation for lightning observation inaugurated in the exact same year, which together form an exceptional occurrence of pure resonance in the 1970s.

The "Culture of Showing" and Photography

One of the core elements of radicalism in 1960s art in Japan was ephemerality. In Anti-Art, object-based works more often than not did not survive beyond their displays and performative practices left few material traces. In Non-Art of the post-Yomiuri years this tendency accelerated, especially in the wilderness, as exemplified by Matsuzawa Yutaka's immaterial conceptualism as well as the performative land art of GUN and The Play. The ephemerality of Non-Art in Japan echoed the global tendencies generally described as "dematerialization."

In this regard, GUN's *Event to Change the Image of Snow* in 1970 can most saliently be compared with Dennis Oppenheim's snow projects of 1968–1969, not only because the American artist's works in part inspired the Japanese group (see chapter 4), but also because his snow works and theirs shared a few commonalities. His snow works were ephemeral (often lasting no more than 24 hours, though longer than GUN's 30 minutes), he recognized the importance of photography early on,[43] and his work was featured in the popular media.

GUN's snow event is discussed in detail in chapter 4. Oppenheim produced nine works around the border of the American state of Maine and the Canadian province of New Brunswick (figure 6.8, plate 18). Born in the state of Washington in 1938, the artist spent most of his life on the West Coast until 1967 when he married Phyllis Jalbert, whose family lived in this snowy northern region near the U.S.-Canadian border.[44] He conceived a series of "cuts" into snow as formalist exercises and executed them with the help of his wife and her family members, using hand tools such as chainsaws.[45] (The relative limitations of his economic means aligned him more closely to GUN than Smithson or Heizer.) He was fascinated with the national border that politically separates two countries, and many of his cuts illuminated this invisible yet present delineation. His titles such as *Boundary Split* and *Time Line* speak of this interest. What separates GUN and Oppenheim crucially is their respective relationships with the mass media.

In the U.S., popular journalism entered the operational equation of American artists with the advent of land art, as recent scholarship demonstrates. Since the 1949 *Life* article on Jackson Pollock, which posed the unthinkable question "Is he the greatest living painter in the United States?,"[46] contemporary art had been an object not of respect but at least of curiosity in the mass media. As art historian Tom Holert observes, thanks to a growing interest in environmental issues and the space age, more thoughtful coverage on land art appeared in the late 1960s, and the popular media were instrumental in the visualization and representation of land works that were difficult for viewers to personally experience; and the land artists slowly learned the usefulness of the mass media for their work.[47] In some cases, the relationship of the artists (most notably Robert Smithson) and the media photographers remained "difficult, often antagonistic" concerning the control of imagery, for the latter tended to disregard the former's intentions in creating spectacular shots.[48] Oppenheim, too, felt the need to take possession of photography of his work and preferred to maintain an informal approach. As history shows, many artists sought to repossess their now-vanished or too-remote-to-visit land works through photography, which could afford them an "afterlife" or "second life," so to speak.[49] That was a natural transition, since the practice of land art was indeed embedded in the art system consisting of exhibitions at both non-profit and for-profit venues, the art market, collectors, and other benefactors.[50] Thus, it was well within the artists' prerogative to display photographs of their land works. Some even transformed documentary photographs into panels and other secondary objects that would stand in for the original works. Oppenheim for one was systematic in his production of related panels: he always included detailed data on the work (including how he made it), a map, and at least one overall view, with additional procedural shots (figure 6.8, plate 18).[51]

In this operational context, media exposure would then be only one piece of the puzzle that is land art. Being in a national magazine might have been exciting, but that was superfluous to the artists' intention. The situation was quite different in Japan, where the art system, both institutional and commercial, was at best weak. To counter this situation, Japanese vanguard artists created what I call the "culture of showing," in which the mass media played an integral role. For these artists, media attention was practically their only option for gaining any kind of reward; and they often worked closely with supportive photojournalists. GUN's snow event culminated this local tangent: their primary goal was to make it into an illustrated magazine and other popular outlets—a few pages of color reproduction were far more desirable than a tiny monochrome photo in *Bijutsu techō*, for example. From the beginning, public exposure was their intended reward in an otherwise rewardless (*mushō*)[52] world of vanguard art in Japan, for which the art market was practically nonexistent.[53] Unlike Oppenheim, GUN at the time did not exhibit the photographs of their snow event or make an object as such out of them.[54]

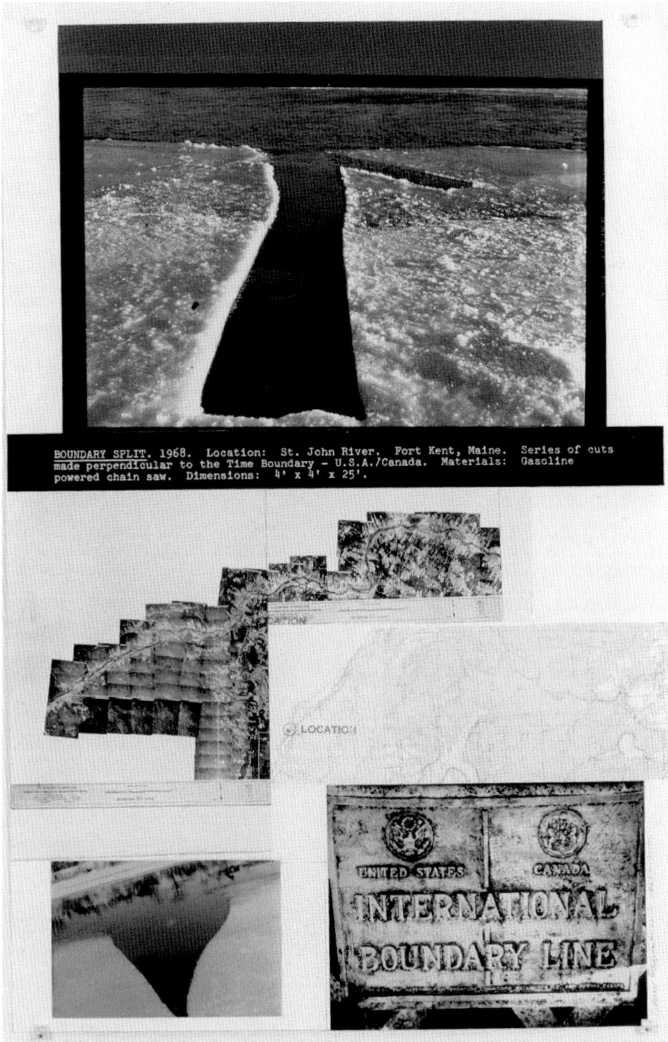

FIGURE 6.8
Dennis Oppenheim, *Boundary Split*, 1968. "Location: St. John's River, Fort Kent, Maine. Series of cuts perpendicular to the Time Boundary U.S.A./ Canada. Gasoline powered chain saw. Dimensions: 4 × 4 × 25 feet." Black and white and color photography, hand-stamped topographic map, aerial map, text on rag board; 60 × 40 inches. © Dennis Oppenheim. Courtesy Dennis Oppenheim Estate. (Also plate 18.)

Although we must avoid oversimplification, it is safe to say that there were two opposing situations in Japan and Euro-America that prompted dematerialization in the late 1960s. Generally speaking, if the increasing marketization of contemporary art compelled American artists to search for dematerialized practices, the lack of any system of commercial reward profoundly informed the experiments of their Japanese counterparts. That is to say, while dematerialization took place in America to "decommodify" art in an increasingly commodified environment, it took place in Japan as a result of an undercommodified environment. An instructive comparison is found between the hole-digging works by Walter De Maria and Group "I." In his 1960 text "Meaningless Work,"[55] published in the Fluxus publication *An Anthology*, De Maria proposed the idea of digging a hole and filling it back in as a meaningless work. His opposition to the commercialization of art in reaction to the growing domination of the art market in the U.S. was unambiguous: he specifically defined his "meaningless works" as "not mak[ing] you money or accomplish[ing] a conventional purpose." In contrast, Group "I," without knowing De Maria's ideas, dug a hole in 1965 on a dry riverbed of the Nagara River as part of *Independent Art Festival* in Gifu (figure 6.9). In land art, scale matters. The Japanese collective's hole was as much as 10 meters wide and 1.5 meters deep. Nine members toiled daily under the scorching summer sun for eight days, then spent two days (the remainder of the 10-day exhibition period) filling it back in to comply with the river law's stipulation that they restore the riverbed's original state.[56] The visiting critics and artists duly noted the significance of their act. Akane Kazuo, a critic from Osaka, the group's home base, characterized their act as a "Sisyphean task," informed by a "pure desire" and "negative energy," that constituted "a biting irony toward the object-dependent act of creation."[57] That is to say, the conventional—and entrenched—notion of what constitutes the work of art was the point of reference to frame the group's futile act. Instead of the art market, it was the modernist idea of art—as strong in Japan as in the U.S., and for that matter in many locales in the world—that prompted their radical departure.

A similar issue can be observed in Matsuzawa Yutaka's proposition that *White Circle* should be a *Painting That Can Be Owned by All Humans* (see figure 2.21). His idea of universal ownership was as radical as Lawrence Weiner's Public Freehold works from 1968 to 1971.[58] Yet Matsuzawa's opposition was directed at a far larger target: postwar materialism and consumerism, wherein anything and everything, including works of art, could be exchanged with money and thus made into a commodity. His solution was to give an egalitarian value to his painting, aiming to take it out of the circuit of commodification altogether. In the absence of a viable market for contemporary art, it would have been meaningless for him to pursue the direction taken by Yves Klein: a symbolic insertion of immateriality into the market through an elaborate transaction ritual involving receipts for "Immaterial Pictorial Sensitivity Zones" (figure 6.5). In other words, although the absence of a market did not prevent

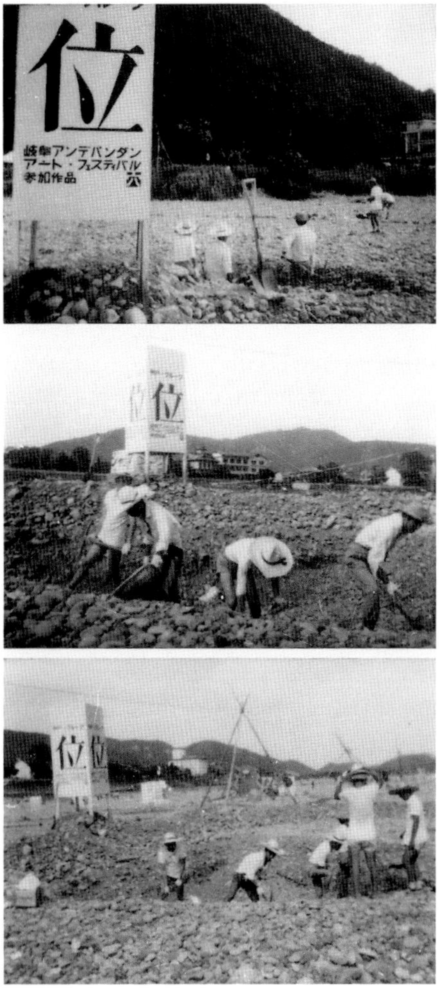

FIGURE 6.9
Group "I," *Hole*, 1965. Documentary photographs of performance art at *Independent Art Festival* in Gifu. © Kawaguchi Tatsuo. Courtesy of Shigeru Yokota Gallery.

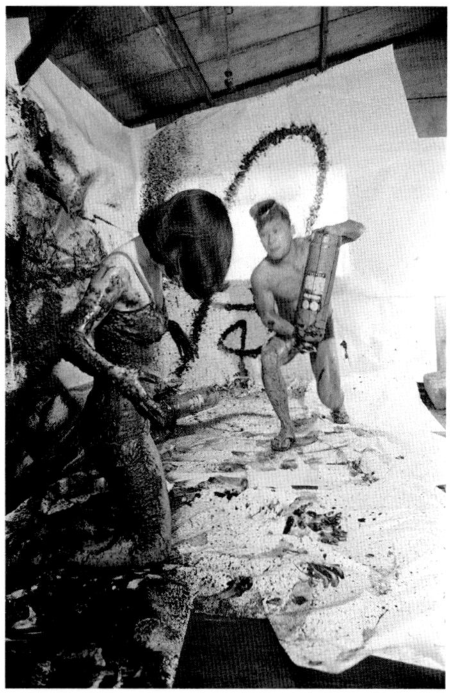

FIGURE 6.10
Ushio Shinohara's "action painting" with an ink-filled fire extinguisher, at Tanaka Shintarō's studio, Tokyo, 1963. Documentary photograph of performance art. © Hirata Minoru.

Matsuzawa from considering the issue of ownership, his options were constrained by his operational environment.

Likewise, GUN's desire for publicity must be put in context—specifically, the "culture of showing" in 1960s Japan.[59] In a nutshell, given the state of the market for contemporary art, vanguard artists had practically no expectations of selling their works, even though there was no shortage of venues to show them in. With the mainstreaming of contemporary art, the number of venues was growing, ranging from rental galleries to such large-scale exhibitions as Mainichi's domestic biannual. Yet as late as 1972 Lee Ufan pointed out the absence of a market as a serious structural issue:

> In brief, in foreign countries [read: Euro-America], [art] is directly tied to making a living. Should you break a pane of glass with a stone [like I did], somebody would buy it. Regardless of their styles and practices, artists over there can eat by being artists. Of course they won't make a fortune, but when, say, Christo covered a beach with tent fabric, somebody stepped forward to buy his idea. Unlike those artists, Japanese artists toil with no economic foundation. That's how different it is between here and there.[60]

Since selling was definitely out of the equation, they had a more realistic hope to show than to sell in creating their works. One consequence of this was unabashed showmanship, combined with radical experimentalism, that prioritized showing and sometimes paid little consideration to anything else. The early examples range from Gutai's shrewd publicity campaign with the American *Life* magazine and Japanese media outlets[61] to numerous outrageous Anti-Art works at the Yomiuri Independent Exhibition (figure 1.7). The meaningless acts of Group "I," too, formed a part of the culture of showing. Even Mono-ha can be understood in this context: the lack of sales possibilities prompted Sekine Nobuo to make a daring experiment with *Phase—Mother Earth*, which was realized at a magnificent height of 270 cm, or some nine feet. He later explained the scale for this and other works: "I can also say this. That is, [our reality is that] we can make works but we cannot sell them. I, for one, [make my works] on the assumption that they won't sell. Or, rather, I don't think about selling at all. Why? Because thinking about it too much will keep me from what I must do now. So, I don't care if they won't sell. I will do what I want to do."[62]

The "culture of showing" contrasts a "culture of selling" wherein the work of art assumes a commodity status. The Japanese attitude of giving almost total priority to "showing" was intensified among those who worked in performative veins, for the obvious reason that their acts in essence generated few commodifiable objects. This was in marked contrast to the situation of Oppenheim, Vito Acconci, and other practitioners of land and performance art in New York: for them, documentary photographs could be marketable objects in and of themselves; they could also make photographs into document panels and such. Compounding the situation in Japan, even in the realm of photography the commodification of prints lagged far behind Euro-America, with priority given to the print media of photobooks and magazine features.[63] In the absence of an art market, many Japanese vanguards turned to a different kind of marketplace: the mass media, especially the print media that had seen the exponential growth of general-interest weeklies and other periodical publications, including *manga* weeklies, since the end of the 1950s.

The de facto originator of the culture of showing was Ushio Shinohara, who famously declared in his autobiography, *The Avant-Garde Road*, of 1968:

> The spiritual freedom that arises from the rewardless act [*mushō no kōi*] of Art with a capital A [*geijutsu*] is nothing but a thing of the past. That is why I propelled the members of my group [Neo Dada] into the spotlight of 20th-century mass media. In front of an interviewer's microphone, a serious discussion of Art is useless. He who loudly says something shocking wins. In front of a camera, he must not hesitate but start dancing naked.[64]

A particular event that inspired Shinohara dates to September 1957. (He did not see Gutai's legendary demonstrations in October 1955). The French artist Georges Mathieu's public demonstration of action painting at the show window of the Shirokiya Department Store in Tokyo. The young Japanese artist was impressed as much by the Informel painter's showmanship and speed as by the sheer presence of numerous cameras clicking away at his every action; then and there, Shinohara saw "a new way of being an artist."[65] Beginning with his appearance as a "Rockabilly Painter," in *Shūkan Sankei*, a general-interest weekly, in 1958,[66] his action-based publicity stunts were colorfully recounted in his 1968 autobiography (figure 6.10). Having read Shinohara's accounts, Horikawa and GUN members revered the Anti-Art hero as an important model to emulate. Staging a series of Happenings during the first year of the group's history, the members were certainly conscious of publicity effects, even though theirs were a modest effort compared with Shinohara's bravado; but Horikawa's stone mailing proved to fascinate the media quite unexpectedly (figure 6.11).

Event to Change the Image of Snow marked an apex of the culture of showing, with all the prerequisites converging to make a bold idea into a memorable feat: performance-based land art, collectivism, and collaboration with a sympathetic photographer. In general, performances were relatively low-budget endeavors that could generate a huge visual impact,[67] both in terms of the action per se and any resulting byproducts, as embodied by Shinohara's "Rockabilly Painter." Furthermore, when several artists joined forces, they could achieve a scale larger than a single artist could, as with *Hole* by Group "I." In fact, collectivism in postwar Japan took a new turn in the post-Yomiuri years, with the proliferation of performative works.[68] Instead of

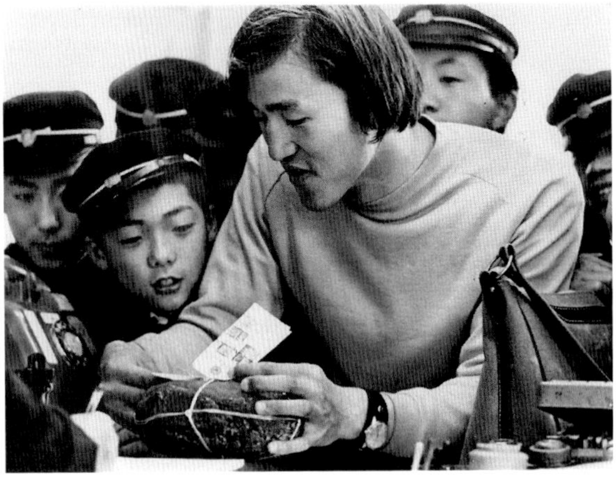

FIGURE 6.11
Horikawa Michio preparing his stone mailing to Prime Minister Satō Eisaku on May 3, 1970. Documentary photograph taken by a Mainichi Newspapers reporter. Photo courtesy of Horikawa Michio.

functioning as exhibition societies in which their members customarily showed their individual works, the post-Yomiuri collectives more routinely worked together under single group identities, beginning with Hi Red Center.[69] Since numbers have power in collectivism, the Ritualist collectives, such as Zero Dimension, frequently created an intercollective alliance in their anti-Expo projects, which produced an anarchic but extraordinary segment of the culture of showing. (Collectivism will be further discussed later in this chapter.)

Last but not least, the proactive involvement of photographers was vital for successes in the culture of showing. Contemporary artists found allies in vanguard-friendly photojournalists such as Hirata Minoru and Hanaga Mitsutoshi, who played a crucial role as agents of mediation between the artists and the print media.[70] Not only did they document the performative works, a task usually expected of photographers, but they also approached magazine editors to pitch article ideas and helped generate publicity for those artists. Publicity may have been as fleeting as their works, but it became the most tangible reward for them. During the 1960s, Hirata produced nearly 30 magazine articles on what he called "art in action" by vanguards ranging from Hi Red Center to Yoko Ono to Ritualists. While avidly chronicling social and genre scenes of the 1960s, Hanaga followed vanguard exhibitions and action-based activities, including Anti-Art performances, Butoh dance, and underground theater.[71] Working with GUN in remote Niigata, the Tokyo-based Hanaga became a veritable member and acted as a producer-cum-promoter; he facilitated the procuring of permission to use the dry riverbed, solicited the donation of pigments, and brought the project to its fruition as a magazine article (see chapter 4).

* * *

The culture of showing may embody a facet of a certain impenetrability the non-Japanese viewer may feel in avant-garde art in Japan. In 1987, reviewing *Japon des avant gardes*, a landmark survey at the Centre Pompidou, the French critic Catherine Millet characterized the vanguard extremism on display as "gone to the point of no return," unconstrained by the Western "classical humanism and Judeo-Christian thought."[72] The Big Three critic Tōno Yoshiaki found this Westerner's observation tantamount to calling the artists "*kamikaze* pilots who rushed forth, never to return" and undertook "one suicide mission after another."[73] Little doubt that such a sense of inscrutability is an obstacle for world art history. If the culture of showing does not entirely explain all the decisions Japanese artists made in their radical practices, however, it does offer a glimpse into the operational environment that affected them. One of our goals in narrating an amplified global story for 1960s art is to retrieve those apparent *kamikaze* practitioners from an abyss of history and securely land them in a field of world art history.

Together in Nature Nearby

The study of resonance often falls into a gray area, as history writing is no precise science. In some instances, the degree of connection is hard to ascertain (as with the case of Akasegawa Genpei's Capitalist Realism); in others, an international connection and a local tradition coexisted (as in the case of GUN's snow event). Thanks to the increased flow of information, the awareness of international contemporaneity markedly grew, especially toward 1970 and beyond, and Japanese artists were more likely to know, if only selectively and superficially, what was going on in Euro-America. (The one-way flow of information was a fact of life at the time; one may argue that this continues to be a problem even in the 21st century despite the qualitative growth of informational flow.) Such uncertainty nonetheless confounds a basic chronological ordering. It is rare to find such a perfect case of resonance, with two practitioners having a similar idea without either knowing what the other was doing, as in a pair of lightning-related works from the same year of 1977: Walter De Maria's *The Lightning Field* and The Play's *Thunder*.

Representing pinnacles of land art in their respective locales, the two works cannot be more different beyond the shared element of observing lightning. Like Smithson and Heizer, De Maria relied on the sponsorship of a willing funder (the Dia Art Foundation) to acquire a tract of land at Quemado in western New Mexico (figure 6.12).[74] Here he created a permanent installation consisting of 400 polished stainless steel poles, 2 inches in diameter (produced by a fabricator to the artist's specification), which are spread in a grid formation at intervals of 200 feet on the barren flatland (erected by laborers). The artist devised a strict viewing protocol for visitors to follow: how to travel to Quemado, how many visitors are allowed to stay at one time at a cabin provided and view the work (six at most), and how long they should stay there (24 hours); the foundation has maintained the work and administered the visits since 1977. Whether or not they see lightning hit one or more of the poles, visitors may still find the experience of a vast Southwest landscape dotted by minimalist poles to be transcendental.

The Play's *Thunder* centered on a pyramid-shaped temporary installation on Mount Jūbu, in Kyoto (figure 6.13). It began as a one-off idea in 1977 but grew into a 10-year project that ended in 1986. Tackling thunder was a logical step for them after their *Wind* in 1976 (figure 3.15), because the pairing of wind and thunder had been a traditional subject of Japanese art since ancient times, the most famous example being *Wind God and Thunder God* depicted in the famed 17th-century screen by Tawaraya Sōtatsu, the founder of Rinpa. Not far from the point where they embarked for *Current of Contemporary Art* (1969) on the Uji River, the 683-meter-high mountain is part of a hiking course. It is easily accessible from a nearby train station; a half-hour bus ride is followed by an hour's walk before one reaches the mountaintop.[75] The group's resources for *Thunder* included their own labor and time to construct the structure with logs (figure 6.14), which were rented from a lumberyard, on land surrounded by tea farms that produce Uji's superb crops of green tea. (They got permission from the

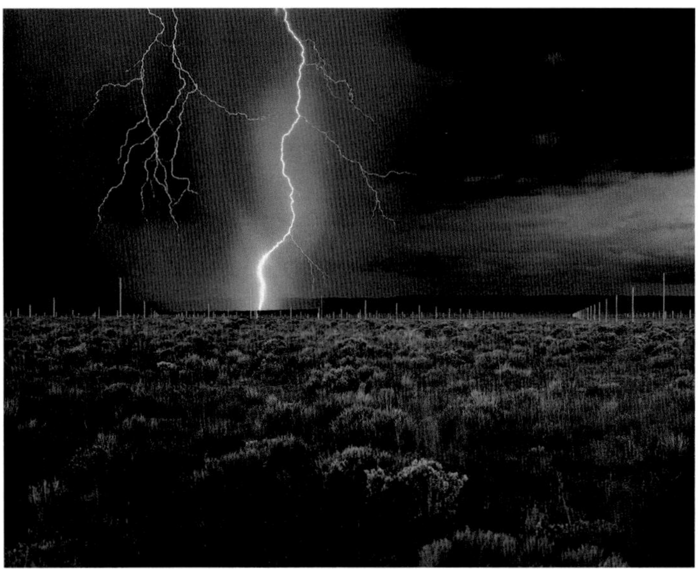

FIGURE 6.12
Walter De Maria, *The Lightning Field*, 1977. Long-term installation, western New Mexico. Photo: John Cliett © The Estate of Walter De Maria. Courtesy Dia Art Foundation, New York.

landowner for the site's annual summer use; for 1981 and 1982 they tried nearby Mount Ōmine, but returned to Mount Jūbu after 1983.) As they built the pyramid—20 meters long on each side and equipped with a lightning rod atop—and subsequently lingered on the site, they were visited by their associates and curious visitors, with whom they waited for lightning to hit. Year after year, with their hallmark "farmer-like"[76] persistence, they built the structure in June, waited for the whole summer in vain, and dismantled it in September. Over the 10 years, altogether 50 people were involved in construction, and over five hundred people shared the "time of waiting."[77]

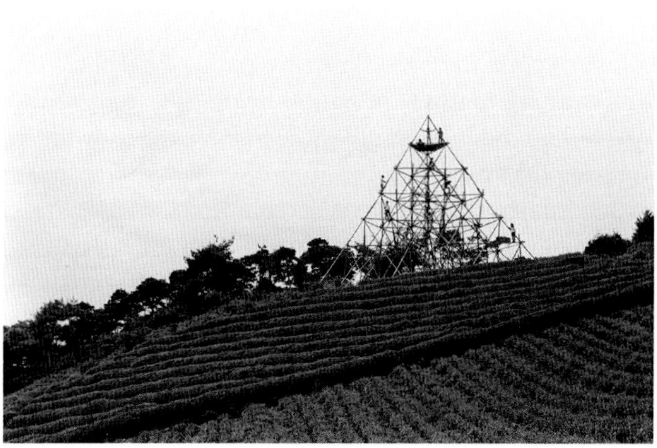

FIGURE 6.13
The Play, *Thunder*, 1977–1986. Installation view on Mount Jūbu, Kyoto, in 1977. © The Play.

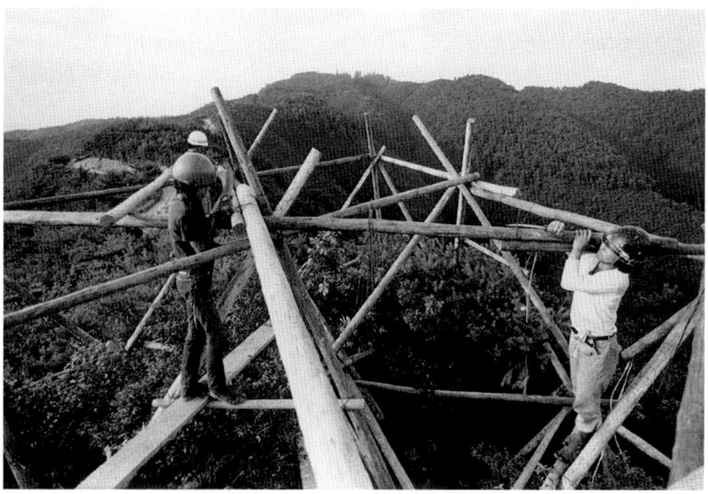

FIGURE 6.14
The Play members constructing *Thunder* on Mount Jūbu, 1977. © The Play.

De Maria's *The Lightning Field* is aligned with Smithson's *Spiral Jetty* as a monumental work of almost "authoritarian"[78] authorship in a remote place, both evoking the sublime and transcendent nature of the Romanticist tradition.[79] These features decisively set it apart from The Play's *Thunder*. Above all, the remoteness of nature and landscape, both physical and metaphysical, is a major ingredient of American Earthworks, as the title of the 2013 exhibition *Ends of the Earth* aptly suggests.[80] As with GUN, a collective authorship characterized The Play. Granted, the group made long-distance trips on a few occasions (e.g., into the Pacific Ocean for *Voyage: Happening in an Egg* in 1968; to Minami Daitōjima for *Torroko* in 1974; and to Hokkaidō for *Wind: Wandering in the Wind* in 1976). Still, "ends of the earth" was an alien idea to them. Rather, the majority of their projects were staged within the six Kansai prefectures of western Japan and in principle were reachable by public transportation (see map in figure 3.6). In short, working together in nature nearby—as opposed to working solo in nature faraway—was a modus operandi of Japanese land art, with its restorative affect offering respite from the everyday.

To understand local factors that informed this character, let us first look at "nature nearby." Geographically, while The Play was particularly blessed with the rich diversity of the natural environment in Kansai, nature—mountains and rivers—exists in proximity to urban areas all over Japan. Even Tokyo, a densely populated modern metropolis, is not far from its natural backyard of Musashino to the west. The closeness and affinity with nature has been built into Japanese culture since ancient times, as the country's literature attests. Indeed, Ikemizu Keiichi, a lead member of The Play who reflected on their relationship with nature, echoes this:

> The nature that we have been engaged with is more close to us and humanized than harsh, yet it is something we cannot go against. Therein, we always breathe in sync with nature's breath. For example, when we are riding well on the flow of a river, our breathing is perfectly synchronized with the river's breathing. And we sense that we are alive as a part of the living nature. [...] And that [sensation] confirms the life of all living beings on the earth and continues to flow when added to a larger undercurrent of our everyday life.[81]

However, we must avoid reducing Ikemizu's observation to certain clichés (for example, the Japanese outlook on nature is to coexist with it), for this would constitute nothing but a facile cultural essentialism that superficially contrasts Eastern and Western views of nature. Rather, we need to examine how Japanese artists operated within a set of historical, social, and cultural parameters in which they found themselves and attempted to gain firsthand experiences of nature nearby. In an operational context of 1960s Japan, "nature nearby" above all represented resources that were accessible (easy to travel to), available (theoretically open for public use), and affordable (incurring practically no cost to use). When vanguard artists wanted to go beyond the accepted norm and defy the status quo, nature nearby was as appealing as the urban streets (also accessible, available, and affordable).

A two-decade lineage of nature nearby began with the precedent set by Gutai, which organized four outdoor exhibitions in 1955–1956, including a pine-forested city park[82] and a beach (table 6.2). Still, it should be noted that the establishment credentials in Ashiya of the group's leader Yoshihara Jirō gave a different meaning to "available" and "affordable" than would be the case for less established practitioners. Importantly, the first Japanese example of hole digging occurred at the 1956 outdoor exhibition, with Yoshihara Michio presenting *Discovery*, a shallow hole dug in the ground with a light radiating from the bottom (figure 6.15). This is arguably among the first works of sculptural land art in postwar Japan.[83] In 1962, the next hole digging took place, when Kyūshū-ha, based in the northern Kyūshū area, staged an overnight performance program, *Grand Gathering of Heroes*, on the Momoji sand beach in Fukuoka. During the night event, Miyazaki Junnosuke quietly dug six or seven square holes, each about six feet deep, while other members and associates were drinking and staging wild actions. Miyazaki thus carved out a place in postwar Japanese art as a forerunner who conflated land art and performance art. His hole digging was doubly rewardless in that those attending the program barely paid attention (and no photograph is extant) and the holes gave way to nature, with the rising tide washing them away.[84]

TABLE 6.2
Gutai's Outdoor Exhibitions (1955–1956)

1955	
July 25–August 6	*The Experimental Outdoor Exhibition of Modern Art to Challenge the Mid-Summer Sun* Ashiya Park, Ashiya; organized by Ashiya City Art Association
1956	
April 6–8	Photo shoots for *Life* magazine Yoshihara Oil Mill factory and Imazu Beach, Nishinomiya
April 9	*One Day Only Outdoor Art Exhibition* A U.S.-bombed ruin of Yoshihara Oil Mill factory, Amagasaki
July 27–August 5	*Outdoor Gutai Art Exhibition* Ashiya Park, Ashiya

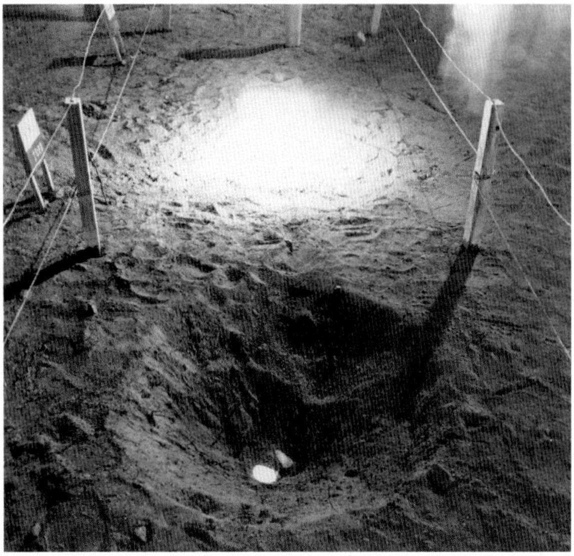

FIGURE 6.15
Yoshihara Michio, *Discovery* (front) and *Shining Water* (back), 1956. Installation view at *Outdoor Gutai Art Exhibition*. © Naomi Yoshihara and the former members of the Gutai Art Association; photo courtesy of Ashiya City Museum of Art & History.

In the use of nearby nature in Japanese land art, dry riverbeds are significantly prevalent as sites for performative works. A few major examples have been looked at in this book: *Hole* by Group "I," sited along the Nagara River at *Independent Art Festival* in 1965 (figure 6.9) and GUN's *Event to Change the Image of Snow* performed along the Shinano River in 1970 (figure 0.3). In addition, the three rivers flowing from Kyoto and Osaka were thematized by The Play in *Current of Contemporary Art* (1969), *Sheep* (1970), and *Ie: The Play Have a House* (1972), with riverbeds offering camping space in the last two (figures 3.8, 3.11, 3.13). The dry riverbed has historically been a zone of social and cultural freedom that goes back to medieval Kyoto, where the dry riverbed of the Kamo River was a venue for popular entertainment including early Kabuki theater (figure 6.16, plate 19).[85] As exemplified by the Nagara River, the dry riverbeds are also frequent sites of recreational activities for ordinary people; it is not unusual to find baseball fields, playgrounds, parks, and even farms on the riverbeds.

If the remote desert stands in for nature in American land art, the nearby dry riverbed represents nature for its Japanese counterpart. The first to claim the dry riverbed in postwar Japanese art was Sightseeing Art Research Institute (Kankō Geijutsu Kenkyūjo), a duo of painters, Nakamura Hiroshi and Tateishi (Tiger) Kōichi, in Tokyo. Their choice was a dry riverbed of the Tama River, an hour's ride by commuter train on the Chūō Line from Shinjuku, where they staged their first joint exhibition on March 30, 1964.[86] The one-day project was a direct consequence of the cancellation of the Yomiuri Independent Exhibition: Tateishi, who had made a successful debut in the

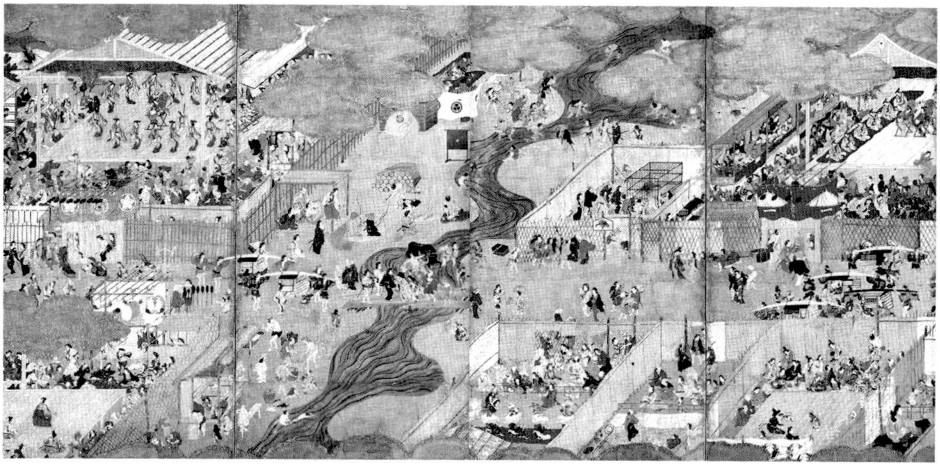

FIGURE 6.16
Entertainment on the Riverbed at Shijō, unknown artist, 17th century, Japan. Pair of two-panel screens, color on paper with gold leaf; 164.4 × 172.8 cm each. Collection of Seikadō Bunko Art Museum, Tokyo. Photo courtesy of Seikadō Bunko Art Museum Image Archives/DNPartcom. (Also plate 19.)

1963 independent exhibition, had an ambitious plan to show a 4 × 6-meter neon painting of Mount Fuji at the now-aborted 1964 independent exhibition. The devastated Tateishi solicited the assistance of Nakamura, nine years his senior, and they quickly founded a two-person collective to present his humongous Mount Fuji painting made of tin plate (neon proving too costly). The young artist scouted a few outdoor places, including a forested mountain in Kawasaki and a public pier in downtown Tokyo. But he settled on the dry riverbed, likely because of its accessibility and certainly because of its affordability; and its availability was insured by their guerrilla strategy (they sought no permission from authorities), which echoed Anti-Art street performances by Hi Red Center and Zero Dimension. The result was a panoramic *Sightseeing Art on the Tama River*, which featured *Mount Fuji of Universal Brotherhood*, as well as a Grand Canyon, a hidden fortress, and even an "imperial viewing platform." The whole effort amounted to a landscape within landscape. Although Tateishi's obsession with Mount Fuji can be interpreted through the mountain's ambiguous status as the icon of both wartime and postwar Japan,[87] his Pop-inflected imagination[88] made the whole exhibition a work of pictorial land art, if you will.[89]

Sightseeing Art on the Tama River indisputably belongs to the culture of showing. Following the routine practice among vanguards of discarding their works after display—a distinct symptom of the culture of showing (see the previous section)—Tateishi abandoned his masterpiece, *Mount Fuji of Universal Brotherhood*, due to a lack of storage space. Still, one significant difference was that publicity was not their goal, the exhibition having been born out of their genuine desire to show Tateishi's Mount Fuji. Acting as a promoter of the young artist, Nakamura filmed the pictorial landscape, added shots he had taken at the American air base in neighboring Tachikawa, and created a short documentary, *Das Kapital* (figure 6.17).[90] An awareness of the need to produce and control the visual representation of their exhibition was not new. For example, Gutai consistently had their members photograph and film their exhibitions and other programs throughout their 18 years of existence. Still, this documentary material was no more than records. In 1960s Japan, it was in fact rare for an artist to make a self-contained work as such from his documentary material of his own show or work, as discussed in the previous section.[91]

A comparable effort was made in the wilderness in 1970 by Katō Yoshihiro, the leader of Zero Dimension, who produced a feature-length 120-minute 16mm film as a compilation of the group's rituals: *White Hare of Inaba*, shot by the video artist Ōe Masanori. One of the memorable scenes showed location shots on the beach of Kujūkurihama, nearby nature for Tokyoites. The photographer Hirata Minoru accompanied Zero Dimension to the seaside and memorialized their activities in still photos separately from Katō's film (figure 6.18).

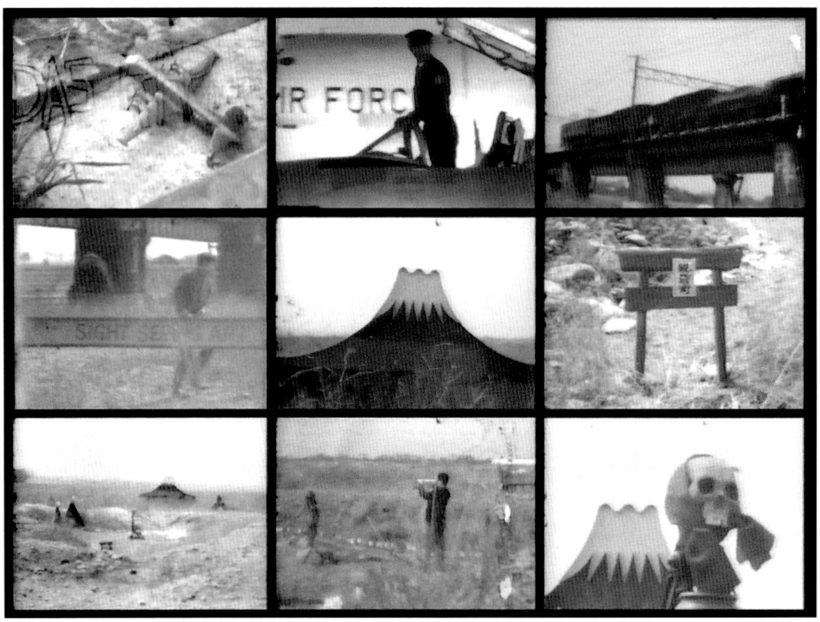

FIGURE 6.17
Nakamura Hiroshi, *Das Kapital*, 1964 (select frames). Film, 11 minutes. Collection of National Research Institute for Cultural Properties, Tokyo.

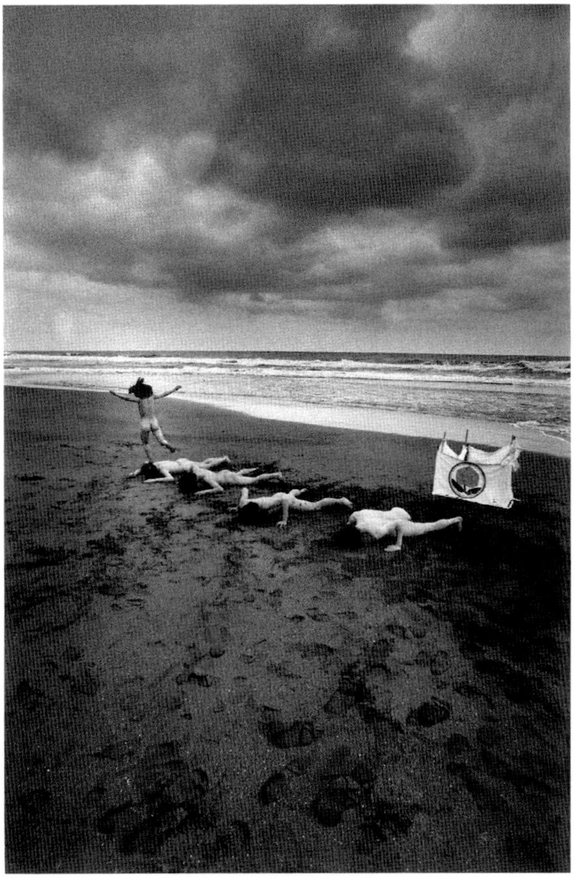

FIGURE 6.18
Zero Dimension's location filming of *White Hare of Inaba* at Kujūkurihama, March 15, 1970. Documentary photograph of performance art. © Hirata Minoru.

The riverbank landscape made by Tateishi and Nakamura is a key work of collective land art. A new form of collaborative collectivism flourished in the post-Yomiuri years. In an environment less hectic and less vulnerable to the authorities than that of the urban streets, this form of collectivism further evolved into what may be characterized as "communalism." Its most philosophical representative was Group "I," who interrogated the issue of singular authorship in *Hole* to the extent that individuality was subsumed not just by collectivity but by anonymity (figure 6.9). In fact, their group name itself embodied their concern. Upon their first exhibition, they explained:

> Our name "I" is *i* [位] of *tan'i* [unit 単位], *i* of *ichi* [position 位置], *i* of *isō* [phase 位相].
> That is to say, we loosely mean
> Each one of us is a unit within the multitude
> And is positioned within it.[92]

Digging a hole and filling it back in was a rewardless task par excellence, but they desired to "capture the world beyond individualism" through this "purposeless" act.[93] If there was a reward, it was the collaboration in and of itself and the "self-liberation" it brought about, as member Kawaguchi Tatsuo would later recall.[94]

Following *Hole*, Group "I" made an intensive investigation of anonymity, mostly through their indoor exhibitions, in their short active life through 1968. The group never explicitly declared the dissolution of its communal bond. In retrospect, it continued in an inactive or dormant mode, until it regrouped in 1974 and 2004. The Play turned the communal idea of working together into a practical and enduring mode while making nature nearby their primary habitat (see chapter 3). Year after year, they discussed a project idea together, realized it together, and afterward reflected on it together; this annual rhythm of operation was reinforced in the 10-year project of *Thunder* (figure 6.19). Their collectivism was open, not closed like the usual artists' groups. In the members' minds, their supporters and other benefactors were part of the group, as were the past members who were no longer with them for one reason or another. The group kept a measured attitude toward publicity and actively devised their own channels of communication through project reports, newsletters, posters, fliers, and other ephemera, so that their experiences would not remain merely personal but help "plow people's everyday life."[95] These documents that carried their original thoughts and words were in turn made into exhibition displays and artists' books for greater circulation.

Different modes of working "together in nature nearby" culminated the radicalism in the wilderness of 1960s Japan. Though not a land artist per se, Matsuzawa Yutaka, too, was a quintessential practitioner of "together in nature nearby." The most

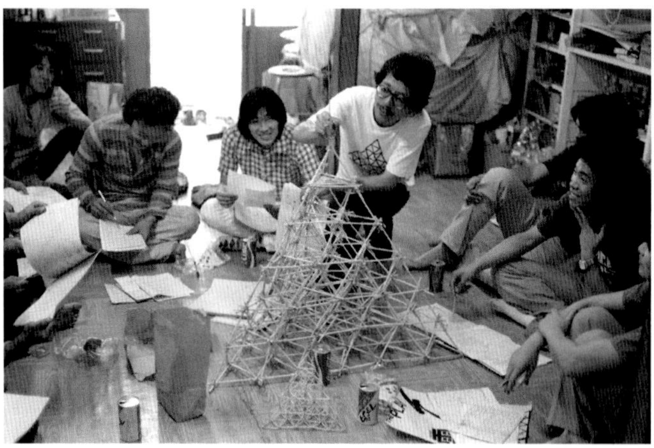

FIGURE 6.19
The Play members working on models for *Thunder*, c. 1977. © The Play.

physical manifestation of this was his Sensuiiri Meditation Platform, which was built on a mountain near his residence in Shimo Suwa and served as a site of his sound communion, *On'e*, with his loosely organized Nirvana School. The members gathered together, traveling certain distances to come to the site to spend time with Matsuzawa and like-minded colleagues. An artist's nature nearby could often be a nature faraway for others; yet Japan's geography made it not too onerous for willing visitors to make a trip. Better yet, in Matsuzawa's *kannen* conceptualism, travel might be performed not by the body but by the mind. When, for example, he sent the second Postcard Painting, titled *Fundamental Painting Exhibition to Be Shown to the Lake*, in August 1967, the mailing was more than an exhibition announcement. It was an open "uninvitation" for the recipient to travel in his or her mind to "steal a glimpse" of the artist's invisible communications to the lake. It is again useful to consider land art across an entire spectrum, from the most physical, bodily, and ontological to the most ephemeral, phenomenological, and even parapsychological. Japan's land art expanded the territory of the mind as it extended the physical reach of art.

* * *

In the dynamic decade of the 1960s, artists in many parts of the world inventively responded to their respective local conditions in their endeavor to transcend the modernist strictures of art. Let us bring Smithson's *Spiral Jetty* back into a direct dialogue with GUN's *Event to Change the Image of Snow*, two defining works of land art in the U.S. and Japan. Expanding on the general comparison we made above, we can see different ways the two practitioners tackled a set of shared issues by pushing their projects to the operational limits imposed upon them in their respective locales. In particular, both confronted distance: GUN as Niigata residents located in the countryside and struggling with nature in everyday life, Smithson as a New Yorker gazing at a remote geology that was part of a vast space-time continuum. Both devised strategies to reduce these distances by fully exploiting the means and resources available to them. The distances thus thematized were not isolated but integral to their lives and thoughts, as well as to their other works. Smithson's "Site/Non-Site" connected the institutional spaces of the museum/gallery with landscapes near and far,[96] whereas GUN's mail-art projects bridged from Tokyo at the center to their remote abode. Then our methodological formulation needs further modification: we are concerned with positions that are "similar yet dissimilar yet similar" in the age of international contemporaneity. Our starting point is similar practices from different locales, which on examination we find were shaped by dissimilar local factors. Yet on a second reading, we may find deeper similarities that link two practices after all. Only by exploring the local closely can we begin to understand the significance of contemporaneous art practices across a newly envisioned global history of art.

EPILOGUE

THREE IN THE WORLD

2008, Norwich: Horikawa Michio

In September–December 2008, the Sainsbury Centre for Visual Arts in Norwich, U.K., presented *On Location: Art, Space, and Place in the 1960s*, an exhibition to explore practices sited outside the gallery walls. The accompanying publication, edited by its curator Simon Dell, pointed to a larger project of world art history in its subtitle: *Siting Robert Smithson and His Contemporaries*.[1] Among the artists included in the show was GUN's Horikawa Michio, whose lone non-Western presence was represented by two stones he mailed from Niigata to London in 2000 and 2001 in conjunction with the Tate Modern's inaugural special exhibition *Century City*. At the Tate Modern, they were shown side by side with his older stones from his *Mail Art by Sending Stones* (1969–1972) and subsequently added to the collection of the museum's archives. His stones proved to be as popular with the media outside Japan as inside: his stone (2000) in the collection of the Getty Research Institute in Los Angeles made a list compiled by the *Guardian* of "1000 artworks to see before you die," along with works by such likely Japanese favorites as Hokusai, Yoko Ono, and Kusama Yayoi.[2]

2009, New York: Matsuzawa Yutaka

In July–October 2009, the Museum of Modern Art in New York held *In & Out of Amsterdam: Travels in Conceptual Art, 1960–1976*, a special exhibition presenting work by artists associated with the Art & Project gallery, in conjunction with the gift of its collections to the museum. The donated items were concurrently shown at the museum's prints collection gallery on the second floor. The entire suite of 156 issues of *Bulletin*, published from 1968 to 1989, was shown, among them three issues by Matsuzawa Yutaka, nos. 21, 42, and 84. Also displayed were two of his mandala collages and a selection from his conceptualist works compiled as *The Whole Works, 1961–1971*. It appears that everything the artist entrusted to Art & Project in 1971 is now housed at the museum in New York. A vitrine that showed his printed works abutted another vitrine that displayed 10 of On Kawara's "I am still alive" telegrams addressed to Adriaan van Ravesteijn, creating a memorable reunion after *Tokyo Biennale 1970*.

2012, Paris: The Play

On June 5, 2012, a crew of 18—which included The Play members and their French and Japanese friends—embarked on an arrow-shaped Styrofoam raft at the Pont de Puteaux in a northeastern suburb of Paris. Reprising the collective's *Current of Contemporary Art* of 1969, they made a trip down the Seine to the island of La Grand Jatte, connecting two loci associated with Parisian modernist movements (Neo-Impressionism and the Puteaux Cubists) (figure 7.1, plate 20). Afterward, the raft was transferred to Le Plateau, an exhibition space of the Frac Île-de-France, for *Mount Fuji Doesn't Exist*, an exhibition curated by Elodie Royer and Yoann Gourmel. This was the pair's second exhibition that included The Play, the first being *Le sentiment des choses* in 2011–2012. In 2014, following the two exhibitions, Royer and Gourmel were instrumental in publishing *Play*, or what the group calls *Big Book*, which combined and expanded on three artist's books they had privately produced in the past.

REGROUPING IN AN OPEN FIELD

History writing is an interface with the past. Like international contemporaneity, history that we narrate reveals as much about how we see the past as about what the past was, if not more. In history writing, too, perception and lived experience may not always coincide with fact. In theory, history writing is never complete and perfect; in practice, correctives are made as we continue to reexamine the past. Since the 1990s, geohistorical correctives have been made in an effort to globalize art history. Mostly in small and sporadic doses, a number of non-Western artists and works have been added to the global (Western) discourse of art history. The three practitioners examined in

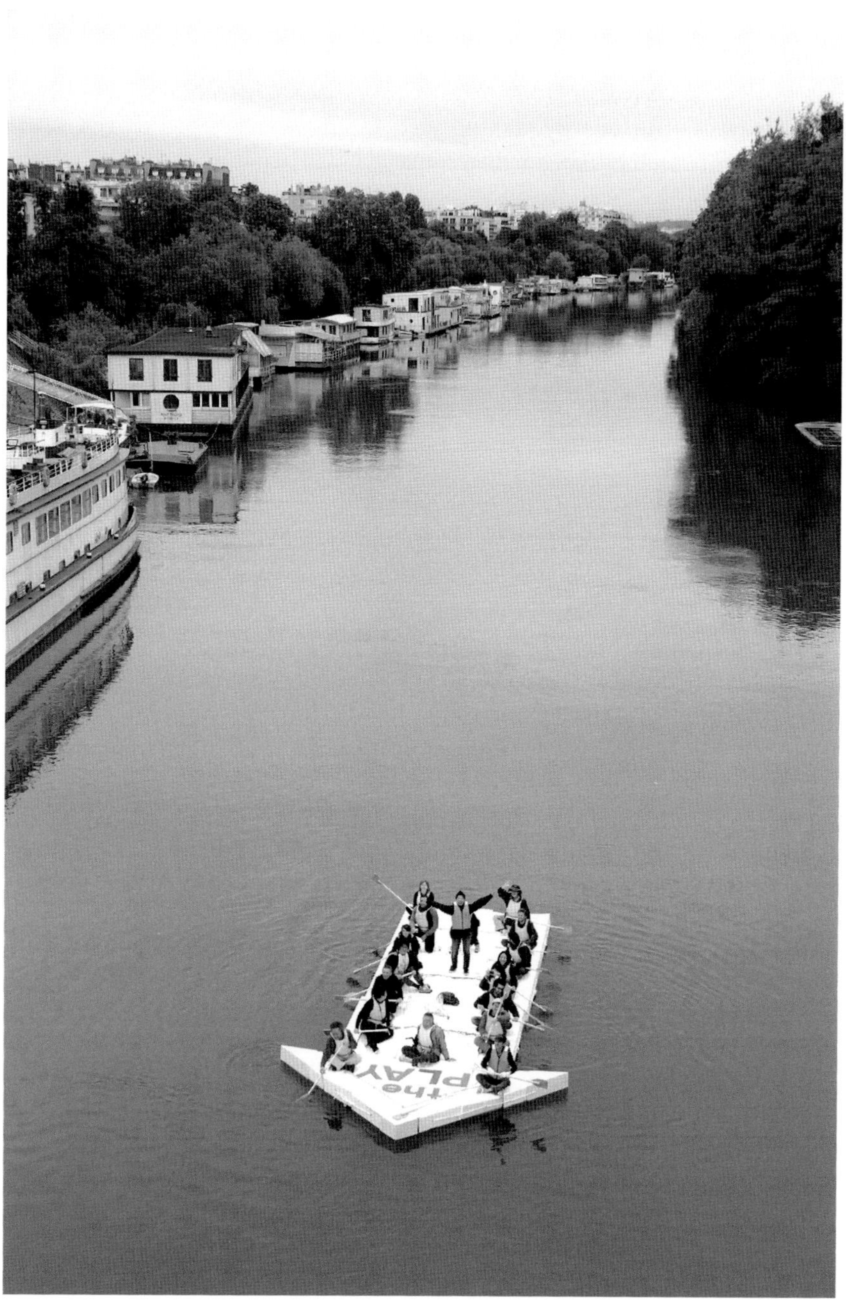

FIGURE 7.1
The Play, *La Seine: Current of Contemporary Art*, 2012. Documentary photograph of performance art. Photo by Minami Takao. © The Play. (Also plate 20.)

this book—Matsuzawa Yutaka, The Play, and GUN—are among those who have benefited from this shift to a certain degree.

This book has made a methodological proposal to "decenter," "amplify," and "regroup" postwar art history by making such additions an integral part of world art history. Key to this methodology is the concept of "international contemporaneity," which derives from the local discourse of 1960s Japan and serves as a geohistorical tool. We have first built a sharable base of local knowledge to understand the practitioners' individual evolutions and frame them in the local histories and contexts that surrounded and enabled their radicalism in the wilderness away from the center of Tokyo. The study of connections has then helped uncover the hitherto unknown and unexplored narrative tangents. A landmark exhibition that made international contemporaneity tangible, *Tokyo Biennale 1970*, serves as a contact point to examine intersecting stories not only of those who showed in the exhibition (Matsuzawa and On Kawara, among others), but also of those who made it happen (Nakahara Yūsuke and Minemura Toshiaki). Partly encouraged by this incoming interface, Matsuzawa orchestrated an outgoing interface by actively networking with international peers through his mail-art campaign *World Uprising*. We have explored internalized interfaces by looking at two discursive events with two markedly different attitudes to imported ideas. In interfacing with Happenings, The Play made an empirical effort to articulate their own idea of Happenings, thereby repossessing both the theory and practice of Happenings. In interfacing with the discourse of Conceptual Art, critics played a normative role, thereby in effect submitting to the dominant discourse. In the study of resonances, we put similar yet dissimilar practices through comparative examination on individual and contextual levels. Matsuzawa's conceptualism is mapped in a spectrum of immateriality through comparison with Yves Klein and Robert Barry, while its broader implications—the issue of modernist painting, the nature of instruction, and the vision for humankind—are considered in juxtaposition with two Japanese pioneers abroad, Yoko Ono and On Kawara. Land art offers entry points to investigate contextual and systemic aspects of 1960s Japan: the culture of showing, often mediated by photography, permeated the lineage of performativity, while the affinity with nearby nature was embraced along with collectivity.

Through the study of connections and resonances, we have regrouped a number of decentered parts and disparate stories. A few strategies for regrouping became more concrete through these studies. We may follow an artist's international footsteps and networking as we have done with Matsuzawa, whose international path was comparable to Gutai's as traced by Ming Tiampo;[3] since the artist himself initiated a "grouping" effort, all we have to do is retrace his path while enhancing it with our accumulated knowledge. When we have a set of similar practices (e.g., the empty gallery and hole digging), it is effective to situate them in a spectrum to tease out their dissimilarities. In a larger framework, knowing diverging local systems and contexts between different regions augments our appreciation of the state of international contemporaneity and enables us to understand how it worked.

These are ways for micro-expansions with fine-tuned subnarratives and details to contribute to loosening up the Eurocentric master narrative. The application is not limited to 1960s Japan. Any locale where international contemporaneity was at work can likewise be investigated. Even where international contemporaneity was scarcely operational, the study of internalized interfaces, especially in discourse, will be instructive, for the assimilation and internalization of Western ideas and practices was part of the learning process in multiple modernisms. Contemporary China's discourse, for example, will be relevant in this inquiry for critically assessing the levels of repossession/autonomy and assimilation/submission in light of a rapid ascent of contemporary art after the Cultural Revolution.

As explained in chapter 1, the works by the three practitioners featured in this book are compared with those by select Euro-American artists, because of their lived experiences and modern Japan's historical circumstances in which it generally looked toward Euro-America as *the* international site of modernism. But comparative counterparts do not have to be Euro-American. For example, GUN's *Event to Change the Image of Snow* can readily be compared with the early actions that Collective Actions Group staged in the countryside after its establishment in Moscow in 1976 (some of them on snow)[4] or the Canadian artist Françoise Sullivan's *Danse dans la Neige* (with the photographer Maurice Perron) in 1948. Horikawa Michio tying up stones as postal parcels may be compared with the Korean Lee Seung-taek who tied up stones beginning in the late 1950s. Or Lee's bold *Wind-Folk Amusement* of 1971 echoes both GUN's snow event and The Play's performative projects in landscape.[5] These comparisons constitute a next step. Yet, as a starting point, this book chose to compare three practitioners to their Euro-American counterparts, for it is imperative to reexamine the problematics of the center-periphery ideology in world art history. In this book, 1960s Japan serves as an analytical pressure point in this endeavor, applied through the methodology of contemporaneity.

* * *

This brings us to an intriguing question on a macro level: How central should the center be in our regrouping effort? It is often said that decentering in the end reinstates the center in our narrative, while the periphery is merely relativized and remains in a soup of multiplicity and alterity. Our study of 1960s art in Japan suggests this question can be recast in more explicitly historical terms: How central was the center (i.e., Euro-America) in the 1960s, retrospectively speaking? If the center is less central than we have thought it was, can we then narrate a history differently? For example, from a periphery? Or even without reference to the center? While these tactics still keep Euro-America as a cardinal point, the decade of the 1960s was when the Euro-American grip on modernism began to weaken, not because the center became weaker but because the perceived periphery became increasingly assertive.

As this book (as well as past scholarship) demonstrates, 1960s Japan offers an exceptional counterpoint by which to examine this question. Japan was not alone, however. Brazil readily comes to mind, with its Neo-Concretism and the mesmerizing body-based and object-based participatory aesthetics of Lygia Clark and Hélio Oiticica. Other non-Western locales—in the Asia-Pacific region and the Middle East, Central and Eastern Europe, and Latin America—can also be plotted according to their respective "time" vis-à-vis the "central time" and further understood in their local circumstances. On the periphery's part, this is by no means an unordered set of alternate stories. Neither Japan nor Brazil nor other non-Western locales were a pale reflection of Euro-America, for each was marked by a unique struggle to devise and materialize its version of modernity. The U.S., too, once held a perceived secondary place with its prewar modernism. We then have to see modernisms themselves in a spectrum, for "modernism" as such is a construct that is never monolithic, constantly evolving over time in many places. This is a larger task of world art history that can merely be suggested here. However, suffice it to say that differences must be assessed not just between modernisms of the center and the periphery, but among modernisms within the periphery as much as within the center, for they are all marked by different trajectories and historical circumstances.[6]

In constructing an alternate narrative, we must proceed cautiously, for the state and nature of international contemporaneity were changing in the postwar decades. In the 1950s, on the one hand, the rise of gestural abstraction depended on the maturation of modernist painting in many locales. A degree of linear progression was strong in this sense, and so was the role of the center, whether in the form of Abstract Expressionism or of Art Informel, as a catalyst for interpoetics. In this regard, the center still held with its front-runner status in modernism in the late 1950s. The state of international contemporaneity was materialized with varying degrees of delay from the center. To capture this delay, we may narrate a history of gestural abstraction from Japan, for example with Shiraga Kazuo and Ushio Shinohara as main "after Pollock/Mathieu" protagonists, and examine resonances among those who similarly took their cue from Abstract Expressionism/Art Informel. This cluster of narrative tangents, through which we assess the extent and natures of interpoetics, can be linked to a cluster of narrative tangents surrounding the center to make a full picture, wherein the center, too, is treated as multifarious sites.

Into the 1960s, on the other hand, conceptualism, performance art, and land art emerged in critiques of the strictures of modernism, as artists in multiple locales began to probe strategies to transcend the status quo, which included the conventions of painting and sculpture, as much as the local situations, be they political, social, or cultural. What is fascinating about 1960s art is that *despite* all the local differences, contemporaneity more often than not binds together practices in widespread places with a resonating overarching challenge—in this case, a challenge to fundamentally call into question the institution of art as codified in modernism. In other words, in the 1960s, modernisms matured in varying degrees, with an increasing number of local times beginning to synchronize and artists in different locales moving in one or more shared directions simultaneously. This constitutes another, higher level of similarity and regrouping. It is a structural similarity because it concerns the very fundamental premise of modernism. This means that we have to magnify our comparative strategy of seeing "similar yet dissimilar yet similar" characters, as touched upon at the end of chapter 6. Here we decenter, amplify, and regroup in two levels of "similar": while the first level offers contact/entrance points to the local, the second offers a collection of larger, possibly decentered frameworks that characterize the 1960s phase of modernism.

Granted, actual circumstances varied from locale to locale in the rise of these new aesthetic strategies. However, if we look at Japan, gestural abstraction was not an absolute prerequisite for them to develop. The case in point in this book is Matsuzawa's conceptualism, which he formulated over a long period of gestation out of his experiments with Surrealist-inflected intermedia, in a critique of modern civilization as a whole. When such ideas and practices as Happenings and Earthworks were transmitted from the putative center, Japan had its own postwar traditions in landscape and action already in place before the foreign imports reached it. The Play, in this book, managed to maintain autonomy of theory and practice in devising their radical voyages as Happenings, and GUN extensively worked through interpoetics to achieve its own locally grounded and internationally relevant practices. Unlike with gestural abstraction, in the cases of land art, performance art, and conceptualism parallel practices evolved in Japan around the same time as in Euro-America, with strong resonances or weak connections to the latter. In retrospect, the center-periphery paradigm was being frayed in a significant manner. Broken was the deep-seated assumption that the center was (in perpetuity) the first and that its influence (always) resulted in imitations.

By incorporating this observation, an alternative narrative for conceptualism can use 1960s Japan—Matsuzawa Yutaka in particular—as a crucial narrative node. (Or we may begin our story from Western Europe or Brazil or wherever international contemporaneity was at work.)[7] Accompanied by a set of pioneers, such as Yves Klein and Robert Rauschenberg (with his "This is a portrait of Iris Clert if I say so" telegram in 1961), Matsuzawa is afforded a distinct place. Another singular group is constituted by Yoko Ono and Fluxus, paralleling these pioneers. After 1964–1965, a number of strains are recognized, including a linguistic type in which such Japanese cognition specialists as Kashihara Etsutomu and Takamatsu Jirō contrast such formalists as Art & Language. An immaterial faction with Matsuzawa, Klein, and Barry contrasts an object-based line encompassing Hi Red Center along with such Latin Americans as Cildo Meireles (*Coca-Cola Project* of 1970). The object line then intersects with a political/activist variety that includes "zero-value" projects by Akasegawa Genpei (*Greater Japan Zero-Yen Note* of 1967), Horikawa Michio (*Zero-Yen Stamp* of 1971), and Meireles (*Zero Dollar* of 1978). A photo-based pool may be large enough to require subdivisions to differentiate the performatively minded (e.g., Nomura Hitoshi's *Dry Ice* of 1969–1970) with the more indexically oriented (e.g., Joseph Kosuth's *One and Three Chairs* of 1965).

This sort of grouping within a movement is not unfamiliar to us as a curatorial strategy. What is new here is that each category will be examined to create a spectrum through "similar yet dissimilar" comparisons. Rather than being absorbed into a vast compendium, each work will be amplified through its narrative tangents and regrouped with other works in this spectrum. The American presence is strong, because of the singular commitment to language and formalism among the practitioners of Conceptual Art, but not dominantly so. It was a localized phenomenon, but all the more so it requires a close study of its internal development,[8] as does that of Matsuzawa and other practitioners and locales that contributed to this narrative.

It goes without saying that aesthetics was not the sole factor that made the center central, as Ming Tiampo astutely demonstrated with her postulation of "cultural mercantilism."[9] In reality, aesthetics is the least problematic issue in our study. As much as geopolitics, discourse, the systems and institutions, and the capitalist market that constituted the art world also contributed to the Euro-American dominance. Even though the state of international contemporaneity in the 1960s was widespread in aesthetic terms, other external aspects were far from being in sync. Most notably, the center's discursive dominance continued, typified by the case of "Conceptual Art," which triumphed over Matsuzawa's claim for *kannen* in Japan, as examined in chapter 5. Japan's art system, institutionally and commercially, barely supported the domestic advancement of *gendai bijutsu* and was ill equipped to promote its internationalization in a sustained manner. In this sense, Japan's state of international contemporaneity was fragile. Eurocentrism operates as an ideological and structural force larger than the sum of these elements, making it a self-perpetuating proposition hard to dismantle.[10] By assessing the strength of the center in the 1960s case by case—the situation with Pop Art, for example, as opposed to that of Conceptual Art[11]—and by exposing its working in the periphery, we may further keep the ingrained Eurocentrism in check in our decentering and regrouping project.

An emblematic manifestation of Eurocentrism involves the canon. Although the shortcomings of the Eurocentric canon are evident, the canon as such nonetheless is hard to do away with. Indeed, since it gives a general shape to history, a well-crafted canon is a useful tool especially for pedagogy and museum display, in which we would like to see our work of world art history incorporated in order to fundamentally shift the paradigm. The proposed methodology of studying "similar yet dissimilar (yet similar)" examples is inherently "group-oriented" in that, rather than looking at individual works as a starting point, we begin with comparisons of a group of works. This suggests a possibility to develop a canon of a sort—a set not so much of "canonical works" as "canonical comparisons," culled from various regions. Again, for postwar art history, Euro-American works such as Smithson's *Spiral Jetty* may remain important, but they will be put through the same process of decentering, amplifying, and regrouping. The process will result in a cluster of connected and resonating works, including, for instance, GUN's *Event to Change the Image of Snow*. At the most rudimentary level, this can be a potential way for regrouping multiple modernisms (here, multiple land arts) in a spectrum and thus constructing a world art history in a tangible manner from bottom up and periphery in.

* * *

Almost a decade has passed since James Elkins rhetorically asked "Is art history global?,"[12] and theories of world art history have been proposed. Desire and aspirations are in place to answer this question in the affirmative. This book has joined the effort and proposed a methodology conceptualized from a "periphery-in" perspective. Ultimately, our goal is to open up a space of investigation without foreclosing avenues of potential expansion.[13] Regrouping can take place in any number of locales. Multiple narratives thus engendered as micro and macro expansions will not be exclusionary but will intersect with and reinforce each other to form a greater matrix of narratives, one (or more) of which will certainly engage Euro-America, a major site of development in postwar art. By opening up, world art historians' inquiries may also be collective as we spread out into multiple locations in the world. Correctives may have to come later, but with a still largely uncharted territory before us, we first have to take a step forward so that we can regroup and compare notes, so to speak. This book is thus not only an invitation to the wilderness of 1960s Japan where radicalism thrived, but also a call for regrouping in an open field where we work, individually and collectively, to repossess radicalism that has abounded in so many locales in the world, whether in the 1960s or before, or onward into the 21st century.

APPENDIX: SELECT TRANSLATION OF MATSUZAWA YUTAKA'S WORKS

ON ANOTHER WORK IN ANOTHER CONTAINER, OR ON CUTTING 1963

Your hard body, a hard container you are in now, a hard work made by me within it. Ah, truly, they will easily collapse and thus are unworthy to place your faith in. Please use your "sense mind" and imagine a you that is the opposite of this soft you. Like an anti-proton as opposed to a proton. Also, side by side with this soft container (you don't have to use the earthly measurements to know their distance), please imagine another container. Like an anti-proton as opposed to a proton. Also please imagine a work opposite to this soft work in this container. Like an anti-proton as opposed to a proton. Now, after communicating with this work in this container, please communicate with another work in another container. Further, please imagine a work that is imaginary [*kyozō*] and located on the border areas of these two containers. Oh, please communicate with that imaginary work present (absent) in it. Information you get thereby is a true Nil that my art can give you. If you cannot come to the container during the exhibition period, please persistently meditate [*shūnen*] toward this container at a given time on a given day (from the future or from the past). My work will communicate with your ψ (psi). This is it. The above relationship is explained in the below diagram [figure 2.13].

A BRIEF REPORT ON THE DISCOVERY OF THE BEGINNING OF *NON-SENSORY PAINTING*
1964

1964.6.4 [sign] To tell you the truth, the past [June] 1, before dawn, I had a sudden revelation, and since then I have been deliberating on it. Now I finally have reached a state where I am confident [about what it meant]. Thus, I am making a brief report on the above titled issue. This struck me so violently like Nil that I felt half of my body paralyzed. This is such a horrifying thought. I beg you not to use common sense in criticizing it. Let me get to the core of the problem. Painting in the past—and of course other types of form making [*zōkei*]—has been conceptualized, created, and appreciated through the five senses. In the future (when will it be?), however, this principle will be completely abandoned and painting will be changed to that which cannot be perceived by the senses. Today, the images of the cosmos and [subatomic] particles are constructed in a way never understood by the senses. Still, using mathematics and language as its tool, contemporary physics is pursuing the existence of such a world. In a similar manner, [sign] *Non-Sensory Painting* brings about a completely new image severed [from painting in the past and existing] solely in a meditating brain. In order to create *Non-Sensory Painting*, humans will soon deploy unimaginable things. You must understand that the relatively liberal deployment of things in the recent paintings is a very, very faint beginning of *Non-Sensory Painting*. Since matters and non-matters used in *Non-Sensory Painting* are tools, they are projected there for use. Like magic objects and words. And only a limited number of people know how to use them, and they will be dissociated from the masses and completely specialized. That is precisely why painting in the future, and for that matter any painting aspiring for the future, today becomes esoteric and assumes a state of discommunication. Today, if we see what mathematicians and physicists are doing, we can see a striking similarity [with *Non-Sensory Painting*]. [three signs] However, it is certain that artists of *Non-Sensory Painting* are pilots toward the final form of humankind. This final form is the state of Nirvana. The state of no difference in energy levels. The state of complete stasis. They are elites in the true sense of the word who will encourage and guide [humankind] along the journey to reach there. They include people in religion, scientists, politicians, artists, and thinkers. What I have discovered this time is only the beginning of the form that *Non-Sensory Painting* will surely take in the future. I am not sure whether there exists any actual work. However, my latest work, *Mandala for the Entrance to Void/Imaginary Space*, may be one such example. It is also possible that it is related to the idea and diagram I made for "imaginary painting" last fall for my Psi-based solo exhibition [at Aoki Gallery in Tokyo]. However, once the discovery is made, I myself am so surprised to see how simple and clear its truth can be. [circle] (Tentative Title) [drawing] [1–9 mandala diagram] [signs] At Void/Imaginary Space Situation Research Center

PSI CORPSE
1964

On Matsuzawa Yutaka's 1964 work *Psi Corpse*—What is *Non-Sensory Painting* (provisional name)?—The work of Nil. *Psi Corpse* is a *Non-Sensory Painting* (provisional name). Thus invisible to the eye. Therefore, even if you try, you cannot find it anywhere. Yet it is positively and absolutely shown in this exhibition. Don't say "Nonsense!" but listen to what I have to say for a while. You are all probably perplexed by the unfamiliar term *Non-Sensory Painting*. Not surprisingly. It was only born the other day on June 4, and has not yet been registered anywhere. Its meaning and concept were communicated to only seven people through a mysterious printed matter, *A Brief Report on the Discovery of the Beginning of Non-Sensory Painting (Provisional Name)*, and nobody else knows about it. What is this *Non-Sensory Painting* of Nil that will obviously be the absolute form of painting in the future? [sign] Flowers in spring, fireflies in summer, colored leaves in autumn, snow in winter. In this exhibition, with your eyes you all perceive that work, one next to it, and one beyond it. You perceive with your ears the work that makes sound over there. However, *Non-Sensory Painting* is different. It cannot be perceived by the five senses. I can hear some people saying such a work that is neither poison nor medicine is meaningless. But is it really so? Somewhere and sometime, you may have heard of the expanding universe or the universe with negative curvature. Or a single electron that simultaneously exists in two places, or an anti-matter that will disappear upon colliding with an ordinary matter. You cannot perceive their images by the senses of your eyes, ears, noses. [sign] Nonetheless, contemporary physicists have proven their existences by means of mathematics and experiments. *Non-Sensory Painting* exists in a similar manner. There it is, overlapping the space of this exhibition in manifold ways. There it is, in your bag, under your ample breasts, at that delicate place beneath your soft clothes. And in the dark depths of your stomach. Or it is sticking onto your cold back. "A leech waited a long time, but food did not come. Finally, the leech rose to chase the food. The food shrank back from the earth's surface, moving upward and upward. The huge-bodied leech vehemently chased it. The rich food fled into space. The leech chased it. Ahead of it, more and more." If you begin to feel strange, is it because of *Psi Corpse* that is a *Non-Sensory Painting*? It is useless even if you cry "No!" and [try to] rub it off.

Non-Sensory Painting surrounds you, saturates you, enters you. You are being invaded by it. Soon, you won't be able to stand or move. You will soon feel that you cannot stand it anymore, that you will die. You will close your eyes and experience Nirvana. You will see in advance the future of the universe and human beings. [sign][sign][sign] I am satisfied that this *Non-Sensory Painting* is far more absurd and bizarre than any fantasy. Because the crazier a new hypothesis is, the more possibility it has of being true. See, your, your XXX is XX. Of course, I could install a tool, whether material or immaterial, of projecting a *Non-Sensory Painting* or an experimental apparatus in this exhibition hall. You may use them and learn to love *Psi Corpse*. However, I did not do so this time. Currently installed at the Void/Imaginary Space Situation Research Center in Suwa, they are unilaterally transmitting to this hall. Into you. Into you. Into you inside you. Into you inside you inside you. Into you inside you inside you inside you. Into you inside you inside you inside y

VOID: COLLECTIVE PARTICIPATION OF "ANTI-CIVILIZATION" SCHOOL 1965

"Statement" by Matsuzawa Yutaka

Have we arrived at an extremely advanced state?
In another hundred years, art in material forms will probably be dropped from the mainstream.
This change will probably take place rapidly.
At this right moment, we must acquire new human powers (psi powers and others) that have already been prepared.
This will occasion the birth of a new humankind and earthly civilization will enter a new stage.
By then, art in material forms will be preserved in vitrines and looked at as curiosities.
From 1964 to 65, a new thought of *Anti-Civilization* put forth in Japan and works informed by it
Are a premature germination of formless art of 200 years from now.
They mark the unknown beginning of the whole meaning and value of the new humankind.
What do you think of this?
We respect that which is invisible to the eye, that which has no form, that which does not exist, that which cannot be touched.
Respect, pect, pect
We despise economic power, political power, physical power, elbow power, brute power,

and vise power.
Let us think of the void [*kū*].
That is the whole character of all the laws.
It is not limited as existence [*yū*] or nonexistence [*mu*, also "nothingness"].
It is a dormant [*myōbuku*] state, neither the path of existence nor that of nonexistence.
Yet it is fixed when captured in each moment
If you say it's there and it's not there, if you say it's not there and it's there
It is a strange "true form."
Not existence, not void, not nonexistence, not non-void
It's a field
It's a reservoir of energy
Neither arising nor ceasing, neither increasing nor decreasing
Should an occasion arise, energy will coalesce and its distinct characteristics will manifest themselves
The state we desire is "all being in void" [*kaizai kokū*], "living in void" [*zaijū kyūchū*]
Dissolve into nirvana [*jakumetsu*] and be invisible, but appear like an apparition at times! times! times!
At that moment (200 years from now), is there anything else that humans want to do?

Non-Sensory Permeation of "Anti-Civilization" through the Structure of the Two World Mandalas

1 Matsuzawa Yutaka, *My Consciousness and Unconsciousness* (Non-Sensory Painting)
2 Oguchi Chikiko, *The most important soft invisible part of ladies walking around at the site of Independent Art Festival and soft invisible matter and spirit covering them* (Invisible Sculpture)
3 Furuta Insa, *Earth, Water, Fire, Wind, Void from August 8 to 19* (Element Painting)
4 Miyasaka Chūshō, *Silence from August 9 to 19* (Formless Painting)
5 Nakamura Anji, *Physiological and Psychological Time from August 9 to 19* (Relativity Sculpture)
7 Komatsu Yoshitaka, *Nagara River and Niagara* (Remote Activation Painting)
9* Takagi Shinpei, *Primary Cosmic Rays Showering over the Site of Independent Art Festival* (Filed Sculpture)
9 Kasahara Inchō, *Empty Is Form Is Empty* (*Kannen* Painting)

The above nine works are arranged in the Diamond World Mandala

10 Matsuzawa Yutaka, *"Anti-Civilization" Exhibition* (Multi-layered Sculpture)
11 Yamada Seishi, *You* (Uncertainty Painting)

12 Misawa Mankō, *Unknown Lost Article at the Site of Independent Art Festival* (Bashful Sculpture)
13 Imai Mokuten, *Three Monsters and Four Bodies* (I Ching Painting)
14 Tsuchihashi Anshin, *Anti-Independent Art Festival* (Anti-World Sculpture)
15 Gomi Chūshin, *Reincarnation* (Parapsychology Painting)
19 Kobayashi Chūchū, *Relationship between Map and Site* (Semantic Painting)
20 Itō Ieyasu, *Communication with a Flying Saucer* (Outer Space Research Sculpture)
21 Kawanishi Kagu, (Psi Painting)

The above twelve works are arranged in the Womb World Mandala.

Translator's note:
*This must be a misprint for "8."

NOTES

PROLOGUE

1. Matsuzawa Yutaka, "Kōya ni okeru andepandan-ten '64" [*Independent '64 in the Wilderness*], *Bijutsu jānaru* [Art journal] (October 1964): 51.

2. Matsuzawa Yutaka, annotation in "Matsuzawa Yutaka nenpu" [Matsuzawa Yutaka's chronology], in *Matsuzawa Yutaka: Supirichuarizumu e / To Spiritualism: Yutaka Matsuzawa 1954–1997*, exh. cat. (Kawaguchi: Kawaguchi Museum of Contemporary Art, 1997). The critic Yoshida Yoshie also quoted a description of the exhibition from the artist's notebook in "Tandoku kōisha no chōgekijō" [Solitary actors in an ultra-theater], *Bijutsu techō* , no. 335 (December 1970): 53–54.

3. Ikemizu Keiichi, quoted in *Shūkan Asahi* [Weekly Asahi], date unknown; reprinted in the *Voyage* section in *Play* (Paris: Bat and Osaka: The Play, 2014), n.p.

4. "2-3 'GUN' saikessei 'Yuki no imēji o kaeru ibento'" [2–3: GUN regrouped with *Event to Change the Image of Snow*], in *GUN: Niigata ni zen'ei ga atta koro / Niigata Contemporary Artists Group and Its Era*, exh. cat. (Nagaoka: Niigata Prefectural Museum of Modern Art, 2012), 45.

5. Yoshihara Jirō, "A Statement by Jirō Yoshihara: Leader of the Gutai," Martha Jackson Gallery press release, September 17, 1958, Archives of the New Gallery, Bennington College, Bennington, VT; quoted from Ming Tiampo, *Gutai: Decentering Modernism* (Chicago: University of Chicago Press, 2011), 2.

6. "Expo Art," or *Banpaku bijutsu*, is a term commonly used in postwar Japanese art history to categorize the technology-oriented intermedia-type works created for Expo '70. See Midori Yoshimoto, "Expo '70 and Japanese Art: Dissonant Voices—An Introduction and Commentary," *Review of Japanese Culture and Society* 23 (December 2011): 1–12.

7. For overviews of postwar Japanese art in English, see Alexandra Munroe, *Japanese Art after 1945: Scream against the Sky* (New York: Abrams, 1994); Thomas R. H. Havens, *Radicals and Realists in the Japanese Nonverbal Arts: The Avant-Garde Rejection of Modernism* (Honolulu: University of Hawai'i Press, 2006); Charles Merewether and Rika Iezumi Hiro, *Art, Anti-Art, Non-Art: Experimentations in the Public Sphere in Postwar Japan, 1950–1970*, exh. cat. (Los Angeles: Getty Research Institute, 2007); and Doryun Chong et al., *Tokyo, 1955–1970: A New Avant-Garde*, exh. cat. (New York: Museum of Modern Art, 2012).

8. "Chihō no zen'ei" was the title of a special feature in *Bijutsu techō*, no. 296 (April 1968).

9. For the history of modern collectivism in Japanese art and how *zaiya* and *zen'ei* operated, see Reiko Tomii, "Introduction: Collectivism in Twentieth-Century Japanese Art with a Focus on Operational Aspects of *Dantai*," *Positions* 21, no. 2 (Spring 2013): 225–267.

10. *Voids: A Retrospective*, exh. cat. (Zurich: JRP; Geneva: Ringier; in association with Paris: Éditions du Centre Pompidou and Centre Pompidou-Metz, 2009). I contributed an essay to *Voids* on the empty gallery exhibitions by Matsuzawa and Hi Red Center, titled "Voiding the Exhibition: Hi Red Center and Matsuzawa Yutaka."

11. *Invisible: Art about the Unseen 1957–2012*, exh. cat. (London: Hayward Gallery, 2012).

12. *Global Conceptualism: Points of Origin, 1950s–1980s*, exh. cat. (New York: Queens Museum of Art, 1999).

13. In the study of contemporaneity in globalizing contemporary art in the 21st century, the body of writing by Terry Smith is especially important, beginning in full force with "Contemporary Art and Contemporaneity," *Critical Inquiry* 32 (Summer 2006): 681–707. My study of "international contemporaneity" dates back to "Historicizing 'Contemporary Art': Some Discursive Practices in *Gendai Bijutsu* in Japan," *Positions* 12, no. 3 (Winter 2004): 611–641.

CHAPTER 1

1. Early efforts include Thomas DaCosta Kaufmann, *Toward a Geography of Art* (Chicago: University of Chicago Press, 2004); James Elkins, ed., *Is Art History Global?* (New York: Routledge, 2007); and David Carrier, *World Art History and Its Objects* (University Park: Pennsylvania State University Press, 2008). More recent studies include James Elkins, Zhivka Valiavicharska, and Alice Kim, eds., *Art and Globalization* (University Park: Pennsylvania State University Press, 2010); Jill H. Casid and Aruna D'Souza, *Art History in the Wake of the Global Turn* (Williamstown, MA: Clark Art Institute; New Haven: Yale University Press, 2014); and James Elkins, *The Impending Single History of Art: North Atlantic Art History and Its Alternatives* (forthcoming).

2. *Art since 1900* by Hal Foster et al. (London: Thames & Hudson) exercises an incrementalism by expanding its non-Western additions from Gutai and Neo-Concretism in the first edition (2004) to such contemporary figures as Ai Weiwei in the 2nd edition (2011). For more on *Art since 1900*, see Elkins, *The Impending Single History of Art* (forthcoming).

3. The most salient examples of this discursive preoccupation can be understood through two questionnaires: "Questionnaire on 'The Contemporary,'" *October* (Fall 2009): 3–124; and "The And: An Expanded Questionnaire on the Contemporary," *Fieldnote 01* (2012): 11–90, http://www.aaa.org.hk/cms/Content/upload/download/fieldnotes/fieldnotes_issue_01_single.pdf (accessed January 23, 2015).

4. Or, to borrow from the critical terminology of Françoise Lionnet and Shu-mei Shih, 1960s Japan was "the becoming minor of Theory"; see the introduction to *The Creolization of Theory*, ed. Lionnet and Shih (Durham: Duke University Press, 2011), 14–15.

5. This was one of the main themes of my "Historicizing 'Contemporary Art': Some Discursive Practices in *Gendai Bijutsu* in Japan," *Positions* 12, no. 3 (Winter 2004): 611–641. Sonal Khullar discusses a similar point in her *Worldly Affiliations: Artistic Practice, National Identity, and Modernism in India, 1930–1990* (Berkeley: University of California Press, 2015), 6.

6. For further discussion on *gendai* in modern Japan, see Tomii, "Historicizing 'Contemporary Art'," 615.

7. Definition from www.merriam-webster.com.

8. Bert Winther-Tamaki looks at this issue from the perspective of artists' production strategies and their manipulation of cultural signifiers in "Six Episodes of Convergence between Indian, Japanese, and Mexican Art from the Late Nineteenth Century to the Present," *Review of Japanese Culture and Society* 26 (December 2014).

9. While I introduced the idea of "interface" in international contemporaneity in "Historicizing 'Contemporary Art'" (613–614), I expanded on James Elkins's negative observation on the presumed limitations of writing the history of multiple modernisms that lack "contact with other people's narratives at all," made in *Art and Globalization*, ed. James Elkins, Zhivka Valiavicharska, and Alice Kim (University Park: Penn State University Press, 2010), 70. To this, I proposed to create contacts through connections and resonances in "Contemporary Art, 'Contemporaneity,' and World Art History," in the same volume (171–175). Whereas "contact points" is a more methodological terminology, "interfaces" factor in the agency of those involved in contacts.

10. Partha Mitter introduced the idea of "structural affinities" in discussing Jemini Roy's primitivism and that of Western counterparts, wherein "neither knew the existence of the other," while examining their difference in "Decentering Modernism: Art History and Avant-Garde Art from the Periphery," *Art Bulletin* 90, no. 4 (December 2008): 543. Structural affinity is a kind of broader resonance to encompass similarities in visual, conceptual, and strategic aspects. My use of "resonances" was inspired by observations, made by postwar American specialists at the *Global Conceptualism* and *Century City* exhibitions, that they saw strong resonances between 1960s art in Japan and in the U.S.

11. "Operation Canaris: 'Mayday for Missing Egg,'" an interview with Herbert Distel by Gabi Zaun-Fertel, http://www.habalukke.ch/zeitung/berena48.html (accessed January 23, 2015).

12. "Gutai Information List," annotated typescript, in Irving Sandler Papers, Getty Research Institute, as described in Ming Tiampo, *Gutai: Decentering Modernism* (Chicago: University of Chicago Press, 2011), 109.

13. Tiampo, *Gutai: Decentering Modernism*.

14. Dore Ashton, "Art: Japan's Gutai Group," *New York Times*, September 25, 1958.

15. This equation was underscored by the center's "cultural mercantilism" as theorized by Ming Tiampo, in which only the center claims legitimacy and originality by consuming and exploiting the periphery. See Tiampo, *Gutai: Decentering Modernism*, 3–5.

16. "Nihon no aryū ni sasaerareta eikō" [Japan's glory upheld by imitators], *Geijutsu Shinchō* (August 1969): 1–28.

17. For a more detailed comparison of Oldenburg and Sekine, see Reiko Tomii, "The Discourse of (L)imitation: A Case Study with Hole-Digging in 1960s Japan," in *Globalization and Contemporary Art*, ed. Jonathan Harris (Boston: Blackwell, 2011), 350–353.

18. Suzaan Boettger, *Earthworks: Art and the Landscape of the Sixties* (Berkeley: University of California Press, 2003).

19. At the outdoor sculpture competition in 1968, the Osaka-based sculptor Fukuoka Michio presented *A Gift from Claes Oldenburg*, a crated quantity of soil the size of Oldenburg's Central Park grave pit.

20. See chapter 2, "The Interpoetics of Distance," in Tiampo, *Gutai: Decentering Modernism*.

21. There was, however, one not too impossible path of information flow, via Nam June Paik, a close associate of Hi Red Center, who was familiar with the German scene having studied in Munich. No piece of evidence to support this path of flow has so far been uncovered.

22. For the German Capitalist Realism, see Elodie Evers, Gregor Jansen, and Magdalena Holzhey, eds., *Leben mit Pop: Eine Reproduktion des Kapitalistischen Realismus / Living with Pop: A Reproduction of Capitalist Realism*, exh. cat. (Cologne: Walther König, 2013).

23. For more on Akasegawa's money work, see Reiko Tomii, "State v. (Anti-)Art: Model 1,000-Yen Note Incident by Akasegawa Genpei and Company," *Positions* 10, no. 1 (Spring 2002): 141–172; and William Marotti, *Money, Trains, and Guillotines: Art and Revolution in 1960s Japan* (Durham: Duke University Press, 2013).

24. See also Jaimey Hamilton Faris's comparative study, "Rooms in Alibi: How Akasegawa Genpei Framed Capitalist Reality," *Art Margins* 4, no. 3 (October 2015): 40–64.

25. Likewise, Midori Yamamura saw a generational and transnational commonality of the postwar years behind the obsessional tendency that Kusama Yayoi shared not only with her Japanese contemporaries (Kudō Tetsumi and Hijikata Tatsumi) but also with her European Zero and Nul peers. See Midori Yamamura, *Yayoi Kusama: Inventing the Singular* (Cambridge, MA: MIT Press, 2015), 52–54.

26. In 2013, the invisible and then theoretical Higgs boson was confirmed by a gigantic tunnel collider at CERN in Switzerland.

27. For a general chronology of Gutai, see Ming Tiampo and Alexandra Munroe, *Gutai: Splendid Playground*, exh. cat. (New York: Guggenheim Museum, 2014).

28. For Yoshihara's writing on Pollock, see Reiko Tomii, "Gutai's Phase Zero: Reading Yoshihara Jirō on Pollock against Takiguchi Shūzō," presented at *Tilting the World: Histories of Modern and Contemporary Asian Art*, a symposium at the University of Sydney and the Art Gallery of New South Wales, November 2013.

29. Among three writings by Yoshihara on Pollock, the most accomplished is "Chūshō kaiga no yohaku" / "Blank of Abstract Painting," *Bokubi* (February 1953): 13.

30. Reiko Tomii, "Murakami Saburō no 'e' no kokoro" / "Murakami Saburō's 'Picture' Mind," in *Murakami Saburo: 70-nendai o chūshin ni / Murakami Saburō: Through the '70s*, exh. cat. (Osaka: ArtCourt Gallery, 2012), 104–110. My new translation of *e* as "picture" and "picturing" rather than as "painting" emerged out of a long discussion at a Gutai workshop co-organized by Harvard University and the Guggenheim Museum in fall 2011.

31. For Gutai's ethics of freedom, see Ming Tiampo, "Please Draw Freely," in Tiampo and Munroe, *Gutai: Splendid Playground*, 45–79.

32. Pedro Erber has made a bifocal study of 1960s art in Brazil and Japan in his *Breaching the Frame: The Rise of Contemporary Art in Brazil and Japan* (Berkeley: University of California Press, 2014). John Clark made a comparative bifocal study in *Asian Modernities: Chinese and Thai Art Compared, 1980 to 1999* (Seattle: University of Washington Press, 2011).

33. The discursive sophistications of 1960s art in Japan is captured by the English translations found in chapter 15 of Alexandra Munroe, *Japanese Art after 1945: Scream against the Sky* (New York: Abrams, 1994), and in Doryun Chong et al., eds., *From Postwar to Postmodern: Art in Japan, 1945–1989—Primary Documents* (Durham: Duke University Press, 2012).

34. Good overviews in English on Japan's politics are given by William Marotti, "Japan 1968: The Performance of Violence and the Theater of Protest," *American Historical Review* 114, no. 1 (February 2009): 97–135, and Oguma Eiji, "Japan's 1968: A Collective Reaction to Rapid Economic Growth in an Age of Turmoil," trans. Nick Kapur with Samuel Malissa and Stephen Poland, *Asia-Pacific Journal* 13, issue 11, no. 1 (March 23, 2015), http://japanfocus.org/-Oguma-Eiji/4300. A digest version of his voluminous and detailed study *1968* (Tokyo: Shin'yōsha, 2009), Oguma's essay outlines the political state of Japan circa 1968 and its specific local contexts, illustrated by news photos and works by such important photographers as Tōmatsu Shōmei and Watanabe Hitomi.

35. For Gutai, see Tiampo, *Gutai: Decentering Modernism*, and Tiampo and Munroe, *Gutai: Splendid Playground.*

36. See William Marotti, *Money, Trains, and Guillotines*, for Anti-Art in and around the Yomiuri Independent Exhibition (especially excellent documentary photographs) and its *Anpo*-inspired political dimension.

37. For the discursive history of Anti-Art, including Miyakawa's formulation, see Reiko Tomii, "*Geijutsu* on Their Minds: Memorable Words on Anti-Art," in *Art, Anti-Art, Non-Art: Experimentations in the Public Sphere in Postwar Japan, 1950–1970* (Los Angeles: Getty Research Institute, 2007), 35–62. For full translation of "After Informel," see Chong et al., *From Postwar to Postmodern*, 105–113.

38. For sample writings by these critics, see Chong et al., *From Postwar to Postmodern*. Miyakawa's discourse of *gendai* will be touched upon later in this chapter in the subsection "Discursive Origins of International Contemporaneity in 1960s Japan."

39. For details of *Model 1,000-Yen Note Incident*, see Marotti, *Money, Trains, and Guillotines* and Tomii, "State v. (Anti-)Art."

40. For a complex relationship of the vanguard cultural practitioners with Expo '70, see "Expo '70 and Japanese Art: Dissonant Voices," special issue guest-edited by Midori Yoshimoto, *Review of Japanese Culture and Society* 23 (December 2011).

41. "Hatsugen suru shinjin-tachi: Hi-geijutsu no chihei kara" [Voices of emerging artists: From the horizon of non-art], special feature, *Bijutsu techō*, no. 324 (February 1970): 12–13. For Mono-ha's discursive practice, see "Artist Roundtable and Writings" in *Requiem for the Sun: The Art of Mono-ha*, ed. Mika Yoshitake, exh. cat. (Los Angeles: Blum & Poe, 2012), 210–227.

42. Koshimizu Susumu, Lee Ufan, Narita Katsuhiko, Sekine Nobuo, Suga Kishio, and Yoshida Katsurō, "'Mono' ga hiraku atarashii sekai" [*Mono* opens a new world], *Bijutsu techō*, no. 324 (February 1970): 34–55; translated in Yoshitake, *Requiem for the Sun*, 211–217.

43. Sekine's candid view on "not making" is found in a roundtable discussion: Ikeda Masuo, Sugai Kumi, Sekine Nobuo, Horiuchi Masakazu, and Tōno Yoshiaki, "Tsukuru koto to tsukuranai koto" [Making and not making], *Bijutsu techō*, no. 315 (July 1969): 176–191.

44. The term "Mono-ha" did not enter art discourse until 1973. However, for simplicity I refer in this publication to "what would be known as Mono-ha" as "Mono-ha." For the name and beginning of Mono-ha, see Yoshitake's essay in *Requiem for the Sun*.

45. KuroDalaiJee (Kuroda Raiji), *Nikutai no anākizumu: 1960 nendai Nihon bijutsu ni okeru pafōmansu no chika suimyaku / Anarchy of the Body: Undercurrents of Performance Art in 1960s Japan* (Tokyo: Grambooks, 2010).

46. I owe this witty terminology to Miwako Tezuka.

47. For Bikyōtō, see Reiko Tomii, "Concerning the Institution of Art: Conceptualism in Japan," in *Global Conceptualism: Points of Origin, 1950s–1980s*, exh. cat. (New York: Queens Museum of Art, 1999), 23–26; Tomii, "Revolution in Bikyōtō's Photography: Naoyoshi Hikosaka and the Group of Five," in *For a New World to Come: Experiments in Japanese Art and Photography, 1968–1979*, ed. Yasufumi Nakamori, exh. cat. (Houston: Museum of Fine Art, 2015), 148–153.

48. For Jikken Kōbō, see Miwako Tezuka, "Experimentation and Tradition: The Avant-Garde Play *Pierrot Lunaire* by Jikken Kōbō and Takechi Tetsuji," *Art Journal* 70, no. 3 (Fall 2011): 64–85; and "Jikken Kōbō and Takiguchi Shūzō: The New Deal Collectivism of 1950s Japan," *Positions* 21, no. 2 (Spring 2013): 351–381.

49. For graphism, a good introduction is given by Michio Hayashi, "Tracing the Graphic in Postwar Japan," in Doryun Chong et al., *Tokyo, 1955–1970: A New Avant-Garde*, exh. cat. (New York: Museum of Modern Art, 2012), 94–119.

50. The confluence of artists and other cultural practitioners in 1960s Japan was forcefully argued by Alexandra Munroe in her *Japanese Art after 1945*. In chapter 7, titled "Circle: Modernism and Tradition," she conceptualized the traditional arts, such as ceramics and calligraphy, as an integral part of the avant-garde in 1950s Japan, which preceded the expanded 1960s and are thus not included in my diagram. By astutely inverting this perspective, Munroe developed an extensive and insightful study on the American relationship to Asian culture and thought in *The Third Mind: American Artists Contemplate Asia, 1860–1989*, exh. cat. (New York: Guggenheim Museum, 2009).

51. Ethics of expression is a new and viable topic of study in postwar Japanese art. See Alexandra Munroe, *Lee Ufan: Making Infinity*, exh. cat. (New York: Guggenheim Museum, 2011), and Tiampo and Munroe, *Gutai: Splendid Playground*.

52. The most important before 1963 was *Gendai bijutsu no jikken / Adventure in Today's Art of Japan*, exh. broch. (Tokyo: National Museum of Modern Art, 1963).

53. The title and subtitle of this survey, each given in Japanese and English, went through revisions. It was not until 1967 that the museum arrived at the well-known form, both in Japanese and English: *Gendai bijutsu no dōkō / Trends in Contemporary Japanese Art*. See "Tenrankai ichiran" [List of all exhibitions], in *Kyoto Kokuritsu Kindai Bijutsukan 50-nen-shi / Fifty Years of the National Museum of Modern Art* (Kyoto: National Museum of Modern Art, 2013).

54. In 1963, two similar programs were held (*Trend of Contemporary Japanese Art* and *Contemporary Trend of Painting: Occident and Japan*), which were streamlined into *Contemporary Trend of Japanese Paintings and Sculptures* in 1964. Hence, the 1970 exhibition became the ninth installment in the series though it was the eighth year.

55. The Nagaoka Contemporary is comparable to Ōhara Museum of Art, founded in 1930 as Japan's first museum of Western modern art by Ōhara Magozaburō, a collector who made his money in the textile business and went on to create a *zaibatsu*.

56. "Goaisatsu" [Greetings], in *Nagaoka Gendai Bijutsukan-shō kaikoten, 1964–1968* [A retrospective of the Museum of Contemporary Art, Nagaoka, Prize Exhibition, 1964–1968], exh. cat. (Niigata: Niigata Prefectural Museum of Modern Art et al., 2002).

57. For the history of Mainichi's biannual exhibitions, see Reiko Tomii, "Toward *Tokyo Biennale 1970*: Shapes of the International in the Age of 'International Contemporaneity,'" *Review of Japanese Culture and Society* 23 (December 2011): 198–201.

58. For Minemura's work, see ibid., 201–203.

59. For the mainstreaming phenomenon from the perspective of artists as an active agency, see Reiko Tomii, "How *Gendai Bijutsu* Stole the 'Museum': An Institutional Observation of the Vanguard 1960s," in *Since Meiji: Perspectives on the Japanese Visual Arts from 1869 to 2000*, ed. J. Thomas Rimer (Honolulu: University of Hawai'i Press, 2012), 144–167.

60. Tokyo Gallery showed Motonaga Sadamasa, Mukai Shūji, Shiraga Kazuo, and Yoshihara Jirō, while Minami Gallery took on Tanaka Atsuko. For the history of the two galleries, see *Shimizu Kusuo to Minami Garō / Kusuo Shimizu & Minami Gallery* (Tokyo: Bijutsu Shuppansha, 1985) and *Tokyo Garō 60-nen / Tokyo Gallery + BTAP 1950–2010* (Tokyo: Tokyo Gallery, 2010).

61. For Takamatsu's life and art, see *Takamatsu Jirō misuterīzu / Takamatsu Jirō: Mysteries*, exh. cat. (Tokyo: National Museum of Modern Art, 2014); *Takamatsu Jirō: Seisaku no kiseki / Jirō Takamatsu: Trajectory of Work*, exh. cat. (Osaka: National Museum of Art, 2015).

62. One of a few surviving works from this exhibition was *Doll Festival*, prominently featured in *The World Goes Pop*, a 2015 exhibition at Tate Modern in London.

63. For Shinohara's life and art, see Hiroko Ikegami and Reiko Tomii, *Shinohara Pops! The Avant-Garde Road, Tokyo/New York*, exh. cat. (Albany: SUNY Press, 2012). His artistically rich yet materially impoverished life is a subject of the 2013 documentary film *Cutie and The Boxer* (dir. Zachary Heinzerling).

64. For example, as Midori Yoshimoto demonstrated, the designer Yokoo Tadanori and others undertook the critique from within at the Textile Pavilion in her "Expo '70 and Japanese Art: Dissonant Voices—An Introduction and Commentary," *Review of Japanese Culture and Society* 23 (December 2011): 1–12. The journal issue also carries a few critical responses to Expo '70 by such contemporary artists as Matsuzawa Yutaka and Akasegawa Genpei in English translation (146–153).

65. Akasegawa Genpei and Matsuda Tetsuo, with Minami Nobuhiro's illustration, "Nihon geijutsu dai-gekisen: Sōretsu emaki (Bijutsu techō 5-gatsu-gō furoku)" [Great battles of the world of *geijutsu* in Japan: A heroic pictorial album, May supplement to *Bijutsu techō*], *Bijutsu techō*, no. 355 (May 1972): n.p. Significantly, neither Akasegawa nor Shinohara was involved in Expo '70.

66. Haryū Ichirō, "Zen'ei geijutsu ni tsukaremashita" [I become weary of avant-garde art], *Geijutsu Shinchō* (August 1962): 151.

67. For more on *Tricks and Vision*, see Mika Yoshitake, "The Language of Things: Relation, Perception, and Duration," in Chong et al., *Tokyo, 1955–1970*, 128–129.

68. One of the exciting developments in recent Japanese-language scholarship is the institutional history in modern art. A superb example, made available to English-language readers, is Satō Dōshin, *Modern Japanese Art and the Meiji State: The Politics of Beauty*, trans. Hiroshi Nara (Los Angeles: Getty Research Institute, 2011).

69. In a fine study of early postwar years, Bert Winther-Tamaki touched upon these two associated terms, translated as "international character/internationality" and "world character," in the art discourse dating back to the war years; see *Art in the Encounter of Nations: Japanese and American Artists in the Early Postwar Years* (Honolulu: University of Hawai'i Press, 2001), 15–16.

70. Takiguchi Shūzō, "Nihon bijutsu to sekai-sei" [Japanese art and world relevance], in *Dai-5kai bijutsu dantai rengō-ten* [Fifth art organization's joint exhibition], exh. cat. (Tokyo: Mainichi Newspapers, 1951), n.p.

71. For Japan's participation in the Venice Biennale, see *Venechia biennāre: Nihon sanka no 40-nen / The Venice Biennale: 40 years of Japanese Participation* (Tokyo: Japan Foundation, 1995).

72. For the discursive importance of the short-lived magazine *Bijutsu hihyō*, see Mitsuda Yuri, "Bijutsu hihyō (1952–57) shi to sono jidai: 'Gendai bijutsu' to 'gendai bijutsu hihyō' no seiritsu" [The *Bijutsu hihyō* magazine and its era: The formation of "contemporary art" and "contemporary art criticism"], *Fuji Xerox Art Bulletin* 2 (2006).

73. Tōno Yoshiaki in Haryū Ichirō, Nakahara Yūsuke, Minemura Toshiaki, and Tōno, roundtable moderated by Okada Takahiko, "Gendai Nihon bijutsu wa dō ugoitaka" [How did contemporary Japanese art move?], special issue of "Nihon no gendai bijutsu 30-nen" [Three decades of contemporary art in Japan], *Bijutsu techō*, no. 436 (July 1978): 17–18.

74. In the 1978 *Bijutsu techō* roundtable (above), Nakahara points this fact out (18). Bert Winther-Tamaki presented a paper on the impact of Mexican modernism in postwar Japan at *Japanese Art since 1945: The 1st PoNJA-GenKon Symposium*, at the Council on East Asian Studies in 2005. See his abstract, "The 'Mexico Boom' in the Japanese Art World, 1955," *Review of Japanese Culture and Society* 17 (December 2005): 113.

75. Takiguchi Shūzō, "Shinsain no kotoba: Kansō" (A juror's word: An impression), *Bijutsu techō*, no. 220 (May 1963): 81.

76. Haryū Ichirō, "Busshitsu to ningen" [Matter and man], *Mizue*, no. 618 (January 1957): 43–47; an excerpt is translated as "Material and Humans," in Chong et al., *From Postwar to Postmodern*, 102–105.

77. Tōno Yoshiaki, "Hitotsu no Anforumeru kan" [One view on Informel], *Bijutsu techō*, no. 134 (December 1957): 107–110.

78. Miyakawa, "Anforumeru igo" [After Informel], *Bijutsu techō*, no. 220 (May 1963): 87.

79. Miyakawa Atsushi, "Anforumeru igo no Nihon no bijutsu: Henbō no suii, montāju-fū ni" [Japanese art after Informel: A course of transformation, as seen in montage], *Bijutsu techō*, no. 227 (October 1963): 51.

80. For more on Miyakawa's discourse of *gendai* and examples by other writers, see Tomii, "Historicizing 'Contemporary Art'," 619–629.

81. Tōno Yoshiaki, *Gendai bijutsu: Porokku igo* [Contemporary art: After Pollock] (Tokyo: Bijutsu Shuppan-sha, 1965).

82. Haryū Ichirō, "Sengo: Kokusaiteki na dōjidaisei no seiritsu e" [Postwar: Toward the formation of international contemporaneity], *Bessatsu Mizue* [Watercolor supplementary], no. 46 (July 1966): 56.

83. Ibid., 59–60.

84. "Sekai ni tsūyō suru Nihon no 12-nin" [12 Japanese artists who can compete internationally], special feature, *Geijutsu Shinchō* (January 1968): 1–16.

85. Haryū Ichirō, "Hihyō no yori takai kinō o" [Wishing art criticism to have a more functional role], *Geijutsu Shinchō* (January 1968): 15.

86. Haryū Ichirō, in Haryū et al., "Gendai Nihon bijutsu wa dō ugoitaka," 18.

87. Haryū Ichirō, "Gendai bijutsu no furontia" [Frontiers of contemporary art], in *Dai 9-kai gendai Nihon bijutsu-ten / The 9th Contemporary Art Exhibition of Japan, 1969*, exh. cat. (Tokyo: Mainichi Newspaper Company, 1969), n.p.

88. For example, Honma Takashi, a curator of the Tokyo Modern, echoed Haryū by using the term in his catalog introduction in *Gendai sekai bijutsu-ten: Higashi to nishi no taiwa / Contemporary Art: Dialogue between the East and the West*, exh. cat. (Tokyo: National Museum of Modern Art, 1969), 5.

89. Ōshima Tatsuo, "Nihon no aryū ni sasaerareta eikō" [Japan's glory upheld by imitators], *Geijutsu Shinchō* (August 1969): 24.

90. Ibid., 28.

91. Fujieda Teruo, "Gendai bijutsu no jōkyō to ronri" [The state and logic of contemporary art], in Hara Eizaburō, Fujieda Teruo, and Shinohara Ushio, *Kūkan no ronri: Nihon no gendai bijutsu* [Logic of space: Contemporary art in Japan] (Tokyo: Buronzusha, 1969), 127–128.

92. Ibid., 129.

93. Lee Ufan, "Hi-taishō sekai eno jikaku" [Self-awareness toward the non-objective world], *Miru* (September 1969): 113.

94. Lee Ufan, in Fujieda Teruo and Lee Ufan (dialogue), "Sakka no shisei to sonritsu no kiban" [Artists' attitudes and the foundation of their existence], *Bijutsu techō*, no. 358 (August/September 1972): 59.

95. In the museum fields, collaborative models of scholarship have been seen in multi-locale exhibition projects since the late 1990s, including *Out of Actions: Between Performance and the Object, 1949–1979* (Museum of Contemporary Art, Los Angeles, 1998) and *Global Conceptualism: Points of Origin, 1950s–1980s* (Queens Museum of Art, 1999). Recent examples relevant to 1960s Japan include *Ends of the Earth: Land Art to 1974* (Museum of Contemporary Art, Los Angeles, 2012) and *Other Primary Structures* (Jewish Museum, 2014), as well as two Pop Art exhibitions, *International Pop* and *The World Goes Pop* (Walker Art Center and Tate Modern, both 2015).

96. Recent scholarship offers a number of publications on non-Western modern and contemporary art. In addition to Erber's *Breaching the Frame* (2014) and Khullar's *Worldly Affiliations* (2015) cited above, those that engage world art history include: Iftikhar Dadi, *Modernism and the Art of Muslim South Asia* (Chapel Hill: University of North Carolina Press, 2010); Joan Kee, *Contemporary Korean Art: Tansaekhwa and the Urgency of Method* (Minneapolis: University of Minnesota Press, 2013); Partha Mitter, *The Triumph of Modernism: India's Artists and the Avant-Garde* (London: Reaktion Books, 2007); and Mari Carmen Ramírez and Héctor Olea, *Inverted Utopias: Avant-Garde Art in Latin America*, exh. cat. (New Haven: Yale University Press; Houston: Museum of Fine Arts, 2004).

97. It is notable that Khullar's formulation of modernism as "worldly affiliation" strongly reflects her subject, modern and contemporary Indian artists, in that "commitment to nationalism" is a core ingredient of her definition. See Khullar, *Worldly Affiliations*, 15. As suggested in epilogue in this book, modernism itself must be understood within a spectrum by factoring such dissimilarities.

CHAPTER 2

1. Unless otherwise noted, Matsuzawa's biography is primarily taken from his "Jihitsu nenpu" [Auto-chronology], *Kikan* [Organ], no. 13, special issue on Matsuzawa Yutaka (1982): 36–73; his interview with Kikuhata Mokuma, "Pusai no hako no naka de" [In the Psi box], *Kikan* (1982): 9–33; and his interview with the author, July 23, 2000.

2. Still to be confirmed, an account by one of his trusted former students has it that in the final days of the war, Matsuzawa received a conscription notice, although he managed to evade it with few consequences. For this long-withheld biographical episode, see Itami Hiroshi, "Matsuzawa Yutaka: Sono shikō no genten" [Matsuzawa Yutaka: An origin of his thought], *Aida*, no. 214 (July 2014): 7. This episode and other minor discrepancies indicate that his autochronology must be further reexamined. In this study, however, I treat the document as the artist's self-image of his life and reference it for my reconstruction of his life where pertinent.

3. Quotes in this paragraph taken from Matsuzawa, "Jihitsu nenpu," 42.

4. Ibid., 45.

5. See his poetry chronology in *Kikan*, special issue (1982), 78–79. The final piece of poetry he composed, in 1961, was a literally "Blank Paper Poem." His poetry is anthologized in *Hoshi mata wa sutorippu shou* [Star or a strip show] (Tokyo: Shoshi Yamada, 2013).

6. Matsuzawa, "Pusai no hako," 18.

7. Matsuzawa Yutaka, "Kyatasutorofī āto ni kankei shite" [A propos Catastrophe Art], *Gendai shi techō* [Contemporary poetry notebook] (1972 November): 18–19.

8. Research on his "chemical painting" is ongoing. An extant exhibition postcard reproducing "chemical painting" from the first exhibition reveals an abstraction in a fairly regular style, while two metal plates matching this description in "Jihitsu nenpu" (page 46) have been found in his family's storehouse, possibly shown at the second Alpha Art Circle exhibition later that year.

9. "A.A.C. manifestou No. 1" [A.A.C. manifesto, no. 1], in *Arufa Geijutsu Jin kessei ten/A.A.C. Exhibition*, exh. broch. (Tokyo: Muramatsu Gallery, 1955), n.p.

10. Matsuzawa, "Jihitsu nenpu," 46.

11. Reiko Tomii, "Snapshots from the Past: Japan Society and *Gendai Bijutsu*—From the Perspective of 1960s Art," in *Making a Home: Japanese Contemporary Artists in New York*, ed. Eric C. Shiner and Reiko Tomii, exh. cat. (New York: Japan Society and Yale University Press, 2007), 36.

12. Matsuzawa, "Jihitsu nenpu," 47.

13. The Matsuzawa Archives at Shimo Suwa contain his correspondence with Pereira; Keiō University Art Center's Takiguchi Shūzō Papers (hereafter Takiguchi Papers) contain Matsuzawa's book review manuscript on Pereira's *The Lapis* (1957).

14. Matsuzawa Yutaka, "Niru no sōzōsha tachi" [Nil creators], unpublished manuscript (ca. 1959) in Takiguchi Papers, centers on the box-based works by Robert Rauschenberg, Joseph Cornell, and H. C. Westermann.

15. Takiguchi mentioned Matsuzawa as one of the promising young artists in "Andepandan no shinjin" [New faces of the Yomiuri Independent Exhibition], *Geijutsu Shinchō* (April 1953): 187.

16. Unless otherwise noted, this paragraph draws from Matsuzawa Yutaka, "Burukkurin yokochō" [Brooklyn streets], *Bijutsu hihyō* (September 1956): 95–96.

17. *National Print Exhibition, 10th Annual. Ten Years of American Prints, 1947–1956* was held at the Brooklyn Museum from May 2 to July 1, 1956.

18. For *trans/formation*, see Anna Vallye, "The Strategic Universality of *trans/formation*, 1950–1952," *Grey Room*, no. 35 (Spring 2009): 28–57.

19. Hamaguchi Tomiharu and Matsuzawa Yutaka, with Haryū Ichirō (interviewer), "Fukashina kūkan eno shikō" [Thinking about invisible space], *Bijutsu jānaru*, no. 51 (October 1964): 29.

20. Matsuzawa, "Pusai no hako," 18.

21. Donald Bain, *Long John Nebel: Radio Talk King, Master Salesman, and Magnificent Charlatan* (New York: Macmillan, 1974), 176–179.

22. Matsuzawa Yutaka, "Saibanetikkusu kara mandara made" [From cybernetics to mandala], *Geijutsu Shinchō* (August 1960): 90.

23. A newspaper clipping of this particular broadcast is also illustrated in ibid., 92. For Yada, see Ralph G. Warren, ed. and introduction, *Yada Speaks: Or, The 500,000 Year Old Wisdom of E Yada di Shi-ite* (Monterey, CA: Angel Press, 1979).

24. Matsuzawa, "Saibanetikkusu kara," 98.

25. Ibid., 91.

26. Ibid., 92.

27. As described in his 1961 flier *On "Meaning of Psi" and "Psi Chamber"* (see figure 2.10).

28. Matsuzawa in Kasai Ei, Maeda Jōsaku, and Matsuzawa Yutaka, with Umehara Masaki (moderator), "Bijutsu to butō to mikkyō" [Art, Butoh, and Esoteric Buddhism], in Inagaki Taruho and Umehara Masaki, *Shūmatsuki no mikkyō* [Esoteric Buddhism in a final era] (Tokyo: Sanpō, 1973), 313.

29. For the history and art of Buddhism, including that of Esoteric Buddhism, a good introduction is Washizuka Hiromitsu et al., *Enlightenment Embodied: The Art of the Japanese Buddhist Sculptor (7th–14th Centuries)*, exh. cat. (New York: Japan Society Gallery, 1997).

30. A detailed theological explanation is given in "Ryōkai mandala" [Two-World Mandalas], http://www.ermjp.com/j/temple/mandara/manda/oshie/oshie8.html (accessed March 20, 2015).

31. Matsuzawa, "Saibanetikkusu kara," 93.

32. Ibid.

33. Matsuzawa recalled that this equation contains five or six ψ's in "Pusai no hako," 23.

34. For all the names invoked in this flier, see Tomii, "Snapshots from the Past," 36–37.

35. He indeed loved all sorts of boxes, collecting myriad paper-made gift boxes and any other types until his death.

36. Matsuzawa, "Pusai no hako," 26.

37. Matsuzawa, in "Dare ga mottomo eikyō o ataetaka" [Who influenced me most], *Bijutsu techō*, no. 431 (March 1978): 107.

38. Matsuzawa, "Fukashina kūkan," 15, 16.

39. Matsuzawa, "Saibanetikkusu kara."

40. This flier apparently was made in a few versions. A version on pale green paper, found in the Matsuzawa Archives, is mentioned in his essay "Kyokūkan Jōkyō Tanchi Sentā" [Void/Imaginary Space Situation Research Center], *Bijutsu jānaru*, no. 61 (October 1967): 22. The other two known versions are "red on brown" (in the author's collection) and "blue on white" (in Aoki Gallery's *Psi Box*, compiled in 1969, and *The Whole Works, 1961–1971*, compiled in 1971 and now in the collection of the Museum of Modern Art, New York).

41. No. 1 of *The Whole Works, 1961–1971*.

42. His rather cryptic invocation of "wings," "thoroughly," and "breast" corresponds to *tsubasa*, *tsubusa*, and *chibusa* in the original Japanese, which together constitute an understated play of rhyme.

43. Matsuzawa Yutaka, letter to Takiguchi Shūzō, envelope postmarked March 2, 1963, in Takiguchi Papers.

44. Notably, Matsuzawa also made a postcard with the same insignia and text, also mailed on the same date, as preserved in Takiguchi Papers.

45. Aoki Gallery opened in September 1961 in Ginza, after the owner Aoki Toshi resigned from Tokyo Gallery. His particular focus was Fantastic Realism of the Vienna School as well as from Nordic countries. See Nakajima Masatoshi, "Takiguchi Shūzō to Aoki Garō" [Takiguchi Shūzō and Aoki Gallery] and chronology, *Yasō* [Night thought], no. 19 (October 1986): 194–196 and 175–183.

46. Notably, he used the word *shūnen*, 執念, which ordinarily means "vengefulness" and "(emotional) attachment." However, his intention seems to combine two characters with their individual meaning: 執 = deeply concerned and 念 = meditate.

47. On the cover of the exhibition catalog, he arranged the title in nine characters in the 3-by-3 mandala format.

48. Miki Tamon, "Geppyō" [Monthly review], *Bijutsu techō*, no 228 (November 1963): 153.

49. Matsuzawa, "Kyokūkan Jōkyō Tanchi Sentā," 22.

50. From this point onward, he received critical attention that was compiled in *Matsuzawa Yutaka: Ψ (pusai) no uchū / Yutaka Matsuzawa: The Cosmos of Ψ (Psi)* (Suwa: Suwa Gensō-sha, 1985).

51. Matsuzawa, "Jihitsu nenpu," 51.

52. Matsuzawa Yutaka, "Busshitsu shōmetsu" [Vanishing of matter], in *Independent Art Festival*, exh. cat. (Gifu: [Organizing Committee], 1965), 17. Notably, Matsuzawa's evolution is concisely described as "from architecture to poetry to vanishing of matter to [work made] prior to vanishing of humans" in an untitled Japanese document from around 1971, paired with an English document (see figure 5.10) in an envelope titled *Post-Nirvana: Our Commune*, which Matsuzawa consigned to Art & Project and now is in the collection of the Museum of Modern Art, New York.

53. Matsuzawa, "Pusai no hako," 23.

54. *Kannen kaiga* (painting) first appears in his statement in the flier-catalog for his solo exhibition at Naiqua Gallery in March 1965; while *kannen tenrankai* (exhibition) first appears in Matsuzawa Yutaka, "Busshitsu shōmetsu: 'Han-bunmei' ten o mite" [Vanishing of matter: After seeing *Anti-Civilization Exhibition*], *Gendai bijutsu* [Contemporary art] (August 1965): 29, and in his work *Anti-Japan: Today's Art Exhibition* (1965).

55. Morita Hajime made an extensive study of *objets* in Japanese art history in *Nihon-obuje 1920–70-nendai danshō* [Japan/*objet*: Fragments from the 1920s–1970s], exh. cat. (Urawa: Urawa Art Museum, 2012).

56. Yoshihara Jirō, "Gutai Art Manifesto" (1957), translated by Reiko Tomii and published in Ming Tiampo and Alexandra Munroe, *Gutai: Splendid Playground*, exh. cat. (New York: Guggenheim Museum, 2014), 18–19.

57. An early example of "Vanish *objets*!" appears in Matsuzawa, "Kyatasutorofī āto," 16. In this 1972 account, he still stated that he had "deliberated on it for three days and three nights." A variation, "Vanish things!" (*mono o kese*), is found in his 1973 roundtable, "Bijutsu to butō to mikkyō," 313–314. In his dialogue with the poet Terayama Shūji for the April 1974 issue of *Geijutsu kurabu*, Matsuzawa comfortably used the phrase "Vanish *objets*!" while explaining it to mean "eliminate material mediation." Terayama Shūji, "Matsuzawa Yutaka," in a three-part interview, "Sakka no konseputo o saguru" [Exploring the artists' concepts], *Geijutsu kurabu* [Art club] (April 1974): 131, 135.

58. Takiguchi Shūzō, "Matsuzawa Yutaka ni manekarete" [Invited by Matsuzawa Yutaka], in *Ψ ni yoru Matsuzawa Yutaka koten* [Matsuzawa Yutaka's solo exhibition according to ψ], exh. cat. (Tokyo: Aoki Gallery, 1963), n.p.

59. For my translation of this work, see Doryun Chong et al., eds., *From Postwar to Postmodern: Art in Japan, 1945–1989—Primary Documents* (Durham: Duke University Press, 2012), 207–208. Two revisions are necessary. First, the beginning should read: "1. Vanishing of Matter," for, as discussed in the previous section, *busshitsu* must not be translated into *objet*. Second, *nenryo no zennō* was mistranslated: "omnipotence of sorts" should instead read "omnipotence of thought."

60. Sigmund Freud, *Totem and Taboo* (1913), trans. A. A. Brill (http://www.gutenberg.org/files/41214/41214-0.txt). The book was first translated into Japanese as *Tōtemu to tabū* in 1928 and has since been available in several editions.

61. Matsuzawa, "Busshitsu shōmetsu: 'Han-bunmei' ten o mite," *Gendai bijutsu*, 29–31.

62. For some examples of the works of Nil in *Anti-Civilization Exhibition*, see Tomii, "Voiding the Exhibition: Hi Red Center and Matsuzawa Yutaka," in *Voids, A Retrospective of Empty Exhibitions*, exh. cat. (Paris: Centre Pompidou, Bern: Kunsthalle, Zürich: JRP/Ringier, 2009).

63. Matsuzawa, "Busshitsu shōmetsu," in *Independent Art Festival*, 17.

64. Yoshida Yoshie, "Matsuzawa Yutaka: Yami o tōtetsu suru kyōdōtai" [Matsuzawa Yutaka: A commune that penetrates the darkness], *Bijutsu techō*, no. 360 (November 1972): 27. Among a handful of sympathetic critics, Yoshida perhaps most accurately comprehended the artist's theoretical thinking process.

65. Matsuzawa, "Sakuhin kaidai: Seimitsu kaiga 'Shiro no mugen 1'" [On my work: *Precision Painting "White Infinity 1"*], *Bijutsu jānaru*, no. 61 (October 1967): 27.

66. Ibid.

67. I owe this insight to Elizabeth Tinsley. She found it more than coincidental that Matsuzawa placed a large circle in his 1965 *Vanishing of Matter: Seeing Anti-Civilization Exhibition*, because it hovers over the text and is reminiscent of the moon image used in the meditation.

68. "Mikkyō meisōhō" [Esoteric Buddhism's meditation methods], *Encyclopedia Kukai*, http://www.mikkyo21f.gr.jp/kukai-ronyu/miyasaka/post-12.html (accessed November 13, 2014). This page is part of the website hosted by Miyasaka Yūkō (宥洪), a son of Miyasaka Yūshō and also a renowned monk and Buddhologist.

69. According to Watanabe Shōkei, an associate of Miyasaka Yūshō's when the monk headed the temple Chishakuin in Kyoto (1999–2007), they worked together to spread the Shingon meditation methods, including *gachirinkan*. In Watanabe's explanation, "First, one looks at the circle and feels the moon in his bosom. Then, one gradually enlarges the circle (moon) and feels the flat moon in three dimensions, as though he is encased inside the moon. One continues to enlarge the moon further, to the size of the room he is in, the house, the town, the Japanese archipelago, the earth, the solar system, and the galactic system. The moon will lose its spherical form and merge with the universe. After enjoying a sublime feeling, he will then reduce the moon in a reverse manner. In the end, he will turn the sphere into the flat disc and return it to the picture. With a deep breath, he ends the meditation." For this information I thank Matsuzawa Haruo, who contacted Watanabe on my behalf and shared with me Watanabe's e-mail to him, dated November 16, 2014.

70. All quotes in this paragraph taken from Matsuzawa, "Sakuhin kaidai."

71. A set of 30 was compiled in a sketchbook, *Precision Painting 30* (1967, now in a private collection), shown as a slide show in a section on Matsuzawa at *Yokohama Triennale* in 2014.

72. Eight circles of identical size are included in Aoki Gallery's *Psi Box*, while one large and one small disc are in *The Whole Works, 1961–1971*.

73. "Bussetsu kanmuryōjukyō" [Shaka's teaching: Meditation of the Buddha of Infinite Life sutra], in *Jōdo sanbukyō* [Three sutras of Pure Land Buddhism] (Kyoto: Honganji Shuppansha, 2013), 295–297.

74. Katō Ikuya, "Matsuzawa Yutaka: Meshia no jigazō" [A messiah's self-portrait], *Bijutsu techō*, no. 314 (June 1969): 174–175.

75. Likely to simulate the act of gazing at the sun in the sky with various landscape backgrounds, he created numerous collages dotted with a single white circle. Some 30 of them, uncatalogued, are in the collection of the Museum of Modern Art, New York (Art & Project/Depot VBVR Gift 1063.2007). The earliest identifiable date is 1967. Most of them bear thumbtack marks, suggesting the possibility that he himself hung them on the wall to practice visualization. Katō Ikuya, in ibid. (page 163), saw some white-circle collages in his *Psi Zashiki Room* in 1969. As of June 2015, a few white-circle collages are still found hanging on the walls at his family house in Shimo Suwa.

76. Kazimir Malevich, "Suprematism," in Herschel B. Chipp, *Theories of Modern Art: A Source Book by Artists and Critics* (Berkeley: University of California Press, 1968), 341.

77. When Matsuzawa taught at Bigakkō in Tokyo, an alternative art school, from 1970 to 1980, he assigned the exercise of *White Circle* by telling his students to gradually enlarge it every week. For his teaching at Bigakkō, see Shimada Yoshiko, "Geijutsu to shikō no jikkenjō: Gendai Shichō-sha to Bigakkō" [Experimental labs: Gendai Shichō-sha and Bigakkō], *Akasegawa Genpei*, a special issue of *Kawade Mook* (October 2014): 207; and Shimada, "Matsuzawa Yutaka," in *Anti-Academy*, ed. Alice Maude-Roxby, exh. cat. (Southampton, UK: John Hansard Gallery, 2013), 52–55.

CHAPTER 3

1. For the etymology of "Happener," see "The Play's Happenings Discourse" in chapter 5.

2. [Preface] to *Play: 1967–80* (Toyonaka and Kyoto: The Play, 1981), n.p.

3. [Preface] to *Play: 1967–73* (Toyonaka: The Play, 1974).

4. [Preface] to *Play: 1967–80*; reprinted in *Play* (Paris: Bat; Osaka: The Play, 2014), n.p.

5. Untitled statement, in *Andepandan '64 ten* [*Independent '64*], exh. cat. (Tokyo: Exhibition Committee, 1964), 1. All quotes in this paragraph from this source.

6. Nishio Ichizō, "Vava ga teian suru neo andepandan fesutibaru ni tsuite" [About a new independent festival proposed by Vava], *Gendai bijutsu*, no. 3 (March 1965): 7.

7. "Andepandan āto fesutibaru—Gendai bijutsu no saiten: Setsuritsu sōkai ni okeru omonaru keika" [*Independent Art Festival—Contemporary Art Festival*: Proceedings of a general meeting to found (the organization committee)] (Gifu: Vava, [1965]), 1.

8. For Kudō's ploy, see Akasegawa Genpei, *Han-geijutsu Anpan* [Anti-Art independent] (1985); pocketbook edition (Tokyo: Chikuma Bunko, 1994), 183–184. For illustrations and more on Kudō's work, see Doryun Chong, *Tetsumi Kudo: Garden of Metamorphosis*, exh. cat. (Minneapolis: Walker Art Center, 2008).

9. For example, see comments by Takiguchi Shūzō and Ide Norio in "Kakujin kakuyō" [Each has his opinion], in *Andepandan '64 ten* [Independent '64], exh. broch. (Tokyo: [Exhibition Committee], 1964), 2.

10. See "Chihō no zen'ei" [Regional avant-garde], special feature, *Bijutsu techō*, no. 296 (April 1968). Many of their works are discussed in KuroDalaiJee (Kuroda Raiji), *Nikutai no anākizumu: 1960 nendai Nihon bijutsu ni okeru pafōmansu no chika suimyaku / Anarchy of the Body: Undercurrents of Performance Art in 1960s Japan* (Tokyo: Grambooks, 2010).

11. *Independent Art Festival*, exh. broch. (Gifu: [Organizing Committee], 1965).

12. Tōno Yoshiaki, "Bodī āto towa nani ka" [What is Body Art?], *Bijutsu techō*, no. 258 (October 1965): 18–19; Ikeda Tatsuo, "Nagaragawa no zen'ei matsuri" [An avant-garde festival at the Nagara River], *Geijutsu Shinchō* (October 1965): 82–83; Akane Kazuo, "Geppyō" [Monthly review], *Bijutsu techō*, no. 258 (October 1965): 131–133.

13. Ikemizu's biography is put together based on *Ikemizu!* (Uji: Ikemizu, 2005) and Ikemizu in Kobayashi Susumu, "Ikemizu Keiichi-shi ni The Play ni tsuite kiku" [Asking Mr. Ikemizu Keiichi about The Play], in *Orutanativu supēsu-ron* [On alternative spaces], ed. Kobayashi (1989); reprinted in the *Yellow Pipe* (1988) section of *Play* (2014), n.p.

14. Ikeda, "Nagaragawa," 82–83; Akane, "Geppyō," 131–132.

15. An announcement and project report bearing the word "Happening" for these two acts are reproduced in *Ikemizu!*, 26–27.

16. Ibid., 17.

17. Ibid., 29.

18. "Gendai bijutsu no saiten" [Contemporary art festival] and "Kansai gendai bijutsu no konnichi" [Kansai's contemporary art today], *Ōru Kansai / All Kwansai* (October 1966): n.p. and 68–72; Minami Enrai, "Gendai bijutsu no saiten" [*Contemporary Art Festival*], *Bijutsu jānaru* [Art journal], no. 59 (1966): 57; "Iki to shōsō no sakka-tachi" [Spirited and impatient artists], *Nihon dokusho shinbun* [Japan readers' newspaper], September 5, 1966.

19. "Kansai gendai bijutsu," 69–70.

20. *Sengo Okayama no bijutsu* [Art of postwar Okayama], exh. cat. (Okayama: Okayama Prefectural Museum of Art, 2002), 100–101.

21. Ikemizu in Kobayashi, "Ikemizu Keiichi-shi ni," 116; reprinted in the *Yellow Pipe* section (1988) in *Play* (2014), n.p.

22. KuroDalaiJee, *Anarchy of the Body*, 47, 77.

23. Ibid., 163.

24. Ibid., 188, 204–205.

25. Ibid., 210.

26. The group name was perhaps derived from Simone de Beauvoir's *Les Mandarins*. See ibid., 563n90.

27. KuroDalaiJee, in ibid., 251.

28. For Gulliver, see *Shūzō Azuchi Garibā / Shuzo Azuchi Gulliver: Ex-Sign*, exh. cat. (Ōtsu: Museum of Modern Art, Shiga, 2010).

29. The number is based on the list of participants in *Play* (2014), although the poster lists 15 names.

30. Descriptions are taken from the *First Play Exhibition* section, in *Play* (2014), n.p.; KuroDalaiJee, *Anarchy of the Body*, 252–254; and Hashimoto Azusa, "Dai 1-kai Play-ten" [First *Play* exhibition], *Kokuritsu Kokusai Bijutsukan nyūsu / The National Museum of Art, Osaka* (August 2014): 6–7.

31. Nakata Kazushige, in the section frontispiece of *First Play Exhibition*, in *Play* (2014), n.p.

32. "Geijutsu no aki" [Fall season of art], *Kōbe shinbun*, September 18, 1967; reproduced in *First Play Exhibition*, in *Play* (2014), n.p.

33. "'Kōdō suru geijutsu' no yagai-ten" [Outdoor exhibition of "action art"], *Asahi gurafu / Asahi Graph* (October 6, 1947); reproduced in *First Play Exhibition*, in *Play* (2014), n.p.

34. Fukuzumi Ren, "Miki Tetsuo intabyū" [Interview with Miki Tetsuo], *HAMArt!* 8 (April 2014):1–6.

35. KuroDalaiJee, *Anarchy of the Body*, 258.

36. Ibid., 279.

37. Oral History Interview with Mizukami Jun, conducted by Sakagami Shinobu, March 21 and 22, 2009, Oral History Archives of Japanese Art (www.oralarthistory.org).

38. Ibid., March 22, 2009.

39. Ikemizu gave a detailed account of *Voyage* in *Ikemizu!*, 47–50, based on his contribution to *Violet Mail*, issued by Miki Tetsuo, and his later recollections. The description of *Voyage* in this section is taken from this account, unless otherwise noted. See also Hashimoto Azusa, "Tamago to Purei" [Egg and The Play], *Kokuritsu Kokusai Bijutsukan nyūsu / The National Museum of Art, Osaka* (October 2014): 6–7.

40. As proposed in the application (*Ikemizu!*, 45).

41. Ikemizu and the group have no document of this notice, perhaps because the school telephoned Ikemizu with this news.

42. Aida Yūji, "Sarumane no harenchi" [Imitation of being shameless], *Osaka shinbun* [1968]; reproduced in the *Voyage* section, in *Play* (2014), n.p.

43. *Ikemizu!*, 50.

44. The Play, "Comment" (1970); reprinted in the *White Cross Manifesto* (1970) section, in *Play* (2014), n.p.

45. However, Anti-Art performers occasionally utilized landscapes as a zone of freedom away from the authorities' watchful eyes, as with the filming of Zero Dimension's *White Hare of Inaba* on a long stretch of sand beach in Kujūkurihama, Chiba Prefecture (figure 6.18). Notably, this took place in their later phase in 1970, when their urban activism waned.

46. Paraphrased from [Preface] to *Play: 1967–80*; reprinted in *Play* (2014), n.p.

47. Nakata Kazushige, police statement (1969); reprinted in the *7 Dimensions* section, in *Play* (2014), n.p.

48. Ikemizu in Kobayashi, "Ikemizu Keiichi-shi," 114; reprinted in the *Yellow Pipe* section (1988), in *Play* (2014), n.p.

49. Membership page in *Play: 1967–80*; reproduced in *Play* (2014), n.p.

50. The list naturally grew in the ensuing years. *Play* (2014) lists five members, 103 former members, 14 institutions and businesses "who offered us deep understanding and cooperation in the realization of our acts," plus four translators for the publication.

51. "Yojigen kara" [From an extra dimension], *Nihon bijutsu kōgei* [Japan art craft] (date unknown); reprinted in *The Play kiroku to genba* [The Play's records and sites] section (1985), in *Play* (2014), n.p.

52. Project description in the section frontispiece of *White Cross Manifesto*, in *Play* (2014), n.p.

53. Ikemizu Keiichi, e-mail to author, April 21, 2015.

54. *White Cross Manifesto*, double-sided poster; reproduced in the *White Cross Manifesto* section, in *Play* (2014), n.p.

55. Japan Expanded Polyethylene Association, "Happō suciróru towa nanika" [What is Styrofoam?], http://www.jepsa.jp/styrofoam/about.html (accessed March 23, 2015).

56. Hashimoto Azusa, "Gendai bijutsu no nagare" [*Current of Contemporary Art*], *Kokuritsu Kokusai Bijutsukan nyūsu / The National Museum of Art, Osaka* (August 2015): 6.

57. Ibid., 7.

58. Project report (1969); reproduced in the *Current* section of *Play* (2014), n.p.

59. Members' schedule (1970) and "Gendai ni bijutsu wa ikinokoreruka: Purei-shi no kojinteki taiken" [Can art survive in contemporary times? Mr. Play's personal experience], *Sandē Mainichi* [Sunday Mainichi] (date unknown); reproduced in the *Sheep* section of *Play* (2014), n.p.

60. "Purei: Nichijō seikatsu tono kyōkai o toriharatte" [The Play takes down the boundaries of everyday life], *Bijutsu techō*, no. 335 (December 1970): 88–89.

61. [Preface] to *Play: 1967–73*, n.p.

62. Project annotation, in the section frontispiece for *Sheep*, in *Play* (2014), n.p.

63. Project report (1972); reproduced in the *Ie* section, in *Play* (2014), n.p.

64. Tōno Yoshiaki, "Za Purei: Nikutai ga kokka ni ninai toki" [The Play: When the body does not resemble the nation], *Mizue* (December 1974): 63.

65. "The Play," *Bijutsu techō*, no. 359 (October 1972): n.p.

66. "The Play: Tent," flier (1974), in Ikemizu Keiichi's archives.

67. Tōno, "Za Purei," 56.

68. Members' schedule, no. 1 (1976); reproduced in the *Wind* section of *Play* (2014), n.p.

69. Ikemizu's statement in report card portfolio (1976); reproduced in ibid.

CHAPTER 4

1. Accounts of Maeyama's biography and GUN's early years have been taken from Oral History Interview with Maeyama Tadashi and Horikawa Michio, conducted by Koh Seong-Jun and Miyata Yūka, June 29 and 30, 2011, Oral History Archives of Japanese Art (www.oralarthistory.org; pre-edited transcripts); and *GUN: Niigata ni zen'ei ga atta koro / Niigata Contemporary Artists Group and Its Era*, exh. cat. (Nagaoka: Niigata Prefectural Museum of Modern Art, 2012).

2. For Ishiko Junzō, see *Ishiko Junzō-teki sekai; Bijutsu hatsu, manga keiyu, kictchu iki / The World of Ishiko Junzō: From Art via Manga to Kitsch*, exh. cat. (Fuchū: Fuchū Art Museum, 2011); and *Gurūpu "Genshoku" to Ishiko Junzō: 1966–1971 / Group "Genshok"" and Ishiko Junzō: 1966–1971*, exh. cat. (Shizuoka: Shizuoka Prefectural Museum of Art, 2014).

3. For Genshoku, see *Gurūpu "Genshoku" to Ishiko Junzō*; and *Mono-ha saikō / Reconsidering Mono-ha*, exh. cat. (Osaka; National Museum of Art, 2005).

4. Exceptions were such metropolitan prefectures as Tokyo and Osaka. For more on regional salons, see Tomii, "Introduction: Collectivism in Twentieth-Century Japanese Art with a Focus on Operational Aspects of *Dantai*," *Positions* 21, no. 2 (Spring 2013): 246–248.

5. *Ashiya shiten / Ashiya City Exhibition 1948–1997* (Ashiya: Ashiya City Art Association, Ashiya City Museum of Art & History, and Ashiya-shi Bunka Shinkō Zaidan, 1997).

6. For Itoigawa's salon, see Koh Seong-Jun, "Gurūpu 'GUN' ga debyū suru made" [Before the debut of GUN], in *GUN: Niigata ni zen'ei ga atta koro*, 12–13; and blog entries for April 21, 2009, and June 19, 2012, in "Horikawa Michio no āto nikki" [Horikawa Michio's art diary], http://d.hatena.ne.jp/niigata-art226/20090421/1240248901 and http://d.hatena.ne.jp/niigata-art226/20120619/1340096492 (both accessed March 25, 2015).

7. *Me* (October 15, 1967): 1; reproduced in *Niigata gendai bijutsuka shūdan GUN no kiseki 1967–1975* [Trajectory of GUN, Niigata's contemporary artists group, 1967–1975] (Jōetsu: Privately published, 2008), 15.

8. Ushio Shinohara, "Zen'ei eno michi" [Road to the avant-garde], 11 parts, *Bijutsu techō*, nos. 263–265, 267–268, 270–274, 275 (February–December 1966); subsequently published as *Zen'ei no michi* (Tokyo: Bijutsu Shuppan-sha, 1968). Accounts of GUN's and individual members' activities after 1969 have been taken from Oral History Interview with Maeyama Tadashi and Horikawa Michio, June 30, 2011; and author's interviews with Maeyama and Horikawa, May 29–30 and December 7, 2012, and June 17, 2014.

9. Miyazawa was the chief editor of *Bijutsu techō* from January 1968 to May 1971.

10. Some tendencies were easier than others to learn from the print media. The ideas and styles of Earthworks and land art were more paper-friendly than those of Conceptual Art, as discussed in chapter 5.

11. Ming Tiampo, *Gutai: Decentering Modernism* (Chicago: University of Chicago Press, 2011), 45–54.

12. For example, see Horikawa in *Niigata gendai bijutsu shūdan GUN to watashi* [GUN, Niigata's contemporary artist group, and I] (Jōetsu: Privately published, 2008), 7.

13. For the mission details of Apollo 11, see NASA, "Apollo 11," http://www.nasa.gov/mission_pages/apollo/missions/apollo11.html (accessed March 25, 2015).

14. Accounts of this work are taken from Horikawa, *Niigata gendai bijutsu shūdan GUN to watashi*, 7–9, unless otherwise noted.

15. Horikawa, "69721115620," statement dated July 26, was first published in his school's student council newspaper (August 9).

16. Horikawa in Oral History Interview with Maeyama Tadashi and Horikawa Michio, June 30, 2011.

17. See Oral History Interview with Niwa Katsuji, conducted by Hon'ami Kiyoshi and Kajiya Kenji, October 31, 2010, Oral History Archives of Japanese Art (www.oralarthistory.org). Niwa also used mail art in his New Year's postcards of 1969, in which he exploited the postal system and inversed the addressee-addresser relationship. This idea was later developed by Maeyama in his mail-art work.

18. Horikawa, interview with author, June 17, 2014.

19. Ishiko Junzō, "'Takamatsu Jirō koten' no mondai teiki" [Questions raised by Takamatsu Jirō's solo exhibition], *Bijutsu techō*, no. 311 (April 1969): 13.

20. Fujieda Teruo, "Kannen no romantisizumu: Busshitsu no shōmetsu" [Romanticism of *kannen*: Vanishing of matter], *Bijutsu techō*, no. 315 (July 1969): 108–109.

21. Horikawa in Oral History Interview with Maeyama Tadashi and Horikawa Michio, June 30, 2011.

22. Horikawa, e-mail to author, August 13, 2014.

23. Lee Ufan, "Kannen no geijutsu wa kanō ka: Obuje shisō no shōtai to yukue" [Is an art of *kannen* possible? The truth and future of the *objet* thought], *Bijutsu techō*, no. 319 (November 1969): 70–79.

24. Ibid., 70.

25. Ibid.

26. Ibid., 79.

27. Horikawa took the design of data cards from Shūsaku Arakawa's "diagram paintings," an example of which the young artist saw in a Japanese edition of Marcel Duchamp's writing, *Maruseru Dushan goroku / To and from Rrose Selavy: Selected Words of Marcel Duchamp*, trans. and ed. by Takiguchi Shūzō (Tokyo: Bijutsu Shuppansha, 1968). This edition includes full-page reproductions of four artworks created for the publication by Arakawa, Duchamp himself, Jean Tinguely, and Jasper Johns.

28. For this collective, see Tomii, "After the 'Descent to the Everyday': Japanese Collectivism from Hi Red Center to The Play, 1964–1973," in *Collectivism after Modernism*, ed. Blake Stimson and Gregory Sholette (Minneapolis: University of Minnesota Press, 2007), 63–64.

29. Armin H. Meyer, American Ambassador, letter to Horikawa Michio, January 23, 1970.

30. As explained in "Kimi mo mēru āto ni sanka shiyō" [Why don't you join and do mail art?], in *Wakamono no ikigai* [Youthful worth of life], ed. Yomiuri Shinbunsha Social Affairs Section (Tokyo: Ēru Shuppansha, 1970), 96–97.

31. Horikawa, data card for *The Nakanomata River Project: 17*, December 13, 1972.

32. Horikawa, "To Apollo 11," handwritten data sheet, July 21, 1969.

33. "Dai-san no wakamono (7): Asobi no hapuningu" [The third youth, no. 7: Playful Happening], *Yomiuri shinbun*, January 8, 1970.

34. Accounts of this project are taken from Horikawa in Oral History Interview with Maeyama Tadashi and Horikawa Michio, June 30, 2011; Ichihasi Tetsuo, Horikawa Michio, and Maeyama Tadashi, "Shuppan ni yosete" [On the publication], in *GUN group: Event to Change the Image of Snow* (Tokyo: Tokyo Gallery, 2009), n.p.; and Horikawa Michio, "'Hyōgen kōi no fukken" [Recovery of the act of expression], *Biiku bunka* (July 1995); reprinted in Horikawa, blog entry for January 9, 2013, in "Horikawa Michio no āto nikki," http://d.hatena.ne.jp/niigata-art226/20130109/1357716184 (accessed March 25, 2015).

35. "Atarashii shizen: Erementarizumu 'Āsuwāku'" [New nature: Elementalism "Earthworks"], special feature, *Bijutsu techō*, no. 315 (July 1969).

36. In the unpaginated illustrated section, both are given the title *Sub-Zero Snow Project.*

37. Maeyama, in Oral History Interview with Maeyama Tadashi and Horikawa Michio, June 30, 2011.

38. Japan Metrological Agency, "Rekidai zenkoku ranking" [Historical records nationwide], http://www.data.jma.go.jp/obd/stats/etrn/view/rankall.php (accessed March 11, 2015).

39. Japan Weather Association, "Yuki no omosa o kangaeru: Gōsetsu no machi Tōkamachi kara" [Thinking about the weight of snow: From the heavy-snow town Tōkamachi], February 9, 2012, https://www.jwa.or.jp/news/docs/2012-02-09.pdf (accessed August 28, 2014).

40. Maeyama, in Oral History Interview with Maeyama Tadashi and Horikawa Michio, June 30, 2011.

41. Ichihashi, Horikawa, and Maeyama, "Shuppan ni yosete."

42. With today's more stringent environmental protection laws, permission would be difficult to secure.

43. Unagami Masaomi, ed., *Yagi Kazuo sakuhinshū* [Works by Yagi Kazuo] (Tokyo: Kyūryūdō, 1969). He also edited *Kawaru iro no mie: Sōgo sayō no jikken* [Changing color appearances: Experiment of interplay] (Tokyo: Color Planning Center, 1970).

44. This figure is given by Hanaga in his uncredited text, "Yuki ni idonda geijutsuka" [Avant-garde artists challenging snow], *Geijutsu seikatsu* (April 1970): 68.

45. "Daisetsugen ni nanashoku no chūshōga" [Seven-color abstract painting on a vast snow field], *Asahi gurafu / Asahi Graph* (March 6, 1970): cover, 3–5.

46. "Yuki ni idonda," *Geijutsu seikatsu*, 65–68.

47. "Daisetsugen," *Asahi Graph*, 4.

48. "Yuki ni idonda," *Geijutsu seikatsu*, 66.

49. Haryū Ichirō, ed., *Kōi ni kakeru / Art of Action and Concept*, no. 11 of *Gendai no bijutsu / Art Now* (Tokyo: Kōdansha, 1972).

50. Accounts of Konishi's life and trial are taken from Konishi Makoto, *Hansen jieikan* [Antiwar self-defense soldier] (Tokyo: Gōdō Shuppan, 1970); and Konishi, ed., *Konishi hangun saiban: Hansen jieikan no tatakai to shōri* [Konishi anti-military trial: An antiwar self-defense soldier's struggle and triumph] (Tokyo: Sanichi Shobō, 1982).

51. Horikawa in Oral History Interview with Maeyama Tadashi and Horikawa Michio, June 30, 2011; Horikawa, *Niigata gendai bijutsu shūdan GUN to watashi*, 14–15.

52. Horikawa's and Maeyama's personal archives contain these works, including self-addressed specimens, which served as "artist's proofs," so to speak.

53. Maeyama was so into "confusion mail art" that he introduced it as teaching material at his middle-school classes during this period; he has preserved many ingenious examples by his students.

54. "Subete no tatakau rōdōsha, gakusei, shimin wa hantei tōsō ni kekki seyo!" [Stand up, all fighting workers, students, and citizens, for the anti-imperialism struggle!], *GUN*, no. 1 (March 10, 1971).

55. "Jinmin no mawari o sutekkā de umeyo!" [Fill the surroundings of people with stickers], *GUN*, no. 1 (March 10, 1971).

56. "70-nendai kaikyū tōsō dotō shingeki e: Zenkoku yūsō sensen no saranaru danketsu o!" [Forcefully advance in the 1970s class struggle: More solidarity for the nationwide Postal Mailing Front], *GUN*, no. 2 (March 20, 1971).

57. For this work, see Tomii, "Rebel with a Cause: Akasegawa Genpei's Greater Japan Zero-Yen Note," in *Appropriation*, ed. David Evans, Documents of Contemporary Art series (Cambridge, MA: MIT Press, 2009).

58. The emperor and the emperor system have been a political rallying point for a number of Japanese artists, including Maeyama and Horikawa. See Arai Hiroyuki, *Tennō āto-ron: Sono bi, "ten" ni tsūzu* [On Emperor art: Its beauty leads to heaven] (Tokyo: Shakai Hyōron-sha, 2014).

59. Yoshihara Jirō, "Chūshō kaiga no yohaku" / "Blank of Abstract Painting," *Bokubi*, no. 21 (February 1953): 13.

CHAPTER 5

1. I am borrowing and adapting a phrase by Allan Kaprow, "communication malfunction," as quoted in Judith F. Rodenbeck, "Communication Malfunction: Happenings and Gutai," in Ming Tiampo and Alexandra Munroe, eds., *Gutai: Splendid Playground*, exh. cat. (New York: Guggenheim Museum, 2014), 265–269.

2. Nakahara Yūsuke, "Ningen to busshitsu" / "Between Man and Matter," in *Ningen to busshitsu: Dai 10-kai Nihon kokusai bijutsu-ten / Between Man and Matter: Tokyo Biennale '70*, exh. cat. (Tokyo: Mainichi Newspapers, 1970), n.p. All quotes from this catalog essay are translated by this author. A full translation is found in Doryun Chong et al., eds., *From Postwar to Postmodern: Art in Japan, 1945–1989: Primary Documents* (New York: Museum of Modern Art; Durham: Duke University Press), 227–231. It should be noted that there are two catalogs for *Tokyo Biennale 1970*, as customary for Mainichi's twin biannuals. The first volume served as an exhibition guide and the second as

documentation, often with the exact same title and format. For the 1970 international exhibition, the covers are different: the first volume carries Nakahira Takuma's photograph of a desolate industrial landscape, while the second has a pitch-black cover.

3. Lucy R. Lippard, *Six Years: The Dematerialization of the Art Object from 1966 to 1972* (Berkeley: University of California Press, 1997), 165. The list gives surnames only, and their names are not indexed.

4. Nakahara, "Ningen to busshitsu" / "Between Man and Matter," n.p.

5. For example, as opposed to 40 artists in its 1970 iteration, *Tokyo Biennale 1967* showed some 500 works by 280 artists from 17 countries. See untitled company's statement, in *Dai 9-kai Nihon kokusai bijutsu-ten / Tokyo Biennale 1967*, exh. cat. (Tokyo: Mainichi Newspapers, 1967), n.p. The 1967 Biennale was the immediate predecessor of the 1970, as the latter (which would have appeared in 1969) was switched with the Mainichi Contemporary in order to present the Tokyo Biennale in the same year as Expo '70: see chapter 1.

6. For this work, see Mika Yoshitake, "Situating *Rust Garden*: Carl Andre in Japan," in *Carl Andre: Sculpture as Place, 1958–2010*, exh. cat. (New York: Dia Art Foundation, 2014), 328.

7. Among the 1969 exhibitions, he personally saw that of the Whitney Museum prior to his appointment as the biennale commissioner in the fall of 1969.

8. For *Tokyo Biennale 1970* and the history of Mainichi's twin biannuals, see Reiko Tomii, "Toward *Tokyo Biennale 1970*: Shapes of the International in the Age of 'International Contemporaneity,'" *Review of Japanese Culture and Society* 23 (December 2011): 198–201.

9. Nakahara, quoted in Minemura Toshiaki, "Dappi suru 'Gendai Nihon bijutsu-ten'" [*Contemporary Art Exhibition of Japan* breaks out of the mold], *Bijutsu techō*, no. 310 (March 1969): 13.

10. Minemura, ibid.

11. Most of the exhibited works are illustrated in *Between Man and Matter*, second volume, n.p.

12. For Nomura Hitoshi, see *Hitoshi Nomura: Early Works*, exh. cat. (New York: McCaffery Fine Art, 2010). The quote is from Nomura, interview with author, April 2, 1996.

13. For discussion of this work, see R[achel] H[ooper], "Kawaguchi Tatsuo," in *For a New World to Come: Experiments in Japanese Art and Photography, 1968–1979*, ed. Yasufumi Nakamori, exh. cat. (Houston: Museum of Fine Art, 2015), 138.

14. Since he sent these postcards without specifying any display method, Minemura devised vinyl sleeves to show both sides (Minemura Toshiaki, interview with author, February 5, 2015). I owe the observation on seriality to Jeffrey Weiss.

15. This number of canvases is given by Anne Wheeler, "Everyday Meditation," in *On Kawara: Silence*, exh. cat. (New York: Guggenheim Museum, 2015), 220. The number of canvases is 96 in the biennale catalog's checklist.

16. *Dai-9kai gendai Nihon bijutsu-ten / The 9th Contemporary Art Exhibition of Japan*, exh. cat. (Tokyo: Mainichi Newspapers, 1969), n.p.

17. Unfortunately, no media are given for the exhibited works in *Gendai bijutsu no dōkō / Trends in Contemporary Japanese Art*, exh. cat. (Kyoto: National Museum of Modern Art, 1969).

18. For example, the modernist sculptor Horiuchi Masakazu was impressed by Matsuzawa's seriousness in a roundtable held to discuss that year's Mainichi Contemporary: Ikeda Masuo, Sugai Kumi,

Sekine Nobuo, Horiuchi Masakazu, and Tōno Yoshiaki, "'Tsukuru koto' to 'tsukuranai koto'" [Making and not making], *Bijutsu techō*, no. 315 (July 1969): 188–189. In this roundtable, the young Sekine Nobuo expressed his interest in Matsuzawa's work with a qualification that he was apprehensive of such "ambiguous" words as "immateriality" (188).

19. Matsuzawa Yutaka, letter to Takiguchi Shūzō, May 2, 1970, in Takiguchi Shūzō Papers (c. 1945–1979), Keiō University Art Center.

20. For the poet Ishikawa Midori's observation on the ethical dimension of Matsuzawa's work, see his "Ryōshi geijutsu: Posuto Hiroshima no seishin gihō" [Quantum art: Post-Hiroshima spiritual methods], in *Supiricharizumu e: Matsuzawa Yutaka / To Spiritualism: Yutaka Matsuzawa, 1954–1997*, exh. cat. (Kawaguchi: Saitō Memorial Kawaguchi Museum of Contemporary Art, 1997), 10–15.

21. Checklist in *Between Man and Matter*, second volume, n.p. The words enclosed in quotation marks are materials listed in the checklist.

22. "'Watashi no shi ni kansuru jakkan no fuen" [Some exegesis on *My Own Death*] / "Some Dilations on 'My Own Death' by Yutaka Matsuzawa," in *Between Man and Matter*, second volume, n.p. Translation adapted by author.

23. Yoshida Yoshie, "Tandoku kōisha no chōgekijō" [Solitary actors in an ultra-theater], *Bijutsu techō*, no. 335 (December 1970): 53–54. Notably, Matsuzawa's entry for the 1964 exhibition was "future death" according to Yoshida's description.

24. *Contemporary Japanese Art: Fifth Japan Art Festival Exhibition*, exh. cat. (New York: Guggenheim Museum, 1970), n.p. For the mist of Kirigamine, see "Suwa-shi kankō gauide" / "Suwa Tourist Information," http://www.suwakanko.jp/nature.php (accessed September 16, 2015).

25. This performance is noted in his 1971 postcard work, *Vanishing/Natural Series (Postcard Painting II-04)*.

26. For the response to *Tokyo Biennale 1970* and its consequences, see Tomii, "Toward *Tokyo Biennale 1970*," 205–206.

27. They are the Museum of Modern Art, Wakayama, and Hyōgo Prefectural Museum of Modern Art, Kobe (now Hyōgo Prefectural Museum of Art).

28. Early large-scale exhibitions of this type were Fukuoka Asian Art Triennale (begun in 1999), Echigo-Tsumari Art Triennial (2000), and Yokohama Triennale (2001).

29. For Art & Project, see Christophe Cherix, ed., *In & Out of Amsterdam: Travels in Conceptual Art, 1960–1976*, exh. cat. (New York: Museum of Modern Art, 2009).

30. Ravesteijn visited his parents in Japan that spring for some two months, because his father, an investment banker, had just moved there. I owe this information to Christophe Cherix, who talked to Ravesteijn on my behalf. Cherix, e-mail to author, January 2, 2015.

31. Nakahara Yūsuke, "Me ni mienai geijutsu" [Art invisible to the eye], *Bijutsu techō*, no. 342 (May 1971): 51–52.

32. See Kynaston L. McShine, ed., *Information*, exh. cat. (New York: Museum of Modern Art, 1970), 14, and "Information (July 2 through September 20, 1970): Checklist* (not including films)," photocopy held in MoMA's Library.

33. *1871–1981: Utopier & Visioner*, exh. cat. (Stockholm: Moderna Museet, 1971).

34. As noted in his 1970 postcard work, *Vanishing/Natural Series (Postcard Painting II-01).*

35. Matsuzawa Yutaka, "Yakusha atogaki" [Translator's note], *Geijutsu kurabu* [Art club] (April 1974): 190. "Translation" here refers to the Japanese translation of Weiner's interview with Willoughby Sharp for *Avalanche* (182–190).

36. Matsuzawa Kumiko, conversation with author, June 15, 2015. The entire trip was meticulously chronicled by Matsuzawa's eldest daughter Kumiko, who made a photo album filled with photographs she took and other original documents in the Matsuzawa Archives, Shimo Suwa.

37. Words by Ravesteijn quoted in Matsuzawa, "G&G-shi tono itchūya" [A day and night with Gilbert & George], *Bijutsu techō*, no. 360 (November 1972): 210. This essay is followed by Kumiko's photographs of the pair in action (212–213), and the pair's writing and work (209, 214–227).

38. Matsuzawa Yutaka, *Pusai āto shūgō* [Psi art gathering], flier (1969).

39. Matsuzawa Yutaka, "Jihitsu nenpu" [Auto-chronology], *Kikan* [Organ], no. 13 (1982): 55.

40. As chronicled by his postcard works, *Vanishing/Natural Series (Postcard Painting II-02),* dated 1970, and *Vanishing/Natural Series (Postcard Painting II-10),* dated 1971.

41. Matsuzawa, "Jihitsu nenpu," 60.

42. As referenced in his 1971 postcard work, *Vanishing/Natural Series (Postcard Painting II-04).*

43. They are now housed at the Museum of Modern Art, New York, as part of a gift from Art & Project in 2007.

44. The gift of Art & Project to the Museum of Modern Art, New York (1063.2007), includes four sets of large envelopes, all marked "Post-Nirvana: Our Commune" and each containing the two diagrams, along with Yoshida Yoshie's English text "Post-Nirvāna: Our Commune." Although the Japanese diagram contains more specific information, I have used the English version to discuss the group's mapping here.

45. "Sekai hōki" [World uprising], call for entries, *Bijutsu techō*, no. 360 (November 1972): 50. The archival material of the *World Uprising* campaign has recently been compiled by the World Uprising Organization Committee in conjunction with *The Final Art Thoughts Workshop Presents: World Uprising Exhibition—A Project for the 22nd Century* held at Bunpōdō Gallery in Tokyo in 2014. See http://sekaihouki-matuzawa.jimdo.com/world-uprising (accessed December 30, 2014).

46. As noted in his 1971 postcard work, *Vanishing/Natural Series (Postcard Painting II-05).*

47. "Komyūn e" [Toward commune], special feature, *Bijutsu techō*, no. 360 (November 1972): 25–104.

48. "Sekai hōki" / "The World Up-Rising 1972, 1973," *Geijutsu kurabu*, no. 8 (April 1974): 153–181.

49. Matsuzawa Yutaka, "Katasutorofī ni tsuite" [On catastrophe], *SD* (January 1973): 24–25.

50. A related checklist was shown at the 2014 *World Uprising* exhibition in Tokyo.

51. For example, "Katasutorofī āto ni kankei shite: Jinrui no metsubō o mae ni" [In reference to Catastrophe Art: Before the demise of humankind], *Gendai shi techō* [Contemporary poetry notebook] (November 1972): 14–20; "Katasutorofī ni tsuite" [On catastrophe], *SD* (January 1973): 24–25.

52. "Katasutorofī āto, Catastrophe Art," *Bijutsu techō*, no. 365 (March 1973): 183–214.

53. *Catastrophe Art from the East*, exh. cat. (Milan: Centro Culturale S. Fedele, 1972).

54. Matsuzawa, "Jihitsu nenpu," 63.

55. Ibid., 67–68.

56. Chronology in *To Spiritualism*, 59–60.

57. Yoshihara Jirō, "Gutai Art Manifesto," trans. Reiko Tomii, in Tiampo and Munroe, *Gutai: Splendid Playground*, 18.

58. Most notably, Murakami Saburō made several conceptualist experiments in the mid-1950s, but never pursued it; he only returned to conceptualism in the early 1970s, after he had left Gutai. See *Murakami Saburō: Through the '70s* (Osaka: Art Court Gallery, 2013).

59. For her writing on Shiraga Kazuo, see Ming Tiampo, "Shiraga's International Art of a New Era," in *Kazuo Shiraga*, exh. cat. (New York: Mnuchin Gallery, 2015), 16–18.

60. Ming Tiampo, *Gutai: Decentering Modernism* (Chicago: University of Chicago Press, 2011), 94–97.

61. Allan Kaprow, *Assemblage, Environments & Happenings* (New York: Abrams, 1966), 212; quoted and rephrased in Rodenbeck, "Communication Malfunction," 265–269.

62. "Internalized interfaces" differs from "interpoetics" as a theoretical construct. As reconceptualized by Ming Tiampo, "interpoetics" illuminates "positive effects" of consciously improving or building upon preceding works, while keeping in check "negative effects" or the so-called "influences" from the normative center. In contrast, "internalized interfaces" encompasses both positive and negative effects that took root after transplantation and were processed either consciously or unconsciously.

63. See Midori Yoshimoto, "From Space to Environment: The Origins of *Kankyō* and the Emergence of Intermedia Art in Japan," *Art Journal* 67, no. 3 (Fall 2008): 25–45.

64. Shiraga Kazuo, "Kōi koso" [Action only], *Gutai 3* (October 20, 1955); English translation by Reiko Tomii, in *Kazuo Shiraga: Six Decades*, exh. cat. (New York: McCaffrey Fine Art, 2009), 60–61.

65. Haryū Ichirō, ed., *Kōi ni kakeru / Art of Action and Concept*, no. 11 of *Gendai no bijutsu / Art Now* (Tokyo: Kōdansha, 1972). It is not unusual that the English title given by the publisher/editor differed from the literal meaning of the Japanese title.

66. In writing this paragraph, I have benefited from the detailed study by KuroDalaiJee (Kuroda Raiji) on the usages of these words and their implications as outlined in this paragraph. See KuroDalaiJee, *Nikutai no anākizumu: 1960 nendai Nihon bijutsu ni okeru pafōmansu no chika suimyaku / Anarchy of the Body: Undercurrents of Performance Art in 1960s Japan* (Tokyo: Grambooks, 2010), 66–76.

67. Ibid., 66.

68. For Shinohara's "action art," see Reiko Tomii, "Shinohara Ushio's Action in Three Modes," in *Shinohara Pops! The Avant-Garde Road, Tokyo/New York*, exh. cat. (Albany: SUNY Press, 2012), 27–35.

69. For example, the critic Haryū Ichirō used the term to characterize her work in "Zen'ei geijutsu ni tsukaremashita" [I become weary of avant-garde art], *Geijutsu Shinchō* (August 1962): 148. Yoko Ono's rejection of the term can be found in her 1966 lecture "To the Wesleyan People," reprinted in *YES Yoko Ono*, exh. cat. (New York: Japan Society, 2000), 289.

70. "Hapuningu towa nanika?" [What is Happening?], *Bijutsu techō*, no. 282 (May 1967): 130–140.

71. "Happening," special feature, *Bijutsu techō*, no. 301 (August 1968): 77–107.

72. "Happener" is generally considered a Japanese neologism, along with another word, "Happenist," as KuroDalaiJee observes (*Anarchy of the Body*, 68). However, Kaprow himself used the term, for example in his 1967 essay in *ARTnews*, "Pinpointing Happenings"; repr. in *The Blurring of Art and Life*, ed. Jeff Kelley (Los Angeles: University of California Press, 2003), 85. Although Kaprow appeared to have rarely used the term in published texts, art historian Judith Rodenbeck has observed that the artist and his colleagues used it colloquially by 1961 (e-mail to author, January 4, 2015). A possible link between New York and Tokyo was Ay-O, close to Kaprow, who made a temporary return to Tokyo in 1966–1967.

73. "Hapuningu towa nanika?," 130.

74. KuroDalaiJee, *Arnachy of the Body*, 67.

75. Ikemizu Keiichi, "Watashi ni totte hapuningu towa nanika" [What Happenings mean to me], *Miru* (September 1969): 114.

76. Kaprow, "The Education of an Un-Artist, Part I (1971)," in *The Blurring of Art and Life*, 97–109.

77. Kaprow, "Pinpointing Happenings," 84.

78. Miki Tetsuo, reprinted in the *Marshmallows & Hot Air* section (1969), in *Play* (2014), n.p.

79. Sekine Nobuo, in Ikeda et al., "'Tsukuru koto' to 'tsukuranai koto,'" 179.

80. Lee Ufan, "Hi-taishō sekai eno jikaku" [Self-awareness toward the non-objective world], *Miru* (September 1969): 112–113.

81. Lee Ufan, "Sekai to kōzō: Taishō no gakai (gendai bijutsu ronkō)" [World and structure: Collapse of the object (on contemporary art)] *Dezain hihyō / The Design Review*, no. 9 (June 1969): 121–133; trans. Stanley N. Anderson in *Lee Ufan: Marking Infinity*, exh. cat. (New York: Guggenheim Museum, 2011), 102–110. In this translation, *hapunā* is translated as "creators of Happenings" (108).

82. *Shigusa-sha* appears in Lee Ufan, "Sonzai to mu o koete: Sekine Nobuo-ron" [Beyond being and nothingness: On Sekine Nobuo], in *Deai o motomete: Atarashii geijutsu no hajimari ni* [In search of encounter: At the dawn of a new art] (Tokyo: Tabata Shoten, 1971), 117–173. English translation by Reiko Tomii as "Beyond Being and Nothingness: On Sekine Nobuo," in *Review of Japanese Culture and Society* 25 (December 2013): 236–259.

83. For Mono-ha's performative nature, see Reiko Tomii, "Six Contradictions of Mono-ha," *Review of Japanese Culture and Society* 25 (December 2013): 212–220.

84. This paragraph is based on Ikemizu, "Watashi ni totte."

85. In contrast, Lee's title was *zōkei sakka*, which literally means "form-making artist," as opposed to "painter" and "sculptor."

86. Ikemizu, untitled statement, in *2nd Han Setouchi gendai bijutsu-ten* [*2nd All Setouchi Contemporary Art Exhibition*], exh. cat. (Okayama: Setouchi Gendai Bijutsu no Kai, et al., 1968), n.p.

87. Ikemizu, "Watshi ni totte," 114.

88. A significant resonance is felt between Ikemizu's theorization and Yoko Ono's 1966 lecture "To the Wesleyan People," in which she outlined her definition of instruction-based event while rejecting the term Happening (see above, note 69).

89. Mizukami Jun, "Hapuningusu ni kansuru 9-ko no kisoteki sengen" [9 basic statements on Happenings], *The Play* 1 (April 1969): front page.

90. Mizukami, "It Happens / With Reactions," *The Play* 1 (April 1969): front page.

91. Judith F. Rodenbeck, *Radical Prototypes: Allan Kaprow and the Invention of Happenings* (Cambridge, MA: MIT Press, 2011), 136.

92. Nakahara Yūsuke credited Matsuzawa's *kannen* as an inspiration for his essay on "idea" in art. See Nakahara, "Aidea toshiteno geijutsu" [Art as idea], *SD* (July 1968): 16.

93. The earliest reference to Conceptual Art was made by Fujieda Teruo in "Atarashii mono no owari: Gendai geijutsu no jōkyō" [The end of the new: The state of contemporary art], *Bijutsu techō*, no. 307 (January 1969): 54. Interestingly, Fujieda translated it as *gainen-teki geijutsu*, although this translation did not gain currency until later.

94. Suzuki Katsuo characterized 1969 as "year one of Conceptual Art," in "Nihon ni okeru 'konsepuchuaru āto' gannen: 1969-nen no gensetsu kūkan kara" [Year one of Conceptual Art in Japan: The discursive space of 1969], *Bijutsu fōramu 21 / Bijutsu Forum 21* 30 (2014): 78–83. However, as this section demonstrates, it is more accurate to call it "year one of *kannen*."

95. *Kannen* (観念) and *gainen* (概念) as excerpted from *Daijirin*, 3rd ed. (2006), in kotobank.jp. For Nishi Amane, see for example Thomas R. H. Havens, *Nishi Amane and Modern Japanese Thought* (Princeton: Princeton University Press, 1970).

96. Lee Ufan, in Fujieda Teruo and Lee Ufan (dialogue), "Sakka no shisei to sonritsu no kiban" [Artists' attitudes and the foundation of their existence], *Bijutsu techō*, no. 358 (August/September 1972): 59.

97. This differentiation is based on the 1999 exhibition *Global Conceptualism*, which through examples from different regions of the world defined "conceptualism" as a broader set of strategies against the status quo. For the capitalization of movement names in world art history, see Tomii, "Toward a New Understanding of 'mono-ha': Or Where to Locate Haraguchi Noriyuki in 1970s Art in Japan," in *Noriyuki Haraguchi*, exh. cat. (New York: Fergus McCaffrey, 2014), 70–71.

98. For the discursive history of Conceptual Art, see Alexander Alberro and Blake Stimson, eds., *Conceptual Art: A Critical Anthology* (Cambridge, MA: MIT Press, 1999).

99. Untitled curatorial statement, *Gendai bijutsu no dōkō / Trends in Contemporary Japanese Painting and Sculpture*, exh. cat. (Kyoto: National Museum of Modern Art, 1966), n.p.

100. See "Tenrankai ichiran" [List of all exhibitions], in *Kyoto Kokuritsu Kindai Bijutsukan 50-nenshi / Fifty Years of the National Museum of Modern Art* (Kyoto: National Museum of Modern Art, 2013), 72.

101. "Gendai bijutsu no dōkō" [Trends in contemporary art], in *Gendai bijutsu no dōkō / Trends in Contemporary Art*, exh. cat. (Kyoto: National Museum of Modern Art, 1969), n.p.

102. "Gendai bijutsu no dōkō" [Trends in contemporary art], in *Gendai bijutsu no dōkō / Trends in Contemporary Art*, exh. cat. (Kyoto: National Museum of Modern Art, 1970), n.p.

103. This usage is most saliently demonstrated by Miki Tamon, then a curator of the Tokyo Modern, a sister institution of the Kyoto Modern, in "Gendai bijutsu no ichidanmen" [An aspect of contemporary art], *Miru* (August 1969): 108.

104. In reviews of the Mainichi Contemporary and the *Trends* survey, some terminological confusion arose as artists and critics tried to use the English term in transliterated *katakana*. Other than *Konsepuchuaru āto* (corresponding to Conceptual Art), we can find *Konseputo āto* (Concept Art) and *Konsepushon āto* (Conception Art).

105. Haryū Ichirō, "Bijutsu jihyō: Geijutsu no unmei ni tsuite" [Art review: On the fate of art], *Sansai* (June 1969): 54; Miyazawa Takeyoshi, "Editā no nōto kara" [From the editor's notes], *Bijutsu techō*, no. 315 (July 1969): 25.

106. Haryū, "Bijutsu jihyō," 55.

107. For example, Ishiko Junzō, "Gendai bijutsu no teiryū" [Undercurrents of contemporary art] (1969); repr. in *Ishiko Junzō chosakushū 2: Imēji-ron* [Ishiko Junzō's writing: On imagery] (Tokyo: Rappasha, 1986), 224.

108. Miyazawa, "Editā no nōto kara," 25. As the chief editor of *Bijutsu techō*, he ran special features on Air Art and Earthworks in its June and July issues.

109. Lee Ufan, "Kannen no geijutsu wa kanō ka: Obuje shisō no shōtai to yukue" [Is an art of *kannen* possible? The truth and future of *objet* thought], *Bijutsu techō*, no. 319 (November 1969): 70–79.

110. Oral History Interview with Fujieda Teruo, conducted by Kajiya Kenji and Adachi Gen, June 30, 2013, Oral History Archives of Japanese Art (www.oralarthistory.org).

111. Fujieda Teruo, "Atarashii hyōgen eno shikō" [Toward new expressions], *Bijutsu techō*, no. 329 (July 1970): 65.

112. Minemura Toshiaki, "'Ima, koko ni' shisshite" [Insisting on "here, now"], *Sansai* (August 1970): 70–75, excerpted and translated by Mika Yoshitake as "Insisting on the 'Here and Now,'" in Chong et al., *From Postwar to Postmodern*, 231–233.

113. Hayami Takashi, "'Jikan' e: Montāju-fū ni" [Toward "time": À la montage), *Bijutsu techō*, no. 375 (December 1973): 187–210.

114. Fujieda Teruo, "Chi-teki hyōgen no dakkan e" [To take back intellectual expression], *Bijutsu techō*, no. 342 (May 1971): 101. This essay was part of the *Bijutsu techō*'s special feature on Conceptual Art (see note 118).

115. This characterization in the editor's notes to "Gainen geijutsu," special feature, *Geijutsu kurabu* [Art club] (April 1974): 224.

116. "Gainen geijutsu," special feature, *Geijutsu kurabu* [Art club] (April 1974): 4–215.

117. Nakahara Yūsuke, "Konsepuchuaru ātosukēpu" [Conceptual artscape], *Geijutsu kurabu* [Art club] (April 1974): [6].

118. "Gainen no geijutsu, geijutsu no gainen" [Art of concept, concept of art], special feature, *Bijutsu techō*, no. 342 (May 1971): 42–105.

119. Nakahara, "Me ni mienai geijutsu," 50–52.

120. Lee, "Hi-taishō sekai eno jikaku," 113.

121. Lee Ufan, in Fujieda Teruo and Lee Ufan (dialogue), "Sakka no shisei to sonritsu no kiban," 67. Throughout this dialogue, Lee made a series of important systemic observations.

CHAPTER 6

1. See *Voids: A Retrospective*, exh. cat. (Zurich: JRP; Geneva: Ringier; in association with Paris: Éditions du Centre Pompidou and Centre Pompidou-Metz, 2009).

2. While Barry's engagement with invisible matter (most famously, inert gases) was intensive, his interest in parapsychology appears not to have been fully developed. At his lecture at Hunter College MFA Campus, New York, March 11, 2015, I asked him about *Telepathic Piece*, and he answered that he visited a telepathy foundation in a gallery building on 57th Street in New York City; he thought telepathy might be something he could work in; and he once did a public demonstration of telepathically communicating something to the audience at Franklin Furnace. What he remembers as a "telepathy foundation" must have been the Parapsychology Foundation, once located at 29 West 57th Street, which is listed in Louis Khourey, "Eileen Garrett: The Skeptical Medium," *TAT Journal* 2, no. 2 [1979]; reproduced at http://www.searchwithin.org/download/eileen_garrett.pdf (accessed April 3, 2015). For the Parapsychology Foundation, founded in 1951, see their website, http://www.parapsychology.org, and Carlos S. Alvarado, Eileen Coly, Lisette Coly, and Nancy L. Zingrone, "Fifty Years of Supporting Parapsychology: The Parapsychology Foundation (1951–2001)," *International Journal of Parapsychology* 12, no. 2 (2001): 1–26; reproduced at http://www.parapsychology.org/dynamic/info/PFIJP122Alvarado.pdf (accessed April 3, 2015).

3. I extract the description of Klein's exhibition from the catalog entry and Denys Riout, "Exaspérations 1958," in *Voids*, 35–36 and 37–46.

4. For more on *Closing Event*, see Reiko Tomii, "Voiding the Exhibition: Hi Red Center and Matsuzawa Yutaka," in *Voids*, 427–432.

5. One visitor later recounted that he had seen a banner bearing the exhibition title inside the gallery. I owe this recollection by Shirani Nariaki to Hosoya Shūhei, who interviewed him at a talk program, "60's Seiji/geijutu no zen'ei towa nan datanoka, sono 1" [What was the avant-garde in politics and art in the 1960s?], Ōkubo Area Center, Tokyo on September 13, 2014, and e-mailed to author, September 22, 2014.

6. The invitation text was composed by Pierre Restany; as translated and quoted in Riout, "Exaspérations 1958," 37.

7. Yves Klein, "Chelsea Hotel Manifesto" (1961), http://www.yveskleinarchives.org/documents/chelsea_us.html (accessed March 3, 2015). The same passage is published as "I Was Introduced to the Void by the Rebuffed Nothingness," in *Overcoming the Problematics of Art: The Writings of Yves Klein*, trans. Klaus Ottmann (Putnam, CT: Spring Publications, 2007), 198.

8. *Myōbuku* (冥伏) is a term associated with Sōka Gakkai, a new Buddhist movement, founded in 1937 and expanded in the postwar decades by its third leader, Ikeda Daisaku. The word is not included in the Digital Dictionary of Buddhism (buddhism-dict.net/ddb/index.html) or Kotobank (https://kotobank.jp/), a comprehensive Japanese dictionary portal. In Ikeda Daisaku and Arnold Toynbee, *21-seiki eno taiwa* [Conversations for the 21st century] (Tokyo: Bungei Shunjū, 1975), Ikeda built on the idea of Mahayana Buddhism that life and death are two different manifestations of the same Life that transcends time and space and resides in two states—the manifested state of what we usually consider "life" and the "dormant" (*myōbuku*) state of "death." In light of Matsuzawa's insatiable intellectual curiosity and his liberal manner of adapting useful ideas from any sources, it would be of little surprise if he had read literature of Sōka Gakkai.

9. Entry on Madhyamaka in *Digital Dictionary of Buddhism* (buddhism-dict.net/ddb/index.html).

10. Yves Klein, "Preparation and Presentation of the Exhibition on April 28, 1958 at the Iris Clert Gallery, 3 rue des Beaux-Arts, Paris 'The Refinement of Sensibility in the First Material State into Stabilized Pictorial Sensibility' The Pneumatic Period (Some Details Have Been Omitted)," in Klein, *Overcoming the Problematics of Art*, 47.

11. Ibid., 56.

12. Ibid., 55.

13. Barry, lecture at Hunter College, March 11, 2015.

14. Liz Kotz, *Words to Be Looked At: Language in 1960s Art*, paperback edition (Cambridge, MA: MIT Press, 2010), 222.

15. Barry, lecture at Hunter College, March 11, 2015.

16. Miyata Kunio, "Garō manifesuto" [Gallery manifesto]; reproduced in *Naiqua Garō: '60-nendai no zen'ei* [Naiqua Gallery: 1960s avant-garde], exh. cat., ed. Miyata Yūka and Kuroda Shūichi (Kyoto: Kyoto University of Art and Design Museum, 2000), 21.

17. A recent retrospective at Hunter College's 250 Hudson Street Gallery suggests the importance of Barry's origin in Minimal Art in his subsequent evolution in Conceptual Art. *Robert Barry: All the Things I Know ... 1962 to the Present*, exh. cat. (New York: Hunter College Art Galleries, 2015).

18. Seki Naoko uncovered new information on Ono's prewar biography, especially her early music education at Jiyū Gakuen, in *Yoko Ono: From My Window*, exh. cat. (Tokyo: Museum of Contemporary Art, 2015).

19. See Bruce Altshuler, "Instructions for a World of Stickiness; The Early Conceptual Work of Yoko Ono," in *YES Yoko Ono*, exh. cat. (New York: Japan Society, 2000), 64–71. Notably, for her exhibition at George Maciunas's AG Gallery, Ono would whisper her instructions to the visitor in person, making her paintings more participatory.

20. The critic Takiguchi Shūzō was a potential link, for the two artists sent him their important works, but more archival research is necessary to draw any conclusion on their knowledge of each other.

21. Oral History Interview with Yasunao Tone, conducted by Yoshimoto Midori and Reiko Tomii, February 5, 2013, Oral History Archives of Japanese Art (www.oralarthistory.org).

22. Jeffrey Weiss correctly observed the significance of the medium of painting in Kawara's art, which set him apart from his New York peers of Conceptual Art. See Weiss, "Bounded Infinity," in *On Kawara: Silence*, exh. cat. (New York: Guggenheim Museum, 2015), 33.

23. Some of them were shown by Midori Yamamura in the exhibition she guest-curated, *Grapefruit: Yoko Ono in 1964* (Ise Culture Foundation Gallery, New York), in 2004.

24. Of note are two koan-like poems that differently conceived of the human body, in Ono, "To the Wesleyan People"; reprinted in *YES Yoko Ono*, 291.

25. See *Reversible Destiny: Arakawa/Gins*, exh. cat. (New York: Guggenheim SoHo, 1997).

26. For Akasegawa's populism, see Reiko Tomii, "Akasegawa Genpei as a Populist Avant-Garde: An Alternative View to Japanese Popular Culture," *Kontur*, no. 20 (2010), PDF accessible from http://kontur.au.dk.

27. This phrase is taken from the press release of the Guggenheim Museum for *On Kawara: Silence* (dated December 22, 2014). Curator Jeffrey Weiss, who organized the exhibition, confirmed that this phrase was a composite paraphrase based on his conversations with On Kawara (e-mail to author, March 4, 2015).The artist was notoriously reclusive, but when he met art world persons in his studio and home he was also incessantly chatty, as I myself witnessed as a "spurned" art historian (he refused to be part of the Japanese section for *Global Conceptualism*) and subsequently as a

translator. The quoted phrase struck me as a succinct summary of his art, based on the body of work he produced as well as my personal encounters with him. For a rare glimpse into how the artist's mind worked, see Yamada Satoru, "Harukanaru taiga o meguru hateshinaki tabi: Kawara On no tame no mikan no tekisuto (2006-nen)" [An endless travel around a remote great river: An unfinished text for On Kawara (2006)], *Rear*, no. 33 (2014): 98–105. This essay is written as though the artist were speaking to us on myriad subjects in the humanities and sciences that interested him, from art to politics to cosmology. For his personal demeanor, see Watanabe Shin'ya, "Kawara On-san tono omoide" [Memory of On Kawara], *Rear*, no. 33 (2014): 109–115. Watanabe recalls a few meetings with Kawara.

28. On Kawara, "Genga itten eno gimon" [Question about the unique original painting], *Bijutsu techō*, no. 140 (April 1958): 24–25; "Insatsu kaiga" (Printed painting), supplementary issue on "Kaiga no gihō to kaiga no yukue" [Painting: Techniques and its future], *Bijutsu techō*, no. 155 (March 1959): 86, 89.

29. Examples of his "printed painting" were included in the second section focusing on the 1950s in *Bijutsu ni buru! Besuto serekushon Nihon kindai bijutsu no 100-nen / Art Will Thrill You! The Essence of Modern Japanese Art* (National Museum of Modern Art, Tokyo) in 2012.

30. Anne Wheeler, "Paris–New York Drawings," in *On Kawara: Silence*, 51.

31. On Kawara, *Aru katarogu no tame no imi no hairetsu / Composition of Words for a Catalogue*, in *Zaigai Nihon sakka-ten: Yōroppa to Amerika / Exhibition of Japanese Artists Abroad: Europe and America*, exh. cat. (Tokyo: National Museum of Modern Art, 1965), n.p. To this exhibition he sent a three-panel *Title* of 1965.

32. I translated an excerpt from Yamamoto Kajin, *Uchū ishiki no tetsugakuteki kenkyū* [A philosophical study of cosmic consciousness] (Tokyo: Kasumigaseki Shobō, 1974), for *On Kawara: Consciousness/Meditation/Watcher on the Hills* (Birmingham, U.K.: Ikon Gallery; Dijon: Le Consortium, with Les Presses du Réel, 2002).

33. I translated an excerpt from Inomata Shūji, *Nyū saiensu no paradaimu: 21-seiki no tame no purinkipia* [Paradigm of new science: Principia for the 21st century] (Tokyo: Gijutsu Shuppan, 1987), for *On Kawara: Paintings of 40 Years* (New York: David Zwirner Gallery, 2004).

34. I translated an excerpt from Matsui Takafumi, *Uchūjin to shite no ikikata: Asutorobaiorojī eno shōtai* [How to live as aliens: An introduction to astrobiology] (Tokyo: Iwanami Shinsho, 2003), for *On Kawara: 10 Tableaux and 16,952 Pages* (Dallas: Dallas Museum of Art, 2008).

35. One connection is documented: Kawara contributed one telegram, received by Matsuzawa on July 22, 1970, for his *Nirvana* exhibition; the image is reproduced in the album section of "Gainen no geijutsu, geijutsu no gainen" [Art of concept, concept of art], special feature, *Bijutsu techō*, no. 342 (May 1971): n.p. Kawara appeared to have held Matsuzawa in high regard among his Japanese contemporaries, according to Nose Yōko, who conducted a series of private conversations with Kawara in her capacity as a curator of the Toyota Municipal Museum of Art (conversation with author, February 17, 2015).

36. For details of the production of the work, see Anne Wheeler, "One Million Years," in *On Kawara: Silence*, 163.

37. *Information*, exh. cat. (New York: Museum of Modern Art, 1970), n.p.

38. Kawara's working method as characterized by Jeffry Weiss, "Introduction," in *On Kawara: Silence*, 25.

39. Midori Yoshimoto's *Into Performance: Japanese Women Artists in New York* (New Brunswick: Rutgers University Press, 2005) is one such study. As for broader diaspora study, DAAN (Diasporic Asian Art Network) has been active in the study of Asian American art. Of particular note are Alexandra Chang, *Envisioning Diaspora: Asian American Visual Arts Collectives from Godzilla, Godzookie to the Barnstormers* (Hong Kong: Timezone 8 Editions, 2008), and Margo Machida, *Unsettled Visions: Contemporary Asian American Artists and the Social Imaginary* (Durham: Duke University Press, 2008). The idea of "Japanese American art," however, is still nascent in the discipline of art history in Japan.

40. For interpretation of his refusal, see Susan Stewart, "Annal and Existence: On Kawara's Date Inscriptions," in *On Kawara: Silence*, 177n5.

41. In 1960s Japan, the lucky few in the mainstream such as Takamatsu Jirō and later Sekine Nobuo were exceptions to the rule, representing a lethargic marketization of contemporary art. In colloquial terms, American starving artists had at least *theoretical* chances for financial gain from their works, while Japanese starving artists had no such luxury at all.

42. For example, see Philipp Kaiser and Miwon Kwon, eds., *Ends of the Earth: Art of the Land to 1974*, exh. cat. (Los Angeles: Museum of Contemporary Art; Munich: Haus der Kunst, 2013), 97–117.

43. Dennis Oppenheim, in Willoughby Sharp, "Discussions with Oppenheim, Heizer, Smithson," *Avalanche* (Fall 1970): 3; reprinted in Germano Celant, *Dennis Oppenheim: Explorations* (Milan: Charta, 2001), 45.

44. "Chronology," in Alanna Heiss, *Dennis Oppenheim: Selected Works 1967–90*, exh. cat. (New York: P.S.1, 1991), 186.

45. Nicolas Slawny, "Interview with Dennis Oppenheim about *Annual Ring*," transcript from a radio interview, June 2, 1998; courtesy of Dennis Oppenheim Studio/Archive.

46. "Jackson Pollock: Is He the Greatest Living Painter in the United States?," *Life* (August 8, 1949): 42–45.

47. Tom Holert, "Land Art's Multiple Sites," in Kaiser and Kwon, *Ends of the Earth*, 97–117.

48. Ibid., 100.

49. I have proposed photography as the "afterlife" of performance art in "Hirata Minoru's 'Action, the 1960s: 'Foto āto' no rironteki kōsatsu" / "Hirata Minoru's Action, the 1960s: A Theoretical Consideration as 'Photo Art,'" in *Minoru Hirata: Action, the 1960s*, exh. cat. (Tokyo: Taka Ishii Gallery, 2014), 58–61/62–65.

50. Philipp Kaiser and Miwon Kwon, "Ends of the Earth and Back," in Kaiser and Kwon, *Ends of the Earth*, 22–27.

51. Amy Plumb Oppenheim, interview with author, April 30, 2015.

52. Taken from Ushio Shinohara's word; see discussion later in this section.

53. In contrast, there was a functioning market for *Nihonga* and *yōga*, two modern forms of painting practices.

54. It was only in 2009 that they put together a portfolio of prints.

55. La Monte Young, ed., *An Anthology* (New York: La Monte Young and Jackson Mac Low, 1963); reprinted in *Theories and Documents of Contemporary Art: A Sourcebook of Artists' Writings*, ed. Kristine Stiles and Peter Selz (Berkeley: University of California Press, 1996), 526.

56. For details of Group "I," see *Gurūpu "I"* [Group "I"], exh. cat. (Kobe: Hyōgo Prefectural Museum of Art, 2004).

57. Akane Kazuo, "Geppyō" [Monthly reviews], *Bijutsu techō*, no. 258 (October 1965): 132.

58. Lucy Soutter, "Perhaps When Reproduced," *Arc*, no. 14 (Summer 2010): 30–34.

59. For a full discussion of the culture of showing, see Reiko Tomii, "The Culture of Showing: The Operational Context for Nomura Hitoshi's Early Works," in *Hitoshi Nomura: Early Works*, exh. cat. (New York: McCaffery Fine Art, 2010), 68–79.

60. Lee Ufan, in Fujieda Teruo and Lee Ufan (dialogue), "Sakka no shisei to sonritsu no kiban" [Artists' attitudes and the foundation of their existence], *Bijutsu techō*, no. 358 (August/September 1972): 69.

61. Before their encounter with Michel Tapié, most members had little concern for selling their work. It should be noted, however, that Yosihara did not seek publicity for the sake of publicity, but used the occasions of media exposure as "assignments" for members to think beyond conventional art making.

62. Sekine in Ikeda Masuo, Sugai Kumi, Sekine Nobuo, Horiuchi Masakazu, and Tōno Yoshiaki, "Tsukuru koto to tsukuranai koto" [Making and not making], *Bijutsu techō*, no. 315 (July 1969): 180. The work elicited much attention at *1st Kobe Suma Rikyū Park Contemporary Art Exhibition* of 1968. On the ground that it was not a permanent, thus collectible, sculpture, his ephemeral work missed the grand prize and was awarded a lesser prize.

63. For Japan's photobook tradition, see Kaneko Ryūichi and Ivan Vartanian, *Japanese Photobooks of the 1960s and '70s* (New York: Aperture, 2009).

64. Ushio Shinohara, *Zen'ei no michi* [The avant-garde road] (Tokyo: Bijutsu Shuppan-sha, 1968), 78–79.

65. Ushio Shinohara, "On Mathieu and *Boxing Painting*," in Hiroko Ikegami and Reiko Tomii, *Shinohara Pops! The Avant-Garde Road, Tokyo/New York*, exh. cat. (Albany: SUNY Press, 2012), 104.

66. "Rokabirī gaka" [Rockabilly painter], *Shūkan Sankei* [Weekly Sankei] (April 27, 1958): 39–41. The episode is described in Shinohara, *Zen'ei no michi*, 30–35.

67. I owe this observation to Jane DeBevoise, who pointed out to me that performance was "a low cost solution to a high risk opportunity" in Chinese art in the 1980s and 1990s, where a similar no-market situation existed before marketization kicked in (DeBevoise, e-mail to author, February 27, 2015).

68. In performative land art, a rare individual work is a series of fire-and-smoke-based works by Yamamoto Keigo in Fukui Prefecture. See Yamamoto Keigo and Sakamoto Hirofumi, "Yamamoto Keigo eno intabyū" [An interview with Yamamoto Keigo], in *Shoki bideo āto saikō / Retrospective Exhibition of the Early Video Art*, exh. cat. (Nagoya: Nagoya Shimin Gallery Yata, 2006), 101.

69. For the post-Yomiuri collectivism, see Reiko Tomii, "After the 'Descent to the Everyday': Japanese Collectivism from Hi Red Center to The Play, 1964–1973," in *Collectivism after Modernism*, ed. Blake Stimson and Gregory Sholette (Minneapolis: University of Minnesota Press, 2007), 44–75.

70. The degree of self-documentation varied from practitioner to practitioner. Gutai had members photograph and film their activities, as did The Play. Among Anti-Art collectives, Zero Dimension had its member Kitade Yukio (Tonbo) serving as a staff photographer.

71. "Hanaga Mitsutoshi nenpyō" [Hanaga Mitsutoshi's chronology], a typescript by the photographer's estate. Hanaga's work has recently been compiled into portfolios by the Hanaga Mitsutoshi Project Executive Committee, which also organized a series of exhibitions at Gallery Kochūten in Nagoya and the Tokyo Art Fair (both in 2014) and Aoyama Meguro in Tokyo (2015).

72. Catherine Millet, "Watashi-tachi no yumemita radikarizumu: Kikan fukanō na chiten to shite" [A radicalism we dreamt of: As a point of no return], *Bijutsu techō*, no. 577 (April 1987): 151. In this essay, Millet reviewed the 1986–1987 exhibition at Centre Pompidou, *Japon des avant gardes*.

73. Tōno Yoshiaki, "Sengo Nihon no zen'ei geijutsu" [Postwar Japanese avant-garde art], *Asahi shinbun*, April 21, 1987, evening edition.

74. Description of the work and site derives from Dia Art Foundation's website, "Walter De Maria, *The Lightning Field*" (overview and visitor information), http://www.diaart.org/sites/page/56/1375 and http://www.diaart.org/sites/page/56/1301 (accessed February 23, 2015).

75. "Rekishiteki shizen kankyō hozen chiiki Jubusan" [Historical nature preservation area: Mount Jūbu], in "Kyoto-fu" / "Kyoto Prefecture Web Site," http://www.pref.kyoto.jp/shizen-kankyo/hozen07.html (accessed February 24, 2015).

76. Paraphrased from [preface] to *Play: 1967–80* (Toyonaka and Kyoto: The Play, 1981), n.p.

77. The section frontispiece to *Thunder* in *Play* (Paris: Bat; Osaka: The Play, 2014), n.p.

78. This strong adjective derives from John Beardsley, "Art and Authoritarianism: Walter De Maria's 'Lightning Field,'" *October* 16 (Spring 1981): 35–38.

79. As pointed out by Robert Rosenblum, "A Postscript: Some Recent Neo-Romantic Mutations," *Art Journal* 52, no. 2 (Summer 1993): 74–84. As early as 1969, Fujieda Teruo also saw a Romanticist tendency in American Earthworks in "Kannen no romantisizumu: Busshitsu no shōmetsu" [Romanticism of idea: Vanishing of matter], *Bijutsu techō*, no. 315 (July 1969): 78–113.

80. Kaiser and Kwon, *Ends of the Earth: Art of the Land to 1974.*

81. Ikemizu Keiichi, statement after *Canoe* (1974); reprinted in the Canoe section of *Play* (2014), n.p.

82. This park, Ashiya Park, is not on a dry riverbed but along the bank of the Ashiya River. The slim river has very narrow and stony dry riverbeds, which are flanked by elevated traffic and pedestrian roads on either side. The well-maintained elongated park runs east of the riverside road, stretching four blocks from north to south.

83. At Gutai, Shiraga's engagements with mud also make early examples of land art. His *Challenging Mud* of 1955 was a class unto itself as a "performance painting" on land (figure 1.4), while in the 1956 outdoor exhibition he wrapped mud with vinyl sheets to make a circular and an oval mound, which were additional "firsts." See "Kazuo Shiraga: Scrap Book 1953–1965," in *Kazuo Shiraga* (New York: Dominique Lévy; Antwerp: Alexel Voordt Gallery, 2015), n.p. [2 album pages dated 1956.7].

84. *Miyazaki Junnosuke*, exh. cat. (Fukuoka: Fukuoka Art Museum, 1998).

85. From late spring to early autumn, the restaurants on the Kamo's west bank in downtown Kyoto have temporary "river floors" (*kawadoko*) for cooler dining experiences. In 1969, the Kamo's dry riverbed became an exhibition site when *Outdoor Plastic Art '69* (Yagai zōkei '69) was held during the less crowded period of October–November. The exhibition, which followed *First Kyoto Outdoor*

Sculpture Exhibition '68 held at the city's popular Okazaki Park, would morph into an annual experimental film/video exhibition in 1970, under the umbrella title *Exhibition of Contemporary Plastic Art / Gendai no zōkei*, which would include the legendary 1972 edition subtitled *Equivalent Cinema*. See *Re: Play 1972/2015: "Eizō hyōgen '72" ten, saien / Restaging "Expression in Film '72,"* exh. cat. (Tokyo: National Museum of Modern Art, 2015).

86. For Sightseeing Art Research Institute, see Kikkawa Hideki and Reiko Tomii, "Mount Fuji at the Tame River: Sightseeing Art Research Institute's Outdoor Exhibition in 1964," in *Postwar: Art between the Pacific and Atlantic, 1945–1965*, ed. Okwui Enwezor, Ulrich Wilmes, and Atreyee Gupta (forthcoming in 2016).

87. "Universal brotherhood" in its title is translated from *hakkō ichiu* (literally "eight directions under one roof"), which was a key ideology that fueled Japan's aggression into neighboring Asian countries with an express goal of establishing a "Greater East Asian Co-Prosperity Sphere." A national symbol since ancient times, Mount Fuji was turned into an imperialist divine symbol in wartime Japan, while it symbolized the endurance and renewal of the country in postwar Japan.

88. For Tateishi and Pop Art, see Ikegami Hiroko, "'Drink More?' 'No, Thanks!': The Spirit of Tokyo Pop," in *International Pop*, ed. Darsie Alexander, exh. cat. (Minneapolis: Walker Art Center, 2015), 170.

89. After *Sightseeing Art on the Tama River*, from 1964, a lineage of artists engaged in a variety of artistic ways with the Tama River, as Tokyo's foremost feature of nearby nature: e.g., for conceptualism, Takamatsu Jirō's *Stone and Numeral* in 1969 (figure 4.5), and for performance art, Cai Guo-Qiang's *Project for Extraterrestrials No. 1* of 1989. See *Tamagawa de/Tamagawa kara, āto suru / At/From Tamagawa 1964–2009*, exh. cat. (Fuchū: Fuchū Art Museum, 2009).

90. A practitioner of Reportage Realism in the 1950s, Nakamura Hiroshi continued to examine the state of Japanese society in his work in the 1960s. The film's title was taken from Karl Marx's famous treatise.

91. In the same year, the filmmaker Jōnouchi Motoharu created *Shelter Plan*, a 16-mm film documenting Hi Red Center's *Shelter Plan*, but he was not a member.

92. "Gurūpu 'I' ni tsuite" [About Group "I"] (1965); reprinted in *Gurūpu "I"*, 8.

93. Hirai Shōichi, "Gurūpu 'I': Sekai o meguru shikō" [Group "I": Thought about the world], in *Gurūpu "I"*, 5.

94. Kawaguchi Tatsuo, quoted in ibid.

95. Paraphrased from [preface] to *Play: 1967–80*, n.p.

96. Before expanding his land art to a monumental scale, Smithson also tapped into New Jersey, his home state, as what may be called "landscape nearby," in both manmade and nature-made states. See Ann Reynolds, *Robert Smithson: Learning from New Jersey and Elsewhere* (Cambridge: MIT Press, 2003), and Kelly Baum, *New Jersey as Non-Site*, exh. cat. (Princeton: Princeton University Art Museum, 2013).

EPILOGUE

1. Simon Dell, ed., *On Location: Siting Robert Smithson and His Contemporaries* (London: Black Dog, 2008).

2. "Artists Beginning with M (Part Two)," October 28, 2008, http://www.theguardian.com/artanddesign/2008/oct/29/1000-artworks-to-see-before-you-die-art; and "1000 Artworks to See Before You Die: Where to Find Them," October 28, 2008, http://www.theguardian.com/artanddesign/2008/oct/29/1000-artworks-to-see-before-you-die-where-to-find-them (accessed March 19, 2015).

3. Tiampo performed this study under the rubric of "line of flight" in *Gutai: Decentering Modernism* (Chicago: University of Chicago Press, 2011), 76–97.

4. For the group, see Octavian Eşanu, with foreword by Boris Groys, *Transition in Post-Soviet Art: The Collective Actions Group before and after 1989* (Budapest: CEU Press, 2013).

5. For Lee's work, see *Lee Seung-taek: Non-Material Works* (Seoul: ICAS Publishing, 2004) and *Seung-taek Lee: Think Reform* (Seoul: Gallery Hyundai, 2014).

6. To just name a few possible topics, a significant contextual issue concerns varying attitudes toward such underlying ideas as nationalism, internationalism, and postcolonialism. (One example involves different postwar attitudes toward nationalism between India and Japan, as touched upon in chapter 1, note 97.) Another historical aspect is different senses of history in separating the modern from the contemporary.

7. The installation of *Global Conceptualism* at the Queens Museum of Art in 1999 began with a parallel presentation of Japan and Western Europe on the right and left, respectively, of an aisle, before introducing North America.

8. In commenting on *Global Conceptualism*, Terry Smith has cautioned about the danger of "reverse reductionism" that might result from the relativization of Euro-American Conceptual Art; see his "One and Three Ideas: Conceptualism Before, During, and After Conceptual Art," *E-flux Journal* (November 2011); http://www.e-flux.com/journal/one-and-three-ideas-conceptualism-before-during-and-after-conceptual-art (accessed April 12, 2015). I am in agreement with Smith that we must be vigilant against reductionism, reverse or otherwise, and hope that my proposition for an open field of world art history that embraces not "reductionism" but "expansionism" will genuinely help us broaden our inquiries.

9. Tiampo, *Gutai: Decentering Modernism*, 3–5; see above, chapter 1, note 15.

10. In this respect, a fine work in post-revisionist art history is Hiroko Ikegami, *The Great Migrator: Robert Rauschenberg and the Global Rise of American Art* (Cambridge, MA: MIT Press, 2010).

11. For the reexamination of Pop Art from a global perspective, see Darsie Alexander, ed., *International Pop*, exh. cat. (Minneapolis: Walker Art Center, 2015), and Jessica Morgan and Flavia Frigeri, eds., *The World Goes Pop*, exh. cat. (London: Tate Modern; New Haven: Yale University Press, 2015).

12. James Elkins, ed., *Is Art History Global?* (New York: Routledge, 2007).

13. In my effort to "open up," a distant yet definite spiritual forebear is John Clark, who more than two decades ago authored "Open and Closed Discourses of Modernity in Asian Art," in *Modernity in Asian Art*, ed. John Clark (Sydney: Wild Peony, 1993), 1–17.

SELECT BIBLIOGRAPHY

This bibliography selectively compiles works cited in this publication to facilitate an overview and further research.

Japanese sources are cited in a bilingual format throughout this volume. If a publication has a title listed in more than one language on the title page (or sometimes on the cover, spine, copyright page, etc.), all of them are listed, with transliterated Japanese first, followed by English and other language(s), if any, separated by a slash: e.g., *Nikutai no anākizumu / Anarchy of the Body*. For publications that appeared with Japanese title only, I have provided translated titles following the Japanese titles, enclosed in square brackets: e.g., *Gendai bijutsu* [Contemporary art]. This format helps differentiate officially given English titles, which routinely appear in library catalogs such as the Japanese CiNii and OCLC's WorldCat, from translations provided by myself. Frequently cited periodicals included in the Glossary are not accompanied by bracketed translation here.

In Japanese museum publications, names of authorial editors or curators are frequently not given in publication data. This is because the collective authorship of a given institution, or an entity such as an "exhibition committee," is assumed. Likewise, Japanese newspapers and magazines routinely carried unsigned texts, presumably produced by the editorial staff. They are by no means "anonymous" texts, but institutionally authored texts. For this reason, these are cited here without author's names.

ARCHIVAL SOURCES (PUBLIC)

Keiō University Art Center
Minemura Toshiaki Papers
Takiguchi Shūzō Papers (c. 1945–1979)

National Art Center, Art Library, Tokyo
The Play Document (719J, P71 610026)

Oral History Archives of Japanese Art http://www.oralarthistory.org)
Fujieda Teruo, conducted by Kajiya Kenji and Adachi Gen (June 30, 2013)
Maeyama Tadashi and Horikawa Michio, conducted by Koh Seong-Jun and Miyata Yūka, June 29 and 30, 2011 (pre-edited transcripts)
Mizukami Jun, conducted by Sakagami Shinobu, March 21 and 22, 2009
Niwa Katsuji, conducted by Honnami Kiyoshi and Kajiya Kenji, October 31, 2010
Tone, Yasunao, conducted by Yoshimoto Midori and Reiko Tomii, February 5, 2013

PUBLISHED SOURCES

1. By and on Matsuzawa Yutaka

Catastrophe art from the East. Exh. cat. Milan: Centro Culturale S. Fedele, 1972.

Hamaguchi Tomiharu, and Matsuzawa Yutaka, with Haryū Ichirō (interviewer). "Fukashina kūkan eno shikō" [Thinking about invisible space]. *Bijutsu jānaru* [Art journal], no. 51 (October 1964): 14–37.

Itami Hiroshi. "Matsuzawa Yutaka: Sono shikō no genten" [Matsuzawa Yutaka: An origin of his thought]. *Aida*, no. 214 (July 2014): 6–8.

Kasai Ei, Maeda Jōsaku, and Matsuzawa Yutaka, with Umehara Masaki (moderator). "Bijutsu to butō to mikkyō" [Art, Butoh, and Esoteric Buddhism]. In Inagaki Taruho and Umehara Masaki, *Shūmatsuki no mikkyō* [Esoteric Buddhism in a final era], 303–349. Tokyo: Sanpō, 1973.

Katō Ikuya. "Matsuzawa Yutaka: Meshia no jigazō" [A messiah's self-portrait]. *Bijutsu techō*, no. 314 (June 1969): 162–175.

Matsuzawa Yutaka. *Hoshi mata wa sutorippu shou* [Star or a strip show]. Tokyo: Shoshi Yamada, 2013.

"Matsuzawa Yutaka." Special issue. *Kikan* [Organ], no. 13 (1982).

Matsuzawa Yutaka: Ψ (pusai) no uchū / Yutaka Matsuzawa: The Cosmos of Ψ (Psi). Suwa: Suwa Gensō-sha, 1985.

Matsuzawa Yutaka: Supirichuarizumu e / To Spiritualism: Yutaka Matsuzawa 1954–1997. Kawaguchi: Kawaguchi Museum of Contemporary Art, 1997.

Ψ ni yoru Matsuzawa Yutaka koten [Matsuzawa Yutaka's solo exhibition according to ψ]. Exh. cat. Tokyo: Aoki Gallery, 1963.

Yoshida Yoshie. "Post-Nirvāna: Our Commune." Unpublished typescript. 1971.

———. "Matsuzawa Yutaka: Yami o tōtetsu suru kyōdōtai" [Matsuzawa Yutaka: A commune that penetrates the darkness]. *Bijutsu techō*, no. 360 (November 1972): 26–48.

2. By and on The Play

Fukuzumi Ren. "Miki Tetsuo intabyū" [Interview with Miki Tetsuo]. *HAMArt!* 8 (April 2014): 1–6.

Hashimoto Azusa. Serialized articles on The Play. In *Kokuritsu Kokusai Bijutsukan nyūsu / The National Museum of Art, Osaka* (August 2014–).

Ikemizu! Uji: Ikemizu, 2005.

Play. Paris: Bat; Osaka: The Play, 2014. [Aka *Big Book*, this volume combines *Black Book* (1981) and *Blue Book* (1991) and extends the content to 2014.]

"The Play." *Bijutsu techō*, no. 359 (October 1972): n.p.

Play: 1967–73. Toyonaka: The Play, 1974. [Aka *Copy Book*].

Play: 1967–1980. Toyonaka and Kyoto: The Play, 1981. [Aka *Black Book*].

Play: 1981–1990. Toyonaka and Kyoto: The Play, 1991. [Aka *Blue Book*].

Tōno Yoshiaki. "Za Purei: Nikutai ga kokka ni ninai toki" [The Play: When the body does not resemble the nation]. *Mizue* (December 1974): 54–63.

3. By and on GUN

GUN: Niigata ni zen'ei ga atta koro / Niigata Contemporary Artists Group and Its Era. Exh. cat. Nagaoka: Niigata Prefectural Museum of Modern Art, 2012.

Horikawa Michio. "Horikawa Michio no āto nikki" [Horikawa Michio's art diary]. Blog entries, http://d.hatena.ne.jp/niigata-art226/. Cited in "Maeda Jōsaku sensei no hapuningu ('69.8)" [Maeda Jōsaku's Happening, August 1969], April 21, 2009, http://d.hatena.ne.jp/niigata-art226/20090421/1240248901; "Maeyama Tadashi, 1," June 19, 2012, http://d.hatena.ne.jp/niigata-art226/20120619/1340096492.

———. "Hyōgen kōi no fukken" [Recovery of the act of expression]. *Biiku bunka* (July 1995). Reprinted in "Yuki āto no konseputo kakujū ni mukete, 2" [To expand on the concept of snow art, 2], January 9, 2013, http://d.hatena.ne.jp/niigata-art226/20130109/1357716184.

———. *Niigata gendai bijutsu shūdan GUN to watashi* [GUN, Niigata's contemporary artist group, and I]. Jōetsu: Privately published, 2008.

Ichihasi Tetsuo, Horikawa Michio, and Maeyama Tadashi. *GUN Group: Event to Change the Image of Snow*. Portfolio and booklet. Tokyo: Tokyo Gallery, 2009.

4. Primary Sources on 1960s Art in Japan

Akasegawa Genpei. *Han-geijutsu anpan* [Anti-Art independent]. 1985; pocketbook edition, Tokyo: Chikuma Bunko, 1994.

———, and Matsuda Tetsuo, with Minami Nobuhiro's illustration. "Nihon geijutsu dai-gekisen: Sōretsu emaki (Bijutsu techō 5-gatsu-gō furoku)" [Great battles of the world of *geijutsu* in Japan: A heroic pictorial album, May supplement to *Bijutsu techō*]. *Bijutsu techō*, no. 355 (May 1972): n.p.

Andepandan '64 ten [*Independent '64*]. Exh. cat. Tokyo: [Exhibition Committee], 1964.

Ashiya shiten / Ashiya City Exhibition 1948–1997. Ashiya: Ashiya City Art Association, Ashiya City Museum of Art & History, and Ashiya-shi Bunka Shinkō Zaidan, 1997.

Contemporary Japanese Art: Fifth Japan Art Festival Exhibition. Exh. cat. New York: Guggenheim Museum, 1970.

Dai-9kai gendai Nihon bijutsu-ten / The 9th Contemporary Art Exhibition of Japan. Exh. cat. Tokyo: Mainichi Newspapers, 1969.

Dai 9-kai Nihon kokusai bijutsu-ten / Tokyo Biennale 1967. Exh. cat. Tokyo: Mainichi Newspapers, 1967.

Dai 10-kai gendai Nihon bijutsu-ten / The 10th Contemporary Art Exhibition of Japan 1971. Exh. cat. Tokyo: Mainichi Newspapers, 1971.

Fujieda Teruo. "Atarashii hyōgen eno shikō" [Toward new expressions]. *Bijutsu techō*, no. 329 (July 1970): 49–65.

———, Hara Eizaburō, and Shinohara Ushio. *Kūkan no ronri: Nihon no gendai bijutsu* [Logic of space: Contemporary art in Japan]. Tokyo: Buronzusha, 1969.

———, and Lee Ufan. "Sakka no shisei to sonritsu no kiban" [Artists' attitudes and the foundation of their existence]. *Bijutsu techō*, no. 358 (August/September 1972): 54–73.

"Gainen geijutsu." Special issue. *Geijutsu kurabu* [Art club] (April 1974).

"Gainen no geijutsu, geijutsu no gainen" [Art of concept, concept of art]. Special feature. *Bijutsu techō*, no. 342 (May 1971): 42–105.

Gendai bijutsu no dōkō / Trends in Contemporary Japanese Art. Exh. cat. Kyoto: National Museum of Modern Art, 1969; 1970.

Gendai bijutsu no saiten [Contemporary art festival]. Exh. broch. Sakai: [Organizing Committee], 1966.

"Happening." Special feature. *Bijutsu techō*, no. 301 (August 1968): 77–107.

"Hapuningu towa nanika?" [What is Happening?]. *Bijutsu techō*, no. 282 (May 1967): 130–140.

Haryū Ichirō. "Hihyō no yori takai kinō o" [Wishing art criticism to have a more functional role]. *Geijutsu Shinchō* (January 1968): 15.

———, ed. *Kōi ni kakeru / Art of Action and Concept.* Gendai no bijutsu / Art Now, vol. 11. Tokyo: Kōdansha, 1972.

———. "Sengo: Kokusaiteki na dōjidaisei no seiritsu e" [Postwar: Toward the formation of international contemporaneity]. *Bessatsu Mizue* [Watercolor supplementary], no. 46 (July 1966): 56–60.

———, Nakahara Yūsuke, Tōno Yoshiaki, and Minemura Toshiaki, with Okada Takahiko (moderator). "Gendai Nihon bijutsu wa dō ugoitaka" [How did contemporary Japanese art evolve?]. *Bijutsu techō*, no. 436 (July 1978): 3–56.

Hayami Takashi. "'Jikan' e: Montāju-fū ni" [Toward "time": À la montage]. *Bijutsu techō*, no. 375 (December 1973): 187–210.

Ikeda Masuo, Sugai Kumi, Sekine Nobuo, Horiuchi Masakazu, and Tōno Yoshiaki. "'Tsukuru koto' to 'tsukuranai koto'" [Making and not making]. *Bijutsu techō*, no. 315 (July 1969): 176–190.

Independent Art Festival. Exh. broch. Gifu: [Organizing Committee], 1965.

Kawara, On. "Genga itten eno gimon" [Question about the unique original painting]. *Bijutsu techō*, no. 140 (April 1958): 24–25.

———. "Insatsu kaiga" (Printed painting). Supplementary issue on "Kaiga no gihō to kaiga no yukue" [Painting: Techniques and its future]. *Bijutsu techō*, no. 155 (March 1959): 82–126.

Lee Ufan. "Kannen no geijutsu wa kanō ka: Obuje shisō no shōtai to yukue" [Is an art of *kannen* possible? The truth and future of the *objet* thought]. *Bijutsu techō*, no. 319 (November 1969): 70–79.

Minemura Toshiaki. "'Ima, koko ni' shisshite" [Insisting on "here, now"]. *Sansai* (August 1970): 70–75. Excerpted and translated by Mika Yoshitake as "Insisting on the 'Here and Now,'" in *From Postwar to Postmodern*, ed. Doryun Chong et al., 231–233. New York: Museum of Modern Art, 2012.

Miyakawa Atsushi. "Anforumeru igo" [After Informel]. *Bijutsu techō*, no. 220 (May 1963): 86–96. Translated by Mika Yoshitake as "After Informel," in *From Postwar to Postmodern*, ed. Doryun Chong et al., 105–113. New York: Museum of Modern Art, 2012.

———. "Anforumeru igo no Nihon no bijutsu: Henbō no suii, montāju-fū ni" [Japanese art after Informel: A course of transformation, as seen in montage]. *Bijutsu techō*, no. 227 (October 1963):49–64.

"Nihon no aryū ni sasaerareta eikō" [Japan's glory upheld by imitators]. Special feature. *Geijutsu Shinchō* (August 1969): 1–28.

Ningen to busshitsu: Dai 10-kai Nihon kokusai bijutsu-ten / Between Man and Matter: Tokyo Biennale '70. 2 vols. Exh. cat. Tokyo: Mainichi Newspapers, 1970. [The two volumes are differentiated by their covers, with the first bearing Nakahira Takuma's photograph and the second in black.]

"Sekai ni tsūyō suru Nihon no 12-nin" [12 Japanese artists who can compete internationally]. Special feature. *Geijutsu Shinchō* (January 1968): 1–16.

Shinohara Ushio. *Zen'ei no michi* [Avant-garde road]. Tokyo: Bijutsu Shuppan-sha, 1968.

Shiraga Kazuo. "Kazuo Shiraga: Scrap Book 1953–1965." In *Kazuo Shiraga*, 216–268. New York: Dominique Lévy; Antwerp: Alexel Voordt Gallery, 2015.

Tōno Yoshiaki. *Gendai bijutsu: Porokku igo* [Contemporary art: After Pollock]. Tokyo: Bijutsu Shuppan-sha, 1965.

Yoshida Yoshie. "Tandoku kōisha no chōgekijō" [Solitary actors in an ultra-theater]. *Bijutsu techō*, no. 335 (December 1970): 49–63.

Yoshihara Jirō. "Chūshō kaiga no yohaku" / "Blank of Abstract Painting." *Bokubi*, no. 21 (February 1953): 12–15.

———. "Gutai Art Manifesto." 1956. Trans. Reiko Tomii. In Ming Tiampo and Alexandra Munroe, *Gutai: Splendid Playground*, 18–19. Exh. cat. New York: Guggenheim Museum, 2014.

5. Other Sources on Modern and Contemporary Art

Alberro, Alexander, and Blake Stimson, eds. *Conceptual Art: A Critical Anthology*. Cambridge, MA: MIT Press, 1999.

Alexander, Darsie, ed. *International Pop*. Exh. cat. Minneapolis: Walker Art Center, 2015.

Arai Hiroyuki. *Tennō āto-ron: Sono bi, "ten" ni tsūzu* [On Emperor art: Its beauty leads to the heavens]. Tokyo: Shakai Hyōron-sha, 2014.

Baum, Kelly. *New Jersey as Non-Site*. Exh. cat. Princeton: Princeton University Art Museum, 2013.

Beardsley, John. "Art and Authoritarianism: Walter De Maria's 'Lightning Field.'" *October* 16 (Spring 1981): 35–38.

Boettger, Suzaan. *Earthworks: Art and the Landscape of the Sixties*. Berkeley: University of California Press, 2003.

Buskirk, Martha, et al. *Hitoshi Nomura: Early Works*. Exh. cat. New York: McCaffery Fine Art, 2010.

Camnitzer, Luis, Jane Farver, and Rachel Weiss, eds. *Global Conceptualism: Points of Origin, 1950s–1980s*. Exh. cat. New York: Queens Museum of Art, 1999.

Carrier, David. *World Art History and Its Objects*. University Park: Pennsylvania State University Press, 2008.

Casid, Jill H., and Aruna D'Souza. *Art History in the Wake of the Global Turn*. Williamstown, MA: Sterling and Francine Clark Art Institute; New Haven: Yale University Press, 2014.

Celant, Germano. *Oppenheim: Explorations*. Milan: Charta, 2001.

Chang, Alexandra. *Envisioning Diaspora: Asian American Visual Arts Collectives from Godzilla, Godzookie to the Barnstormers*. Hong Kong: Timezone 8 Editions, 2008.

Cherix, Christophe, ed. *In & Out of Amsterdam: Travels in Conceptual Art, 1960–1976*. Exh. cat. New York: Museum of Modern Art, 2009.

Chong, Doryun, ed. *Tetsumi Kudo: Garden of Metamorphosis*. Exh. cat. Minneapolis: Walker Art Center, 2008.

———, et al., eds. *From Postwar to Postmodern: Art in Japan 1945–1989*. New York: Museum of Modern Art, 2012.

———, et al. *Tokyo, 1955–1970: A New Avant-Garde*. Exh. cat. New York: Museum of Modern Art, 2012.

Clark, John. *Asian Modernities: Chinese and Thai Art Compared, 1980 to 1999*. Seattle: University of Washington Press, 2011.

———. "Open and Closed Discourses of Modernity in Asian Art." In *Modernity in Asian Art*, ed. John Clark, 1–17. Sydney: Wild Peony, 1993.

Copeland, Mathieu, et al., eds. *Voids, A Retrospective of Empty Exhibitions*. Exh. cat. Paris: Centre Pompidou; Bern: Kunsthalle; Zurich: JRP/Ringier, 2009.

Dadi, Iftikhar. *Modernism and the Art of Muslim South Asia*. Chapel Hill: University of North Carolina Press, 2010.

Elkins, James. *The Impending Single History of Art: North Atlantic Art History and Its Alternatives*. Forthcoming.

——, ed. *Is Art History Global?* New York: Routledge, 2007.

——, Zhivka Valiavicharska, and Alice Kim, eds. *Art and Globalization*. University Park: Penn State University Press, 2010.

Erber, Pedro. *Breaching the Frame: The Rise of Contemporary Art in Brazil and Japan*. Berkeley: University of California Press, 2014.

Eşanu, Octavian. *Transition in Post-Soviet Art: The Collective Actions Group before and after 1989*. Budapest: CEU Press, 2013.

Evers, Elodie, Gregor Jansen, and Magdalena Holzhey, eds. *Leben mit Pop: Eine Reproduktion des Kapitalistischen Realismus / Living with Pop: A Reproduction of Capitalist Realism*. Exh. cat. Cologne: Walther König, 2013.

Faris, Jaimey Hamilton. "Rooms in Alibi: How Akasegawa Genpei Framed Capitalist Reality." *Art Margins* 4, no. 3 (October 2015): 40–64.

Govan, Michael. *Reversible Destiny: Arakawa/Gins*. Exh. cat. New York: Guggenheim SoHo, 1997.

Gurūpu "Genshoku" to Ishiko Junzō: 1966–1971 / Group "Genshok"" and Ishiko Junzō: 1966–1971. Exh. cat. Shizuoka: Shizuoka Prefectural Museum of Art, 2014.

Gurūpu "I" [Group "I"]. Exh. cat. Kobe: Hyōgo Prefectural Museum of Art, 2004.

Harris, Jonathan, ed. *Globalization and Contemporary Art*. Boston: Blackwell, 2011.

Havens, Thomas R. H. *Radicals and Realists in the Japanese Nonverbal Arts: The Avant-Garde Rejection of Modernism*. Honolulu: University of Hawai'i Press, 2006.

Heiss, Alanna. *Dennis Oppenheim: Selected Works 1967–90*. Exh. cat. New York: P.S.1, 1991.

Hoffmann, Jens, and Joanna Montoya. *Other Primary Structures*. Exh. cat. New York: Jewish Museum, 2014.

Ikegami, Hiroko. "'Drink More?' 'No, Thanks!': The Spirit of Tokyo Pop." In *International Pop*, 165–180, 362–365. Exh. cat. Minneapolis: Walker Art Center, 2015.

——. *The Great Migrator: Robert Rauschenberg and the Global Rise of American Art*. Cambridge, MA: MIT Press, 2010.

——, and Reiko Tomii. *Shinohara Pops! The Avant-Garde Road, Tokyo/New York*. Exh. cat. Albany: SUNY Press, 2012.

Ishiko Junzō-teki sekai: Bijutsu hatsu, manga keiyu, kitchu iki / The World of Ishiko Junzō: From Art via Manga to Kitsch. Exh. cat. Fuchū: Fuchū Art Museum, 2011.

Kaiser, Philipp, and Miwon Kwon, eds. *Ends of the Earth: Art of the Land to 1974*. Exh. cat. Los Angeles: Museum of Contemporary Art; Munich: Haus der Kunst, 2013.

Kaneko Ryūichi, and Ivan Vartanian. *Japanese Photobooks of the 1960s and '70s*. New York: Aperture, 2009.

Kansai no bijutsu / Art in Kansai, 1950s–1970s. Exh. cat. (Kobe: Hyōgo Prefectural Museum of Modern Art, 1994).

Kaprow, Allan. *The Blurring of Art and Life*. Ed. Jeff Kelley. Berkeley: University of California Press, 2003.

Kee, Joan. *Contemporary Korean Art: Tansaekhwa and the Urgency of Method*. Minneapolis: University of Minnesota Press, 2013.

Khullar, Sonal. *Worldly Affiliations: Artistic Practice, National Identity, and Modernism in India, 1930–1990*. Berkeley: University of California Press, 2015.

Kikkawa Hideki, and Reiko Tomii. "Mount Fuji at the Tame River: Sightseeing Art Research Institute's Outdoor Exhibition in 1964." In *Postwar: Art between the Pacific and Atlantic, 1945–1965*, ed. Okwui Enwezor, Ulrich Wilmes, and Atreyee Gupta. Forthcoming.

Klein, Yves. *Overcoming the Problematics of Art: The Writings of Yves Klein*. Trans. Klaus Ottmann. Putnam, CT: Spring Publications, 2007.

Kotz, Liz. *Words to Be Looked at: Language in 1960s Art*. Paperback edition. Cambridge, MA: MIT Press, 2010.

KuroDalaiJee (Kuroda Raiji). *Nikutai no anākizumu: 1960 nendai Nihon bijutsu ni okeru pafōmansu no chika suimyaku / Anarchy of the Body: Undercurrents of Performance Art in 1960s Japan*. Tokyo: Grambooks, 2010.

Lee Seung-taek: Non-Material Works. Seoul: ICAS Publishing, 2004.

Lionnet, Françoise, and Shu-mei Shih, eds. *The Creolization of Theory*. Durham: Duke University Press, 2011.

Lippard, Lucy R. *Six Years: The Dematerialization of the Art Object from 1966 to 1972*. Berkeley: University of California Press, 1997.

Machida, Margo. *Unsettled Visions: Contemporary Asian American Artists and the Social Imaginary*. Durham: Duke University Press, 2008.

Marotti, William. "Japan 1968: The Performance of Violence and the Theater of Protest." *American Historical Review* 114, no. 1 (February 2009): 97–135.

———. *Money, Trains, and Guillotines: Art and Revolution in 1960s Japan*. Durham: Duke University Press, 2013.

McShine, Kynaston L., ed. *Information*. Exh. cat. New York: Museum of Modern Art, 1970.

Merewether, Charles, and Rika Iezumi Hiro. *Art, Anti-Art, Non-Art: Experimentations in the Public Sphere in Postwar Japan, 1950–1970*. Exh. cat. Los Angeles: Getty Research Institute, 2007.

Minoru Hirata: Action, the 1960s. Exh. cat. Tokyo: Taka Ishii Gallery, 2014.

Mitsuda Yuri. "Bijutsu hihyō (1952–57) shi to sono jidai: 'Gendai bijutsu' to 'gendai bijutsu hihyō' no seiritsu" [The *Bijutsu hihyō* (Art criticism) magazine and its era: The formation of 'contemporary art' and 'contemporary art criticism'"]. *Fuji Xerox Art Bulletin* 2 (2006).

Mitter, Partha. "Decentering Modernism: Art History and Avant-Garde Art from the Periphery." *Art Bulletin* 90, no. 4 (December 2008): 549–555.

———. *The Triumph of Modernism: India's Artists and the Avant-Garde*. London: Reaktion Books, 2007.

Miyata Yūka, and Kuroda Shūichi, eds. *Naiqua Garō: '60-nendai no zen'ei* [Naiqua Gallery: 1960s avant-garde]. Exh. cat. Kyoto: Kyoto University of Art and Design Museum, 2000.

Miyazaki Junnosuke. Exh. cat. Fukuoka: Fukuoka Art Museum, 1998.

Morgan, Jessica, ed. *The World Goes Pop*. Exh. cat. London: Tate Modern, 2015.

Munroe, Alexandra. *Japanese Art after 1945: Scream against the Sky*. New York: Abrams, 1994.

———. *Lee Ufan: Making Infinity*. Exh. cat. New York: Guggenheim Museum, 2011.

———. *The Third Mind: American Artists Contemplate Asia, 1860–1989*. Exh. cat. New York: Guggenheim Museum, 2009.

———, and Jon Hendricks. *YES Yoko Ono*. Exh. cat. New York: Japan Society, 2000.

Murakami Saburō: Through the '70s. Osaka: Art Court Gallery, 2013.

Nagaoka Gendai Bijutsukan-shō kaikoten 1964–1968 [A retrospective of the Museum of Contemporary Art, Nagaoka, Prize Exhibition 1964–1968]. Exh. cat. Niigata: Niigata Prefectural Museum of Modern Art et al., 2002.

Nakajima Masatoshi. "Takiguchi Shūzō to Aoki Garō" [Takiguchi Shūzō and Aoki Gallery]. *Yasō* [Night thought], no. 19 (October 1986): 194–196. There is also a chronology on pp. 175–183.

Nakamori, Yasufumi, ed. *For a New World to Come: Experiments in Japanese Art and Photography, 1968–1979*. Exh. cat. Houston: Museum of Fine Art, 2015.

Nihon-obuje 1920–70-nendai danshō [Japan/*objet*: Fragments from the 1920s–1970s]. Exh. cat. Urawa: Urawa Art Museum, 2012.

Oguma Eiji. "Japan's 1968: A Collective Reaction to Rapid Economic Growth in an Age of Turmoil." Trans. Nick Kapur with Samuel Malissa and Stephen Poland. *Asia-Pacific Journal* 13, issue 11, no. 1 (March 23, 2015), http://japanfocus.org/-Oguma-Eiji/4300.

"Questionnaire on 'The Contemporary.'" *October* 130 (Fall 2009): 3–124.

Ramírez, Mari Carmen, and Héctor Olea. *Inverted Utopias: Avant-Garde Art in Latin America*. Exh. cat. New Haven: Yale University Press; Houston: Museum of Fine Arts, 2004.

Reynolds, Ann. *Robert Smithson: Learning from New Jersey and Elsewhere*. Cambridge, MA: MIT Press, 2003.

Rimer, J. Thomas, ed. *Since Meiji: Perspectives on the Japanese Visual Arts from 1869 to 2000*. Honolulu: University of Hawai'i Press, 2012.

Rodenbeck, Judith F. "Communication Malfunction: Happenings and Gutai." In Ming Tiampo and Alexandra Munroe, *Gutai: Splendid Playground*, 265–269. Exh. cat. New York: Guggenheim Museum, 2014.

———. *Radical Prototypes: Allan Kaprow and the Invention of Happenings*. Cambridge, MA: MIT Press, 2011.

Rosenblum, Robert. "A Postscript: Some Recent Neo-Romantic Mutations." *Art Journal* 52, no. 2 (Summer 1993): 74–84.

Satō Dōshin. *Modern Japanese Art and the Meiji State: The Politics of Beauty*. Trans. Hiroshi Nara. Los Angeles: Getty Research Institute, 2011.

Schimmel, Paul, ed. *Out of Actions: Between Performance and the Object 1949–1979*. Exh. cat. Los Angeles: Museum of Contemporary Art, 1998.

Sengo Okayama no bijutsu [Art of postwar Okayama]. Exh. cat. Okayama: Okayama Prefectural Museum of Art, 2002.

Seung-taek Lee: Think Reform. Seoul: Gallery Hyundai, 2014.

Shimada Yoshiko. "Geijutsu to shikō no jikkenjō: Gendai Shichō-sha to Bigakkō" [Experimental labs: Gendai Shichō-sha and Bigakkō]. *Akasegawa Genpai*, special issue. *Kawade Mook* (October 2014): 200–214.

———. "Matsuzawa Yutaka." In *Anti-Academy*, ed. Alice Maude-Roxby, 52–55. Exh. cat. Southampton, UK: John Hansard Gallery, 2013.

Shimizu Kusuo to Minami Garō / Kusuo Shimizu & Minami Gallery. Tokyo: Bijutsu Shuppansha, 1985.

Shiner, Eric C., and Reiko Tomii, eds. *Making a Home: Japanese Contemporary Artists in New York*. Exh. cat. New York: Japan Society; New Haven: Yale University Press, 2007.

Shoki bideo āto saikō / Retrospective Exhibition of the Early Video Art. Exh. cat. Nagoya: Nagoya Shimin Gallery Yata, 2006.

Shūzō Azuchi Garibā / Shuzo Azuchi Gulliver: Ex-Sign. Exh. cat. Ōtsu: Museum of Modern Art, Shiga, 2010.

Slawny, Nicolas. "Interview with Dennis Oppenheim about *Annual Ring*." Unpublished transcript form a radio interview, June 2, 1998.

Smith, Terry. "Contemporary Art and Contemporaneity." *Critical Inquiry* 32 (Summer 2006): 681–707.

———. "One and Three Ideas: Conceptualism Before, During, and After Conceptual Art," *E-flux Journal* (November 2011). http://www.e-flux.com/journal/one-and-three-ideas-conceptualism-before-during-and-after-conceptual-art (accessed April 12, 2015).

Soutter, Lucy. "Perhaps When Reproduced." *Arc*, no. 14 (Summer 2010): 30–34.

Stimson, Blake, and Gregory Sholette, eds. *Collectivism after Modernism*. Minneapolis: University of Minnesota Press, 2007.

Suzuki Katsuo. "Nihon ni okeru 'konsepuchuaru āto' gannen: 1969-nen no gensetsu kūkan kara" [Year one of Conceptual Art in Japan: The discursive space of 1969]. *Bijutsu fōramu 21 / Bijutsu Forum 21* 30 (2014): 78–83.

Takamatsu Jirō misuterīzu / Takamatsu Jirō: Mysteries. Exh. cat. Tokyo: National Museum of Modern Art, 2014.

Takamatsu Jirō: Seisaku no kiseki / Jirō Takamatsu: Trajectory of Work. Exh. cat. Osaka: National Museum of Art, 2015.

Tamagawa de/Tamagawa kara, āto suru / At/From Tamagawa 1964–2009. Exh. cat. Fuchū: Fuchū Art Museum, 2009.

Tezuka, Miwako. "Experimentation and Tradition: The Avant-Garde Play *Pierrot Lunaire* by Jikken Kōbō and Takechi Tetsuji." *Art Journal* 70, no. 3 (Fall 2011): 64–85.

———. "Jikken Kōbō and Takiguchi Shūzō: The New Deal Collectivism of 1950s Japan." *Positions* 21, no. 2 (Spring 2013): 351–381.

"The And: An Expanded Questionnaire on the Contemporary." *Fieldnote 01* (2012): 11–90. http://www.aaa.org.hk/cms/Content/upload/download/fieldnotes/fieldnotes_issue_01_single.pdf (accessed January 23, 2015).

Tiampo, Ming. *Gutai: Decentering Modernism*. Chicago: University of Chicago Press, 2011.

———, and Alexandra Munroe. *Gutai: Splendid Playground.* Exh. cat. New York: Guggenheim Museum, 2014.

Tokyo Garō 60-nen / Tokyo Gallery + BTAP 1950–2010. Tokyo: Tokyo Gallery, 2010.

Tomii, Reiko. "Akasegawa Genpei as a Populist Avant-Garde: An Alternative View to Japanese Popular Culture." *Kontur*, no. 20 (2010). PDF accessible from http://kontur.au.dk.

———. "Historicizing 'Contemporary Art': Some Discursive Practices in *Gendai Bijutsu* in Japan." *Positions* 12, no. 3 (Winter 2004): 611–641.

———. "'International Contemporaneity' in the 1960s: Discoursing on Art in Japan and Beyond." *Japan Review*, no. 21 (2009): 123–147. http://shinku.nichibun.ac.jp/jpub/pdf/jr/JN2103.pdf.

———. "Introduction: Collectivism in Twentieth-Century Japanese Art with a Focus on Operational Aspects of *Dantai*." *Positions* 21, no. 2 (Spring 2013): 246–248.

———. "State v. (Anti-)Art: Model 1,000-Yen Note Incident by Akasegawa Genpei and Company." *Positions* 10, no. 1 (Spring 2002): 141–172.

———. "Toward *Tokyo Biennale 1970*: Shapes of the International in the Age of 'International Contemporaneity.'" *Review of Japanese Culture and Society* 23 (December 2011): 198–201.

———, and Fergus McCaffrey. *Kazuo Shiraga: Six Decades.* Exh. cat. New York: McCaffrey Fine Art, 2009.

Vallye, Anna. "The Strategic Universality of *trans/formation*, 1950–1952." *Grey Room*, no. 35 (Spring 2009): 28–57.

Venechia biennāre: Nihon sanka no 40-nen / The Venice Biennale: 40 years of Japanese Participation. Tokyo: Japan Foundation, 1995.

Volk, Alicia. *In Pursuit of Universalism: Yorozu Tetsugorō and Japanese Modern Art.* Berkeley: University of California Press; Washington, DC: Phillips Collection, 2010.

Watanabe Shin'ya. "Kawara On-san tono omoide" [Memory of On Kawara]. *Rear*, no. 33 (2014): 109–115.

Weintraub, Max, Sarah Watson, and Annie Wischmeyer, eds. *Robert Barry: All the Things I Know … 1962 to the Present.* Exh. cat. New York: Hunter College Art Galleries, 2015.

Weisenfeld, Gennifer. *Mavo: Japanese Artists and the Avant-Garde, 1905–1931.* Berkeley: University of California Press, 2002.

Weiss, Jeffrey, with Anne Wheeler. *On Kawara: Silence.* Exh. cat. New York: Guggenheim Museum, 2015.

Winther-Tamaki, Bert. *Art in the Encounter of Nations: Japanese and American Artists in the Early Postwar Years.* Honolulu: University of Hawai'i Press, 2001.

———. "Six Episodes of Convergence between Indian, Japanese, and Mexican Art from the Late Nineteenth Century to the Present." *Review of Japanese Culture and Society* 26 (December 2014).

———. "The 'Mexico Boom' in the Japanese Art World, 1955." *Review of Japanese Culture and Society* 17 (December 2005): 113.

Yamada Satoru. "Harukanaru taiga o meguru hateshinaki tabi: Kawara On no tame no mikan no tekisuto (2006-nen)" [An endless travel around a remote great river: An unfinished text for On Kawara (2006)]. *Rear*, no. 33 (2014): 98–105.

Yamamura, Midori. *Grapefruit: Yoko Ono in 1964*. Exh. cat. New York: Ise Culture Foundation Gallery, 2004.

———. *Yayoi Kusama: Inventing the Singular*. Cambridge, MA: MIT Press, 2015.

Yoko Ono: From My Window. Exh. cat. Tokyo: Museum of Contemporary Art, 2015.

Yoshimoto, Midori, ed. "Expo '70 and Japanese Art: Dissonant Voices," special issue. *Review of Japanese Culture and Society* 23 (December 2011).

———. "From Space to Environment: The Origins of *Kankyō* and the Emergence of Intermedia Art in Japan." *Art Journal* 67, no. 3 (Fall 2008): 25–45.

———. *Into Performance: Japanese Women Artists in New York*. New Brunswick: Rutgers University Press, 2005.

Yoshitake, Mika, ed. *Requiem for the Sun: The Art of Mono-ha*. Exh. cat. (Los Angeles: Blum & Poe, 2012).

———. "Situating *Rust Garden*: Carl Andre in Japan." In *Carl Andre: Sculpture as Place, 1958–2010*, 324–335. Exh. cat. New York: Dia Art Foundation, 2014.

INDEX

Note: Plates appear following page 92.